OBJECTIVE MEASUREMENT:
Theory Into Practice

edited by

Mark Wilson

Graduate School of Education
University of California, Berkeley

ABLEX PUBLISHING CORPORATION
NORWOOD, NEW JERSEY

Library of Congress Cataloging-in-Publication Data

Objective measurement : theory into practice / edited by Mark Wilson.
　　p.　cm.
　　"Selected from among the 41 papers presented at the Fifth International Objective Measurement Workshop (IOMW5), held . . . at the University of California, Berkeley, on March 25 and 26, 1989"–Pref.
　　Includes bibliographical references and index.
　　ISBN 0–89391–727–3. — ISBN 0–89391–814–8 (pbk.)
　　1. Psychometrics—Congresses.　2. Psychometrics—Data　processing—Congresses.　3. Educational　tests　and　measurements—Congresses. I. Wilson, Mark.　II. International Objective Measurement Workshop (5th : 1989 : University of California, Berkeley)
BF39.024　1991
150'.1'5195—dc20　　　　　　　　　　　　　　　　　　　91–16210
　　　　　　　　　　　　　　　　　　　　　　　　　　　　CIP

Ablex Publishing Corporation
355 Chestnut St.
Norwood, NJ 07648

Table of Contents

Preface

The chapters in this volume (with two exceptions) were selected from among the 41 papers presented at the Fifth International Objective Measurement Workshop (IOMW5), held in Tolman Hall at the University of California, Berkeley, on March 25 and 26, 1989. The full set of papers is given in the Appendix. A comparison of that list with the chapter titles will provide some hints that several of the chapters underwent considerable alteration for this volume. The Workshop (as is discussed by Ben Wright in Chapter 2) is primarily a forum for participants to report on their recent work and receive quick feedback; the papers are often presented with little of the background they would need for a broader audience. Hence, the major task in gathering these papers into this volume was to provide such background, add some essential readings in the reference lists of the chapters, and to make the more technical parts of the papers more accessible. Nevertheless, the final set of chapters represents a very wide range both in terms of topic and technicality. To help make sense of this potentially confusing breadth, the chapters have been grouped into three "themes": measurement practice, measurement theory, and mathematical and statistical applications to measurement. Within each theme, chapters have been organized (roughly) according to the technical demands on the reader. Thus, in measurement practice, a dichotomous application is presented first, followed by a polytomous application, followed by a polytomous application involving a more complex model. Of course, there are many ways that academic researchers can find to make their subjects more complicated, and the order given reflects no more than one person's notion of "technical demand."

The selection of the papers was carried out in part by the IOMW5 participants themselves—some did not feel their work was ready for publication, some papers were already moving towards publication elsewhere. From those that remained, the chapters in this volume were chosen to represent the richness and depth of research in the field of objective measurement on the eve of the 1990s. Measurement is the link between the qualitative models of theorists (in whatever substantive discipline is under investigation) and the quantitative analysis of data. Spanning this link, one way to classify measurement activities is by the predominance of substantive discipline, measurement itself, or techniques applied to measurement.

Thus, the selection includes a group of chapters (4 through 9) that illustrate the application of objective measurement methods to a variety of fields—personality psychology, a sociological study of school environment, personnel management, pain research, motor performance, and curriculum development. These chapters emphasize practice over theory, showing how the measurement process contributes valuable perspectives on substantive theory, and how it can be used to feedback information about substantive theory.

Another group of chapters (10 through 14) offers examples of contributions to measurement theory. Three of them describe the development of new measurement models that extend objective measurement into new domains—to learning contexts, rank-ordered data, and multidimensional profiles composed of subtests. These are complemented by a study of the use of objective measurement to examine the construct validity of items, and an exploration of the impact of test anxiety and item order on measurements.

The final group of chapters (15 through 18) examines recent developments in mathematical and statistical applications to measurement. Here we see a number of mathematical programming techniques applied to test assembly, parameter estimation, and generalizability theory. Also, we see optimal sample design procedures applied to parameter estimation, and the use of decision theory to examine a classical ATI problem.

The first group of chapters (1, 2, and 3) is somewhat idiosyncratic. The first two chapters are the two exceptions noted above which were not presented at the workshop. Chapter 1 is an attempt to summarize briefly the approach to measurement that brings together the otherwise very diverse groups of researchers and practitioners that assemble at the workshops every two years. Chapter 2 is an essay on the history of the workshops by their founder and guiding spirit, Ben Wright. Chapter 3 is a discussion of objective measurement from the perspectives of ancient and modern philosophical traditions.

While these chapters span a wide spectrum of topics from objective measurement, they hardly exhaust the field. There are notable gaps—

for example, matters of fit occupy somewhat less of a place in this collection than they would in a truly representative collection. Hopefully, any imbalances will be overcome in future collections of papers from IOMW6 and beyond.

Acknowledgments

Many people contributed to the publication of this volume; I thank you all, and hope that the final product is worthy of your efforts. Initial planning input came from David Andrich, Richard Smith, Wim van der Linden, and Ben Wright. Acting Dean Bill Rohwer of the Graduate School of Education at the University of California, Berkeley, graciously volunteered the facilities of Tolman Hall for the Workshop and supported the Workshop and this volume by allocating secretarial assistance. Barbara Nakakahira and Shelly Okimoto supervised communications throughout the process. Hoi Suen, Wim van der Linden, and Ben Wright each helped review and revise several of the chapters. All of the chapter authors displayed a very cooperative spirit in making (sometimes several rounds of) alterations to their manuscripts. In particular, I would like to thank Martijn Berger and Wim van der Linden, and Jos Adema, Ellen Boekkooi-Timminga, and Noud Gademann for reworking their Workshop presentations to produce completely original papers for this volume. Finally, Barbara Bernstein of Ablex Publishing Corporation has guided the volume from concept to publication with both good humor and high professional competence.

part I

Introduction

chapter 1

Objective Measurement: The State of the Art

Mark Wilson
Graduate School of Education
University of California, Berkeley

It would seem only reasonable that a volume entitled *Objective Measurement* should make clear why the variety of measurement that it represents should deserve the qualification "objective." As Wright (Chapter 2) explains, the papers collected here were presented at a workshop of objective measurement practitioners and theorists. This chapter has been prepared to give background for the term "objective measurement," to direct the reader to more extensive sources, and to suggest some of the directions for research in this topic in the years to come.

"Objectivity" as a necessary feature of measurement is old and venerable, but the term has many meanings (e.g., Webster's [Gove, 1965] gives eight that could be applied to measurement in one way or another). The meaning that is being ascribed to "objective" in the context of this volume is quite specific. "Objective measurement" means that, in a situation where a certain class of stimuli (e.g., items) are being used to measure certain individuals:

> The comparison between two stimuli should be independent of which particular individuals were instrumental for the comparison; and it should also be independent of which other stimuli within the considered class were or might also have been compared. Symmetrically, a com-

parison between two individuals should be independent of which particular stimuli within the class considered were instrumental for the comparison; and it should also be independent of which other individuals
were also compared, on the same or on some other occasion. (Rasch, 1961,
pp. 330–331)

Thus, it should not matter who else is measured when you are measured, nor should it matter which particular measuring instruments
are used to measure you, so long as they all belong to the relevant class
(Wright, 1968). Rasch named this quality "specific objectivity" (Rasch,
1966), and he showed that if the probabilistic relationship between an
individual's responses to an item and an underlying variable were
governed by one of a family of mathematical relationships, then specific objectivity would hold (Rasch, 1960). He demonstrated this for a
Poisson model of misreadings and one for speed, and also for a logistic
model of dichotomous test responses. This last is commonly known as
the "Rasch model" in his honor, and measurement that seeks to adhere
to the standard of specific objectivity is also known as "Rasch measurement" or "objective measurement." He also demonstrated that, under
certain rather essential conditions, these are the *only* models that can
result in specific objectivity, a result which was broadened and
clarified by Andersen (1973) and Fischer (1974). (See also Chapters 3
and 14, respectively, for more detailed discussions of these points.)

To see the import of specific objectivity, consider the limitations that
hold in situations where it does not obtain. For example, in standardized testing, based on traditional test theory, an individual's percentile
score will depend on who else is present in the reference group, as well
as which particular items are used. Thus, the results of a standardized
test are only interpretable with respect to the original norming sample, and when the items are constant from year to year. This sort of
problem can be partially addressed with the complicated techniques of
test equating, but these are only available at great cost. In contrast,
the most common measurement instruments in education—classroom
tests—are typically composed of different items at each administration, are given to a school population that is constantly changing in its
make up so that norming samples more than a few years old are worse
than irrelevant, and must be constructed and interpreted with very
little dollar investment. The interpretation of standardized tests is so
sensitive to the composition of the original reference group and the
original sample of items that it has led to an ossification of tests and
testing and a broad public dissatisfaction with the practice of standardized testing. In contrast, where a set of items has been found
appropriate for an objective measurement model, these items may be

used to form an item bank and then reassembled into many different subtests, each of which yields common-scale measures. Measures of an individual become independent of who is measured along with the examinee, and changing reality may be implemented by fractional adjustments to the parameters of items in the bank.

That specific objectivity is not attained simply by postulating more complicated mathematical models is illustrated by considering what happens when the Birnbaum two-parameter logistic model (1968) is used. For this model, the relative difficulty of items must change for individuals of differing ability. In objective measurement, the item difficulty order is used as a way of criterion-referencing and construct-validating the test (see, for example, Chapters 4, 5, 6, and 8). This essential feature of good test development technique is not available when the Birnbaum model is used as the basis for measurement. Another example of the problems that arise with the use of tests that are not designed to the specific objectivity standard is that the estimate of an individual's ability is based not on their raw score, but on a complex scoring formula involving varying item parameters. This means that two individuals with the same raw score may not be estimated to have the same ability. While esoteric arguments may be made that estimates gained by such methods have better statistical properties, this will be of little interest to the examinee who cries "Unfair!" when he or she realizes that an examinee with the same score was admitted to a college from which he or she was excluded. In contrast, all objective measurement models are based on a response scoring formula (counting right answers) that is known to the examinee and that is in fact the sufficient statistic for the parameter estimates of the objective measurement model.

Some who comment on the issues surrounding measurement claim that the choice of a model is a purely technical matter—"get the one that fits best and forget the rest," "don't try to interpret parameters, just estimate abilities." This approach will sometimes lead to smaller standard errors in estimates of person abilities, if only because more item parameters are used. However, such a position ignores the historical development of measurement in the social, behavioral, and physical sciences, which is a story of the selection, rejection, and adaptation of measurement standards (Andrich, 1978b, 1985, 1989a, 1989b). These measurement standards encapsulate our beliefs about what it means to measure something. The arena of discourse concerning such matters is philosophy (see Chapter 3) and substantive theory, rather than statistical technicality. Specific objectivity may seem a tough standard, but, as the chapters in Part II of this volume demonstrate, adherence to it does enhance the quality of measurement.

Of course, specific objectivity is not the only standard that one needs to apply in order to attain good measurement. Specific objectivity must be applied in concert with the traditional standards of testing (AERA, APA, & NCME, 1985), many of which are clarified and simplified in an objective measurement framework. Rather than give an account of the procedures that implement these standards, the reader is directed to the chapters in Part II of this volume, and in particular, Chapter Four. Further accounts of objective measurement practice are given in Wright and Stone (1979) and Wright and Masters (1981).

Given this basis, what is the focus of exciting work in objective measurement as we enter the 1990s? The first focus is addressed in Part II of this volume—the continuing investigation of how to apply existing objective models in a broad range of contexts. This is the dynamism which is at the heart of objective measurement. It is out of real measurement situations that the original ideas for objective measurement arose, and consideration of such situations will be the instigator of future advances.

Needless to say, new applications will occasionally throw up puzzles that don't fit standard approaches. This leads to the second focus—the development of new models within the objective measurement tradition. Historical examples of such new models are the Linear Logistic Test Model (Fischer, 1973), the Rating Scale Model (Andrich, 1978a), and the Partial Credit Model (Masters, 1982). This is continued in this volume by the models described in Chapters 12, 13, and 14, respectively

A third focus is exemplified by the chapters in Part IV of this volume—the application of new mathematical and statistical methods to measurement problems. These developments are an indication that the activity of measurement is not different from other research activities involving mathematical and statistical concepts. The major advance represented in these chapters is the recognition that the diverse methods of mathematical programming may be applied at a number of crucial points in the measurement procedure to make the procedure more rigorous and more flexible.

A new and promising focus is introduced in Chapters 10 and 11, respectively. In this development, which is only just beginning to gain some prominence in the research community, the old barrier between the theory of measurement and theory in the substantive discipline is starting to crumble. In Chapter 10 we see that distinction blurring as results from measurement are used to inform cognitive theory and consequently to inform the practice of item development. Chapter 11 raises the important issue of which personal and contextual variables should be considered a part of the measurement model when he investigates the impact of test anxiety and item order on performance. It remains to be resolved whether a factor such as test anxiety should be used to *modify* a measurement, or whether it should remain an extra piece of information external to the measurement.

Historically, the standards of measurement, both those promulgated by professional organizations and the requirement of specific objectivity, have been seen as independent of the substantive discipline in which the application is to take place. It is possible to go beyond this division and incorporate the theory that is the basis for a substantive investigation into measurement practice, and even to use it as the basis for development of the measurement model (Wilson & Mislevy, 1989). This is illustrated by recent work on the use of mixture models to investigate a situation where objective measurement (in the form of a Rasch model) is assumed to hold only for *some* individuals. For example, Mislevy and Verhelst (in press) postulate two classes of individuals, one a Rasch class, and one a random guesser class; another example is provided by Wilson (1989), where successive Piagetian stages are the basis for successive Rasch classes. Although these ideas are grounded in the concept of specific objectivity, they go beyond specific objectivity. The challenge will be to incorporate the important advance that such ideas promise while preserving the foundation of objective measurement. Philosophical work, such as that exemplified in Chapter 3, will be necessary before the true import of these developments will become clear.

REFERENCES

AERA, APA, NCME. (1985). *Standards for educational and psychological testing*. Washington, DC: APA.

Andersen, E.B. (1973). Conditional inference for multiple-choice questionnaires. British *Journal of Mathematical and Statistical Psychology, 26*, 31–44.

Andrich, D. (1978a). A rating formulation for ordered response categories. *Psychometrika, 43*, 561–573.

Andrich, D. (1978b). Relationships between the Thurstone and Rasch approaches to item scaling. *Applied Psychological Measurement, 3*, 449–460.

Andrich, D. (1985). An elaboration of Guttman scaling with Rasch models for measurement. In N. Brandon Tuma (Ed.), *Sociological methodology* (pp. 33–80). San Francisco: Jossey-Bass.

Andrich, D. (1989a). Distinctions between assumptions and requirements in measurements in the behavioral sciences. In J.A. Keats, R. Taft, R.A.

Heath, & S.H. Lovibond (Eds.), *History, systems and mathematical psychology* (pp. 7–16). Amsterdam: North-Holland, Elsevier.

Andrich, D. (1989b). Constructing fundamental measurements in social psychology. In J.A. Keats, R. Taft, R.A. Heath, & S.H. Lovibond (Eds.), *History, systems and mathematical psychology* (pp. 17–26). Amsterdam: North-Holland, Elsevier.

Birnbaum, A. (1968). Some latent trait models and their use in inferring an examinee's ability. In F.M. Lord & M.R. Novick (Eds.), *Statistical theories of mental test scores* (pp. 397–479). Reading, MA: Addison-Wesley.

Fischer, G.H. (1973). The linear logistic test model as an instument in educational research. *Acta Psychologica, 37*, 359–374.

Fischer, G.H. (1974). *Einfuhrungin die theorie psychologischer tests.* Vienna: Verlag Hans Huber.

Gove, P.B. (1965). *Webster's third new international dictionary.* Springfield, MA: Merriam.

Masters, G.N. (1982). A Rasch model for partial credit scoring. *Psychometrika, 47*, 149–174.

Mislevy, R.J., & Verhelst, N. (in press). Modeling item responses when different subjects employ different solution strategies. *Psychometrika.*

Rasch, G. (1960). *Probabilistic models for some intelligence and attainment tests.* Copenhagen: Denmarks Paedagogiske Institute. (Reprinted by University of Chicago Press, 1980)

Rasch, G. (1961). On general laws and the meaning of measurement in psychology. *Proceedings of the Fourth Berkeley Symposium on Mathematical Statistics and Probability, 4*, 321–333.

Rasch, G. (1966). An individualistic approach to item analysis. In P.F. Lazarsfeld & N.W. Henry (Eds.), *Readings in mathematical social science* (pp. 89–108). Chicago: Science Research Associates.

Wilson, M. (1989). Saltus: A psychometric model of discontinuity in development. *Psychological Bulletin, 105*(2), 276–289.

Wilson, M., & Mislevy, R.J. (1989). *Test theory for measuring understanding and learning.* Paper presented at the Educational Testing Service Invitational Symposium on Language Acquisition and Language Assessment, Princeton, NJ.

Wright, B.D. (1968). Sample-free test calibration and person measurement. *Proceedings of the 1967 Invitational Conference on Testing Problems.* Princeton, NJ: Educational Testing Service.

Wright, B.D., & Stone, M. (1979). *Best test design.* Chicago: MESA Press.

Wright, B.D., & Masters, G.N. (1981). *Rating scale analysis.* Chicago: MESA Press.

chapter **2**

The International Objective Measurement Workshops: Past and Future

Benjamin D. Wright
Department of Education
University of Chicago

THE PAST

Georg Rasch succeeded to immortality in the fall of 1980 one week before the University of Chicago reprint of "Probabilistic Models for Some Intelligence and Attainment Tests" (Rasch, 1980) reached his island home. That seminal volume took 20 years to reprint because Georg could not surrender the possibility of improving it. Thirty-five years have passed since those Friday morning seminars in Erik Thomsen's office at the Danish Institute for Educational Research were recorded, transcribed by Georg's daughter, Lotte Prien, and translated into English by Gustav Leunbach. Georg's incomparable voice still rings from the book's glorious pages as fresh and incisive as ever. For those who rallied to the first *International Objective Measurement Workshop* in the following Spring of 1981, the past was Georg's great beginning.

---

* If this chapter is useful, credit Mark Wilson, Richard Smith, Mike Linacre, and David Andrich. If not, blame me.

THE MOTIVE

How did we meet Georg? He was visiting professor of statistics at the University of Chicago in the spring of 1960. I was the sole survivor of his 24 surprising lectures on measurement. The statisticians found his originality hard to swallow. The social scientists found his mathematics hard to follow. I was lucky. I stayed and listened and then, for 20 years, spent hundreds of exciting hours working with Georg in Denmark, Chicago, and Australia.

Bruce Choppin joined us in Copenhagen in 1965 where we spent two months at Georg's blackboard. David Andrich met Georg when Georg returned to Chicago for three months in 1972 and David spent another six months with Georg at his summer home on Laeso Island in 1977. Graham Douglas met Georg in Perth when Georg was visiting professor of education and statistics at the University of Western Australia in 1974. Our last mortal contact with Georg was in June 1979 when David went to Laeso to tape Georg's autobiography (Wright, 1980a, 1988d).

THE NAME

Why "International Objective Measurement Workshop"?

International? We came from England, Australia, and America. Bruce was teaching Rasch measurement in Israel and Indonesia. We hoped to involve Europeans who used Rasch models: Gerhard Fischer, Arnold van den Wollenberg, Hans Spada, Leo van der Kamp, Wim Van der Linden, Eddy Roskam.

Workshop? We wanted to go beyond titillating one another with fait accompli. We wanted to work together in lively, informal discussions from which surprising new work would evolve.

Objective Measurement? What other topic in social science method is more in need of clarification and communication? Those who use Rasch methods know what "objective measurement" means. But there are others who attempt "measurement" with tools which we deduce from theory and observe in practice do not and cannot produce objective measures. They insist that the Rasch Model is no more than a one-parameter simplification of their three-parameter model in which guessing and discrimination are enshrined as the "really important" item parameters (Wright, 1984; Andrich, 1989a).

SPRING 1981: IOMW1

David, Bruce, Graham, and I convened IOMW1 in Judd 111, University of Chicago, in April 1981, to remember Georg, to inspire one another, and to get on with measurement. No program survives. But Richard Smith recalls that David showed how Georg's measurement model was the necessary and sufficient stochastic realization of Guttman's conjoint order definition of scalability (Guttman, 1950a) and how Guttman's, much admired but never implemented, principal components of scale analysis (Guttman, 1950b) could be realized in a useful way by a Rasch model for rating scales (Andrich, 1985a). Important work on David's "extended logistic model" followed (Andrich, 1982, 1985b, 1988b). The mathematics are developed and explained by David's student and colleague, Pender Pedler (1988).

Bruce used the history of thermometry to show how the idea of a variable depends on the ways of its realization (Choppin, 1985a). At first, each way of observing heat defined a different "heat" variable. Then, through centuries of painstaking research, inspired thinking, and careful comparison, the many "heats" were united into one "temperature" derived from the idea of molecular motion. Bruce's story foretells the patience and persistence we will have to apply to reduce the many scattered variables of social science to a few decisive ones.

Graham deduced a conditional estimation procedure for the Rasch (1961) parameters of polytomous observations. Then he demonstrated that the resulting conditional estimates could never become better enough than their more accessible unconditional equivalents (Wright & Panchapakesan, 1969; Wright & Douglas, 1977a, 1977b; Linacre, 1987c, 1989b) to justify the trouble they required (Douglas, 1978, 1980; Wright, 1988e).

In pursuit of persuading social scientists, they could construct measures (and hence quantitative inferences and the scientific knowledge they empower) as solid as any enjoyed by physicists, I explained the inferential equivalence of individual questioning, multiple questionnaire equating, and general question banking, and urged the construction and maintenance of working integrations of questionnaires and tests into easily accessible and systematically self-correcting item banks (Wright, 1977; Wright & Bell, 1984).

Ron Mead proved that significant variation in item discrimination signals multidimensionality in the data. He also showed how parameterizing item discrimination forces multidimensionality into the analysis, thus contradicting and confounding the unidimensionality attempted in a concomitant specification of only one person parameter.

Geoff Masters introduced the important and much to be built upon topic of partial credit analysis. He showed how his partial credit model specialized the rating-scale parameters to individual items and then explored its application to "answer-until-correct" data (Masters, 1982, 1987, 1988a; Masters & Wright, 1982, 1984; Wright & Masters, 1982, pp. 152–179).

SUMMER 1982: IOMW2

David Andrich convened IOMW2 at the University of Western Australia on August 2–4, 1982. This three-day affair was sponsored by UWA, Murdoch University, and the Western Australia State Department of Education, preceded by a special issue of *Education Research and Perspectives* (Andrich & Douglas, 1982), announced by an official program and inaugurated by the UWA Vice-Chancellor, a physicist. Two afternoons and evenings were spent analyzing, discussing, and interpreting data brought by participants. Fifty-two Australians, Hok Siang Ng and Swee Phua (Singapore Ministry of Education), T. Theunissen (CITO, Netherlands), Richard Smith (American College Testing), and I participated. Figure 2.1 lists the program and participating institutions.

```
                    THE IOMW2 PROGRAM

Ben Wright         Simplicity in Calibrating & Measuring
Geoff Masters      The Partial Credit Model
David Andrich      The Model with Scale and Location
Graham Douglas     Invariance and Objectivity
George Morgan      Bayes Estimation of Rasch Measures
Richard Smith      The Analysis of Person Fit
Barry Kissane      Objectivity and the Study of Change
Pender Pedler      Dependence and Local Correlation
```

```
             PARTICIPATING INSTITUTIONS

University of Chicago, Western Australia State
Department of Education, Australian Council for
Educational Research, Netherlands National Institute
for Educational Measurement, American College Testing,
Murdoch University, Singapore Ministry of Education.
```

Figure 2.1. The IOMW2 Program and Participating Institutions

David proved that Thurstone's (1928, 1931) ideals for invariant-scale construction are realized through Rasch rating-scale analysis (Andrich, 1978a, 1978b, 1978c). He also showed how Rasch measurement makes final sense of the famous attenuation paradox (Andrich, 1985b). A UNESCO assignment kept Bruce away, but he sent a paper on "Realistic Characteristic Curves for Multiple Choice Items" in which he showed how students in different countries differed in their use of identical multiple-choice distractors (Choppin, 1983b, 1985b). Graham deduced the statistical model which follows from the measurement requirements of "Invariance and Objectivity."

Since many IOMW2 participants were new to Rasch measurement, I worked through the basic steps of the measuring/calibrating process, emphasizing their conceptual simplicity and easy practice (Wright & Stone, 1979, pp. 28–45). To clarify fit analysis I visualized the implications of person misfit with a "fitbox." (The low boundary of a fitbox is the lowest measure the person would get were they denied their lucky guesses on items too hard for them. The high boundary is the measure the person would get were they forgiven their careless errors on items too easy for them.) A fitbox covers all reasonable measures a person's performance could imply. When, as is usual, the fitbox is tighter than the estimated measure bracketed by a couple of standard errors, it seems safe to conclude that a valid measure has been obtained.

During a concomitant (Misha Strassberg) University of Western Australia Lecture on "The Natural Origin of Scientific Thinking and Measurement," I started a theory for the evolution of scientific thinking built on the logical progression from *naming* to *counting* to *ordering* to *measuring* and showed how this psychology of measurement could be anchored in Piagetian cognitive and Freudian psychosexual development.

Geoff Masters (Western Australian State Education Department) broadened his exposition of partial credit modeling and described a successful application of partial credit analysis to school data (Mossenson, Hill, & Masters, 1987). Geoff also demonstrated that statistical invariance of individual item step difficulties over different samples of students was obtainable in practice (Masters, 1984a; Masters & Evans, 1986).

Pender Pedler and David applied their mathematical work on rating-scale response components to the problem of "Independence, Dependence and Local Correlation" and demonstrated how content-related clusters of dichotomous items that manifest local dependence can be salvaged for objective measurement by compounding the responses they elicit into a cluster score modeled as a rating scale (Andrich, 1985b; Pedler, 1988; Wilson, 1988).

Richard Smith proved the practical equivalence of likelihood ratio and Pearson chi-square fit statistics (Smith & Hedges, 1982) and summarized his studies of the statistics of person fit analysis (Smith, 1985, 1986, 1988). Richard showed that simulated null distributions of standardized residuals and unbiased mean squares were normal enough in the relevant segments of their tails to support most global fit decisions. He also stressed the inferential advantage of basing fit analysis on a priori, theory-based item partitions (Smith, 1990).

SPRING 1985: IOMW3

It took two and a half years to collect IOMW3. The Chicago site of the American Educational Research Association meeting expedited participation. IOMW3 convened in Judd 111, University of Chicago, on March 26–28, 1985. Australia and the Netherlands were well represented.

The invitation encouraged papers on the contribution of measurement to science, additivity and fundamental measurement, models for response step calibration, the analysis of hierarchy, procedures for missing data, Bayesian estimation, fit statistics for inliers and outliers, the implications of overfit, diagnostic residual analysis, classroom computer-based tailored testing, school system item banking, curriculum mapping, and rehabilitation evaluation. Figure 2.2 lists the program and participating institutions.

SPRING 1987: IOMW4

Once more in Judd 111, University of Chicago, April 15–17, 1987, this time celebrated, at Mark Wilson's suggestion, by a Thai banquet at Tipsuda where we drank many toasts to Georg and one another. The program and participating institutions are listed in Figure 2.3.

SPRING 1989: IOMW5

Mark Wilson started planning IOMW5 at AERA in the spring of 1988. He convened us in Tolman Hall, University of California, Berkeley, March 25–26, 1989. Thanks to Mark, IOMW5 was also celebrated with a Thai banquet. The program and accomplishments of IOMW5 are documented in the chapters and abstracts printed in this book.

```
                    THE IOMW3 PROGRAM

Ben Wright          Theory of Objective Measurement
David Andrich       Unifying Measurement Theory
Eddy Roskam         Deriving the Rasch Model
Ivo Molenaar        Non-Parametric Ability Estimation
Paul Kelley         Cutting Scores from Item Banks
  Carolyn Iwamoto
Dick Woodcock       Verifying Construct Validity
Vivian Erviti       Rating Scales for Medical Students
  Jennifer Pappas
Matthew Schulz      Assessment of Visually Impaired
David MacArthur     Measuring over Repeated Testing
George Morgan       Bayesian Rasch Measures
Jenni Bosma         Algorithms for Adaptive Testing
Judy Burry          Measuring Teacher Effectiveness
Geoff Masters       Partial Credit Applications
Wim v.d.Linden      Analyzing Paired Comparisons
Mark Wilson         Identifying & Measuring Hierarchies
Mike Linacre        Making Measurement Accessible
Marty Grosse        How Objectivity Enables Certification
Larry Ludlow        Managing Teacher Certification
John de Jong        Item Selection from Pretests
Richard Smith       Assessing Partial Knowledge
```

```
              PARTICIPATING INSTITUTIONS

University of Western Australia, Netherlands Catholic
University, University of Groningen, National Board of
Medical Examiners, Veterans Administration, University
of California at Los Angeles, Australian Council for
Educational Research, Institute for Educational
Research, University of Kansas, University of Melbourne,
University of Twente, MEDIAX, Boston College,
Netherlands National Institute for Educational
Measurement, Johnson O'Connor Foundation, Malaysian
Ministry of Education, Singapore Ministry of Education
```

Figure 2.2.   The IOMW3 Program and Participating Institutions

SUMMARY

The history, philosophy, and meaning of measurement are our foundations and these essential lines of investigation and communication,
introduced at IOMW1 by Bruce, David, and myself, continue to be

```
                    THE IOMW4 PROGRAM

Richard Smith       Sex Differences in Math Tests
Barry Kissane       The Effect of Calculators on Math
Mary Lunz           Analysis of Inter-Judge Reliability
Matthew Schulz      One-Step Vertical Equating
Mike Linacre        Ratings by Several Raters
Bill Fisher         Gadamer and Rasch on Objectivity
Richard Gershon     Calibrating Words
  David Schroeder
George Ingebo       Item Calibration Stability
  Chad Karr
Fred Forster        Fixed Parameter Model Applications
  George Ingebo
Wim v.d.Linden      Sample Designs for Rasch Estimation
Mike O'Brien        The Effects of Misfit on Measuring
Barbara Dodd        Adaptive Testing with Rating Scales
Kathy Green         Item Banking in a Small Classroom
Dennis Wisniewski   Distractor Analysis
David MacArthur     Mathematical Models of Pain
Henk Kelderman      Loglinear Models for Test Equating
Geoff Masters       Charting Student Progress
  Mark Wilson
Marty Grosse        Analyzing Item and Person Fit
Christa Winter      Measuring Math Problem Solving
```

```
              PARTICIPATING INSTITUTIONS

Educational Testing Service, Murdoch University,
American Society of Clinical Pathologists, Chicago
Public Schools, Johnson O'Connor Foundation, Portland
State University, Portland Public Schools, University
of Twente, Columbia University, University of Texas,
University of Wyoming, Pontiac Public Schools,
Veterans Administration, University of California at
Berkeley, University of Melbourne, National Board of
Medical Examiners and the Malaysian Ministry of
Education.
```

Figure 2.3. The IOMW4 Program and Participating Institutions

pursued by Eddy Roskam (Roskam & Jansen, 1984), Bill Fisher (1988a, 1988b), Mike Linacre (1989d), and George Engelhard (1984). IOMW5 devoted a section to this topic. Bill Fisher's explanation of the Platonic roots of Rasch separability is particularly illuminating and provocative (see Chapter 3 in this volume).

By now we have established, beyond a shadow of a doubt, that whenever the generic *criteria for measurement* identified by physicists (Campbell, 1920) and mathematicians (Luce & Tukey, 1964) and demanded by the founders of psychometrics (Thorndike, 1927; Thurstone, 1928, 1931; Guilford, 1936; Guttman, 1950a) are actually put into requirement, then only the Rasch model can be deduced (Brogden, 1977; Perline, Wright, & Wainer, 1979; Roskam & Jansen, 1984; Wright & Linacre, 1987; Wright, 1985, 1988a, 1988b, 1989a, 1989b). Far from being a special case of some superfluous affectation, the Rasch model is the necessary and sufficient process for measurement. It follows that only data that can be made to fit a Rasch model can be used to construct measures.

In particular this means that

1. Whenever one counts on raw scoring, counts right answers or Likert-scale categories, then one is collecting data from which only a Rasch model can construct measures.
2. Whenever one estimates a regression analysis, growth curve, confidence interval, significance test, or means and standard deviations and so requires quantification of the dependent variable sufficiently linear and invariant to justify the necessary arithmetic, then one requires measures of the kind only Rasch models produce.

Our mathematical foundations continue to consolidate and simplify. IOMW1 furnished Ron Mead's exposition of the multi-dimensionality signaled by variation in item discrimination. Way back in 1965, Bruce and I had learned from bitter experience that variation in item discrimination is impossible to estimate without the imposition of unreasonably arbitrary constraints. (Cross-weighing observed responses by ability estimates when discrimination is estimated and then by discrimination estimates when ability is estimated produces a regenerative feedback which escalates to infinity (Wright, 1977, pp. 103–104).)

Even more important is the realization that modeling variation in item discrimination denies the development of construct validity. Variation in item discrimination forces ICCs to cross so that the meaning of the variable cannot be based on the difficulty ordering of item content. When there is no unique item ordering on which to build meaning or with which to benchmark standards, then construct validity and criterion referencing disappear. This means that whenever one aspires to understand the meaning of one's variables in terms of the item content by which they are defined, then one has decided to work with a model which specifies that ICCs do not cross, a Rasch model.

IOMW2 provided Graham's deductions of Rasch polytomous models from objectivity. This was followed by Eddy Roskam's IOMW3 deduction of the simple Rasch model from stochastic conjoint order. During IOMW5 I provided three easy-to-follow simplifications of the deductions of the model from Fisher sufficiency (Wright, 1989a), Thurstone invariance (Wright, 1988a, 1989b), and Campbell concatenation (Wright, 1985, 1988b). Finally, Mike Linacre capped the IOMW5 discussion with a complete generalization of the measurement models which follow from objectivity (Linacre, 1989d).

As for the measurement models themselves, although most contemporary application uses the simplest Rasch model for dichotomous data, Georg's foresight (Rasch, 1961) has flowered into a host of more complicated and more versatile, yet practical, elaborations. We have programmed and applied not only models for rating scales and partial credit scoring (Wright & Mead, 1976; Masters, 1982; Wright & Masters, 1982; Wright & Linacre, 1984; Linacre, 1987b, 1987c, 1989b, 1989c, 1989e; Wright, Linacre, & Schulz, 1989), but also David's extended linear model for, among other applications, the management of local dependence (Andrich, 1985b; Pedler, 1988).

The modeling of guessing as an item parameter, so fashionable among those who adore complexity as the hallmark of science, is rapidly collapsing as an actual practice. This is because *guessing cannot and need not be estimated as an item asymptote.* Guessing is neither necessary nor useful as an item characteristic. When guessing actually occurs, it is always a person-response anomaly, manifested occasionally by a few individuals on a few items which baffle or rush them (Wright, 1977, pp. 110–112). Only recurring lucky guessing on multiple choice items can disturb measurement. But when guesses are lucky, the consequences in the responses of the lucky guesser are clearly visible improbable right answers. Whenever something must be done about the few lucky guesses which actually do occur in multiple-choice item response data, the few persons responsible for those few occurrences are easy to find and reasonable corrections for any interference with measurement are easy to apply (Wright & Stone, 1979, pp. 170–190).

The famous challenge of developmental discontinuity was taken up by Mark Wilson's SALTUS model (Wilson, 1984, 1985, 1989). The elusive puzzle of how to deal with Thurstone/Coombs unfolding was clarified and resolved by David (Andrich, 1985c, 1988a, 1989b). Finally, during IOMW4 and IOMW5, Mike Linacre showed us a mathematical model and an efficient accompanying PC-computer program for the analysis of the kind of many-faceted data which the intermediation of judges always produces (Linacre, 1987d, 1989a, 1989c, 1989d, 1989e, 1990b; Lunz, Wright, Stahl, & Linacre, 1989a, 1989b; Lunz, Wright, & Linacre, 1990).

The pairwise method of estimation described by Georg Rasch in the 1950s (Rasch, 1980, pp. 171–172) and the mainstay of Bruce's work (Choppin, 1968, 1976, 1979, 1981, 1983a) was revived by Wim van der Linden in IOMW3 (van der Linden, 1988), but with a seeming "tied ranks" problem, and then returned to by Mike Linacre in IOMW5 as a generalized model for, even incomplete, rank orders in which there is no ties problem (see Chapter 12 in this volume). IOMW5 brought Bob Jannarone's conjunctive measurement model (see Chapter 13 in this volume) with help from Henk Kelderman and Cees Glas' models for multivariate ability distributions (see Chapter 14 in this volume).

Many new and useful statistical procedures emerged during these years. IOMW1 began with Bruce's and Graham's implementations of the pairwise and marginal conditional procedures outlined by Georg. This led to Wim's mathematical work (van der Linden & Eggen, 1988) and Mike's model for analyzing rank orders (Linacre, 1989a, 1989e). Henk Kelderman gave his first report on the log linear approach during IOMW3 and brought that to fruition during IOMW5 with a convenient computer program and clear explanations of how to think through the structure of the measurement model and relate this to the options of the log linear analysis (Kelderman, 1986a, 1986b, 1988; Kelderman & Macready, 1988).

Computer programs to apply these procedures have become plentiful. At IOMW1 we saw output from Bruce's PAIR (Choppin, 1983a) and Ron's BICAL (Wright & Mead, 1976; Wright, 1988e). By IOMW2 we were looking at applications of Geoff's DICOT (Masters, 1984b). Mike brought PC-MICROSCALE (Wright & Linacre, 1984) to IOMW3. At IOMW4 we saw analyses performed by PC-CREDIT (Masters & Wilson, 1988), MSCALE (now BIGSCALE: Wright, Linacre, & Schulz, 1989), MFORMS (Schulz, 1988), and FACETS (Linacre, 1989c). Results from many computer programs were exhibited at IOMW5 where there was a section devoted to their demonstration (Horabin, 1989).

Concern with the statistics of fit to the model and the validation of how well particular data could serve measurement were ubiquitous. Joe Ryan urged the necessity and value of fit analysis during IOMW1. At IOMW2 Richard Smith outlined all there was to say about person performance fit and I made misfit visible with fit boxes. The practical use of misfit analyses to clarify variables, improve items, and qualify measures became an active part of every application reported. The study of fit continues (Douglas & Wright, 1990; Smith, 1990; Schulz, 1987, 1990).

Computer adaptive testing made its first appearance in Jenni Bosma's IOMW3 report of her use of CAT in grade school classrooms (Bosma, 1985). Barbara Dodd and Bill Koch reported on CAT with rating scales during IOMW4 and IOMW5 and Richard Gershon (1989) used data collected by CAT for his study of test anxiety (see Chapter 11 in this volume).

Item banking was featured in all five workshops. Bruce outlined its importance for international comparisons in IOMW1 (Choppin, 1968, 1976, 1979, 1981). I developed its necessity for quantitative theory in education or psychology during IOMW2 (Wright, 1977, 1980b; Wright & Bell, 1984) and Geoff showed how it could be done with partial credit items (Masters, 1984a; Masters & Evans, 1986). During IOMW4, Matt Schulz demonstrated the simple and efficient one-step item banking and simultaneous vertical test equating which was possible with the MSCALE and MFORMS computer programs (Schulz, 1988). The wide-ranging yet eminently practical northwest item-banking accomplishments of George Ingebo, Fred Forster, and Chad Karr were reported during IOMW4 and IOMW5 (Ingebo, 1989).

Finally, the rich potentials of mapping performance, so essential to the comprehension and communication of test results, were brought into IOMW1 by Dick Woodcock's KEYMATH form (Connolly, Nachtman, & Pritchett, 1971), extended in IOMW3 with the detailed variable maps of Dick's reading mastery test (Woodcock, 1973) and expanded in IOMW4 by the charts of student progress developed by Geoff, Mark, and George Morgan (Masters, Morgan, & Wilson, 1987). Realizations of Rasch measurement mapping can be found in Colin Elliott's *British Ability Scales* (1981) and Dick's *Woodcock-Johnson Psycho-Educational Battery* of intelligence and achievement tests (Woodcock, 1989).

SPRING 1991: IOMW6

What will materialize in Judd 111, University of Chicago, March 30 to April 1, 1991, during IOMW6?

The philosophical, scientific, and logical foundations of Rasch measurement will continue to deepen and strengthen. The fundamental connections with the measurement work of Norman Campbell, R.A. Fisher, Thurstone, Guttman, and with simultaneous conjoint additivity will become better understood and easier to communicate. The necessity and sufficiency of the Rasch relation for any kind of measurement will become clearer and easier to explain.

The obvious and important differences between raw scores and constructed measures will be better understood and more widely heeded. Scores (counts of observed replications) are necessary for measurement. For practical efficiency, they also need to be statistically sufficient. But scores, as they stand,

1. Distort the arithmetic necessary for most statistical analyses because they are not linear,
2. Muddy results because the empirical coherence of the observations counted is not validated,
3. Mislead interpretation because they are not qualified by a sample-free estimate of their individual precision, and
4. Obstruct inference because their numerical meaning remains limited to the particular items actually taken (for any comparability at all every person must take exactly the same items in exactly the same way) (Wright & Linacre, 1989a, 1989b).

The currently celebrated activity of evaluating differential item functioning by a haphazard gaggle of contrasting methods will subside into a routine aspect of diagnostic fit analysis based on a priori partitions of items and persons (Linacre, 1987a; Linacre & Wright, 1989; Smith & Kramer, 1989). There will be significant progress in the use of item content to develop construct validity (Lunz, 1989; Lunz & Stahl, 1989) and also in the quantitative analysis of item components (Smith, 1987; Green & Smith, 1987).

The Rasch analysis of more than two facets—the simultaneous calibration, not only of items, but also of judges, tasks, times, and settings—will be illustrated by provocative and surprising analyses. The potential stability of judge calibrations, not only within but also between judge-intermediated examinations, will be demonstrated by Mary Lunz and others (Linacre, 1989d).

The immense potential and essential practicality of computer adaptive testing will further unfold (Bosma, 1985; Linacre, 1987b, 1990a; Wright, 1988c; Masters, 1988b; Gershon, 1989). Mary Lunz will show that many examinees can take many tests tailored to their many individual behaviors on many different computers at many different sites at many different times and yet produce quantitatively comparable measures on the common scale defined by the calibrated bank of items used to implement the many tests.

The extensive possibilities for constructing sensitive yet practical scoring keys for complicated but natural problem-solving performances will unfold, and the creative potential in incremental collaboration of scoring key development and partial credit analysis will be demonstrated (Julian & Wright, 1988).

Progress in our competence to invent new and ever more sensitive and useful observation models and, in particular, to measure problem-solving ability, professional performance, and the functional status of the physically and mentally disabled will become manifest, particularly in the work of Ray Adams, Geoff Masters, Matthew Schulz, Anne Fisher, and Ellen Julian.

Rasch measurement software workable on any everyday personal computer will be even easier to obtain and to use and even more convenient, versatile, and informative (Linacre, 1987b, 1989c; Wright, 1988c; Gershon, 1989).

There will be new and surprising Rasch applications in fields far from Education or Psychology (Stahl, 1989).

We will have an exciting time!

REFERENCES

Andrich, D. (1978a). Relationships between the Thurstone and Rasch approaches to item scaling. *Applied Psychological Measurement, 2*, 451–462.

Andrich, D. (1978b). Application of a psychometric rating model to ordered categories which are scored with successive integers. *Applied Psychological Measurement, 2*, 581–594.

Andrich, D. (1978c). A rating formulation for ordered categories. *Psychometrika, 43*, 561–573.

Andrich, D. (1982). An extension of the Rasch model for ratings providing both location and dispersion parameters. *Psychometrika, 47*, 105–113.

Andrich, D. (1985a). An elaboration of Guttman scaling with Rasch models for measurement. In N. Brandon Tuma (Ed.), *Sociological methodology* (pp. 33–80). San Francisco: Jossey-Bass.

Andrich, D. (1985b). A latent trait model for items with response dependencies: Implications for test construction and analysis. In S. Embretson (Ed.) *Test design: Contributions from psychology, education and psychometrics* (pp. 245–273). New York: Academic Press.

Andrich, D. (1985c). The construction of a probabilistic model for the psychological scaling of unfolding choice data. In E.E. Roskam (Ed.), *Measurement and personality assessment* (pp. 21–38). Amsterdam: North-Holland, Elsevier.

Andrich, D. (1988a). The application of an unfolding model of the PIRT type for the measurement of attitude. *Applied Psychological Measurement, 12*, 33–51.

Andrich, D. (1988b). A general form of Rasch's extended logistic model. *Applied Measurement in Education, 1*, 363–378.

Andrich, D. (1989a). Statistical reasoning in psychometric models and educational measurement. *Journal of Educational Measurement, 26*, 81–90.

Andrich, D. (1989b). A probabilistic item response theory model for unfolding preference data. *Applied Psychological Measurement, 13*, 193–216.

Andrich, D., & Douglas, G.A. (Eds.). (1982). Rasch models for measurement in educational and psychological research. *Education Research and Perspectives, 9*, 5–118.

Bosma, J. (1985). *The effects of adaptive question selection and detailed feedback on learning and teaching with microcomputers*. Chicago: University of Chicago, Department of Education, MESA.

Brogden, H.E. (1977). The Rasch model, the law of comparative judgement and additive conjoint measurement. *Psychometrika, 42,* 631–634.

Campbell, N.R. (1920). *Physics: The elements.* London: Cambridge University Press.

Choppin, B.H. (1968). An item bank using sample-free calibration. *Nature, 219,* 870–872.

Choppin, B.H. (1976). Recent developments in item banking. In D.N.M. de Gruiter & L.J.T. Van der Kamp (Eds.), *Advances in psychological and educational measurement.* New York: Wiley.

Choppin, B.H. (1979). Testing the question: The Rasch formula and item banking. In M. Ragget, P. Ragget, & C. Tutt (Eds.), *Assessment and testing of reading: Problems and practices.* London: Ward Lock.

Choppin, B.H. (1981). Educational measurement and the item bank model. In C. Lacey & D. Lawton (Eds.), *Issues in evaluation and accountability.* London: Methuen.

Choppin, B.H. (1983a). *A fully conditional estimation procedure for Rasch model parameters* (CSE Tech. Rep. No. 196). Los Angeles: UCLA. (ERIC ED 228267)

Choppin, B.H. (1983b). *Extracting more information from multiple choice tests: Analytic techniques for the answer-until-correct mode.* Los Angles: UCLA. (ERIC ED 227175)

Choppin, B.H. (1985a). Lessons for psychometry from thermometry. *Bruce Choppin on Measurement and Education, Evaluation in Education, 9,* 9–12.

Choppin, B.H. (1985b). A two-parameter latent trait model. *Bruce Choppin on measurement and education, Evaluation in Education, 9,* 43–62.

Connolly, A.J.,Nachtman, W., & Pritchett, E.M. (1971). *KEYMATH: Diagnostic Arithmetic Test.* Circle Pines, MN: American Guidance Service.

Douglas, G.A. (1978). Conditional maximum-likelihood estimation for a multiplicative binomial response model. *British Journal of Mathematical and Statistical Psychology, 31,* 73–83.

Douglas, G.A. (1980). Conditional inference in a generic Rasch model. In *Proceedings of the invitational conference on the improvement of measurement in education and psychology.* Melbourne, Australia: Australian Council for Educational Research.

Douglas, G.A., & Wright, B.D. (1990). Response patterns and their probabilities. *Rasch Measurement SIG Newsletter, 3*(4).

Elliott, C.D. (1981). *The British Ability Scales.* Windsor, Great Britain: NFER.

Engelhard, G. (1984). Thorndike, Thurstone and Rasch: A comparison of their methods of scaling psychological tests. *Applied Psychological Measurement, 8,* 21–31.

Fisher, W. (1988a). *Philosophical hermeneutics and fundamental measurement.* Chicago: University of Chicago, Department of Education, MESA.

Fisher, W. (1988b). Recent developments in the philosophy of science pertaining to problems of objectivity in measurement. *Rasch Measurement SIG Newsletter, 2*(2).

Gershon, R.C. (1989). *CAT administrator (computer program).* Chicago: Micro Connections.

Green, K.E., & Smith, R.M. (1987). A comparison of two methods of decomposing item difficulties. *Journal of Educational Statistics, 12*, 369–381.

Guilford, J.P. (1936). *Psychometric method.* New York: McGraw-Hill.

Guttman, L. (1950a). The basis for scalogram analysis. In S.A. Stouffer et al. (Eds.), *Measurement and prediction* (pp. 60–90). New York: Wiley.

Guttman, L. (1950b). The principle components of scale analysis. In S.A. Stouffer et al. (Eds.), *Measurement and prediction* (pp. 312–361). New York: Wiley.

Horabin, I. (1989). TESTCALC. *Rasch Measurement SIG Newsletter, 3*(1).

Ingebo, G. (1989). Rasch and educational research: Opportunity and obligation. *Rasch Measurement SIG Newsletter, 3*(1).

Julian, E.R., & Wright, B.D. (1988). Measuring physician competence with computerized patient simulations. *Applied Measurement in Education, 1*, 294–318.

Kelderman, H. (1986a). *Item bias detection using the loglinear Rasch model* (Research Rep. 86–2). Enschede, Netherlands: University of Twente.

Kelderman, H. (1986b). *Common item equation using the loglinear Rasch model* (Research Rep. 86–9). Enschede, Netherlands: University of Twente.

Kelderman, H. (1988). *Loglinear multidimensional IRT models for polytomously scored items* (Research Rep. 88–17). Enschede, Netherlands: University of Twente.

Kelderman, H., & Macready, G. (1988). *Loglinear latent class models for detecting item bias* (Research Rep. 88–10). Enschede, Netherlands: University of Twente.

Linacre, J.M. (1987a). *Mantel-Haenszel and the Rasch statistic* (MESA Memorandum No. 39). Chicago: University of Chicago, MESA Psychometric Laboratory. (ERIC ED 281 859)

Linacre, J.M. (1987b). *UCAT: A BASIC computer-adaptive testing program* (MESA Memorandum No. 40). Chicago: University of Chicago, MESA Psychometric Laboratory. (ERIC ED 280 895)

Linacre, J.M. (1987c). Estimation: Iteration and convergence. *Rasch Measurement SIG Newsletter, 1*(1).

Linacre, J.M. (1987d). *An extension of the Rasch model to multi-faceted situations.* Chicago: University of Chicago, MESA.

Linacre, J.M. (1989a). Rasch analysis and rank ordering. *Rasch Measurement SIG Newsletter, 2*(4).

Linacre, J.M. (1989b). Rasch model parameter estimation with the extra-conditional algorithm. *Rasch Measurement SIG Newsletter, 3*(1).

Linacre, J.M. (1989c). *FACETS computer program for many-faceted Rasch measurement.* Chicago: MESA Press.

Linacre, J.M. (1989d). *Many-faceted Rasch Measurement.* Chicago: MESA Press.

Linacre, J.M. (1989e). *FRANK Computer Program for Rasch Analysis of Rank-ordered Data.* Chicago: MESA Press.

Linacre, J.M. (1990a). Computer-adaptive testing in the classroom. In J. Keeves (Ed.), *The International Encyclopedia of Education: Supplementary Volume Two.* Oxford: Pergamon Press.

Linacre, J.M. (1990b). Measurement of judgements. In J. Keeves (Ed.), *The International Encyclopedia of Education: Supplementary Volume Two.* Oxford: Pergamon Press.

Linacre, J.M., & Wright, B.D. (1989). The equivalence of Rasch PROX and Mantel-Haenszel algorithms. *Rasch Measurement SIG Newsletter, 3*(2).

Luce, R.D., & Tukey, J.W. (1964). Simultaneous conjoint measurement: A new type of fundamental measurement. *Journal of Mathematical Psychology, 1,* 1–27.

Lunz, M.E. (1989). Constructing examinations from calibrated item variables. *Rasch Measurement SIG Newsletter, 3*(2).

Lunz, M.E., & Stahl, J.A. (1989). Content validity revisited: transforming job analysis data into test specifications. *Evaluation and the Health Professional, 12,* 192–206.

Lunz, M.E., Wright, B.D., Stahl, J.A., & Linacre, J.M. (1989a). *Equating practical examinations.* Paper presented at National Council on Measurement in Education Annual Meeting, San Francisco. (ERIC TM 012968).

Lunz, M.E., Stahl, J.A., Wright, B.D., & Linacre, J.M. (1989b). *Variations among examiners and protocols on oral examinations.* Paper presented at the American Educational Research Association Meeting, San Francisco. (ERIC TM 012988).

Lunz, M.E., Wright, B.D., & Linacre, J.M. (1990). Measuring the impact of judge severity on examination scores. *Applied Measurement in Education.*

Masters, G.N. (1982). A Rasch model for partial credit scoring. *Psychometrika, 47,* 149–174.

Masters, G.N. (1984a). Constructing an item bank using partial credit scoring. *Journal of Educational Measurement, 21,* 19–32.

Masters, G.N. (1984b). DICOT: Analyzing classroom tests with the Rasch model. *Educational and Psychological Measurement, 44,* 145–150.

Masters, G.N. (1987). Measurement models for ordered response categories. In R. Langeheine & J. Rost (Eds.), *Latent trait and latent class models.* New York: Plenum.

Masters, G.N. (1988a). The analysis of partial credit scoring. *Applied Measurement in Education, 1,* 279–297.

Masters, G.N. (1988b). Education measurement: Prospects for research and innovation. *Australian Educational Researcher, 15,* 23–34.

Masters, G.N., & Evans, J. (1986). Banking non-dichotomously scored items. *Applied Psychological Measurement, 10,* 355–367.

Masters, G.N., Morgan, G., & Wilson, M.R. (1987). *Charting student progress.* Melbourne: University of Melbourne, Centre for the Study of Higher Education.

Masters, G.N., & Wilson, M.R. (1988). *PC-CREDIT.* Melbourne: University of Melbourne, Centre for the Study of Higher Education.

Masters, G.N., & Wright, B.D. (1982). Defining a fear-of-crime variable: A comparison of two Rasch models. *Education Research and Perspectives, 9,* 18–32.

Masters, G.N., & Wright, B.D. (1984). The essential process in a family of measurement models. *Psychometrika, 49,* 529–544.

Mossenson, L.T., Hill, P.W., & Masters, G.N. (1987). *Tests of reading comprehension (TORCH).* Hawthorne, Australia: Australian Council for Educational Research.

Pedler, P. (1988). *Accounting for psychometric dependence with a class of latent trait models.* Perth, Australia: University of Western Australia, Department of Education.

Perline, R., Wright, B.D., & Wainer, H. (1979). The Rasch model as additive conjoint measurement. *Applied Psychological Measurement, 3,* 237–256.

Rasch, G. (1980). *Probabilistic models for some intelligence and attainment tests.* Chicago: University of Chicago Press. (Original work published 1960)

Rasch, G. (1961). On general laws and the meaning of measurement in psychology. In *Proceedings of the Fourth Berkeley Symposium on Mathematical Statistics and Probability* (pp. 321–333). Berkeley: University of California Press.

Roskam, E.E., & Jansen, P.G.W. (1984). A new derivation of the Rasch model. In E. Degreef & J. Van Buggenhaut (Eds.), *Trends in mathematical psychology* (pp. 293–307). Amsterdam: Elsevier Science Publishers B.V. North-Holland.

Schulz, M. (1987). *Functional assessment in rehabilitation.* Chicago: University of Chicago, Department of Education, MESA.

Schulz, E.M. (1988). MFORMS: A Rasch computer program for one-step item banking. *Rasch Measurement SIG Newsletter, 1*(2).

Schulz, E.M. (1990). Functional assessment of fit of data to the Rasch model. *Rasch Measurement SIG Newsletter, 3*(4).

Smith, R.M. (1985). Validation of individual response patterns. *International Encyclopedia of Education* (pp. 5410–5413). Oxford: Pergamon Press.

Smith, R.M. (1986). Person fit in the Rasch Model. *Educational and Psychological Measurement, 46,* 359–372.

Smith, R.M. (1987). Assessing partial knowledge in vocabulary. *Journal of Educational Measurement, 24,* 217–231.

Smith, R.M. (1988). The distributional properties of Rasch standardized residuals. *Educational and Psychological Measurement, 48,* 657–667.

Smith, R.M. (1990). Theory and practice of fit in Rasch measurement. *Rasch Measurement SIG Newsletter, 3*(4).

Smith, R.M., & Hedges, L.V. (1982). A comparison of likelihood ratio and chi-square tests of fit in the Rasch model. *Education Research and Perspectives, 9,* 44–54.

Smith, R.M., & Kramer, G.A. (1989). Utilizing response pattern analysis in making admission decisions. *Rasch Measurement SIG Newsletter, 2*(4).

Stahl, J.A. (1989). Archaeology and objective measurement. *Rasch Measurement SIG Newsletter, 3*(3).

Thorndike, E.L. et al. (1927). *The measurement of intelligence.* New York: Bureau of Publications, Teachers College, Columbia.

Thurstone, L.L. (1928). The measurement of opinion. *Journal of Abnormal and Social Psychology, 22,* 415–430.

Thurstone, L.L. (1931). Measurement of social attitudes. *Journal of Abnormal and Social Psychology, 26,* 249–269.

van der Linden, W.J. (1988). *Optimizing incomplete sampling designs for item response model parameters* (Research Rep. 88–5). Enschede, Netherlands: University of Twente.

van der Linden, W.J., & Eggen, T.J.H.M. (1988). *The Rasch model as a model for paired comparisons with an individual tie parameter* (Research Rep. 88–9). Enschede, Netherlands: University of Twente.

Wilson, M. (1984). *A psychometric model of hierarchical development.* Chicago: University of Chicago, Department of Education, MESA.

Wilson, M. (1985). *Measuring stages of growth.* Hawthorne, Australia: Australian Council for Educational Research.

Wilson, M. (1988). Detecting and interpreting local item dependence using a family of Rasch models. *Applied Psychological Measurement, 12,* 353–364.

Wilson, M. (1989). Saltus: A psychometric model of discontinuity in cognitive development. *Psychological Bulletin, 105,* 276–289.

Woodcock, R.W. (1973). *Woodcock reading mastery tests.* Circle Pines, MN: American Guidance Service.

Woodcock, R.W. (1989). *Woodcock-Johnson psycho-educational battery—revised.* Allen, TX: DLM Teaching Resources.

Wright, B.D. (1977). Solving measurement problems with the Rasch model. *Journal of Educational Measurement, 14,* 97–116.

Wright, B.D. (1980a). Foreword. In G. Rasch (Ed.), *Probabilistic models for some intelligence and attainment tests* (pp. ix-xix). Chicago: University of Chicago Press.

Wright, B.D. (1980b). Afterword. In G. Rasch (Ed.), *Probabilistic models for some intelligence and attainment tests* (pp. 185–196). Chicago: University of Chicago Press.

Wright, B.D. (1984). Despair and hope for educational measurement. *Contemporary Education Review, 1,* 281–288.

Wright, B.D. (1985). Additivity in psychological measurement. In E. Roskam (Ed.), *Measurement and personality assessment* (pp. 101–112). Amsterdam: North-Holland.

Wright, B.D. (1988a). The model necessary for a Thurstone scale. *Rasch Measurement SIG Newsletter, 2*(1).

Wright, B.D. (1988b). Campbell concatenation for mental testing. *Rasch Measurement SIG Newsletter, 2*(1).

Wright, B.D. (1988c). Practical adaptive testing (PAT). *Rasch Measurement SIG Newsletter, 2*(2).

Wright, B.D. (1988d). Georg Rasch and measurement. *Rasch Measurement SIG Newsletter, 2*(3).

Wright, B.D. (1988e). The efficacy of unconditional maximum likelihood bias correction. *Applied Psychological Measurement, 12,* 315–318.

Wright, B.D. (1989a). Deducing the Rasch model from the traditional requirement that counting right answers be sufficient. *Rasch Measurement SIG newsletter, 3*(1).

Wright, B.D. (1989b). Deducing the Rasch model from Thurstone's requirement that item comparisons be sample-free. *Rasch Measurement SIG Newsletter, 3*(1).

Wright, B.D., & Bell, S. (1984). Item banks: What, why, how. *Journal of Educational Measurement, 21*, 331–345.

Wright, B.D., & Douglas, G.A. (1977a). Best procedures for sample-free item analysis. *Applied Psychological Measurement, 1*, 281–294.

Wright, B.D., & Douglas, G.A. (1977b). Conditional versus unconditional procedures for sample-free item analysis. *Educational and Psychological Measurement, 37*, 573–586.

Wright, B.D., & Linacre, J.M. (1984). *MICROSCALE: Rasch Analysis Computer Program*. Westport, CT: Mediax Inc.

Wright, B.D., & Linacre, J.M. (1987). Rasch model derived from objectivity. *Rasch Measurement SIG Newsletter, 1*(1).

Wright, B.D., & Linacre, J.M. (1989a) Observations are always ordinal: Measures, however, must be interval. *Archives of Physical Medicine and Rehabilitation, 70*, 857–860.

Wright, B.D., & Linacre, J.M. (1989b) The differences between scores and measures. *Rasch Measurement SIG Newsletter, 3*(3).

Wright, B.D., & Linacre, J.M., & Schulz, M. (1989). *BIGSCALE: Rasch analysis computer program*. Chicago: MESA Press

Wright, B.D., & Masters, G.N. (1982). *Rating scale analysis*. Chicago: MESA Press.

Wright, B.D., & Mead, R.J. (1976). *BICAL: Calibrating items with the Rasch model* (MESA Memorandum No. 23). Chicago: University of Chicago, MESA Psychometric Laboratory.

Wright, B.D., & Panchapakesan, N. (1969). A procedure for sample-free item analysis. *Educational and Psychological Measurement, 29*, 23- 48.

Wright, B.D., & Stone, M.H. (1979). *Best test design*. Chicago: MESA Press.

chapter **3**

Objectivity in Measurement: A Philosophical History of Rasch's Separability Theorem*

William P. Fisher, Jr.
Research Associate
Department of Research and Evaluation
Marianjoy Rehabilitation Center

POSITIVISM AND POSTPOSITIVISM

Positivism holds that facts exist in a manner that is strictly independent from human preconceptions and values. Newton (1952, pp. 369, 404) was the epitome of positivist philosophy when he held that science has no need for hypotheses in the observation of facts (Burtt, 1925, pp. 215–220). Descartes helped make Newton's positivism possible by appearing to say that the recognition of facts did not require advance notions of what counts as valid knowledge. Descartes (1971, pp. 183–184) denied that he had discounted entirely the role of such preconceptions, but said that their simplicity and self-evidence precluded

---

* The author is grateful for the financial support of the Spencer Foundation and the helpful criticisms that emerged from dialogues with Benjamin Wright, David Tracy, Paul Ricoeur, and Sophie Haroutunian-Gordon, but must take responsibility for this thought experiment himself.

philosophical attention. The fact that scientific measurement was formulated in this way, on the basis of seemingly self-evident factuality, led to a sense of the natural as simply given and obvious to anyone who could think.

In the 20th century, positivism suffered a series of setbacks. Today it appears that scientific facts are not self-evident to any thinking person anywhere in any time, and that scientists must have prior notions of the whole to which parts belongs in order to observe specific facts. The necessity of taking into account the historical, linguistic, and sociocultural factors that make observation possible (Heelan, 1983b, 1983c) when defining objectivity has greatly complicated the problem of determining what an adequate conceptualization of it would look like. Many of those who consider themselves the guardians of objectivity fear that considering it as part and parcel of the moral context in which it emerges will render it bankrupt, and there are those who appear to oppose any effort aimed at articulating the discourse of objectivity as just another voice in an inherently anarchic hubbub (Feyerabend, 1977, 1981). On the other hand, criticisms of the way objectivity is represented are often just, true, and objective, a point that sometimes seems to be lost on those critics who go to extremes in their conclusions as to what possibilities may remain for objectivity in measurement. For instance, those who say that objectivity is doomed because language and culture play a role in its constitution seem to have conveniently forgotten that their observation of historical contingency is itself factual, and that it is one permeated by the forces making up our contemporary cultural and political context. The philosophy of science and the epistemology of the social sciences are caught in a dilemma wherein it is just as legitimate to say "anything goes" as to replace rigor with rigidity. Neither skepticism nor dogmatism can be decisively justified, however. The former position refuses to recognize the validity of anything outside of the specific context of its emergence, and the latter holds that constancy is imposed upon all contexts in like fashion, from the outside and in the name of some uninvolved authority. However, absolute relativism posits itself as not relative, and absolutism is relativized as soon as it is observed to emerge in some contexts but not others.

The problem of mitigating the opposition between absolute relativism and relative absolutism is especially pointed in social science. The effect of the methodological dilemma in social science has been the emergence of a variety of interpretive, qualitative approaches, in which the local negotiation of meaning is often the focal point of interest. Many who advocate interpretive social science dogmatically avoid quantitative approaches, as if the meaning of numbers is not negotiated via dialogue and metaphor. A more critical approach to method shows that the problem is not that quantification is itself inherently one-sided and blind to the birth and evolution of facts, but that too little attention has been accorded the way mathematical models represent (or fail to represent) the location of the numbers used on a measurement scale. It is most important to notice that the circular process by which objectivity in measurement is established is usually overlooked in social science, and so the rigor that defines science as science is lost.

By simply assuming that numerical data represent a constant and invariant unit in the phenomenon of interest, most quantitative research in social science is positivistic in practice even when its rhetoric is not. Even if statistics computed from data read off an instrument with low validity and reliability do not distribute differently than the same statistics computed under conditions of perfect measurement, these statistics are of no use in trying to understand the structure of a phenomenon (Baker, Hardyck, & Petrinovich, 1966, p. 306; Townsend & Ashby, 1984, pp. 398–400). Despite the fact that it is frequently ignored, the justification of the assignment of numbers to qualities is the first task of measurement (Suppes & Zinnes, 1963, p. 4). The inescapable necessity of the justification of measuring and measured in science has been repeatedly asserted in 20th-century social measurement (Angoff, 1960; Duncan, 1984; Guttman, 1950; Loevinger, 1947; Thorndike et al., 1926, p. 1; Thurstone, 1928), and practical and easy-to-use methods for achieving that justification, have been delineated by Rasch (1960, 1961, 1966, 1977) and Wright (1968, 1977; Wright & Stone, 1979; Wright & Masters, 1982). In this chapter, two accounts of the justification of measuring with measured will be traced from their early formulations in the origin of geometry. Then, the contrast between these two accounts will be used to interpret Rasch's separability theorem. Finally, data constituting a rudimentary test of the separability theorem will be analyzed.

TIGHTENING THE FOCUS ON THE PROBLEM

The Pythagorean Metaphysics of Positivism

Conceptual resources useful for the resolution of philosophy's dilemma have emerged from examinations of the historical settings in which the notions of science and objectivity crystallized, dissolved, and recrystallized (Burtt, 1925; Gadamer, 1980; Heidegger, 1967; Husserl, 1970). Among the groups in ancient Greece making important and early contributions to this dynamic were the Pythagoreans; their influence has been felt throughout the development of modern science in at least two ways. First, the Pythagoreans set the stage for positivism by asserting that the world is numerically constituted in and of itself. Saying "the world is number," the Pythagoreans held that everything is made up of indivisible, elementary spatial units (Burtt, 1925, p. 42). This sense of objective existence led to the notion of the natural as given, and to an inordinately strong focus on methodological rules as the sole criteria necessary to meet for the discernment of objective facts (Heidegger, 1967, 1982; Burtt, 1925). By the time of Descartes (1961), it seemed that precise rules could be laid down and followed such that they always and everywhere produced the same results.

The misplaced stress on methodology follows from an inadequate appreciation of the second major Pythagorean contribution to the history of science, the respect mathematicians hold to this day for simplicity, elegance, and parsimony. This respect can be traced to the ancient Greek sense of the meaning of mathematics: the simplest, most elegant, and most parsimonious solution is valued because it is the one in which the separation of figure from meaning, of signifier from signified, is most cleanly and clearly effected. For reasons such as these, Copernicus belonged to Pythagorean societies and Pythagorean influences can be seen in Kepler and Galileo's works (Rutherford, 1984, pp. 112–113; Burtt, 1925, pp. 60, 36–71, 88); from this point of view, Copernicus' question was not, "Does the earth move?" Instead,

> He simply included the earth in the question which Ptolemy had asked with reference to the celestial bodies alone; what motions should we attribute to the earth in order to obtain the simplest and most harmonious geometry of the heavens that will accord with the facts? (Burtt, 1925, pp. 50–51)

Because facts appeared to be given and not contextually constituted, the Cartesian emphasis on method and the Pythagorean understanding of the world as number led to Newton's positivistic rejection of any role for hypotheses in the focusing of scientific questions (Burtt, 1925, pp. 215–220). Contextual factors, such as language and culture, were simply not included in considerations of what constitutes objectivity in science, so the dialectical interplay and convergence of figure and meaning that attends their separation was ignored. Facts were God-given, and even though Descartes (1971, pp. 183–184) admitted that we must have some prior notion of what existence and understanding are in order for us to recognize them as such, he held that philosophers overcomplicate these matters, and that they are really too simple and self-evident to be put on record. Because of this misplaced emphasis on what seems to be completely obvious, the mathematical respect for simplicity inadvertently led to the positivist assumption that what is objective is what can be proven.

Method and Objectivity

As a result of the "victory of method over science" (Nietzsche, 1967, p. 261) and the "forgetfulness of Being" (Heidegger, 1962) fostered by the one-sided, positivist account of science, technical know-how threatens to completely outstrip moral understanding. Heidegger's work plays an important role in the task of turning this situation around because it is an effort aimed at putting on record what Descartes saw fit to leave off (Heidegger, 1982, p. 125). The need for an enumeration of what was too simple and self-evident for Descartes to record has been pointed out in the 20th century many times and in many ways, from Gödel's meta-mathematics to Kuhn's (1970) elaboration of the structure of scientific revolutions: the capacity to recognize objective truth (culturally contextualized and limited as it is) always exceeds the capacity of method to prove it, as method itself compels us to admit (Weinsheimer, 1985, p. 52). The first objection to Descartes' omission is that methodological skill alone does not include the capacity to imagine interesting and provocative research questions (Gadamer, 1975, 1976). The second objection is that researchers do more than just follow rules in the production and analysis of phenomena; their training and their practice is a matter of playing with and around problems and technologies, such that instruments become extensions of the body, bringing things into focus (Ackermann, 1985; Heelan, 1983a, 1983b, 1983c, 1985; Ihde, 1979; Kuhn, 1961; Lynch, 1985).

These objections begin to suggest a strategy for recovering what Descartes left off the record when we inquire after the meaning of his (Descartes, 1961, p. 16) observation that what the ancient Greeks "recognized as mathematics was very different from that which people accept in our times." In this passage he remarks that whatever "truly" mathematical devices they may have had, those devices must have been very simple. This construal of Greek mathematics has been sharply rebutted by Whitehead (1968, p. 179), who contends that

it is a mistake to think that the Greeks discovered the elements of mathematics, and that we have added the advanced parts of the subject. The opposite is more nearly the case; they were interested in the higher parts of the subject and never discovered its elements.

When the formulators of modern science discovered the elements of mathematics, its higher parts were forgotten and disregarded as irrelevant to the obvious utility and effectiveness of the numerical formulae. These higher parts included the ontological reasons for the restrictions placed by Plato on the instruments appropriate to geometry; forgetting these reasons allowed the seemingly simplest and most obvious, self-evident explanation of the effectiveness of mathematics to suffice in the Newtonian account of science. Our problem, as Husserl (1970; Derrida, 1978) showed, is how to recover the ancient, more advanced account of mathematics and use it to reconstruct how the extension of geometry into the mathematization of nature came about. Only by articulating the structure of mathematical and technological existence will we be able to understand why Plato restricted the instruments of geometry to the compass and straightedge, so that we may then devise similarly productive restrictions for the instruments of social science.

The Platonic Metaphysics of the Academy

To begin, we need to inquire further into the difference between ancient and modern mathematics. Though Plato was intellectually indebted to the Pythagoreans, recent readings of him (Burtt, 1925, p. 53; Gadamer, 1980; Heidegger, 1967) suggest that his relation to them was more critical than usually has been thought. Though it is true that Plato sought to ally himself with the Pythagoreans' mathematical rigor against the Sophists' equivocations, he held that the Pythagorean love and worship of mathematics had clouded their thinking (Gadamer, 1980, pp. 30–36). Plato's critique of the Pythagoreans is the heretofore scarcely tapped resource we need for the examination of ideas concerning the problem of defining objectivity in a useful and meaningful way. The etymology of our word "mathematics" expresses how this is so and makes possible application of Plato's insight to our own problems concerning philosophy's dilemma and objective measurement in social science. *Ta mathemata*, ancient Greek for what we call mathematical entities, have two primary qualities: (a) they can be taught and learned, and (b) they are learned through what is already known (Heidegger, 1967, p. 75). Hence, *ta mathemata* is often translated as curriculum, and *mathema* as learning (Bell, 1931, p. 58; Bochner, 1966, p. 255; Dantzig, 1955, p. 25; Descartes, 1961, p. 17; Heath, 1931, p. 5; Miller, 1921, pp. 78, 17; Wilder, 1965, p. 284). Before the Greeks, number was just one of many mathematical entities, and held no special interest. For instance, the Egyptians added together numbers only in association with the units they were held to represent (bushels of grain, liters of water, etc.); they did not recognize that 2 + 2 = 4 no matter which unit is involved (Suppes & Zinnes, 1963, p. 4). Number was like any other thing that endured beyond specific situations, could be learned, was sharable across interpersonal relations, and facilitated community and commerce.

In dialogues such as the *Meno* and the *Phaedo*, Plato stressed, in Pythagorean fashion, how all learning is a form of remembering and "re-cognizing" something that must have been already known. Where Plato differs from the Pythagoreans is in asserting the ideality of geometrical relationships (Burtt, 1925, p. 68). Gadamer (1980, p. 35) agrees that

> precisely therein lies the limitation of the Pythagorean explanation of number and world: Pythagoreans take numbers and numerical relations for existence itself and are unable to think of the noetic order of existence by itself.

As Gadamer continues on to say, science derives its very possibility from ideality. Because all understanding is a matter of "re-cognizing" what has already played itself out in the relationships in which one is involved, Plato's focal interest is on how learning occurs through what is already known: how the fore-structures of knowledge dialectically converge with the things themselves such that linguistic, numeric, and geometric figures separate from the meaning they carry. This is why, over the entrance to his Academy, Plato put the words "Let no one enter here who is not yet educated in mathematics." In saying this, Plato made mathematics, in the sense of that which can be taught and is learned through what is already known, the metaphysical presupposition of all "academic" knowledge (Heidegger, 1967, p. 76) because it is what is most fundamental to the event of understanding.

Thus Plato's dictum had nothing to do with a mere ability to calculate, as is so often assumed in the modern conception of mathematical knowledge. Instead, Plato saw that the crucial issue of philosophy resided in what seems self-evident in mathematics, namely, that geometrical and numerical figures mediate the conversational exchange of questions and answers such that each converges with, and cleanly separates from, the others and the meaning they carry (Derrida, 1982, p. 229; Ricoeur, 1977, p. 293; Gadamer, 1975, p. 366). Focusing attention on the way things represent themselves through figures, Plato restricted the use of instruments in geometry to the compass and straightedge, thereby allowing things to communicate themselves by means of the way measuring and measured converge upon and separate from a common object. This restriction eliminated the mechanical reproduction of figures from geometry because this strategy confuses the conceptual idealities of things with their names, in Pythagorean fashion. Plato's reasons for restricting the instruments of geometry are the same reasons why he placed philosophy in close association with mathematics, namely because

> even he who has not yet seen all the metaphysical implications of the concept of pure thinking but only grasps something of mathematics . . . knows that in a manner of speaking one looks right through the drawn circle and keeps the pure thought of the circle in mind. (Gadamer, 1980, p. 101; cf. Burtt, 1925, p. 42)

Gadamer could easily be paraphrasing Plato. In Book VI of the *Republic* (510d), Plato writes that mathematicians

> make use of the visible forms and talk about them, though they are not thinking of them, but of those things of which they are a likeness, pursuing their inquiry for the sake of the square as such and the diagonal as such, and not for the sake of the image of it which they draw.

From these observations of what mathematicians do, Plato extended the notion of ideality into the definition of the objects of geometry, conceiving of a point as "'an indivisible line,' and a line as 'length without breadth'" (Cajori, 1985, p. 26). These definitions make it most obvious that what is analyzed, or rather, what reveals itself through the dialectical interplay of theory and data mediated by instruments (Ackermann, 1985; Heelan 1983a, 1985; Ihde, 1979), is not the actually divisible line that is drawn out, and which is called a point, but is instead the conceptual ideality of that figure. The crisis brought upon Pythagorean mathematics by the existence of "irrational" numbers was overcome because these numbers live out the same conceptual existence in ideality that rational ones do. The irrationality of the square root of two, for instance, no longer threatened the heart of mathematics because the existence of this number and the line segment it represents no longer depended upon representation as a line segment of precisely drawable length or as a ratio that could be specified exactly.

Ideality and Geometric Rigor

In the same way, the mathematization of sociocultural phenomena requires a conceptual ideality that stands independent of the figures representing it; whether the figures are numeric, geometric, or metaphoric is irrelevant as long as the mathematical metaphysics of academia remain in play. Delineating this ideality and establishing its separation from the figures carrying it is, as Rasch (1960, p. xx) understood, "a huge challenge, but once the problem has been formulated it does seem possible to meet it."

A clearer understanding of the problem follows from a consideration of what happens when figure and meaning remain intertwined. When philosophical or scientific discourse is dissociated from pure ideality as it is obtained in geometrical analyses, it allows its "means to assert themselves as whatever they are, and in pushing to the fore . . . they suppress what is displayed in them" (Gadamer, 1980, p. 105), as was the case with the mechanical devices used by Sophists and Pythagoreans to manipulate and physically transform figures in order to solve otherwise unsolvable problems such as the squaring of the circle. From this point of view, confusion appears as a contextualized confounding of figure and meaning; it may be that every understanding eventually appears to have been a confusion of one kind or another in hindsight, but the recognition that an understanding was confused is itself a new separation of figure and meaning. As Wittgenstein (1980, p. 56) says, we should not be afraid of speaking nonsense, we simply must pay attention to our nonsense; the wider, Platonic sense of mathematical being aims at wagering that what is said plays itself out to be less nonsense than sense, and at constantly checking it for validity against the things themselves (Ricoeur, 1981, pp. 211–212; Hirsch, 1967, p. 174). As Rasch (1960, p. 11) says, we stand in need of measurement models in which chance plays a decisive role because of the impossibility of deterministically predicting human behavior; only when the problem of objective discourse is formulated probabilistically can we approach the rigor of geometry in social measurement.

Because of the need to constantly monitor the extent to which figure and meaning separate, the rigor of geometry "was an indispensable preliminary to the study of philosophy" (Scott, 1960, p. 20) not only for Plato, but for Husserl as well:

> The mathematical object seems to be the privileged example and most permanent thread guiding Husserl's reflection. . . . [on phenomenology] because the mathematical object is *ideal*. Its being is thoroughly transparent and exhausted by its phenomenality. (Derrida, 1978, p. 27; original emphasis)

Husserl takes up the problem of mathematical objectivity in order to begin to overcome science's "loss of meaning for life," which has come

about through Galileo's "fateful omission" of the means by which nature came to be described mathematically (Husserl, 1970). The "great
gap which separates the new [Galilean] science from its classical [Pla-
tonic] original" was that the mathematics of modern science was seen
as strictly numerical, devoid of the moral, political, and aesthetic implications pursued by Plato (Marcuse, 1974, p. 230). The effectiveness
of modern mathematics took on such force that philosophy came to be
irrelevant and unneeded in face of the seeming self-evident way figure
separates from meaning. Science will not regain its meaning for life,
however, until the contemporary and ancient senses of mathematics
are reconnected in the form of a critically constituted domain of human, moral, and cultural investigation.

What this means for contemporary social science is that the conception of the mathematical as strictly numerical—"the numbers don't
remember where they came from" (Lord, 1953, p. 751)—prevents the
introduction of rigor and continues the alienation of human and natural by preventing recognition of the need for instruments that will
allow things to communicate themselves. The instruments of social
science are employed in such a way that thinking is placed before
being, in a Cartesian manner, and therefore succeed only in asserting
themselves, suppressing the (relative and probabilistic) true being of
the phenomena of interest. What is needed is a postpositivist acknowl-
edgment such as Duncan's (1984, p. 221), that "the social roots of social
measurement are in the social process itself," and that we had best
tend to the plant as a whole if it is to survive. The dialectical convergence and separation of figure and meaning is the common focus of
mathematics and philosophy. Objectivity in measurement emerges
from its subterranean course in human history, and begins to flow as
from a source, in Plato. Only when the wider, Platonic sense of mathematics is used to calibrate instruments we can count on to mediate
relations with a relative and probabilistic invariance will the rigor of
geometry be introduced to social science.

THE RESOLUTION OF PHILOSOPHY'S DILEMMA

In looking to Plato and the history of science for a model of objectivity
in measurement, we must immediately recognize that the separation
of figure from meaning is never absolute or perfect. If it was, the
Pythagoreans and positivists would have succeeded in their goals, we
would be building Guttman scales in social science, and the quality of
human life would be much different. On the other hand, historical and

cultural contextualization does not preclude a relatively rigorous separation of figure from meaning within specific contexts, such as conversations, schools, the marketplace, and scientific experiments.

In fact, the larger contextualization is what makes the specific separability possible. History and culture constitute a frame of reference structured by a mostly implicit body of questions through which we are enabled to enter into and learn from new situations. We expect particular sets of relations to follow from particular words and turns of phrase. These expectations guide us by focusing attention on the thing itself, on the line of inquiry, and on the path of meaning. Without history and culture, there is no opening cleared for the emergence of a path, its illumination, nor for its following. With them, however, thoughts do become relatively straight, the dimensions of our interrelations are marked by their limits and meaning emerges as a measure of existence, all of which is demonstrated by the technical success of science. Our problem is that this success has been understood in a manner that prevented it from being steered or directed, even if it appears impossible to control or stop.

The dilemma of being forced to choose between equally unsatisfactory accounts of objectivity is resolved by the dialectical and interactive convergence and separation of question and questioned, measured and measuring, in the flowing creation of meaning. The dilemma is not resolved in the sense that the questions it raises are closed; rather, these questions are brought into higher resolution as heated debate tightens the focus on them. One might also say that the dilemma is resolved in that it has been put back into solution, but we can only expect that new problems will crystalize as the topic cools, demanding that we approach them with a new resolve at some later date.

Circularity and Linearity

At the moment, though, the question is how to turn up the heat higher. How does this stress on the conversational convergence of question and answer, and the contextualized separation of figure from meaning that it facilitates, address practical issues of measurement? First, it is quite significant that Rasch (1960, p. 110), and Luce and Tukey (1964) as well, found that they could achieve their measurement goals only by entering into the nonvicious, hermeneutic circularity of a simultaneous, conjoint formalization of the question and answer parameters of a psychological or educational test. Rasch (1960, p. 110) did not "find it feasible to introduce the two concepts [of ability and difficulty] separately, [but] had to formalize them simultaneously . . . one by means of the other, as it were, and vice versa, without getting into any logical circle." The nonvicious quality of the hermeneutic circle follows from the fact that things are always understood in terms of something already known. As Heidegger (1962, p. 195) put it, this circle

> is not to be reduced to the level of a vicious circle, or even of a circle which is merely tolerated. In the circle is hidden a positive possibility of the most primordial kind of knowing. To be sure, we genuinely take hold of this possibility only when, in our interpretation, we have understood that our first, last and constant task is never to allow our fore-having, fore-sight, and fore-conception to be presented to us by fancies and popular conceptions, but rather to make the scientific theme secure by working out these fore-structures in terms of the things themselves.

Partners to the pedagogic conversations constitutive of *ta mathemata* circle about the object guiding their interaction, their questions and answers converging together upon a common path of meaning that is rigorously independent of the particular words, phrases, persons, places, and times through which they have been represented. Rigor in the separation of figure from meaning does not imply their absolute independence. Rather, this second way in which the object of philosophical discourse addresses practical issues of measurement speaks to the problem of allowing things to communicate themselves by elucidating the depths of the fore-structures of knowledge. We know that we have been successful in giving our discourse up to the self-representative play of the thing itself only when that play can be repeated across specific contexts within a larger cultural arena.

The probabilistic formulation of simultaneous conjoint measurement that Rasch offers in his separability theorem describes a movement of question and answer in measurement analogous to the flow of question and answer in pedagogic dialogue. The probabilistic formulation of conjoint measurement duplicates the specificity of the context in which the convergence and separation of figure and meaning occurs. It can be seen that the "specific object-spheres" of science (Heidegger, 1977, p. 126), the "specific factuality" of language as it is used in conversation (Gadamer, 1975, pp. 403–404), the "specific plurivocity" of texts (Ricoeur, 1981, p. 213), and the "specific objectivity" of data meeting the requirements of Rasch's measurement models (Rasch, 1961, 1966, 1977) all follow from expressions of the hermeneutics of facticity. In any form of rigorous analysis, the spoken and the heard, the written and the read, and the measured and the measuring are each compelled to allow the object of the question and answer interaction take over and direct the course of the exchange.

Just as any oral or written message requires the convergence and separation of figure and meaning to be communicated, so too does numerical communication require the same convergence and separation of the questions and answers conveying it. Just as verbal communication demands a repeatable unity of meaning that maintains an invariant size and order all along the path followed in dialogue, so, too, does the meaningfulness of number require the convergence and separation of the structure of the number line with that of the phenomenon of interest. Rasch has provided a simple, elegant, and parsimonious model of how we can engage ourselves in our first, last, and constant task of making the scientific theme secure by working out the fore-structures of knowledge in terms of the things themselves:

> On the basis of [one of the equations in the measurement model being analyzed] we may estimate the item parameters independently of the personal parameters, the latter having been replaced by something observable, namely, by the individual total number of correct answers. Furthermore, on the basis of [the next equation] we may estimate the personal parameters without knowing the item parameters which have been replaced by the total number of correct answers per item. Finally, [the third equation] allows for checks on the model [another equation] which are independent of all the parameters, relying only on the observations. (Rasch 1961, p. 325; 1960, p. 122)

This separability theorem follows from the event that occurs in the convergence of questions with answers along a line of meaning played out by the thing itself through the interactive, mutual implication and unity of subject and object. When questions and answers point together at a common object, it becomes possible to position the questions along the arrow of meaning (to estimate the item parameters) free of concern for the particular persons responding (the person parameters), because these latter have been replaced by groups of observed responses (the individual total number of answers in a category—right or wrong, true or false, agree or disagree, and so on—per person) which could have been provided by anyone versed in the necessary background of social practices. Conversely, the convergence of question and answer also makes it possible to position the persons along the path delineated by the thing itself (to estimate the person parameters) without knowing which particular questions have been asked of them (the item parameters) because these have been replaced by monotonous strings of responses (the total number of correct answers per item) that might have resulted from any questions that point together along a common line of inquiry. Finally, we can check the extent to which the thing itself dominated the process of question and answer (the model) free from concern for the particular questions asked and persons responding (all the parameters) by examining the extent to which the responses keep the scientific theme secure by living up to our requirements for measurement. This last amounts to checking to see which person measures or item calibrations may be dependent upon some idiosyncracy of the person or item; hence it is a way of monitoring the extent to which measuring and measured have converged and separated. It can also be interpreted as a strategy for keeping the question alive and preventing it from being derailed by hidden agenda or unexamined prejudices.

Despite the circular process by which we become engaged in dialogue or measurement, there nevertheless remains a detachment of the meaning of what is said and done from the author's intention, from the instance of the saying, writing, and doing, from the particular speaker, writer, reader, or listener involved, and from the particular words, and vocal or writing style, conveying that meaning. Of course, this detachment is not absolute, and virtually any meaning can be shown to depend in some way or another upon something unique to a particular context. Science does not merely assert detachment blindly, however; it is the search for the limits of that detachment and therefore it is irrevocably concerned with unity, the way phenomena hang together and belong to a world. What Rasch's separability theorem makes possible is a way of keeping questions open to refutation, and of focusing our questioning activity on live topics. What reading Plato shows is that the separation of figure from meaning is an essential assumption not only whenever numbers are understood to represent something, but whenever communication is attempted. We cannot speak and listen, or read and write, without assuming a convergent coming together of thoughts and things in a flow of linguistic, historical, and cultural conceptualizations that have lived rigorously independent of the particular instances of their occurrence.

Contrasting Approaches to Rigor in Measurement

Rasch's approach to measurement differs markedly from both its closest and more distant relatives; for one thing, it is easier to put into practice than any of them. Rasch's formulation is very different from even the closely related approaches described by Thurstone (1928, 1959), Guttman (1950), and by Luce and Tukey (1964; see Andrich, 1978, 1985; Englehard 1984; Brink, 1972; Brogden, 1977; Perline, Wright, & Wainer, 1979), primarily because it is probabilistic. For instance, Guttman would have us model social measurement in a way that adheres as strictly as possible to the deterministic structure of physical measurement, wherein a seemingly absolute convergence and separation of measured with measuring is obtained. However, this results in the unreasonable requirement that questions maintain an absolutely invariant order of difficulty. Guttman seeks to emulate the one-sided, positivist account of natural science and extend it into social science by trying to cut off, instead of follow, the interaction of question and answer, and the mutual implication of subject and object. Luce and Tukey incorporate this mutual implication into their formulation of simultaneous, conjoint measurement as a new form of fundamental measurement, but they, like Guttman, neglect the need for a probabilistic model of this interaction. Without a probabilistic formulation, any model of fundamental measurement that aims to be applicable to human affairs will necessarily fail to hold for any but the simplest and most trivial of variables. Accordingly, it is appropriate that Hirsch (1967, p. 174) refers to probability as "the staple of the historical sciences," meaning that there is no final, all-encompassing account that tells the story of any human experience, but that there are only more or less likely stories useful for making sense out of things.

Rasch would agree with Hirsch's assessment, having himself gone so far as to say that "models are not meant to be true" (Rasch 1964, pp. 2, 3, 24; 1960, pp. 37–38). He points out that even the apparently deterministic measurement models of classical physics are not absolutely true, but hold only within particular margins of error; these error terms, Rasch (1960, p. 115) says, can be interpreted as probability distributions. In saying this, Rasch is countering the Cartesian and Newtonian claim that signifying figures, such as instruments, texts, and metaphors, can be completely disentangled from their signified meaning. Because context is so important to the emergence of clearly delineated meaning, the use of Rasch's measurement models requires due stress upon the arrangement of an observational situation likely to produce the convergence and separation of figure and meaning, and instrument and sample.

Arranging observational situations is analogous to the way natural scientists create phenomena via experimental procedures (Galison, 1988; Hacking, 1983, 1988; Heelan, 1988, 1989; Lynch, 1985). Heidegger (1977) calls this the work of enframing, the framework through which images of the things themselves come into view. Things come into view insofar as they are mathematical, in the wider, Platonic sense of being represented by figures but not dependent upon particular exemplars or persons for them to convey their meaning. At this point it is possible to imagine a useful paraphrase of the question Copernicus posed. Turning from a geometry of the heavens to one of social spheres and orbits, we can ask what structure should be attributed to the abilities, attitudes, and behaviors of people in order to obtain the simplest and most harmonious geometry of the social world that will accord with the facts, as these facts emerge from within the social world itself.

Rasch's answer to this question, as well as the historically effective answers of Plato and Copernicus, is, given that new facts are created from the transformation of what is already known within the framework of a particular cultural context, that the simplest and most harmonious geometry of the social world requires a clarity that can be provided only by instruments that do not inordinately vary in the size and order of their units depending upon the particular sample measured. Rasch therefore attributes the following structure to human abilities:

> A person having a greater ability than another should have the greater probability of solving *any* item of the type in question, and similarly, one item being more difficult than another one means that for *any* person the probability of solving the second item correctly is the greater one. (Rasch, 1960, p. 117; original emphases)

Attitudes and behaviors must also be arranged to be observed in a framework that conforms to the same probabilistic principles if objectivity in measurement is to take hold. Any generalization or comment about data that asserts or assumes a meaningfulness extending beyond the particular group of respondents involved in a study at one particular time and place assumes that the meanings signified by the questions making up an instrument have converged together upon a common line of meaning, and that this meaning is rigorously independent of these particular questions and the event of their interaction with these particular people at this particular time.

It follows, then, that the most important principle of fundamental measurement realized in Rasch's work is that objective comparisons require questions and answers to share a relatively constant order. Numerical comparisons are meaningful only to the extent that they embody such an order. To have calibrated a line of meaning is to have a number line that conforms to the structure of a phenomenon such that a single unit is (relatively and probabilistically) invariantly repeated along the dimension of interest. Only on such a line are sample-free instruments and measures provided, but it is a rare thing to see social researchers attempt to justify their assumptions in this regard. There are those who contend that Rasch's mathematics demands too much in the way of restrictive "assumptions" to be usefully applied to the data of social science (Goldstein, 1979; Lord, 1983; Hambleton & Rogers, 1989); the fact is, however, that these alleged "assumptions" are *assumed* to hold only by those who do not make them explicit requirements for objectivity in measurement. Fit to Rasch's measurement models is the simplest and most practical way of making the sufficient and necessary tests that justify the claim to objectivity in measurement (Douglas & Wright, 1986; Wright & Douglas, 1986).

In contrast to the simplicity and ease of use associated with Rasch's measurement models, there are approaches more distantly related to Rasch's than Guttman's or Luce and Tukey's that seem to go out of their way looking for complications to draw into the problem Rasch called "huge" to begin with. It could even be said that the two- and three-parameter models (so-called because they include extra parameters describing item functions in addition to the difficulty parameter) advocated in Item Response Theory (IRT) are self-defeating in that the mathematics of these models close off virtually any possibility of meeting the requirements of measurement. The convergence and separation of question and answer are prevented by the inclusion of extra terms that destroy the possibility of fulfilling the cancellation axiom, as described below. Two- and three-parameter IRT models therefore are not concerned with pursuing the geometric rigor made possible when data meet the requirements specified by Rasch's separability theorem.

For example, following Rasch's explication of the observational framework necessary for objectivity in measurement, the comparison of the abilities or attitudes of two people can be accomplished only in relation to a task that has a probabilistically constant difficulty. We then have a comparison of each person's ability (or attitude) (b_n and b_m) with the difficulty (d_t) of the task in question, and can subtract one of these from the other in such a way that the difficulty of the item cancels out:

$$
\begin{array}{rcl}
g_{nt} & = & b_n - d_t \\
- g_{mt} & = & b_m - d_t \\
\hline
g_{nt} - g_{mt} & = & b_n - b_m
\end{array}
$$

When we say, "This child does well in arithmetic," by arithmetic we do not mean just the items on a particular test, we mean any kind of arithmetic problem that the child may encounter. The test is assumed to provide an instrument-free view of arithmetic ability (by those who do not *require* it to do so) analogous to the way that the compass and straightedge facilitate unobstructed views of geometrical figures. The fact that arithmetic ability may vary according to context (grocery store vs. home vs. school vs. street vs. work) is interesting, and measures accounting for these variations are needed, but quantitative approaches that deliberately confound figure and meaning will only make our already huge problems insurmountable. The instruments of educational measurement are technologies capable of providing a clear view of abilities and how they vary, but when a second parameter is used to describe the item's discrimination, it is impossible to remove the influence of the item from the comparisons made, leaving the difference between the persons' abilities or attitudes dependent upon the particular item used:

$$
\begin{array}{r}
g_{nt} = a(b_n - d_t) \\
- g_{mt} = a(b_m - d_t) \\
\hline
g_{nt} - g_{mt} = a(b_n - b_m)
\end{array}
$$

Item discrimination and guessing parameters violate the most basic requirements of mathematics and measurement, repeating the Pythagorean error of allowing the mechanics of the instrumentation to obstruct the view of the thing itself, rather than transparently facilitating that view. By allowing instruments to present themselves in the place of the things supposed to be communicated, multiparameter IRT "model[s] destroy the possibility of explicit invariance of the estimates of the person and item parameters" (Andrich, 1988, p. 67), which is to say that they preclude the justification of measured with measuring necessary for objective comparisons. It is here that the wider, moral sense of mathematical thinking emphasized by Plato comes to bear most plainly on the problems of social measurement. The justification of measured and measuring is a matter of social justice to the same extent that it is one of scientific accuracy.

The ostensible reason for including a second- or third-item parameter is to try to second-guess the item writers and the test takers by including terms that will trap inordinate variation by modeling it into what is supposed happens in the question-and-answer process. The effective result, however, is to defeat the goal of measuring abilities and to facilitate the retention of items and response sets that do not participate in the delineation of the line of inquiry, but are slanted in a different direction. Hambleton and Rogers (1989, p. 148) proclaim that the three-parameter IRT model virtually always fits test data, and that the "Rasch model" rarely does. What can this mean but that double standards are taken for granted and that there must be some criterion other than the thing itself which is determining test content?

That there is such a criterion is made evident by Jaeger (1987) in his presentation of two sides in the "Rasch debate." Jaeger (1987, p. 8) juxtaposes Wright's (1968) willingness to allow the conceptualization of the variable to be tested by the way it plays itself out through the question-and-answer process with Lindquist's (1953) demand that scaling methods be prevented from determining item content. According to Lindquist (1953, p. 35; also see Goldstein, 1979, p. 218), test analysts have "no business monkeying around" with "sacrosanct" content definitions that have been "handed down" from on high by the authorities deemed responsible for such things. This one-sided imposition of preconceptions on educational variables can only be aided by scaling methods that accept their questions as God-given and too simple to require critical engagement, in the manner prescribed by Descartes and Newton's approaches to data. To say with Lindquist, Goldstein, and multiparameter IRT advocates that method must be prevented from determining content is to presume that scientific authority is always and everywhere imposed on the relations studied from outside of them as an absolute given. The historical transformations of reason show, however, that scientific authority emerges from within the relation of measured and measuring, and that facts are not given, but instead emerge from a struggle in which the scientist forces data to fit a theory, which is not to say that data can be made to fit any theory that comes along (Kuhn, 1961, 1970). Instead of being glad that test items can more regularly be made to fit the three-parameter IRT model than the requirements for measurement modeled by Rasch, one should wonder just how many double and triple standards are being applied in contemporary education in the name of sacrosanct theories handed down from on high.

In addition to confounding the requirements for rigorous objectivity in measurement, advocates of two- and three-parameter IRT models admit that these models are hard to use and understand, that they require large numbers of respondents, making them expensive and time-consuming, and that there are no easy-to-use computer programs for their application (Hambleton & Rogers 1989, p. 158; see the discussion in Wright, 1984, p. 286, for more of these kinds of admissions). These same writers admit that Rasch measurement is easy to do and understand (Hambleton & Cook, 1977, p. 88), that it works well with low numbers of respondents (Lord, 1983), making it inexpensive and fast, and that there are easy-to-use computer programs available for analyzing data (Hambleton & Cook, 1977, p. 76; see the discussion in Wright, 1984, p. 286, for more). In short, multiparameter IRT and the deterministic models of Guttman and Luce and Tukey have the common failing of deploying a notion of objectivity in measurement that ignores the contextual exigencies of meaning in favor of maintaining the depleted myth of an unquestionable authority that stands outside of the question-and-answer process. What we need, however, is to trust the interplay of question and answer as a means of determining what the point of any ongoing conversation is at the moment, and in order to monitor the twists and turns we take on the path of meaning.

CONCLUDING COMMENTS

Numerical convergence with and separation from things are fairly simple matters to establish, as Rasch, Wright, and others have repeatedly shown. However, we must not let Descartes mislead us into regarding these relative simplicities as trivialities unworthy of attention. These simplicities are the air we breathe, the water we drink, and the food we eat. They are the very substance of our social, political, and economic lives, which means that they are the most difficult things to focus on, because we are immersed in them. Immersion in the issues that matter most to cultural life presents the difficulty of not simply supposing that what has been said or written has provoked the convergence and separation of figure and meaning. Instead, we must demonstrate that this has happened, and we must constantly check and recheck that the fore-structures of meaning are not presented to us by popular fancies, but are worked out in terms of the things themselves. The seeming self-evident factuality of the measures produced in classical, Newtonian physics allowed conceptualizations of the relations between numbers and things to be lax. But the work of science nevertheless continued to be focused almost exclusively upon the creation and use of new phenomena through the replication of measures and the calibration of instruments. This work continued to be successful in spite of the gap that existed in the philosophical understanding of why it was successful.

More problematic was the fact that the lax conceptualization of the role and importance of structure in number was carried into social studies as part of the assumptions of statistical methodology. Forms of testing and social measurement can be found in the most ancient and non-Western civilizations, but only after modern science took shape were efforts aimed at devising a moral or political arithmetic focused in the sense that we understand them today. Though Christian Thomasius, for one, did what we now call a study of interrater reliability in 1692 (McReynolds & Ludwig, 1984), no one assigned much importance to the phenomenological aptness or construct validity of the numbers used as measures until fairly recently. For instance, Fisher (1932, p. 2) held that proper experimental design and research methodology alone would transform the social studies into sciences. But all of the examples he used to demonstrate how this would be accomplished involved numbers read off the calibrated instruments of biology, chemistry, and physics. Thus, statistical methods were transferred into social science with no eye on the existential meaning of the numbers involved; that is, no one asked whether numbers actually represented constant amounts of some one thing. Through no fault of their own, social scientists inherited a gap in measurement thinking that has great consequences for their work, but was hardly noticed in the fields from which it came. This gap becomes glaringly obvious, however, when social measurement is mapped directly onto the structure of physical measurement in the manner of Guttman (1950) and Murphy, Murphy, and Newcombe (1937), as has been shown by Wilson (1989a).

Husserl (1970, p. 49) called the gap in Galileo's articulation of the mathematization of nature the "fateful omission;" following from his efforts, Heidegger, Gadamer, and Ricoeur have sought to continue the "demythologization of science," as Gadamer (1981, p. 150) puts it. The work of these philosophers is most often used by those who would avoid positivism in social science by turning toward more descriptive, interpretive or qualitative methods. Husserl's lifelong interest in mathematics and the explicit interests of the latter three writers in the problems of science and technology make their works far more applicable to problems of quantification than has been widely appreciated (Heelan, 1983a, 1983c, 1985, 1988; Ihde, 1979). The main points of overlap between their work and the requirements of objectivity in measurement are:

1. *Convergence*—the nonvicious, hermeneutic circularity that holds in the simultaneous, conjoint formalization of the parameters describing the measured and the measuring; and
2. *Separation*—the requirement that, within the framework of a general context, the meaning of something cannot depend upon who said or wrote it, where or when it was said, who else was around when it was said, who asked about it, nor upon the particular words and turns of phrase used to express it.

These two factors have been referred to as the "paradox of unity and separation" (Brenneman, Yarian, & Olson, 1982, p. 6). The seemingly unanswerable question asks just how it could be that we can ever come together as a community and decide upon common units of meaning when each of these units can be infinitely divided or added into still other units we also unhesitatingly call wholes. It can only follow that convergence can never be absolutely complete. If it were, there would be no need for language; our unity would leave no need for speaking or writing. Similarly, our separation cannot be absolutely complete. Again, if it were, there would be no need for language; our alienation would leave speaking and writing useless.

Objectivity must therefore exhibit the features of a tin-can telephone theory of communication: just the right amount of mediating tension is needed to balance convergence and unity with separation and difference. Too much tension breaks the lines of communication, measurement, standards, and meaning, resulting in speechless alienation. Not enough tension introduces a laxity into communication that lets us say anything we want without testing it against the things themselves. This results in a sort of speechless unity wherein we believe ourselves together on a point but have not said or heard anything.

The Rasch models of fundamental measurement are the best hope we have for a direction-finding compass capable of guiding us in delineating paths of thinking, in drawing out lines of inquiry, and in regulating the dimensions of social science. It is along these paths, lines, and dimensions that our thinking and communication take place; hence, it is along these story lines that the narratives of our community life are plotted. Data from fields as diverse as paleontology, archeology, sociology (see Chapter 5), industrial quality control, personnel management (see Chapter 6), blind and physical rehabilitation, and studies of myth and metaphor, besides the usual educational and psychological testing data, have been usefully fitted to the requirements of measurement, and several very informative, inexpensive and easy-to-use computer programs are available (Wright, Linacre, & Schultz, 1990; Wright & Linacre, 1990; among others).

Mathematical proofs of the sufficiency and necessity of these requirements for objectivity in measurement exist (Rasch, 1960; Luce & Tukey, 1964; Wright & Douglas, 1986; Douglas & Wright, 1986), and Wilson (1988, 1989a, 1989b) has elaborated upon the superior utility and practicality of data meeting these requirements, but a simple and graphic demonstration of how the fulfillment of these requirements relates to the traditional conception of measurement, such as that of length, is needed. The following experiment was devised with this purpose in mind. Centimeter measures of various small objects were compared with the logit values (Rasch's formulation of the log odds units used to express both person ability and item difficulty) made from a ruler with unequally sized units. Unequal unit sizes were used because of the need to duplicate a fundamental problem of social research in the sphere of natural science, namely, the near-impossibility of inventing test or questionnaire items of equally spaced difficulties. The question this little project seeks to answer, therefore, is whether unevenly spaced articulations of a variable can be used to create an interval scale. Length is the obvious variable to use because it has a commonly accepted interval structure that can be used to test the linearity of the logit measures.

Unevenly spaced units were drawn onto the edge of a sheet of paper and used to create a data matrix by asking whether the various objects were longer than, at, or not up to each mark. Each object measured was assigned a marker which varied depending upon whether it was longer than (2), at (1), or not up to (0) the unit in question. The following is an example of the resulting data:

Object n 22222100000000000.

This object surpassed five of the unevenly spaced units, and was judged to be at the sixth one, and not up to the last eleven. The pattern of object n's data is, of course, a perfect Guttman scale; once a lower category is assigned, the data never go back up to a higher one. Because Rasch analyses are not designed to deal with perfectly formed data, a small amount of random variation had to be introduced when the data were analyzed via the standard Rasch procedure, using MSCALE (Wright, Congdon, & Rossner, 1988); three of the 37 "responses" to "item" 1, at the far left in "person" (object) n's data shown, were changed from 2s to 1s, and this "item" was excluded from further consideration with no effect on the results. Then the logits were plotted against the centimeter measures.

The results (see Figures 3.1 and 3.2) show the relationship of Rasch-calibrated units (logits) and centimeters to be virtually one to one. Figure 3.1 shows the plot of centimeter and logit values for the unevenly spaced units drawn on the paper ruler; these are equivalent to test items or survey questions. Figure 3.2 shows the plot of centimeter and logit values for the 37 objects measured, which include the height and width of an ashtray, the diagonal of a computer monitor, the height and thickness of books, and so on; these correspond to the person abilities or attitudes measured by a test or survey. The data in the upper right of each figure are merely indicative of object lengths going off the end of the improvised ruler; these are equivalent to test items so difficult that no person answers them correctly or rates them in the highest category of a rating scale. The overall linearity of the centimeter/logit plots demonstrates that data fitting the Rasch model produce interval scales equivalent to those in the physical sciences, just as Luce and Tukey (1964) called for.

An important aspect of this final point is that its achievement by Rasch involved a convergence of his thought with the historical source

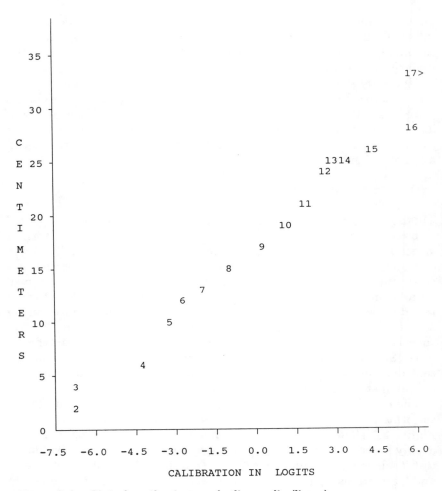

Figure 3.1.   Plot of centimeters vs. logits—units (items).

of objectivity in measurement, not with efforts aimed at mimicking the analytic methods of physics. In understanding that models are not meant to be true, but always remain on trial, in giving chance a decisive role in social measurement, and in allowing the hermeneutic circle to hold sway in the dynamic interaction of question and answer, Rasch's achievement in no way partakes of a one-sided, reductive instrumentalism; his work forces us to recognize the instructive and conversational dimension of objectivity in measurement that has heretofore been ignored, but which will be the crux of any truly human science.

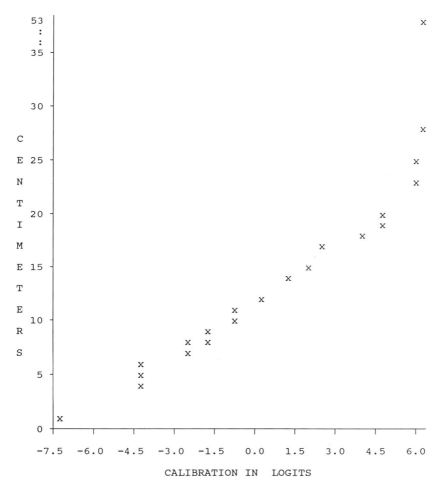

Figure 3.2.   Plot of centimeters vs. logits—objects (examinees). (An *x* may represent more than one object.)

REFERENCES

Ackermann, J.R. (1985). *Data, instruments, and theory: A dialectical approach to understanding science.* Princeton, NJ: Princeton University Press.

Andrich, D. (1978). Relationships between the Thurstone and Rasch approaches to item scaling. *Applied Psychological Measurement, 2,* 449–460.

Andrich, D. (1985). An elaboration of Guttman scaling with Rasch models for measurement. In N.B. Tuma (Ed.), *Sociological methodology* (pp. 33–80). San Francisco: Jossey-Bass.

Andrich, D. (1988). *Rasch models for measurement*. Newbury Park, CA: Sage.

Angoff, W.H. (1960). Measurement and scaling. S.V. In C.W. Harris (Ed.), *Encyclopedia of educational research*. New York: Macmillan.

Baker, B.O., Hardyck, C.D., & Petrinovich, L.F. (1966). Weak measurements vs. strong statistics: An empirical critique of S.S. Stevens' proscriptions on statistics. *Educational and Psychological Measurement, 26*, 291–309.

Bell, E.T. (1931). *The queen of the sciences*. Baltimore: Williams & Wilkins.

Bochner, S. (1966). *The role of mathematics in the rise of science*. Princeton, NJ: Princeton University Press.

Brenneman, W.L., & Yarian, S.O., with Olson, A.M. (1982). *The seeing eye: Hermeneutical phenomenology in the study of religion*. University Park, PA: Pennsylvania State University Press.

Brink, N.E. (1972). Rasch's logistic model vs. the Guttman model. *Educational and Psychological Measurement, 32*, 921–927.

Brogden, H.E. (1977). The Rasch model, the law of comparative judgment and additive conjoint measurement. *Psychometrika, 42*, 631–634.

Burtt, E.A. (1925). *The metaphysical foundations of modern science*. New York: Harcourt, Brace & Co.

Cajori, F. (1985). *A history of mathematics*. New York: Chelsea.

Dantzig, T. (1955). *The bequest of the Greeks*. London: George Allen & Unwin.

Derrida, J. (1978). *Edmund Husserl's "origin of geometry": An introduction* (J.P. Leavey, Jr., trans.). Stony Brook, NY: Nicholas Hayes.

Derrida, J. (1982). White mythology: Metaphor in the text of philosophy. In *Margins of philosophy* (pp. 207–271) (A. Bass, Trans.). Chicago: University of Chicago Press.

Descartes, R. (1961). *Rules for the direction of the mind* (L.J. Lafleur, trans.). Indianapolis: Bobbs-Merrill.

Descartes, R. (1971). *Philosophical writings* (E. Anscombe & P. Geach, Eds. and trans.). Indianapolis: Bobbs-Merrill.

Douglas, G.A., & Wright, B.D. (1986). *The two category model for objective measurement* (Research Memorandum No. 34). Chicago: University of Chicago, MESA Psychometric Laboratory.

Duncan, O.D. (1984). *Notes on social measurement: Historical and critical*. New York: Russell Sage Foundation.

Englehard, G., Jr. (1984). Thorndike, Thurstone, and Rasch: A comparison of their methods of scaling psychological and educational tests. *Applied Psychological Measurement, 8*(1), 21–38.

Feyerabend, P. (1977). *Against method*. London: New Left Books.

Feyerabend, P. (1981). How to defend society against science. In I. Hacking (Ed.), *Scientific revolutions* (pp. 156–167). Oxford: Oxford University Press.

Fisher, R. (1932). *Statistical methods for research workers* (4th ed.). London: Oliver & Boyd.

Gadamer, H.-G. (1975). *Truth and method* (G. Barden & J. Cumming, Eds., W. Glen-Doepel, trans.). New York: Crossroad.

Gadamer, H.-G. (1976). *Philosophical hermeneutics* (David E. Linge, Ed. and trans.). Berkeley: University of California Press.

Gadamer, H.-G. (1980). *Dialogue and dialectic: Eight hermeneutical studies on Plato* (P.C. Smith, trans.). New Haven, CT: Yale University Press.

Gadamer, H.-G. (1981). *Reason in the age of science* (F.G. Lawrence, Trans.). Cambridge, MA: MIT Press.

Galison, P. (1988). Philosophy in the laboratory. *The Journal of Philosophy, 85*(10), 525–527.

Goldstein, H. (1979). Consequences of using the Rasch model for educational assessment. *British Educational Research Journal, 5*(2), 211–220.

Guttman, L. (1950). The basis for scalogram analysis. In S.A. Stouffer et al. (Eds.), *Studies in social psychology in World War II. Volume 4: Measurement and prediction* (pp. 60–90). New York: John Wiley & Sons.

Hacking, I. (1983). *Representing and intervening: Introductory topics in the philosophy of natural science*. Cambridge: Cambridge University Press.

Hacking, I. (1988). On the stability of the laboratory sciences. *The Journal of Philosophy, 85*(10), 507–514.

Hambleton, R.K., & Cook, L.L. (1977). Latent trait models and their use in the analysis of educational test data. *Journal of Educational Measurement, 14*(2), 75–96.

Hambleton, R.K., & Rogers, H.J. (1989). Solving criterion-referenced measurement problems with item response models. *International Journal of Educational Research, 13*(2), 145–160.

Heath, T.L. (1931). *A manual of Greek mathematics*. Oxford: Clarendon Press.

Heelan, P. (1983a). Natural science as a hermeneutic of instrumentation. *Philosophy of Science, 50*(2), 181–204.

Heelan, P. (1983b). Perception as a hermeneutical act. *Review of Metaphysics, 37*(1), 61–75.

Heelan, P. (1983c). *Space-perception and the philosophy of science*. Berkeley: University of California Press.

Heelan, P. (1985, March 16). *Interpretation in physics: Observation and measurement*. Unpublished manuscript. Philadelphia: Greater Philadelphia Philosophy Consortium.

Heelan, P. (1988). Experiment and theory: Constitution and reality. *The Journal of Philosophy, 85*(10), 515–524.

Heelan, P. (1989). After experiment: Realism and research. *American Philosophical Quarterly, 26*(4), 297–308.

Heidegger, M. (1962). *Being and time* (J. Macquarrie & E. Robinson, trans.). New York: Harper & Row.

Heidegger, M. (1967). *What is a thing?* (W.B. Barton, Jr. & V. Deutsch, Trans.). South Bend, IN: Regnery.

Heidegger, M. (1977). *The question concerning technology and other essays* (W. Lovitt, Trans.). New York: Harper & Row.

Heidegger, M. (1982). *Nietzsche. Vol. 4: Nihilism* (D.F. Krell, Ed., F.A. Capuzzi, trans.). San Francisco: Harper & Row.

Hirsch, E.D. (1967). *Validity in interpretation*. New Haven, CT: Yale University Press.

Husserl, E. (1970). *The crisis of European philosophy and transcendental philosophy* (D. Carr, Trans.) Evanston, IL: Northwestern University Press.

Ihde, D. (1979). *Technics and praxis.* Boston: D. Reidel.

Jaeger, R.M. (1987). Two decades of revolution in educational measurement!? *Educational Measurement: Issues and Practice, 6*(2), 6–14.

Kuhn, T.S. (1961). The function of measurement in modern physical science. *Isis, 52*(168), 161–193.

Kuhn, T.S. (1970). *The structure of scientific revolutions* (2nd ed.). Chicago: University of Chicago Press.

Lindquist, E.F. (1953). Selecting appropriate score scales for tests (Discussion). *Proceedings of the 1952 Invitational Conference on Testing Problems.* Princeton, NJ: Educational Testing Service.

Loevinger, J. (1947). A systematic approach to the construction and evaluation of tests of ability. *Psychological Monographs, 61*(4, Whole No. 285).

Lord, F. (1953). On the statistical treatment of football numbers. *American Psychologist, 8,* 750–751.

Lord, F. (1983). Small N justifies Rasch model. In D.J. Weiss (Ed.), *New horizons in testing* (pp. 51–61). New York: Academic Press.

Luce, R.D., & Tukey, J.W. (1964). Simultaneous conjoint measurement: A new kind of fundamental measurement. *Journal of Mathematical Psychology, 1*(1), 1–27.

Lynch, M. (1985). Discipline and the material form of images: An analysis of scientific visibility. *Social Studies of Science, 15*(1), 37–66.

McReynolds, P., & Ludwig, K. (1984). Christian Thomasius and the origin of psychological rating scales. *Isis, 75,* 546–553.

Marcuse, H. (1974). On science and phenomenology. In A. Giddens (Ed.), *Positivism and sociology* (pp. 225–236). London: Heinemann.

Miller, G.A. (1921). *Historical introduction to mathematical literature.* New York: The Macmillan Company.

Murphy, G., Murphy, L.B., & Newcombe, T.M. (1937). *Experimental social psychology.* Westport, CT: Greenwood Press.

Newton, I. (1952). *Opticks* (4th ed.). New York: Dover.

Nietzsche, F. (1967). *The will to power* (Walter Kaufman & R.J. Hollingdale, trans., Walter Kaufman, Ed.). New York: Vintage Books.

Perline, R., Wright, B.D., & Wainer, H. (1979). The Rasch model as additive conjoint measurement. *Applied Psychological Measurement, 3*(2), 237–255.

Rasch, G. (1960). *Probabilistic models for some intelligence and attainment tests.* Chicago: University of Chicago Press. (Reprinted, 1980).

Rasch, G. (1961). On general laws and the meaning of measurement in psychology. *Proceedings of the Fourth Berkeley Symposium on Mathematical Statistics and Probability, 4,* 321–333. Berkeley: University of California Press.

Rasch, G. (1964). *Objective comparisons.* Lecture given at the UNESCO seminar, Voksenasen, Oslo, Norway.

Rasch, G. (1966). An item analysis which takes individual differences into account. *British Journal of Mathematical and Statistical Psychology, 19,* 49–57.

Rasch, G. (1977). On specific objectivity: An attempt at formalizing the request for generality and validity of scientific statements. *Danish Yearbook of Philosophy, 14*, 58–94.

Ricoeur, P. (1977). *The rule of metaphor: Multi-disciplinary studies of the creation of meaning in language* (R. Czerny, trans.). Toronto: University of Toronto Press.

Ricoeur, P. (1981). *Hermeneutics and the human sciences.* (J.B. Thompson, trans.). Cambridge: Cambridge University Press.

Rutherford, W. (1984). *Pythagoras: Lover of wisdom.* Wellingborough, Northamptonshire, Great Britain: The Aquarian Press.

Scott, J.F. (1960). *A history of mathematics.* London: Taylor & Francis.

Suppes, P., & Zinnes, J.L. (1963). Basic measurement theory. In R. Duncan Luce, R.R. Bush, & E. Galanter (Eds.), *Handbook of mathematical psychology* (pp. 1–76). New York: John Wiley & Sons.

Thorndike, E.L., et al. (1926). *The measurement of intelligence.* New York: Columbia University Teacher's College Press.

Thurstone, L.L. (1928). Attitudes can be measured. *American Journal of Sociology, 33*, 529–554. (Reprinted in L.L. Thurstone, *The measurement of values.* Chicago: University of Chicago Press, 1959).

Thurstone, L.L. (1959). *The measurement of values.* Chicago: University of Chicago Press.

Townsend, J.T., & Ashby, F.G. (1984). Measurement scales and statistics: The misconception misconceived. *Psychological Bulletin, 96*, 2, 394–401.

Weinsheimer, J.C. (1985). *Gadamer's hermeneutics: A reading of "truth and method."* New Haven, CT: Yale University Press.

Whitehead, A.N. (1968). *Essays in science and philosophy.* New York: Greenwood Press.

Wilder, R.L. (1965). *Introduction to the foundations of mathematics.* New York: John Wiley & Sons.

Wilson, M. (1988). Using the partial credit model to investigate responses to structured subtests. *Applied Measurement in Education, 1*(4), 319–344.

Wilson, M. (1989a). A comparison of deterministic and probabilistic approaches to measuring learning structures. *Australian Journal of Education, 33*(2), 127–140.

Wilson, M. (1989b). Empirical examination of a learning hierarchy using an item response theory model. *Journal of Experimental Education, 57*(4), 357–371.

Wittgenstein, L. (1980). *Culture and value* (G.H. von Wright, in collaboration with H. Nyman, Eds., and P. Winch, trans.). Chicago: University of Chicago Press.

Wright, B.D. (1968). Sample-free test calibration and person measurement. In *Proceedings of the 1967 Invitational Conference on Testing Problems.* Princeton, NJ: Educational Testing Service.

Wright, B.D. (1977). Solving measurement problems with the Rasch model. *Journal of Educational Measurement, 14*(2), 97–116.

Wright, B.D. (1984). Despair and hope for educational measurement. *Contemporary Education Review, 3*(1), 281–288.

Wright, B.D., & Douglas, G.A. (1986). *The rating scale model for objective measurement* (Research Memorandum No. 35). Chicago: University of Chicago, MESA Psychometric Laboratory.

Wright, B.D., & Linacre, J.M. (1990). *FACETS: A computer program for many-faceted Rasch analysis*. Chicago: MESA Press.

Wright, B.D., Linacre, J.M., & Schultz, M. (1990). *BIGSCALE: A Rasch-model rating scale analysis computer program*. Chicago: MESA Press.

Wright, B.D., & Masters, G. (1982). *Rating scale analysis*. Chicago: MESA Press.

Wright, B.D., Congdon, R., & Rossner, M. (1988). *MSCALE: A Rasch program for ordered categories*. Chicago: MESA Press.

Wright, B.D., & Stone, M. (1979). *Best test design*. Chicago: MESA Press.

part II

Measurement Practice

Using Rasch Procedures to Understand Psychometric Structure in Measures of Personality

Michael L. O'Brien
Fordham University

Historically, objective tests of personality traits have been constructed informally and interpreted normatively. For example, the Minnesota Multiphasic Personality Inventory (MMPI) (Hathaway & McKinley, 1967), developed by criterion scoring, is interpreted by norm referencing an examinee's total score. As such, a single standard score or percentile may be estimated for each trait being measured. Since norms are based on total scores, only a description of the *level* of a person's trait may be interpreted. However, the *pattern within* the person's responses to a given scale may also contain valuable information. Regretably, traditional procedures ignore this potentially useful aspect of responses. To utilize response patterns when interpreting personality traits, it is necessary to focus on the psychological *process* which underlies the variable measured by the scale. Thus, enhanced psychometric procedures focus prescriptively on the structure of a personality variable in terms of item severity (i.e., "intensity" or "difficulty"). Persons are measured by observing their individual response to a given item and prescribing the outcome probabilistically. Thus, both a level and a pattern within a personality trait may be measured, providing more information for interpretation. The goal of my current work is to suggest a synthesis of methods which facilitate both level and pattern interpretations of a given personality trait.

Focus on structure within a psychological variable stems from Thurstone's (1927) revision of Fechner's work in psychophysics. Thurstone argued that *all* mental tests, including personality tests, measure an underlying psychological continuum. As such, personality test items reflect a structure of intensity and psychological theory that is used to predict the relative severity of any given representative item within a domain of items reflecting the trait being measured. Test development, as seen from Thurstone's method, incorporates expert judgment of item severity. In the cognitive domain (e.g., in the development of an achievement test), this procedure is commonplace, in the personality domain, it is rare. For example, if one wished to introduce an item to a math test such as "$2 \times 2 = $ _____," the focus would first address whether this item is valid for the test objectives and then on how difficult the item appears to be, given a curriculum. The anticipated item difficulty reflects the complexity of skill measured by this item relative to other skills represented by other test items. It is necessary to make this judgment before any sense can be made about the pattern of a person's responses to the test items. Therefore, personality test development could be enhanced by incorporating a procedure which focuses on expected item severities, given a theory about how people function with the personality trait being measured.

It is my present purpose to offer a revision of some aspects of personality test construction and validation so that the limitations of solely normative procedures can be relieved. This takes the form of five procedural steps. I provide an example of how my current work with the measurement of narcissistically abused personality reflects the use of the steps.

PROCEDURAL STEPS

Step 1—Scale Development

To define a personality variable, one begins by identifying a body of literature in which the construct is discussed. The step between a personality theory and a personality test is that the former is operationalized into the latter. That is, psychological theory leads to psychological measurement—not the other way around, as is the case with the traditional criterion-scoring method.

Theory defines the scope and interconnections of a psychological trait with other traits. One begins to operationalize a theory by specifying a domain of items thought to reflect the variable being measured (Anastasi, 1988). Here, it is often useful to delineate specific objectives or diagnostic criteria for item writers. For example, one might devise a measure of a personality disorder from reading the relevant psychoanalytic literature and then using the diagnostic criteria from the DSM-III-R (APA, 1988).

Items reflect specific experiential samples of the variable in a person's life. Whereas a diagnostic criterion for a particular disorder may be dichotomized as present or absent, a person may experience a range of severity within different circumstances around the same problem. For example, one might experience a diagnostic feature of depression, such as hopelessness, in different ways and with varying severity according to various environmental stimuli. A depressed person may, for example, experience intense hopelessness upon the death of a loved one, whereas the loss of a summer home in Vermont is met with mild or absent hopelessness. For another depressive, the reactions may be reversed or even equivalent under similar circumstances. Experience is referential, not absolute. Therefore, diagnostic criteria should be viewed as "subdomains," each containing many experiential samples and a range of likely severities.

Item writers are thus summoned to produce a pool of items meeting the specifications of the diagnostic criteria. Each item writer needs to be thoroughly familiar with the literature underlying the diagnostic criteria and, ideally, should have experienced a treatment situation in which the trait was observed.

The item pool is now ready for another review—this time for likely severity. This integral part of Step 1 requires the expert panel to make predictions regarding the likely severity of each item when calibrated. The panel members should read each item and from their expertise assign an a priori rating which reflects their expectation of the item's severity (see, for example, O'Brien & Hampilos, 1988). The rating is based upon predictions implied from the relevant literature and from the experience of the panel members who worked clinically with the trait being measured. Many types of rating scales may be used to assign severity ratings; however, the Global Assessment of Functioning Scale (GAF Scale) within the DSM-III-R is quite effective for rating items which measure pathological disorders (see Figure 4.1). Just as achievement test items reflect a curriculum based on learning theory, personality test items reflect a functioning based on psychological theory. The process of expert rating should occur independently of knowledge from the empirical step below.

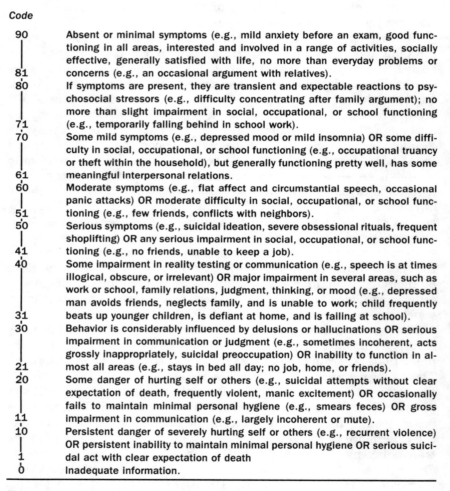

Global Assessment of Functioning Scale (GAF Scale)

Consider psychological, social, and occupational functioning on a hypothetical continuum of mental-health illness. Do not include impairment in functioning due to physical (or environmental) limitations. See p. 20 for instructions on how to use this scale. (*Note:* Use intermediate codes when appropriate, e.g., 45, 68, 72.)

Code

90 — Absent or minimal symptoms (e.g., mild anxiety before an exam, good functioning in all areas, interested and involved in a range of activities, socially effective, generally satisfied with life, no more than everyday problems or concerns (e.g., an occasional argument with relatives).

81

80 — If symptoms are present, they are transient and expectable reactions to psychosocial stressors (e.g., difficulty concentrating after family argument); no more than slight impairment in social, occupational, or school functioning (e.g., temporarily falling behind in school work).

71

70 — Some mild symptoms (e.g., depressed mood or mild insomnia) OR some difficulty in social, occupational, or school functioning (e.g., occupational truancy or theft within the household), but generally functioning pretty well, has some meaningful interpersonal relations.

61

60 — Moderate symptoms (e.g., flat affect and circumstantial speech, occasional panic attacks) OR moderate difficulty in social, occupational, or school functioning (e.g., few friends, conflicts with neighbors).

51

50 — Serious symptoms (e.g., suicidal ideation, severe obsessional rituals, frequent shoplifting) OR any serious impairment in social, occupational, or school functioning (e.g., no friends, unable to keep a job).

41

40 — Some impairment in reality testing or communication (e.g., speech is at times illogical, obscure, or irrelevant) OR major impairment in several areas, such as work or school, family relations, judgment, thinking, or mood (e.g., depressed man avoids friends, neglects family, and is unable to work; child frequently beats up younger children, is defiant at home, and is failing at school).

31

30 — Behavior is considerably influenced by delusions or hallucinations OR serious impairment in communication or judgment (e.g., sometimes incoherent, acts grossly inappropriately, suicidal preoccupation) OR inability to function in almost all areas (e.g., stays in bed all day; no job, home, or friends).

21

20 — Some danger of hurting self or others (e.g., suicidal attempts without clear expectation of death, frequently violent, manic excitement) OR occasionally fails to maintain minimal personal hygiene (e.g., smears feces) OR gross impairment in communication (e.g., largely incoherent or mute).

11

10 — Persistent danger of severely hurting self or others (e.g., recurrent violence) OR persistent inability to maintain minimal personal hygiene OR serious suicidal act with clear expectation of death

1

0 — Inadequate information.

Figure 4.1.   Samples of GAF Scale from DSM-III-R.

A final component in Step 1 is the traditional prediction of the total test score with external measures of the same sample of examinees. These predictions, often referred to as concurrent, predictive, or construct validity, require the test developer to select existing tests to be administered with the pilot items. Here, it is important to comb the literature for relevant interconnections amidst related traits, in which a lawful relationship may be predicted between the newly developed test and existing external tests. Predictions are to be made prior to observing empirical data from the new test.

Once satisfactory progress is made with Step 1, the test items are ready for tryout with a sample of examinees who are representative of the larger population for whom the test is ideally targeted.

Step 2—Item Calibration

Once the items are administered to a group of examinees, known as the calibration sample, the response matrix is prepared for analysis. At this juncture, the real work of psychophysical methods is set into motion. Whereas Thurstone's scaling methods were based on normal deviates, modern psychophysical methods employ log-based, sample-free calibrations and test-free person measurement (Rasch, 1960; Wright, 1968). These methods, known as Rasch models, predict the probable response of a person to an item, given the person's position on the underlying trait and the item's severity in relation to the underlying dimension being measured (Wright & Masters, 1982). Choice of which Rasch model to use depends on the observation format—dichotomous, rating scale, partial credit, and so on (see, for example, Masters & Wilson, 1988; O'Brien, 1986, 1989). Other latent trait methods, known generally as Item Response Theory (IRT) models, fail to estimate person fit. Rather, they force *any* given pattern of responses into a trait-level estimate and thereby limit the interpretation of a person's performance (Wright & Stone, 1979).

Scaling the item calibrations from the calibration sample requires keypunching the response matrix into a computer file and applying a Rasch analysis computer program, such as BICAL (Wright & Mead, 1976). For this discussion, it will be assumed that one is developing a test of a personality disorder. As such, a Rasch analysis will be used to estimate the probability of a person's response to a test item. The response probability is derived from the estimated difference between a person's level of pathology on the underlying trait and the level of severity of an item used to measure the trait. The general form of the Rasch model when item responses are dichotomous is:

$$Pr\,(X_{ni} = 0,1\,/\,b_n,\,d_i) = \frac{\exp\,(X_{ni}\,(b_n - d_i))}{1 + \exp\,(b_n - d_i)} \tag{1}$$

Wherein: X_{ni} is response X (0 or 1) given by person n to item i;

b_n is person n's level of pathology on the underlying trait; and

d_i is item i's level of severity on the underlying trait.

b_n is estimated from the unweighted sum of pathological responses given by each person, and d_i is estimated from one minus the proportion of pathological responses given to each item.

Applying the Rasch model to test data results in an estimate of b for each score (i.e., sum of pathological responses). An estimate of d for each item is calibrated independently from the person measures. However, b and d are expressed on a common, logistic scale, centered at $\bar{d} = 0$. Convenient linear transformations of this logistic scale are given by Wright and Stone (1979). For example, norm-referenced scaling for expressing person measures and item calibrations on the same scale is facilitated from the following Rasch Normative Scaling Unit (NIT) transformations of b and d, respectively:

$$NIT_b = 500 + \frac{(b - \bar{b})}{S_b} \times 100 \tag{2}$$

$$NIT_d = 500 - \frac{\bar{b}}{S_b} \times 100 + \frac{\bar{d}}{S_d} \times 100 \tag{3}$$

These NIT transformations create a norm-based scale with $\bar{b} = 500$ and $S_b = 100$ for the elected norming (i.e., calibration) sample. Item severity is calibrated on the same NIT scale, with $\bar{d} = 500 - \bar{b}\,/\,S_b \times 100$ and $S_d = 100$. The NIT scale is convenient for exposing the confrontation of the norming sample to the test items, as well as for comparing normal vs. clinical samples on the same underlying trait. An illustrative example of these procedures follows later in this chapter.

Items of poor quality are identified through inspecting item fit statistics (Wright & Stone, 1979). These indices are used to flag items for whom the predicted responses were errant. Usually, items which misfit were either miskeyed or tapped into a dimension not intended to be measured by the test. Such items often provide the opportunity for further item editing and expose opportunity for reconsideration of initial test development specifications. For example, one might opt to create a battery of tests rather than a single test to measure a trait with orthogonal dimensions. Large numbers of misfitting items may indicate various problems with the psychological theory on which the items are based and/or problems with the process by which the theory is realized as items.

Upon completion of Step 2, the test developer is left with a set of calibrated items and a measure of each person's level of pathology on the personality disorder trait. In addition, the concurrent measures selected from Step 1 are scored and recorded for each examinee.

Step 3—Item Validation

Finding a "best set" of items does not stop with Step 2. Validity addresses the usefulness of a test for its intended purpose and specification. Hence, one must evaluate whether the predictions made by the expert raters regarding expected item severities are reflected from the item calibrations. A formal procedure for this step is presented and illustrated in O'Brien and Hampilos (1988). A more informal procedure, which is to produce a bivariate plot and estimate the correlation coefficient, is presented later in this chapter. In any case, the test developer uses Step 3 to determine which items may be safely retained for use in the test. Often, insights regarding subtle aspects of certain items and the trait in general are uncovered from this step. Indeed, one misses out on the science of test development when this step is omitted!

Step 4—Person Measure Validation

The observed pattern of responses given by each person is compared against the predicted pattern from the Rasch model. This unique feature of Rasch models, known as the person fit statistic, separates a meaningful total score from one which needs to be clarified from inspecting surprising individual responses (Wright & Stone, 1979). Diagnosis from analyzing individual response patterns given to a single test is the essence of a person measure validation from a Rasch perspective. When the test items pass the stringent requirements of Steps 1 to 3, a misfitting response pattern identified in Step 4 should be taken seriously because it indicates that the misfitting person experiences the variable differently than its usual manifestation. Often, "gaps" exist between levels of the person's experience with the trait—such as an individual who functions well with lone activities but who experiences difficulty with group work. For misfitting persons, the total test score is misleading—the real story lurks amidst the analysis of the content of the response pattern. The analysis of person fit is an integral part of the application of objective measurement through

Rasch models, and is one of its major advantages over other forms of IRT.

Another way to provide evidence of validity is to follow traditional procedures for investigating concurrent, predictive, and construct validity. However, it is recommended that Rasch-based person measures be used instead of total raw scores. It is also wise to produce bivariate plots for pairs of variables in correlation analysis. Useful information is often found from inspecting outliers for whom the correlation fails to hold. It may be possible to explore additional information about such persons which will explain their unusual performance on a scale. Finally, it is useful to depict the relationship between highly correlated variables across the entire range of the trait being measured by the new test. An illustrative example of this procedure appears later in this chapter.

Step 5—Population Congruence

When one intends to use the newly developed test with only one target population, the test is ready upon satisfying Step 4. However, sometimes tests of personality are used in two populations—normal and clinical. In such instances, one should verify that the same test may be used to measure the personality trait of interest. This step requires two procedures. First, items calibrated separately from normal and clinical samples are plotted against an identity line in a bivariate graph and bounded by 95 percent confidence bands. Items falling within the bands are invariant and evidence the same underlying severity calibration. Items outside the bands shift position and have different meaning across the two samples. For purposes of comparing normal and clinical samples, only invariant items should be used for person measurement. A discussion of the procedures for constructing the confidence bands is given in Wright and Stone (1979, p. 96).

The second procedure is to use the invariant items to measure the level of pathology, b, for all persons, regardless of their population membership. One expects to evidence a higher $\bar{b}$ for the clinical sample, given that a trait measuring pathology is involved. Hence, the population congruence requirement of Step 5 is satisfied when the item calibrations are sample invariant and when $\bar{b}$ is higher for the clinical vs. normal sample.

ILLUSTRATIVE EXAMPLE

In this section, a brief example of the use of the procedural steps is presented. The work is based on the development, calibration, and validation of the Narcissistically Abused Personality Dimension (NAPD) of the O'Brien Multiphasic Narcissism Inventory (OMNI) (O'Brien, 1987, 1988). The NAPD scale was developed to measure a personality disorder discussed by Alice Miller (1981, 1984, 1985). Specifically, the narcissistically abused personality theoretically results when, in development, the normal narcissistic needs are *blocked* and the individual is denied nurturance of true needs. Unlike the Narcissistic Personality Disorder described in DSM-III-R, the narcissistically abused personality is marked by tendencies toward looking for others' approval for self-validation, experiencing problems with belongingness, and recognizing others' needs as being of greater importance than one's own. Thus, unlike the exploitative and entitled interpersonal style of the traditional narcissist (Kernberg, 1976), the narcissistically abused personality plays the martyr in relationships and feels compelled to achieve in order to be worthwhile.

Step 1—Scale Development

To initiate the construction of the NAPD scale, the literature on narcissism was extensively reviewed. Expert clinical psychologists who have worked with the disorder were consulted for development of key clinical features to be delineated through the diagnostic criteria for narcissistically abused personality disorder. The criteria identified were: (a) putting others' needs before one's own through martyrdom; (b) imposing patterns of actual or imaginary isolation through social discomfort, fear of rejection, feeling misunderstood, or practicing secretive acts; and (c) feelings of anxiety or reverse entitlement such that others know better how to live and have better lives. These diagnostic criteria will be subsequently referred to as Domains 1, 2, and 3, respectively.

Five item writers were employed and trained for item development from using these three diagnostic domains. Each writer held a masters or doctoral degree in psychology and was familiar with the work of Alice Miller. Ten items for each diagnostic domain were written and the test developer selected the best seven items in each area for pilot testing. Items were written in the Yes/No dichotomous item format to reflect the "either/or" cognitive style of narcissistic individuals.

An expert panel was then convened to rate the items for their expected severity level of pathology. For this rating procedure, the Global Assessment of Functioning Scale (GAF) was used to anchor the expected pathological criteria. For this review, six doctoral-level psychometrics students and two expert clinical psychologists were consulted. Each expert was asked to rate the level of impairment of functioning

	NIT	GAF Domain/Rating	OMNI Item	Probability of Pathological Response: Normal Subjects	Probability of Pathological Response: Clinical Subjects
Severely Pathological ↑	753	2 / 44	34. Would your secretive acts horrify your friends? (Y)	.11	.33
Serious GAF Impairments M_C →	716	2 / 51	48. Do you have problems that nobody else understands? (Y)	.14	.41
High Depression Anxiety	685	3 / 62	25. When confused, do you think of your mother's wishes to help you to resolve your conflicts? (Y)	.18	.54
	656	3 / 66	17. Do you think that movie stars have better lives than you? (Y)	.21	.67
	623	1 / 63	7. Do you tend to feel like a martyr? (Y)	.26	.73
	597	1 / 68	37. Do you find it easier to empathize with others' misfortunes than with those of your own? (Y)	.30	.78
	564	2 / 67	6. Do you find it easy to relax in a group? (N)	.36	.81
Minor GAF Impairments M_N →	551	3 / 57	46. Do you think that going through life is like walking on a tightrope? (Y)	.39	.86
Low Depression & Anxiety	485	2 / 70	28. Do you try to avoid rejection at all costs? (Y)	.52	.95
Mildly Pathological ↓	442	1 /1 82	3. Would you try to please others than to have your own way? (Y)	.61	.98

Note: NIT is the Rasch Normative Scaling Unit; Direction of the pathological response for each item is in parentheses; M_C is the Mean NIT_b level based on Clinical Subjects (n = 256); M_N is the Mean NIT_b level based on Normal Subjects (n = 286).

Figure 4.2. Rasch scaling and response probabilities of normal and clinical subjects on OMNI items measuring the narcissistically abused personality.

that would be expected or typical of a person who responded to a given NAPD item in the pathological direction. The median rating given to each item was assigned to reflect the expected severity level for each item. The NAPD items and their corresponding diagnostic domains and GAF ratings appear in Figure 4.2; a sample of the criteria is given in Figure 4.1.

Traditional hypothetical predictions regarding external measures were made based on the writings in the psychoanalytic literature. Miller (1981) found that her narcissistically abused analysands experienced depression and anxiety. Therefore, the IPAT tests of depression and anxiety, respectively, were selected and expected to correlate positively with the newly developed NAPD test.

Step 2—Item Calibration

Two hundred eighty-six persons served as the calibration sample for the pilot testing. The examinees consisted of 143 undergraduate and graduate students enrolled in psychology courses at two private New York City universities and 143 parents, friends, and siblings of the students. These "normal subjects" constituted a representative balance of sex, age, ethnic, and racial characteristics of the general population for whom the NAPD was targeted. All examinees responded to the 21 NAPD pilot items and the IPAT tests of depression and anxiety, respectively. The resulting item response matrix from the NAPD items was analyzed using the BICAL computer program. Item severity indices and fit statistics were estimated for each item. A NIT_d transformation was applied to each item severity estimate, following the procedures described in the previous section of this chapter. The 21 items were then set aside for further consideration in Step 3 as follows.

Step 3—Item Validation

A NAPD pilot item was considered as "valid," or useful, if it demonstrated an acceptable item mean square fit statistic of 1.3 or lower AND if the GAF Scale rating for the item predicted the NIT_d severity calibration. Further, the final set of NAPD items included a minimum of three items of varying severity from each of the three diagnostic domains. The NIT_d calibrations for the final set of 10 NAPD items are reported in Figure 4.2.

The interrater reliability, estimated from the six raters on 10 items, was estimated to be $\alpha = 0.80$, which was considered as adequate evidence of agreement among the raters (Anastasi, 1988). The median

GAF Scale rating, which is on a scale which is inverse to the NIT_d scale, was predicted to be negatively correlated with the item severity calibrations. The resulting correlation was statistically significant in the expected direction ($r = -0.83$, $p < .001$). Thus, it was possible to understand the variability in the NAPD item severities by applying the a priori GAF Scale descriptions. Test developers might, based on these findings, utilize the GAF Scale for referencing predictions about test items which measure personality disorders.

Step 4—Person Measure Validation

The final set of 10 NAPD items were selected from the calibration sample response matrix and rerun through BICAL to obtain an estimate of each subject's level of narcissistic pathology from the NAPD. A person fit statistic was also estimated from the discrepancy between each person's observed vs. expected pattern of responses to the NAPD items. Interpreting response pattern is a key advantage of the methods proposed in this chapter. An anecdote from a clinical use of OMNI helps to illustrate this advantage. A clinical psychologist administered OMNI to a few patients. A woman, who we'll call Joan, answered only three items in the narcissistic direction. This score would reflect a low level of narcissistically abused personality. With a traditional personality test, one would stop here and conclude that narcissistic abuse is not Joan's problem. However, Joan's response pattern misfit the Rasch model. Why? Because two of the three items which Joan answered in the narcissistic direction were, indeed, mild—expected from persons with a low level of narcissistic abuse. Namely, Joan expressed an interest in pleasing others rather than to have her own way and to try to avoid rejection at all costs. However, the third item that Joan answered in the narcissistically abused direction was the *most* severe item on the scale: that Joan's secretive acts would horrify her friends. It turns out that Joan was an incest victim and her response pattern to the OMNI items reflects a splitting defense in her functioning. On the surface, when in public, Joan is pleasant, accommodating, and seemingly well adjusted. However, when alone, Joan is isolated, fearful, and prone to addictive behaviors that she hides from her friends. She disconnects her phone when she goes on drinking and eating binges and her secret is that she is a lesbian.

Thus, pattern scores lead the test interpreter to potentially important insights which uncover the examinee's own relationship to the personality variable being measured. A valid measure is one which reflects the actual nature of the trait within the individual who is being tested. Rasch fit statistics tell us whether total score, or level per se, is sufficient in understanding a person's level of trait—or, whether through misfit, a person's experience with the trait can be understood usefully in more idiosyncratic terms.

To study validity of total scores, misfitting person responses were removed from the analysis, since these persons related idio-syncratically and their total scores were, therefore, useless. The 272 persons whose person fit statistics fell below 2.0 on NAPD were se-lected for validity study against the external measures of depression and anxiety, respectively. The first correlation between NAPD and the log transformation of the IPAT depression total score was statistically significant in the predicted direction ($r = 0.80$, $p < .001$). The second correlation between NAPD and the log transformation of the IPAT anxiety total score was also statistically significant in the expected direction ($r = 0.69$, $p < .001$). Along the far left column of Figure 4.2, the relationships between the range of the NAPD scale and the exter-nal measures of depression and anxiety are depicted. This presenta-tion is intended to provide the practitioner with a sense of how NAPD content was related to levels of affective disturbances.

Step 5—Population Congruence

Since NAPD measures personality pathology, the scale needs to mea-sure the underlying narcissistically abused personality trait in a simi-lar way for both "normal" and "clinical" samples. Hence, a clinical sample of 256 patients receiving psychotherapy in one of four large outpatient treatment programs in the greater New York City area took the NAPD items (O'Brien, 1988). The clinical sample consisted of pa-tients in their first year of treatment whose primary or secondary diagnosis involved narcissistic pathology. The sample was otherwise of similar demographic characteristics in relation to the normal sample studied previously. To investigate the invariance of NAPD item sever-ities and the mean difference in pathology level between normal and clinical samples, separate BICAL analyses were performed from the response matrices of the two samples.

To study the invariance of the NAPD item severities, a NIT_d index was estimated for each item from normal v. clinical samples. All ten pairs of item severities fell within a 95 percent standard error of the difference from the same underlying NIT_d parameter. Further, the correlation coefficient between the estimates was not different from 1.00 ($r = 0.94$, $p < .001$, $r_{max} = 1.00$; see Wright & Masters, 1982). This result supported strongly the invariant scale positions of the NAPD item severity between normal and clinical samples.

To determine whether the NAPD scale could be shown to measure higher levels of narcissistic pathology for the clinical population in relation to the normal population, mean NIT_b was estimated from the respective samples. The results, as shown in the left column of Figure 4.2, indicated that the mean level of narcissistically abused pathology for the clinical sample was higher than that of the normal group so the scale discriminated levels of narcissistic pathology in the expected direction ($t = 21.88$, $p < .001$).

In the far right columns of Figure 4.2, the probability of a pathological response to each item for the respective samples is reported. These response probabilities provide the Rasch-based expectation of the likelihood that a given individual from either sample would, on the average, respond in a narcissistically disturbed way to a given NAPD item.

CONCLUSION

Developing and analyzing a personality test via the suggested steps should yield important benefits for research and application. Because of the focus on the structure of an underlying personality trait, the researcher can expose the full meaning of the test items within the context of a psychological trait. Personality theories are built upon a notion of how a person functions in situations and predictions of functioning are made explicit in the suggested steps. Further, validity is possible at the item level by verifying the accuracy of predictions of item severity, given expert ratings based on theory and functional criteria. In practical terms, a test interpreter may benefit from analyzing the pattern of a person's responses to the test items. This is especially useful when a person's total score conceals important clinical information. For example, a person with a low total score may have responded positively to a few items indicative of severe pathology. Thus, the pattern score may lead the test interpreter to discover important idiosyncrasies about the person that would have been obscured from having just the total score.

These advantages of the proposed procedural steps are intended to enhance rather than to replace traditional methods of personality testing. When "new" methods such as Rasch models are introduced, researchers and practitioners alike question which, if any, benefits the new method promises over the old one. Perhaps the simple answer is that, with Rasch models, a pattern score within a single trait can be interpreted. In this way, a severity continuum, which is based on psychological theory, is exposed as an important aspect of test development and interpretation. Traditional methods of personality measurement ignore internal structure in this sense and thus limit research and application.

In this chapter, the example from OMNI used items scored dichotomously. Rasch models are now used for other scoring formats, such as rating scales and partial credit hierarchies (Wright & Masters, 1982). In fact, the OMNI-R (O'Brien, 1990) uses a rating-scale scoring format and is now available from the author.

It is hoped that the suggested procedural steps for personality testing benefit the researcher's and practitioner's quest to understand and to interpret personality traits in a more complete way.

REFERENCES

American Psychiatric Association. (1988). *Diagnostic and statistical manual of mental disorders: DSM-III-Revised.* Washington, DC: American Psychiatric Association.

Anastasi, A. (1988). *Psychological testing* (6th ed.). New York: MacMillan.

Hathaway, S.R., & McKinley, J.C. (1967). *Minnesota Multiphasic Personality Inventory.* New York: Psychological Corporation.

Kernberg, O. (1976). *Borderline conditions and pathological narcissism.* New York: Jason Aronson.

Masters, G. N., & Wilson, M. (1988). *PC-CREDIT: A microcomputer program for Partial Credit Analysis.* Computer program and notes prepared for the Annual Meeting of the American Educational Research Association, New Orleans, LA.

Miller, A. (1981). *The drama of the gifted child.* New York: Basic Books.

Miller, A. (1984). *Thou shalt not be aware.* New York: Farrar, Straus & Giroux.

Miller, A. (1985). *For your own good.* New York: Farrar, Straus & Giroux.

O'Brien, M.L. (Ed.). (1986). The development and use of structured tests. *Studies in Educational Evaluation, 12,* 1–88.

O'Brien, M.L. (1987). Examining the dimensionality of pathological narcissism: factor analysis and construct validity of the O'Brien Multiphasic Narcissism Inventory. *Psychological Reports, 61,* 499–510.

O'Brien, M.L. (1988). Further evidence of the validity of the O'Brien Multiphasic Narcissism Inventory. *Psychological Reports, 62,* 879–882.

O'Brien, M.L. (1989). Psychometric issues relevant to selecting items and assembling parallel forms of language proficiency instruments. *Educational and Psychological Measurement, 49,* 347–354.

O'Brien, M.L. (1990). *O'Brien Multiphasic Narcissism Inventory—Revised.* Test and scoring manual available from author.

O'Brien, M.L., & Hampilos, J.P. (1988). The feasibility of creating an item bank from a teacher-made test, using the Rasch model. *Educational and Psychological Measurement, 48,* 201–212.

Rasch, G. (1960). *Probabilistic models for some intelligence and attainment tests.* Copenhagen: Danmarks Pedagogiske Institut (Reprinted by the University of Chicago Press, 1980).

Thurstone, L.L. (1927). A mental unit of measurement. *Psychological Review, 34,* 415–423.

Wright, B.D. (1968). Sample-free test calibration and person measurement. In *Proceedings of the 1967 Invitational Conference on Testing Problems.* Princeton, NJ: Educational Testing Service.

Wright, B.D., & Masters, G.N. (1982). *Rating scale analysis.* Chicago: MESA Press.

Wright, B.D., & Mead, R.J. (1976). *BICAL: Calibrating items with the Rasch model* (Research Memorandum No. 23). Chicago: Statistical Laboratory, Department of Education, University of Chicago.

Wright, B.D., & Stone, M.H. (1979). *Best test design.* Chicago: MESA Press.

chapter **5**

Measuring Changes in the Quality of School Life

Mark Wilson
Graduate School of Education
University of California at Berkeley

The aim of this chapter is to investigate the changes in students' perceptions of their school life that occurred as a result of an intervention program. The consistency of the latent trait definition of a quality of life instrument was investigated before and after a summer intervention program for potential high school dropouts in Louisiana high schools. The establishment of such stability is an important stage in the validation of any instrument, but is especially important with one that is to be used to examine the success of a program using a pretest/posttest design. The subscales of the instrument were used to establish a profile of the school perceptions of a potential high school dropout and then the relative gains of a control and treatment group were examined to assess the impact of the summer intervention program.

Dropping out is becoming an increasingly severe social problem as educational reform and the toughening of educational standards makes it more difficult for marginal students to succeed in school. The Louisiana State Youth Opportunities Unlimited (LSYOU) (Gaston, 1987) program was developed to conduct research on alternative strategies for dropout prevention as well as to gather information on the nature of dropouts and the decision to drop out of school. Many potential dropouts have problems coping with the formal and impersonal structure of most high schools (Cusick, 1973; Wehlage & Rutten, 1984). Thus, LSYOU represented an effort to create an alternative and more supportive organizational structure. In order to achieve this, program teachers, tutors, and counselors undertook in-service training in a counseling curriculum, all class sizes were limited to 13 with a tutor and teacher in each class, students and staff were involved in non-academic activities, and student input to and autonomy within the program were encouraged.

The instrument used is a multiscale assessment of how a student perceives their school life. The Quality of School Life instrument (QSL) (Williams & Batten, 1981) was designed as an application of Burt's conception of quality-of-life assessment (Burt, Fischer, & Christman, 1979) and Spady and Mitchell's model of schooling (Mitchell & Spady, 1977, 1978). They have postulated a four-part system that links Societal Expectations to School Structures and hence to Student Experiences. In the four domains of Societal Expectations, schools are expected to:

1. Nurture and guide each student's sense of social responsibility for the consequences of his or her own personal actions, and for the character and quality of the groups to which the student belongs;
2. Generate and support social integration among individuals across cultural groups and within institutions;
3. Facilitate and certify the achievement of technical competence, in effect, to certify that individuals are capable of doing tasks valued in the society at large; and,
4. Encourage and enhance personal development in the form of physical, emotional, and intellectual skills and abilities (Mitchell & Spady, 1977, p. 9).

The schools respond by developing four types of organizational structures:

1. Supervision structures, which engender the development of social responsibility in students through adjustment to and learning of prevailing social values (Status);
2. Socialization structures, which emphasize student participation in the social system of the school in order to achieve social integration (Identity);
3. Certification structures, which enable students who have reached agreed standards of technical competence to qualify for certificates, rewards, promotions, and the like (Opportunity); and,
4. Instruction structures, which facilitate personal development

through learning and exploration (Adventure) (Williams & Batten, 1981, p. 9).

An exploratory factor analysis was used by Williams and Batten (1981) to assess the multidimensional nature of the QSL instrument, and then the hypothesized structure was tested using confirmatory procedures. It consists of six subscales, two general ones, and four more specific ones that match the Spady-Mitchell domains described above. The two general scales are:

1. General Affect (GA), which taps the nonspecific feelings of happiness and well-being associated with school;
2. Negative Affect (NA), which taps the reverse of GA, depression, loneliness, or restlessness.

The four domains are:

3. Status (ST), which assesses a student's feelings of worth in the social context;
4. Identity (ID), which assesses a student's feelings of growth as an individual;
5. Opportunity (OP), which assesses a student's feelings of increasing adequacy to meet society's standards;
6. Adventure (AD), which assesses a student's feelings of growth through learning.

They also identified a seventh subscale:

7. Teachers (TE), which assesses a student's feelings toward his or her teachers.

METHOD

Sample

Students from three Louisiana parishes were identified by their teachers and principals as being at risk of dropping out. A group of similar students, with roughly the same demographic background, was also obtained from each school. Prior to the beginning of the program, the applicant pool was administered the QSL instrument at a testing session and were told to respond in terms of their present school. Students were then randomly assigned to the treatment and control conditions.

At the end of the program, the control group students were administered a posttest and asked to respond in terms of the school they had attended in the spring. The treatment group students were asked to respond in terms of the academic component of LSYOU. The control group responses were used to test the consistency of student attitudes over the course of the summer and the treatment group responses served to indicate the perception of differences between the regular school and the LSYOU program. Further details of the experimental design are given in Shapiro (1987).

The Instrument

In the initial study by Williams and Batten (1981), it was found that the items developed for the Adventure domain did not adequately identify it as a distinct factor. Eight replacement Adventure items were tried out on this sample. There are 34 items in the scale. The items are all statements with the stem "School is a place where . . . " followed by a specific predicate such as "I feel happy." The response format has four categories: Strongly Disagree, Disagree, Agree, and Strongly Agree. All are scored positively except for the NA subscale which is scored negatively.

Use of this instrument in different geographic, cultural, or developmental contexts raises certain issues of the ability of the respondents to understand the original intent of the instrument's authors because of differences in idiom and word meanings. Consequently each item was examined for appropriateness in the new context. A panel of "local experts" (the group of LSU teachers who were involved in the summer training program) was consulted to recommend alterations in the wording of the items. This process resulted in some adjustment to the wording of several items. The resulting items are shown in Figure 5.1 along with a brief label for each that will be used in subsequent discussion. Relatively complete response sets were obtained for 138 students, 50 in the Control group, and 88 in the Treatment group.

The Analyses

The first part of the analyses was designed to decide whether the QSL instrument displayed the qualities needed to make comparisons between the relative changes in the treatment and control groups. That is, do the seven subscales give consistent item parameters across test and retest (i.e., do the students' perceptions of the structure of the seven latent traits change over summer)? Subject to satisfactory an-

School is a place where . . .

GA1	(LIKE GO)	I really like to be each day
GA2	(HAPPY)	I feel happy
GA3	(PROUD)	I feel proud to be a student
GA4	(INTERESTED)	I am interested in the work we do
NA1	(DEPRESSED)	I feel depressed
NA2	(LONELY)	I feel lonely
NA3	(UPSET)	I get upset
NA4	(RESTLESS)	I feel restless
ST1	(IMPORTANT)	I feel important
ST2	(THINK A LOT)	I know that people think a lot of me
ST3	(CONFIDENCE)	people have confidence in me
ST4	(RESPECT)	I am treated with respect
ST5	(WORTHWHILE)	I feel I have become a worthwhile person
ID1	(UNDERSTAND)	getting together with other people helps me to understand myself
ID2	(LEARN)	I learn a lot about myself
ID3	(GET ALONG)	I learn to get along with other people
ID4	(OTHERS)	I have learned to see other people's points of view
TE1	(HELP)	teachers help me to do my best
TE2	(NOTICE)	teachers take notice of me in class
TE3	(FAIR)	teachers are fair and just
TE4	(CLASS)	teachers treat me fairly in class
TE5	(GRADES)	teachers give me the grades I deserve
OP1	(SUCCESSFUL)	I know I can do well enough to be successful
OP2	(SATISFACTORY)	I know I can reach a satisfactory standard in my work
OP3	(WELL)	I know the sorts of things I can do well
OP4	(HANDLE)	I know how to handle the work
OP5	(SATISFACTION)	I get satisfaction from the schoolwork
AD1	(NEW IDEAS)	I discover interesting new ideas
AD2	(SOLVE)	I like working to solve a problem
AD3	(GROW)	I grow in knowledge and skills
AD4	(MEANINGFUL)	I find the subject matter meaningful
AD5	(INVOLVED)	I can become involved in the work
AD6	(RELATE)	I can relate what I am learning to what I already know
AD7	(NEW THINGS)	I look forward each week to learning something new
AD8	(OTHERS)	I learn to relate my ideas to other peoples' ideas

Figure 5.1.   The QSL items given to the LSYOU students

swers to the above question, the second part of the analyses investigated the following: (a) What is a criterion-referenced description of an average potential dropout according to the QSL subscales, and (b) what changes occurred over summer for the treatment group and the control group? The LSYOU data set was analyzed to assess the extent to which the different contexts resulted in different structures for the latent trait underlying each subscale. Andrich's (1978) Rating Scale Model (RSM) was used, which parametizes each person with a single latent trait parameter β_j, the location of person j on the latent trait, and each item with a parameter δ_i, the location of item i on the latent trait, and with threshold parameters τ_1, τ_2 and τ_3 which characterize the transition from one category to the next. These are combined to give a probability model as in equation (1):

$$\Pr(y_{ij} = n) = \frac{\exp \sum_{k=0}^{n} (\beta_j - (\delta_i + \tau_k))}{1 + \sum_{t=1}^{3} \exp \sum_{k=1}^{t} (\beta_j - (\delta_i + \tau_k))}, \quad n = 0,1,2,3 \qquad (1)$$

where y_{ij} is the response of person j to item i, and

$$\tau_0 = 0, \text{ so that } \exp \sum_{k=0}^{0} (\beta_j - (\delta_i + \tau_k)) = 0.$$

This model makes no assumptions about the unconditional distributions of the persons along the latent trait, but does assume that the model (1) adequately fits the data. Thus to use (1) to compare the QSL subscales under different contexts, one must first check for adequate data model fit. The fit of these data to the RSM has been reported in Wilson (1987), and will not be repeated in detail here.

Item statistics can be compared to check for equivalence of item location estimates, between pretest (δ_1) and posttest (δ_2), and for equivalence of item threshold estimates, also between pretest (τ_1) and posttest (τ_2). These comparisons can be routinized by using the standardized difference between the parameters as given in equations (2):

$$z_\delta = (\delta_1 - \delta_2)/(s_1{}^2 + s_2{}^2)^{1/2}$$

$$z_\tau = (\tau_1 - \tau_2)/(s_1{}^2 + s_2{}^2)^{1/2} \qquad (2)$$

where the subscripts 1 and 2 refer to two different contexts and s refers to the appropriate standard error in each case (Wright & Masters, 1982, p. 115).

Criterion-Referenced Portrait of an Average Potential Dropout

Assuming that the preceding analyses have established the QSL sub-scales as adequate measuring instruments in these circumstances, the method now is quite straightforward (with just one problem): The average of the sample is illustrated with respect to the item definition of the subscales. The one problem is that the analyses used to estimate location on each subscale do not provide a location for students who score either the maximum or minimum possible on each subscale. Effectively, such students are located at plus or minus infinity, respectively. This is overcome by taking the (somewhat conservative) position that these students are best located at the point closest to the mean where their score (either zero or the maximum) becomes more probable than all other scores together (i.e., the point at which the modeled probability of a zero or maximum score is exactly a half). A procedure for finding this point is described in Wilson and Wright (1983), and is followed here. The treatment group is used as the basis for this portrait as it is to be the anchor for the change analyses described below. Each subscale is criterion-referenced by examining the predicted performance of selected students to each item within each subscale. For this study, the average student was chosen. There is no necessity to restrict attention to just the average student in general, it was chosen here for illustrative purposes.

Effects of the Intervention Program

The control group is examined for significant changes using a paired t-test on the subscale estimates. This is done to establish whether the measures can be expected to be stable when there is no systematic treatment. Once stability has been established the treatment group is also examined for significant changes using the same procedure.

RESULTS

The stability over time of the subscale definition was assessed with an internal consistency criterion—by comparing item structure using the RSM. Essentially this is asking the question: Does this group of people perceive the items that make up each subscale in the same way before and after summer? The fit of these data to the model has been examined and found satisfactory except for the fifth Teachers item, TE5 (Wilson, 1987). This item is concerned with whether students think that they get the grades they deserve. The misfit for this item can be

Table 5.1. Item Locations and Pre-to Posttest z Scores

Subscale	Item No.	Pretest Estimate	Posttest Estimate	z-score
GA	1	0.35	0.68	−1.33
	2	0.40	0.20	0.79
	3	−0.68	−0.74	0.23
	4	−0.08	−0.13	0.19
NA	1	0.06	0.05	0.05
	2	−0.54	−0.73	0.84
	3	0.06	0.15	−0.42
	4	0.41	0.53	−0.58
ST	1	−0.30	−0.13	−0.65
	2	0.16	0.20	−0.16
	3	−0.01	−0.52	1.90
	4	0.16	0.45	−1.14
ID	1	0.39	0.19	0.76
	2	−0.26	−0.18	−0.29
	3	−0.23	0.01	−0.87
	4	0.10	−0.02	0.43
TE	1	−0.63	−0.77	0.52
	2	−0.07	−0.35	1.04
	3	0.52	0.75	−0.90
	4	0.18	0.37	−0.75
OP	1	−0.54	−1.08	1.86
	2	−0.54	−0.32	−0.78
	3	−0.09	−0.43	1.20
	4	0.33	0.72	−1.45
	5	0.83	1.11	−1.07
AD	1	−0.21	−0.13	−0.33
	2	0.73	0.68	0.23
	3	−0.75	−0.59	−0.63
	4	0.04	0.15	−0.46
	5	0.02	0.07	−0.21
	6	−0.08	−0.70	2.50
	7	−0.01	0.15	−0.66
	8	0.25	0.36	−0.49

interpreted to indicate that the potential dropouts perceive their teacher's grading practices in a different way from that in which they perceive other teacher characteristics. It was decided to leave this item out of the remaining analyses. Thus, the results for the TE subscale should be considered only tentative.

The question of whether the differences between the item location estimates is statistically significant is assessed using the standardized location differences recorded in the last column of Table 5.1. These standardized differences indicate that (except for the eighth Adventure item—AD8) the item locations are not statistically different.

Hence, we can continue on to the comparison stage for all the subscales except Adventure. Item AD8 concerns student perceptions about whether they can relate new knowledge to old. The difference is quite systematic in the sense that the responses to this item are well modeled by the RSM parameters both before and after the summer, but the item is answered in a consistently more positive way after summer. This difference of 0.52 logits is quite large; for a student with an average attitude towards Adventure it represents a more than three-fold decrease in the odds of a negative response as opposed to a positive response to the item (i.e., Strongly Disagree and Disagree versus Agree and Strongly Agree). Closer examination shows that, for this item, the raw score change for the Treatment group was a gain of 0.30 (Paired t-test: $t = 3.89$ on 86 degrees of freedom, $p < 0.001$) and for the Control group it was 0.14 (Paired t-test: $t = 1.31$ on 48 degrees of freedom, $p = 0.20$). Thus, while both Treatment and Control showed gains on this particular item, only the Treatment gain was statistically significant, so we may ascribe the difference in definition of the Adventure variable between pre- and posttest primarily to a change in the treatment group which occurs for this item over and above any changes that occurred in the rest of the items. Although this indicates a difference in the latent trait definition for this subscale, the majority of the items had similar relative locations for the two occasions indicating that the definition was at least similar. Hence, it was decided to continue with the analyses for this subscale, bearing in mind, as for the Teachers subscale, that any results are at best tentative.

Further features of the IRT item results that can be compared are the threshold estimates which are given in Table 5.2. They give the locations of the thresholds between successive categories of the rating scale. For example, consider the General Affect subscale. If an item is located at 0 logits on the latent trait, the point at which "Disagree" becomes more likely than "Strongly Disagree" is -2.93 on the logit scale; the point when "Agree" succeeds "Disagree" is -0.36 logits; and the point at which "Strongly Agree" succeeds "Agree" is 3.29 logits. The threshold parameters can be interpreted to indicate the relative propensity of an average member of a group to give more or less extreme responses on the Strongly Agree to Strongly Disagree scale. Generally speaking, for a person at a fixed value on the attitude scale, the less spread out the threshold parameters, the more likely it is that more extreme responses will be given. Again, standardized differences are given in the last column, which show that the response structure has remained unchanged for the Negative Affect, Status, Teachers, and Adventure subscales. It has changed in that (all other things being equal) the average student is tending to give less extreme responses for

Table 5.2.   Item Thresholds and Pre-to Posttest z Scores

Subscale	Threshold	Pretest Estimate	Posttest Estimate	z-score
GA	1	−2.93	−2.39	−1.32
	2	−0.36	−0.41	0.25
	3	3.29	2.79	2.44
NA	1	−1.72	−1.23	−1.47
	2	−0.70	−0.61	−0.51
	3	1.92	1.89	0.16
ST	1	−2.28	−2.16	−0.27
	2	−0.41	−0.76	1.65
	3	2.70	2.92	−1.11
ID	1	−2.63	−1.80	−1.70
	2	−0.64	−0.54	−0.50
	3	3.27	2.35	4.99
TE	1	−2.31	−2.41	0.28
	2	−0.76	−0.50	1.27
	3	3.07	2.91	0.71
OP	1	−1.89	−2.80	1.55
	2	−0.83	−0.81	−0.09
	3	2.73	3.61	−5.41
AD	1	−1.73	−1.75	0.06
	2	−0.80	−0.80	0.00
	3	2.53	2.55	−0.17

the General Affect and Identity subscales and more extreme responses for the Opportunity subscale after the summer break.

Criterion-Referenced Portrait of the Average Potential Dropout

The means of the RSM location estimates for the Treatment and Control groups are given in Table 5.3. Comparing the pretests with independent sample t-tests results in nonsignificant differences at the 5 percent level for all the subscales, giving post hoc support for the random allocation of students to the two groups. The RSM locations are by themselves somewhat uninformative. To give them meaning, we can examine how an average potential dropout (as identified for this sample) would answer each item in the subscale according to the IRT parameter estimates.

Figures 5.2 through 5.11 show the relative probabilities of giving each of the responses—Strongly Disagree, Disagree, Agree, and Strongly Agree—to each of the subscales in turn. For the General Affect scale, Figure 5.2 shows that an average sample member will

Table 5.3.   Comparison of IRT Group Estimates

Subscale	Means		t	df	p
	pre	post			
Treatment Group					
GA	1.27	1.35	0.45	82	0.66
NA	−0.98	−1.04	−0.47	83	0.64
ST	1.41	1.40	−0.04	84	0.97
ID	1.69	2.27	2.66	82	0.01
TE	0.93	1.28	1.40	85	0.17
OP	1.67	2.08	2.45	81	0.02
AD	1.50	1.84	1.79	74	0.08
Control Group					
GA	1.16	1.19	0.13	47	0.90
NA	−0.97	−0.97	0.02	45	0.99
ST	1.34	1.21	−0.62	48	0.54
ID	1.62	1.61	−0.87	48	0.39
TE	1.12	1.05	−0.29	46	0.77
OP	1.72	1.59	−0.64	47	0.52
AD	1.27	1.53	1.21	47	0.23

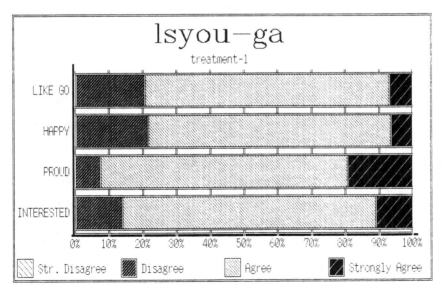

Figure 5.2.   Predicted response probabilities for an average Treatment group student on the General Affect items

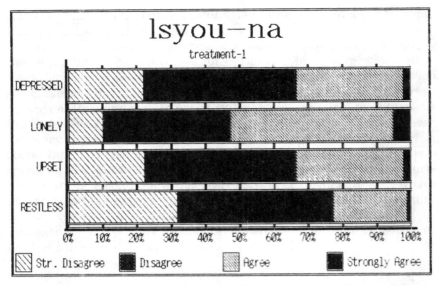

Figure 5.3.   Predicted response probabilities for an average Treatment group student on the Negative Affect items

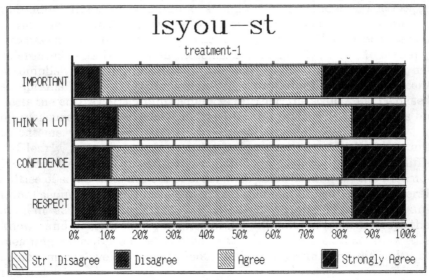

Figure 5.4.   Predicted response probabilities for an average Treatment group student on the Status items

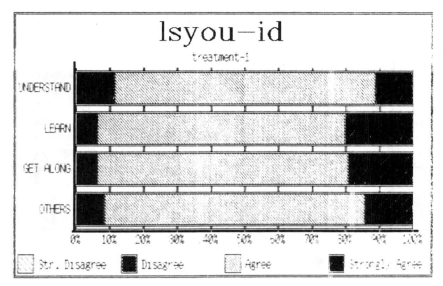

Figure 5.5. Predicted response probabilities for an average Treatment group student on the Identity items

answer predominantly "Agree" to all four items on the subscale. The items LIKE GO and HAPPY are each about twice as likely as the item PROUD to incite a "Disagree" response, with INTERESTED in between the two extremes. (Note: Abbreviations have been used as item labels in an effort to make the discussion more concise. The reader should check Figure 5.1 to see which label goes with each item.) The negative items of the Negative Affect scale have elicited a more even spread of responses than the General Affect Scale, as shown in Figure 5.3. Remember that because these items are negatively oriented, a "Strongly Disagree" here is equivalent to a "Strongly Agree" on the other scales. Here the responses for a typical student are about evenly balanced between "Disagree" and "Agree" for the items DEPRESSED, LONELY, and UPSET, but DEPRESSED and UPSET are about twice as likely to provoke a "Strongly Disagree" response as is LONELY, and RESTLESS is even more likely to provoke a "Strongly Disagree" response and is much less likely to provoke an "Agree" response.

Consider the Status subscale illustrated in Figure 5.4. This is very similar to the General Affect picture with "Agree" predominating for all items and with somewhat less differences between items in the other categories. This is repeated for the Identity subscale in Figure 5.5 and for the Teachers subscale in Figure 5.6, although for the Teach-

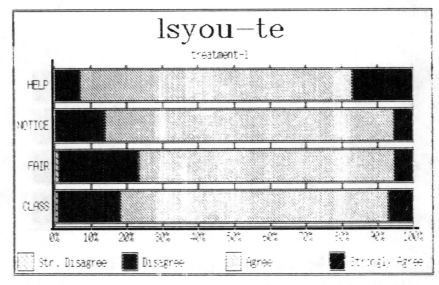

Figure 5.6.   Predicted response probabilities for an average Treatment group student on the Teachers items

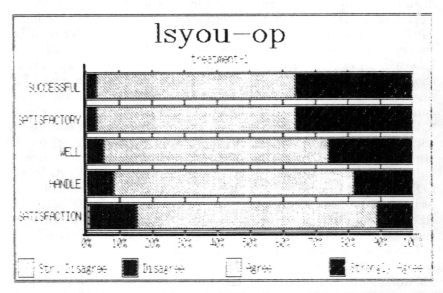

Figure 5.7.   Predicted response probabilities for an average Treatment group student on the Opportunity items

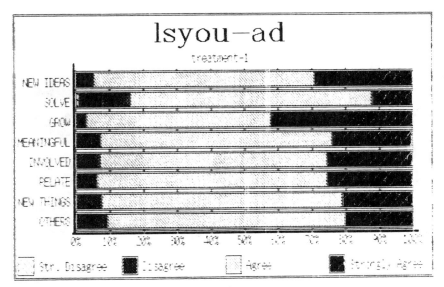

Figure 5.8. Predicted response probabilities for an average Treatment group student on the Adventure items

ers subscale the item HELP is about half as likely as FAIR to incite a "Disagree" response. In Figure 5.7, the Opportunity subscale also shows a predominantly "Agree" response, but the SUCCESSFUL and SATISFACTORY items are much more likely to induce "Strongly Agree" than is SATISFACTION with WELL and HANDLE at intermediate points between. The Adventure subscale also shows a predominance of "Agree" in Figure 5.8, with a considerable tendency for GROW to incite a "Strongly Agree" response reducing down to only a small percentage of SOLVE responses in the "Strongly Agree" category.

Effects of the Intervention Program

In Table 5.3, the Control group displayed no significant change on any of the subscales, which is an indication that the measures are not sensitive to unsystematic treatment. For the Treatment group there are significant differences only for the Identity and Opportunity subscales. These differences are illustrated by comparing Figures 5.9 and 5.10 with Figures 5.5 and 5.7, respectively. For Identity, the mean estimate of location has increased by 0.58 logits. In the case of an average student, this translates into a change for the "Strongly Agree"

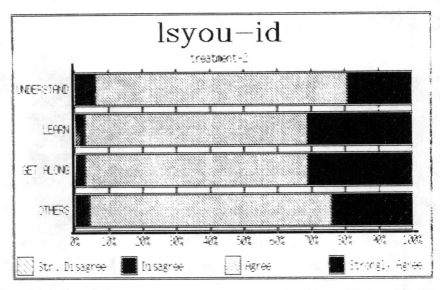

Figure 5.9. **Predicted response probabilities for an average Treatment group student on the Teachers items, posttest**

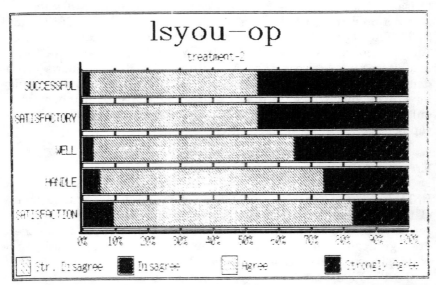

Figure 5.10. **Predicted response probabilities for an average Treatment group student on the Opportunity items, posttest**

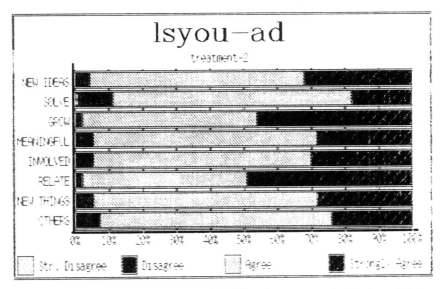

Figure 5.11. Predicted response probabilities for an average Treatment group student on the Adventure items, posttest

category from 11 to 19 percent for UNDERSTAND, 20 to 31 percent for LEARN, 19 to 31 percent for GET ALONG, and 14 to 24 percent for OTHERS. For Opportunity the mean estimate has increased by 0.41 logits which corresponds to a change for the "Strongly Agree" category from 36 to 46 percent for SUCCESSFUL and SATISFACTORY, 26 to 35 percent for WELL, 18 to 26 percent for HANDLE, and 11 to 17 percent for SATISFACTION.

In order to clarify the discussion about the inconsistency in item RELATE in the Adventure subscale, examine the behavior of this item in Figures 5.8 and 5.11. Here all the categories have moved a small amount towards the positive from the pretest to the posttest. However, RELATE has changed from 26 percent probability of inciting a "Strongly Agree" response to a 49 percent probability. This doubling of the relative likelihood of an extreme positive response is the source of the inconsistency displayed in the standardized difference column in Table 5.2.

DISCUSSION

The analyses have shown that we may proceed to make a straightforward interpretation of the results for the subscales other than Teach-

ers and Adventure. The problems with these two are somewhat different. For Teachers, one item, concerning teachers' grading practices,
prompted responses that were decidedly disorderly compared to the
rest of the Teachers items. It seems that, for potential drop-outs,
teacher grading practices constitute part of a different variable to
that defined by the other items. It was decided to use the remaining
set in the analyses that followed, but it must be borne in mind that
using them may be oversimplifying the attitude of potential dropouts
towards teachers, even given the caveat concerning grading practices.
For the Adventure subscale, the problem was not one of fit within the
measurement occasions, but of a dramatic change in location of one
item which far outstripped the others in the scale. This item, which
concerns the student's perception of his or her ability to relate new
knowledge to old, showed a sizeable and statistically significant
change in a positive direction for students in the treatment group
(but not for the control group). This is an important finding concerning the intervention program. However, as the Adventure items did
provoke responses in concordance with the RSM model in each cir-
cumstance, it was decided here too, to display the results for this
scale as a whole. It must be remembered in interpreting the results
that the student definition of the variable "Adventure" shifts somewhat from pre- to posttest.

Turning now to the portrait of an average potential dropout, as
painted by the QSL instrument, we find that such a student displays a
predominance of "Agree" responses in all the positively oriented
scales. The relative difficulty of giving a more positive (or negative)
response to each item within the subscale is represented by the comparison of the "Strongly Agree" (or "Strongly Disagree") responses.
For General Affect, this shows that students found it relatively harder
to respond positively to items that said school was a place where they
were HAPPY or where they LIKE(d) to GO than to the item that said
school was a place where they felt PROUD. For the Status and Identity
items, the item locations are all within two standard errors of a central
point, so making distinctions between the items is not warranted. Essentially, these subscales are composed of items of homogeneous location. For the Teachers subscale, bearing in mind the earlier warning
about these items, the students found it easier to agree that teachers
HELP them than that teachers are FAIR to them. For the Opportunity
subscale, the typical student displayed the same predominance of
"Agree" responses overall, but they also were inclined to "Strongly
Agree" that they can "do well enough to be successful" and that they
can "reach a satisfactory standard." This inclination was considerably
reduced for the item that asked whether they were themselves satis-

fied with their work. For the Adventure subscale on the pretest, the pattern is similar, with the typical student more ready to strongly endorse that they "grow in knowledge and skills" than that they "like working to solve problems" or "learn to relate [their] ideas to others' ideas." The negatively oriented subscale provoked a different response pattern from the typical dropout, with about equal occurrence of "Disagree" and "Agree." Here the student is more likely to "Strongly Disagree" that he or she feels UPSET and DEPRESSED than that he or she feels LONELY or RESTLESS. This type of conceptual mapping of the subscale latent traits is important as it gives a concrete interpretation of the subscales that is necessary if the results are to contribute to the understanding of the complex of variables that constitute "quality of school life."

Lastly, what differences did the intervention program make according to the QSL subscales? The Treatment group showed no statistically significant changes in General Affect, Negative Affect, Status, or with the somewhat flawed Adventure and Teachers subscales. There are statistically significant differences in the Identity and Opportunity subscales and they both indicate positive change over the summer intervention. This change is also substantively significant, giving a uniform increase of about 10 percent in the tendency of a typical potential dropout to "Strongly Agree" with each of the items that constitutes these two subscales. This corresponds to a relative increase ranging from 135 percent to 171 percent over the predicted number of strong agreements at the pretest, where the variation is due to differences among the items.

The potential dropouts identified for the LSYOU program have responded to the summer intervention by considerably increasing their perception of their feelings of growth as an individual, and their increasing adequacy to meet society's standards. In addition, they now perceive that they have a greatly increased ability to relate their newly acquired school knowledge to what they already know. None of these variables showed any comparable change in the control group. The effects of the summer intervention program were not evident in the two general scales, General Affect and Negative Affect, nor were any significant effects displayed in the way the potential students saw their worth in the social context of school, their personal academic development (apart from the special case mentioned above), or their image of their teachers, although there was evidence that the Teachers subscale was not adequate to fully comprehend the complexity of their feelings about teachers. In particular, there was evidence that teachers' grading practices were perceived differently from other teacher characteristics.

In conclusion, the analyses above have illustrated how the RSM can be used to:

1. Assess the consistency of the internal definition of a subscale between pre- and posttests,
2. give a criterion-referenced portrait of the sample subjects with respect to the items in each subscale,
3. give a similarly criterion-referenced account of the changes that occurred according to each subscale.

REFERENCES

Andrich, D. (1978). A rating formulation for ordered response categories. *Psychometrika, 43*, 561–573.

Burt, R.S., Fischer, M.G., & Christman, K.P. (1979). Structures of well-being: Sufficient conditions for identification as restricted covariance models. *Sociological Methods and Research, 8*, 111–120.

Cusick, P. (1973). *Inside high schools.* New York: Holt, Rinehart, & Winston.

Gaston, S. (1987). *LSYOU: The effects of an alternative organizational framework on students at risk for dropping out.* Paper presented at the annual meeting of the American Educational Research Association, Washington, DC.

Mitchell, D.E., & Spady, W.G. (1977). *Authority and the functional structuring of social actions in schools.* Paper presented at the annual meeting of the American Educational Research Association.

Mitchell, D.E., & Spady, W.G. (1978). Organizational contexts for implementing outcome-based education. *Educational Researcher, 7*(7), 9–17.

Shapiro, J.Z. (1987). *Project LSYOU: A summative evaluation.* Paper presented at the annual meeting of the American Educational Research Association, Washington.

Welhage, G., & Rutten, P. (1984). Dropping out: How much do schools contribute to the problem? *Teachers College Record, 87*(3), 374–392.

Williams, T.H., & Batten, M.H. (1981). *The quality of school life* (ACER Research Monograph, No. 12). Hawthorn, Australia: Australian Council for Educational Research.

Wilson, M. (1987). *The structure of the quality of school life: An international comparison.* Paper presented at the annual meeting of the National Council for Measurement in Education, Washington, DC.

Wilson, M., & Wright, B.D. (1983). *Finite measures from perfect scores.* Paper presented at the annual meeting of the American Educational Research Association, Montreal, Canada.

Wright, B.D., & Masters, G.N. (1982). *Rating scale analysis.* Chicago: MESA Press.

chapter **6**

Distinguishing Between Shared and Unique Employee Needs

Ellen R. Julian
National Board of Medical Examiners

Benjamin D. Wright
MESA Psychometric Laboratory
University of Chicago

INTRODUCTION

A survey was conducted of employees' needs for current and potential benefits provided by the organization. A portion of the survey was a nine-item "wish list" of potential benefits to which employees were asked to respond "Very Interested," "Interested," or "Not Interested." The organization wanted to know which benefits were of most interest to the employees. This focus on "measuring" items is in contrast to the usual focus of measuring people. In addition, a method was needed for ensuring that unique patterns of person interest were not lost in the item averages.

The initial analysis of these data (Julian et al., 1988) reported the percentage of respondents selecting each of the three interest levels for all potential benefits. The drawback to this was that the ranking of the benefits is ambiguous because it depends on the interest level by which

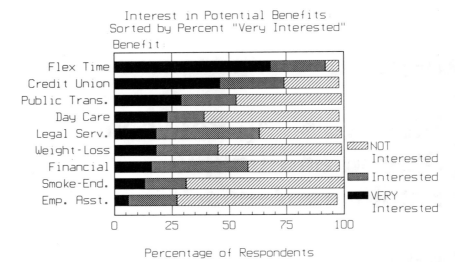

Figure 6.1a.   Interest in Potential Benefits: Sorted by Percent "Very Interested"

they are ranked. Figure 6.1 shows bar charts ordered by the percentage of employees selecting various levels of interest. Figure 6.1a ranks potential benefits by the proportion of people responding "Very Interested." Figure 6.1b ranks them by the proportion responding "Not Interested." Figure 6.1c ranks them by the proportion responding "In-

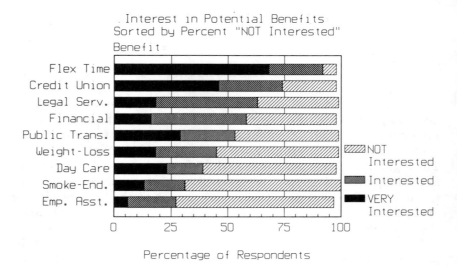

Figure 6.1b.   Interest in Potential Benefits: Sorted by Percent "Not Interested"

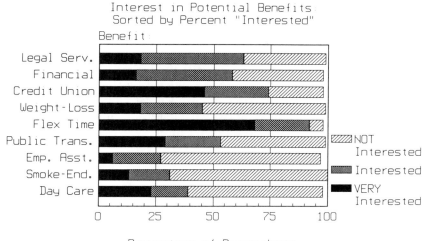

Figure 6.1c.   **Interest in Potential Benefits: Sorted by Percent "Interested"**

terested." These three orderings are different. Each ranking implies a variable, but the three variables implied by Figures 6.1a, b, and c are not the same. If the organizational decision makers are to use these data to select benefits for implementation, which ranking should they use?

The item difficulty estimates from the Rasch partial credit model (RPCM) (Andrich, 1978; Wright & Masters, 1982) provide an unambiguous ranking of the benefits. The RPCM also identifies employees with unexpected patterns of interest, so that only those few patterns need be individually reviewed by the researcher or decision makers.

The RPCM offers five advantages in the analysis of these data. First, it measures both employees and benefits on level of interest. Second, it evaluates how well the potential benefits work together to define a single variable. Third, the RPCM specifies the pattern of employee interest for each benefit. This pattern provides the organizational decision makers with a concise description of which benefits are desired and of the intensity of that interest. A distinction can be made between benefits that would make many employees somewhat happy, and benefits that would make a few employees very happy. The fourth advantage is that the RPCM incorporates the available quantitative data into one overall picture of how much interest exists for each potential benefit. The fifth is that the RPCM analysis identifies employees and benefits that stand out qualitatively as not fitting into that general picture.

The RPCM analysis enables a single, one-page summary description of how each potential benefit relates to persons with different overall levels of interest in benefits. This is the common theme extracted from the data. Then, from an employee's position on the interest scale, it is possible to predict which benefits will be desired. Those employees with unusual patterns of interest are flagged by the analysis for further qualitative review. These employees have identified themselves by responding to one or more of the wish list items differently than the others, for instance, by expressing no interest in any benefit except one. Individual analysis of their particular response patterns brings out their unique benefit needs.

METHOD

The Survey

The Employee Benefits Survey presented a brief summary of the current benefits and, for each area of benefits, asked several questions about satisfaction with the current package. The last page of the survey listed nine potential benefits and asked for an indication of the amount of interest the staff member had in each benefit. Interest was indicated by checking one of three boxes labeled "Very Interested," "Interested," and "Not Interested." This paper presents a Rasch partial credit analysis of this nine-item wish list.

The wish list consisted of "Legal Services" (referral or support), "Child Care/Day Care," "Employee Assistance Program" (drug or alcohol counseling and treatment), "Credit Union," "Financial Services," "Weight-loss Program," "Smoke-ending Program," "Flex Time" (4- or $4^{1}/_{2}$-day work week), and sale of or discount on "Public Transportation" tokens.

Sample

The Employee Benefits Survey was sent to all 155 employees of the organization. Ninety-one percent of the employees, 141, completed and returned the survey. A complete description of the group's demographics is available in Julian et al. (1988).

Analyses

The initial analysis shown in Figure 6.1 (Julian et al., 1988) of the wish list responses was based simply upon the percentage of respondents selecting each level of interest.

A RPCM (Masters, 1982) analysis of these data treated each benefit as an item. All three response categories were used for every item. Responses were coded 0 for "Not Interested," 1 for "Interested," and 2 for "Very Interested." Nine employees failed to respond to one or more benefits. However, the missing data algorithm in MSTEPS (Wright et al., 1987), the RPCM calibration program used, enables the inclusion of these employees in the analysis.

The resulting item difficulties provide an unambiguous ranking of the level of interest in the benefits. Within each benefit item, the response-step difficulties describe the particular pattern of interest for that benefit. The first step is the progression from "Not Interested" to "Interested." The second step is from "Interested" to "Very Interested." The step difficulties values are at the level of overall benefit interest where the most probable level of interest for that benefit goes up one category.

If the difficulty of the first step is greater than that for the second, the step difficulties are "reversed" (Julian & Wright, 1988). Reversal indicates that the middle category, in this case "Interested," is not the most probable response for any level of overall interest, or ability. Instead, employees will most probably be either "Not" or "Very Interested" in these benefits.

A map of the relationship between employee overall interest levels and expected interest in specific benefits was constructed from the MSTEPS item calibrations and employee measures.

How well interest in these nine benefits works as a single variable can be evaluated by several statistics produced by the RPCM calibration. The reliability for persons is the familiar coefficient alpha and indicates how cleanly the highest scoring (most overall interested) and lowest scoring (least interested) employees are separated (Wright & Masters, 1982, pp. 105–108). Person separation is the ratio of the adjusted standard deviation of persons (their standard deviation, corrected for unreliability) to their root mean square error of measurement and indicates how many statistically distinct strata of employee interest can be defined. The separation reliability for items, in turn, indicates how well the "hardest" (to be interested in) benefit items can be separated from the "easiest" (Wright & Masters, 1982, pp. 91–94). In this study, measuring the benefits is more important then measuring the employees, so the item separation and reliability will be of greater interest.

Fit statistics identify people or items that manifest unusual patterns of interest. For each employee response, a predicted level of interest, calculated from the difference between the employee's overall benefit interest level and the benefit item difficulty, is compared with the response actually made. The squared difference is summed across benefit items and when the sum is too large, the employee is identified as misfitting. While it is the overall amount of unexpectedness in a employee's response string which results in their being identified as misfitting, it is the particular pattern of unexpected responses that sheds insight into the unique benefit needs of these people.

For example, on this survey, employees who expressed no interest in any benefit except an unpopular one would have an unusual pattern. Benefits for which only the employees with the lowest level of overall interest expressed a desire would also misfit. The fit statistics reported here are the information weighted fit statistics, called infit. These statistics are used as flags to identify misfitting people or misfitting items. Since their expected value is approximately zero and their expected standard deviation is approximately one, values outside of plus or minus two imply a problem. Large positive infits indicate noise or unexpected variation in the response pattern and large negative infits indicate that the responses were too predictable (Wright & Masters, 1982, p. 100). The interpretation of fit statistics is discussed in Douglas and Wright (1990), Smith (1990), Linacre (1990), and Schulz (1990).

RESULTS

The RPCM calibration of 18 item steps and 137 employees (four wanted either all or none of the benefits) results in an average employee interest measure of -0.36, with an average standard error of 0.56. The negative average interest level indicates that the employees, on the average, accumulated slightly less than half of the possible points from the wish list, suggesting a slight amount of disinterest in these benefits. Person separation is a modest 1.37, yielding a person-separation reliability of .65, but item separation is a substantial 7.65 for an item-separation reliability of .98. This high reliability leaves little room for more than one dimension to be present in these data. Further, the nine benefits can be separated into almost as many strata as there are benefits, suggesting substantial differences in levels of interest among them.

The average item infit is 0.07 with a standard deviation of 0.85. No items have infit statistics greater than ± 2.00. This and the high reliability of item separation indicates that the potential benefits are working together as a single variable, and that there are no discernible competing dimensions of benefits.

The average employee infit is -0.02 with a standard deviation of 1.12. Ten employees have infit statistics higher than $+2.00$ and three are more negative than -2.00. Employees with high positive fit statis-

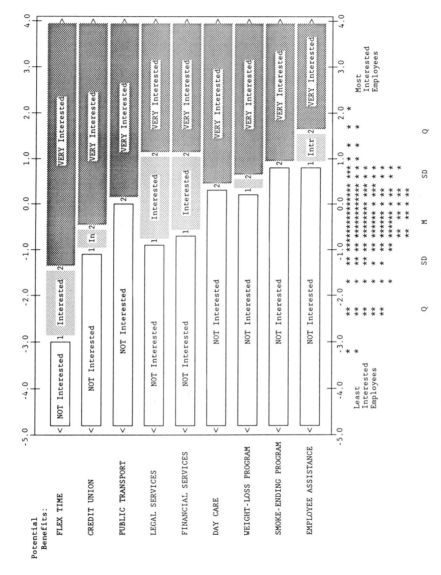

Figure 6.2. RPCM Scaling of Employee Benefits Wish List: The Map

Employee Number		L	D	E	C	F	W	S	F	P	Infit	Interest Level
137											2.87	0.11
	Responses:	0	0	2	0	1	1	2	1	2		
	Residuals:	-2	-1	3	-2	0	0	2	-2	1		
121											2.39	0.34
	Responses:	0	0	2	1	0	2	2	2	1		
	Residuals:	-2	-1	2	-1	-2	1	2	0	0		
78											2.38	-0.62
	Responses:	0	2	2	0	0	0	0	2	0		
	Residuals:	-1	2	4	-1	-1	-1	0	1	-1		
81											2.37	0.11
	Responses:	1	2	2	0	2	0	0	1	1		
	Residuals:	0	1	3	-2	2	-1	-1	-2	0		
46											2.21	-0.11
	Responses:	0	2	0	0	0	2	0	2	2		
	Residuals:	-1	2	-1	-2	-1	2	-1	1	1		
29											2.20	-0.03
	Responses:	2	2	M	2	1	0	1	0	0		
	Residuals:	2	2	M	1	0	-1	1	-4	-1		
140											2.14	-2.27
	Responses:	0	0	0	0	0	0	0	0	2		
	Residuals:	0	0	0	-1	0	0	0	-1	6		
52											2.13	-0.36
	Responses:	1	2	0	0	0	0	2	2	0		
	Residuals:	0	2	-1	-2	-1	-1	3	1	-1		
58											2.09	-1.70
	Responses:	1	0	0	0	0	0	0	0	2		
	Residuals:	1	0	0	-1	-1	0	0	-2	4		
50											2.06	-0.62
	Responses:	0	2	0	0	0	2	0	2	0		
	Residuals:	-1	2	0	-1	-1	2	0	1	-1		

M - missing response

Figure 6.3.   Employees with Unique Needs

tics are the ones who show an idiosyncratic interest or lack of interest in one or more particular benefits. One-hundred-twenty-seven of the employees do fit. The map in Figure 6.2 represents the common pattern produced by the 127 fitting employees. The particular 10 employees who do not fit are analyzed in Figure 6.3. These two figures incorporate all of the information from these data into just two pictures.

The distribution of employee interest is shown across the bottom of the benefit-item map in Figure 6.2. For an employee with a given interest level, it is possible to read up the page from his or her location on the interest scale to predict his or her most likely level of interest in each benefit. For example, an employee at zero would probably not be interested in "Employee Assistance," "Smoke-ending" or "Weight-loss Programs," "Day Care," or "Public Transportation," but would be expected to be very interested in a "Credit Union" and "Flex Time."

The map in Figure 6.2 shows that three benefits, "Day Care," "Public Transportation," and a "Smoke-ending Program," show reversals of their step difficulties. This indicates that there is no level of overall interest for which the most likely response to those benefits is simply "Interested." The most probable response goes directly from "Not Interested" to "Very Interested."

Of the nine potential benefits, all except the above-mentioned three produce two steps. The middle category, "Interested," for the "Credit Union," "Employee Assistance Program," and "Weight-loss Program" are quite small. Only four employees fall in the region on the interest scale where they will be expected to be simply "Interested" in the "Employee Assistance Program." Although their "Interested" regions cover a smaller area on the map in Figure 6.2, about 26 employees will probably be "Interested" in a "Weight-loss Program" and 29 in a "Credit Union."

Three other benefits, "Flex Time," "Legal Services" and "Financial Services," show large "Interested" regions. However, because of the location of their "Interested" region on the overall interest continuum, many more employees will probably be simply "Interested" in the two "Services" than in "Flex Time." Most employees will probably be "Very Interested" in "Flex Time."

Common Needs. The RPCM difficulties estimate an overall level of interest for each potential benefit. The estimated difficulty of each benefit ranks them with respect to the amount of interest expressed by the group. The listing of the potential benefits in Figure 6.2 is in order of descending interest. This ranking is different from any of the three rankings resulting from simply considering the percent of the group expressing any single interest level (in Figure 6.1).

The corporate decision makers can use Figure 6.2 to determine which benefits would be the most welcome, in terms of overall employee interest. Benefits like the "Credit Union," without a large "Interested" area, would be of considerable interest to many employees, but of no interest at all to others. In contrast, a benefit with a similar "Not Interested" region, but with a large "Interested" region and a smaller "Very Interested" region, such as "Legal Services," would be of great interest to only a small number of employees, and of some interest to many. The difference is in how interest is distributed. The decision makers might include the "Credit Union" as a benefit for all employees but make "Legal Services" an option for those who are really interested.

Unique Employee Needs. Figure 6.3 is a list of employees who had infit statistics greater than 2.00. The benefit for which their response is most unexpected is indicated. The top number is their observed response (higher numbers indicate more interest). The bottom number is the amount of unexpectedness in that response.

Employee #137 is unexpectedly interested in the "Employee Assistance Program," as are #78 and #81. Employee #29 is surprising because of a lack of interest in "Flex Time," despite interest in other benefits. Because so many of the respondents favor "Flex Time," only those who wanted no benefits are expected to NOT want "Flex Time." Employee #29 wants many of the other benefits, but not "Flex Time." Employees #140 and #58 are interested in none of the potential benefits except for the "Public Transportation Assistance." Employee #52 is noticeably interested in a "Smoke-ending Program."

The other three misfitting employees, #121, #46, and #50, emphasized extreme responses, one way or the other, for most benefits. This pattern of extremes in most of their responses is what made their total pattern misfit. It suggests that their feelings about differences among the benefits offered are especially strong.

Most of the above qualitative diagnoses might have been made after an item-by-item review of each individual employee's responses to the nine benefits, with reference to the group's preferences. However, 141 sets of responses times nine benefits makes 1,269 responses to evaluate. The accuracy and thoroughness, or even completeness, of such a review might be disappointing. The RPCM offers an extremely efficient and objective way for flagging people with unexpected patterns. Only unusual patterns need be individually reviewed by the researcher or decision makers, in this case, only 10 of 141.

SUMMARY AND DISCUSSION

The RPCM variable map, in Figure 6.2, summarizes all of the quantitative information needed by the organizational decision makers into one, easy-to-understand picture. Decisions about which benefits to implement and how should depend on the shape of employees' interest. The "Credit Union" and "Legal Services" benefits show approximately equal regions of "Not Interested." They differ, however, in their regions of "Interested" and "Very Interested." For the "Credit Union," everyone who is not "Not Interested" is expected to be "Very Interested." In contrast, for "Legal Services" the region in which most employees fell is only "Interested." The decision makers may decide, given equal organizational cost for the two, to make more people very happy by implementing the credit union.

In the initial analysis (Julian et al., 1988), an attempt was made to explain how the pattern of responses was not the same for all benefits, without making reference to the RPCM analyses. Here is that explanation:

> The relative number of respondents checking "Interested" and "Very Interested" gives an indication of the importance of the benefit for those who are interested. For instance, the Employee Assistance Program, Financial Planning, Legal Services, and the Weight Loss Program had much larger proportions selecting "Interested" than "Very Interested." This indicates that more people thought something like "yeah, that'd be ok" than thought "I must have this." (Julian et al., 1988, p. 4)

> In contrast, Child Care, a Credit union and Flex Time had much larger numbers pick "Very Interested" than "Interested." This suggests a real enthusiasm for these benefits on the part of the people who were interested. (Julian et al., 1988, p. 4)

This initial analysis identifies the "Credit Union" and "Flex Time" as benefits without a distinct middle step, whereas the RPCM identifies "Public Transportation" and a "Smoke-ending Program," in addition to "Day Care" which was detected by both analyses. The reason the intuitive analysis identifies different benefits is because it has no way of looking at WHICH people picked each level of interest. Is the group who selected "Interested" from the middle of the overall interest distribution or are they a smattering from all over? The RPCM item structure uses this information.

Most types of analyses of these data would have forced the employees with unique needs into the common pattern. If their idiosyncratic responses had not been flagged and tabled for review, the decision makers would never have known about these employees' unique needs.

The Rasch rating-scale model (Andrich, 1978; Wright & Masters, 1982) might have been considered for the analysis of these data. That is a possibility when all of the "items" have the same number of possible categories. However, that would force the pattern of interest to be the same for all benefits so that the benefits for which that pattern did not function would appear as misfitting. The use of the more detailed RPCM allows each benefit to have a unique interest pattern.

The map of the results of the RPCM calibration of the Employee Benefits Survey wish list section enables an interpretation of the data not possible with a traditional analysis. The decision makers can see at a glance the structure of employees expressed wishes for benefits. They can also evaluate individually the needs of those few employees for whom the common pattern does not fit.

REFERENCES

Andrich, D. (1978). A rating formulation for ordered response categories. *Psychometrika, 43*, 561–573.

Douglas, G. A., & Wright, B. D. (1990, Winter). Response patterns and their probabilities. *Rasch Measurement Special Interest Group Newsletter, 3*(4), 2–4.

Julian, E.R., Cass, J., Davenport, L., Obrzut, L., Powell, G., Riddick, S., & Ross, D. (1988). *Final report of the Employee Benefits Task Force*. Philadelphia: National Board of Medical Examiners.

Julian, E. R., & Wright, B. D. (1988). Using computerized patient simulations to measure the clinical competence of physicians. *Applied Measurement in Education, 1*, 299–318.

Linacre, J. M. (1990, Winter). Where does misfit begin? *Rasch Measurement Special Interest Group Newsletter, 3*(4), 6–7.

Masters, G. N. (1982). A Rasch model for partial credit scoring. *Psychometrika, 47*, 149–174.

Schulz, M. (1990, Winter). Functional assessment of fit. *Rasch Measurement Special Interest Group Newsletter, 3*(4), 7–9.

Smith, R. M. (1990, Winter). Theory and practice of fit in Rasch measurement. *Rasch Measurement Special Interest Group Newsletter, 3*(4), 4–6.

Wright, B. D., & Masters, G. N. (1982). *Rating scale analysis: Rasch measurement*. Chicago: MESA Press.

Wright, B. D., Schulz, E. M., Congdon, R. T., & Rossner, M. (1987). *MSTEPS: A Rasch program for partial credit scoring* [Computer program]. Chicago: University of Chicago, MESA Psychometrics Laboratory.

chapter **7**

Partial-Credit Modeling and Response Surface Modeling of Biobehavioral Data

David L. McArthur
Veterans Affairs Medical Center, Long Beach
and Department of Psychiatry and Human Behavior,
University of California Irvine

Kenneth L. Casey and Thomas J. Morrow,
Veterans Affairs Medical Center, Ann Arbor
and Departments of Neurology and Physiology,
University of Michigan Medical Center

Michael J. Cohen and Steven L. Schandler
Veterans Affairs Medical Center, Long Beach
and Department of Psychiatry and Human Behavior,
University of California Irvine

Stimuli may differ in their relative painfulness; persons may differ in their relative stoicism or squeamishness. Reduced to the simplest terms, most pain measurements require an implicit notion that some recognizable ordering can be made of both stimuli and persons. Without these orderings, formulating a cohesive understanding of people's responses to painful stimuli would be exceedingly difficult. However, pain is possibly the most difficult and complicated but least understood of our sensory experiences (Chapman et al., 1985). In both the experimental laboratory and the clinic, pain is a highly individual phenomenon. Extremes of variability occur even between persons whose physical symptoms and presenting problems seem nearly identical. For several years evidence has been mounting that traditional methods of analysis may not be fully sufficient to explain the complex phenomenon of pain. Rudy (1989) comments on this point:

> Over the past 20 years pain measurement has gained considerably in maturity . . . [T]here has been a proliferation of measures, scales, questionnaires, inventories, observational techniques, and other assessment strategies designed to quantify pain and/or cognitive, behavioral, affective, and physiological consequences of the pain experience. . . . [H]owever, considerable conceptual, theoretical, and methodological vigilance is still needed in the field of pain measurement. (p. 51)

Pivotal aspects of the problem in building a systematic "well-tempered" model for pain measurement include determining the best possible mathematical underpinnings, the minimum number of required parameters, and the serviceability—the ease with which the mathematics solve real measurement problems and best assist both experimental and clinical understanding of the pain experience. Workers in the field of pain measurement have yet to agree how this might be done. For example, one group of investigators studying nerve activity and pain report has relied on five parameters (three which concern wave patterns and another two which reflect proportions) to model the relationship (Fors, Ahlquist, Skagerwall, Edwall, & Haegerstam, 1984; Fors, Edwall, & Haegerstam, 1988). The result is a complex curve that requires one description for one portion of the relationship, then a different description for another portion; the formula that accomplishes this is of necessity quite complicated and the generalized solution remains statistically indeterminate. An entirely different approach to modeling attempts to fit equations to data rather than the other way around, and is typified by classification of pain patients based on concatenating sets of measures, including organic pathology (using assigned values derived from extensive rules about scoring a number of different pathophysiologies), pain behavior (using scores for various activities, pain verbalizations, drug dependencies, and personality features), and other data (Brena, 1984). The total number of parameters in this extended but statistically fragile model appears to be at minimum several dozen.

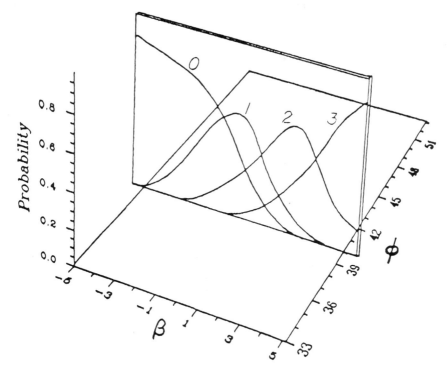

Figure 7.1.   Schematic PCM solution showing response probabilities for each of four rating steps, placed in context of a stimulus continuum

We propose that on both theoretical and practical grounds the Partial-Credit Model (PCM) (Masters, 1982) can be applied to pain response data generated in either the lab or the clinic. Each trial of each stimulus serves as an "item," with each allowable rating considered a step function in a theoretically continuous spectrum of the individual's responsivity to the stimulus. "Items," however, are also arrayed along a theoretically continuous dimension based on stimulus magnitude: Indeed, this facet of the situation can be unambigously measured by physical methods (and need not be estimated). What then becomes available is a set of PCM solutions, one for each stimulus, which can be linked together by stimulus magnitude to create a series of three-dimensional surfaces, one for each step in the rating scale (Figure 7.1).

The results of the PCM analyses arrayed by stimulus magnitude can be readily interpreted as a response surface. Response probabilities are calculated from the conventional PCM

$$P(x|n,i) = \frac{\exp \sum_{j=0}^{x} (\beta_n - \delta_{ij})}{\sum_{k=0}^{m} \sum_{j=0}^{k} (\beta_n - \delta_{ij})}, x = 0,m \qquad (1)$$

where $P(k|n,i)$ is the probability of response k by person n to stimulus i, β_n is the "sensitivity" of that person to stimulation, and δ_{ij} is the propensity of stimulus i to elicit response j relative to response $j - 1$. These probabilities can be entered in a vector whose dimension is determined by the experimenter's initial quantizing of the stimulus continuum. This vector forms the basis for a multidimensional probability function. For analysis of such a surface a methodology known as Response Surface Modeling (RSM)[1] has developed over the last two decades, primarily in the engineering sciences (Box & Draper, 1987; Khuri & Cornell, 1987). RSM's theoretical foundations require extensive use of calculus, but in practice RSM is easily restricted to a "region of interest," in this case bounded by the minimum and maximum stimulus values, a minimum and maximum logit—say, ±5.0, and probabilities from 0.0 to 1.0. These simple restrictions mean that RSM can be recast as a familiar regression equation

$$Z = \omega_0 + \omega_1 X + \omega_2 Y + \omega_3 X^2 + \omega_4 Y^2 + \omega_5 X \cdot Y + \epsilon \qquad (2)$$

in which X, Y, and Z refer to the logit scale, the stimulus scale, and the response probabilities, respectively, while ω are regression weights and ϵ is residual error. Using Equation (2), RSM yields four canonical interpretations based on error-free solutions (i.e., $\epsilon = 0$ and $R^2 = 1.0$). These canonical solutions—a hill, saddle, ridge, and shoulder (Figure 7.2)—provide a guide for considering the pain-stimulus–pain-response interaction from a strictly theoretical standpoint. The canonical solutions differ only in their ω's; the one which corresponds best to psychophysical theory is the ridge since it implies that a maximum response can be elicited by any stimulus given a sufficiently responsive individual. In actual use, if none of the canonical solutions is approximated, (i.e., $\epsilon \gg 0$, $R^2 \ll 1.0$), something else about the pain stimulus and the pain response needs further study.

---

[1] Note that this abbreviation is used to signify something else in Wilson's chapter in this volume.

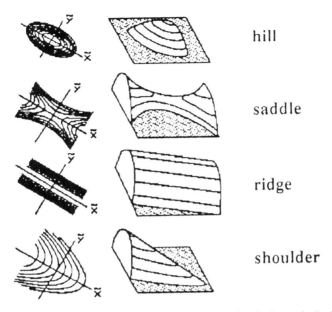

hill

saddle

ridge

shoulder

Figure 7.2.   Response surface modeling: Canonical solutions derivable from a regression equation formed from three terms

METHOD

As part of ongoing studies in pain perception upon heat stimulation of the skin, 14 female and 12 male healthy volunteers, ages 14–59 years, gave informed consent for the experiment. Ambient temperature ranged between 22 and 26°C; temperatures at the skin surface averaged 31.25°C. Each of 10 trials within this protocol consisted of eight stimuli applied to the volar surface of the nondominant forearm for a maximum of five seconds, in random order without replacement with a brief recovery period between each stimulus. The stimulus temperatures selected were 33°, 36°, 40°, 43°, 45°, 47°, 50°, and 52°C. The amount of heat at the thermode tip was controlled by a microprocessor; its value was not known by the participant. Allowable responses were "No sensation of heat," "Warm," "Hot," and "Pain"—the participant was asked to state a single choice out loud, and the response to each separate stimulus was noted by the experimenter. If pain was reported the experimenter withdrew the stimulus immediately. The highest level of stimulation always elicited the rating of "pain" from every participant on every trial, and was dropped for purposes of further analysis since its information content is null.

The resulting three-faceted data matrix (26 persons × 10 trials × 7 stimuli in real-time order) was rearranged (260 cases × 7 items in ascending order of stimulus magnitude) and analyzed with the PCM model using the program MSTEPS (Wright, Rossner, & Congden, 1987). Intermediate values used in production of the response category probability curves for each item were intercepted and recast in terms of four separate three-dimensional matrices of person logits, stimulus magnitudes, and response probabilities. These matrices, one for each of the four allowable ratings, were then separately evaluated by RSM using BMDP 1R (BMDP Statistical Software, 1988).

RESULTS

The lowest level of stimulation, 33°C, seldom produced any response but "No sensation of heat" while 50°C was sufficient to elicit the maximum rating from almost every respondent on all occasions. The overwhelming tendency among respondents was to accurately detect differences in stimulus temperatures even though the order of their presentation within a trial was random. A small percentage of ratings, however, suggested that the natural stimulus order was not recognized by a participant (i.e., adjacent ratings showed either a step reversal or a jump of more than one step). Hubert's Γ (Hubert, 1979, 1984) was applied to matrices of change in ratings between the adjacent stimuli: In every instance Γ was statistically significant, meaning that the participants' production of higher ratings as higher stimulus magnitudes were administered was at no time a completely random process.

PCM analysis resulted in satisfactory model fits (person separation reliability = 0.73, item separation reliability = 0.99). Stimulus calibrations recaptured from the participants' ratings correlated highly with the actual stimulus temperatures ($r = -0.95$). Two individuals with aberrant fit statistics (Wright & Stone, 1979) were both found to be less responsive on several trials than average, and less stable in their ratings overall. Fit statistics for the remaining participants were all within acceptable range. In sum, the PCM analysis provided a fully interpretable outcome for the study of pain perception.

Each participant received 10 trials at each stimulus intensity, and thus imbedded in the study's design is a repeated- measures phenomenon. Repeated-measures analysis of variance using the Rasch person estimates in a participants × trials design revealed a significant trials effect ($F_{9,225} = 2.17$, $p < .05$); post-hoc testing showed a decline in overall ratings from the first two trials to the final trial, reflecting a natural course of moderate stimulus habituation. The presence of such interaction violates a strict interpretation of specific objectivity offered by Fischer (1987). Alternatively, both Embretson's (in press) multidimensional latent trait model for measuring change, in which learning abilities over time are treated as separate dimensions, and Linacre's (1989b) multifaceted model, in which each separate component of the test situation is represented by an independent parameter, deserve attention in this context. To further determine the relative size of the trials effect in the present study, the data were reanalyzed using Linacre's approach (Linacre, 1989a). The largest difference between calibrations for trials was only 1.09 logits, a range smaller than the smallest difference between any pair of stimulus calibrations. Because the trials effect was also smaller than the effects due to differences between subjects, it is ignored in the remaining analysis.

We turn to the next methodological step, the translation of PCM to

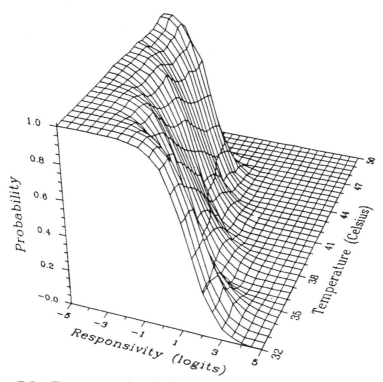

Figure 7.3.   Response surface for "No sensation of heat"

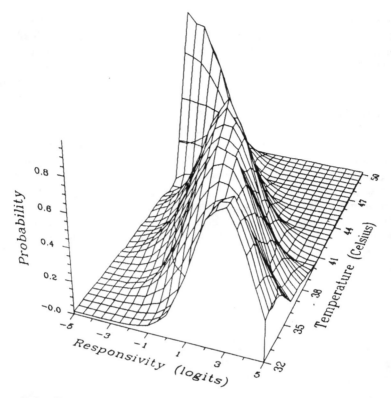

Figure 7.4.   Response surface for "Warm"

RSM. From the probability curves calculated by MSTEPS for each rating step for each stimulus, discrete values taken at every 0.5 logits were preserved as X and Z coordinates, resulting in an 11×7 matrix. Figures 7.3–7.6 present the response surfaces which emerge when these values are placed in the context of the Y coordinate representing stimulus magnitude, after expansion to 21×37 matrices using a smoothing technique called Kriging (Ripley, 1981). The equiprobable ($p = .25$) contours are also shown. Regression analysis using the RSM methodology was performed on the unsmoothed surfaces for each rating step, with Equation (2) as the design model.

RSM analysis of the surface for the lowest rating yielded $R^2 = 0.814$, indicating a very smooth pattern across all stimulus magnitudes for the full range of responsivities. The ridge solution of the canonical RSM is clearly the appropriate error-free analogue. Likewise the surface for the highest rating also was shown to be generally smooth:

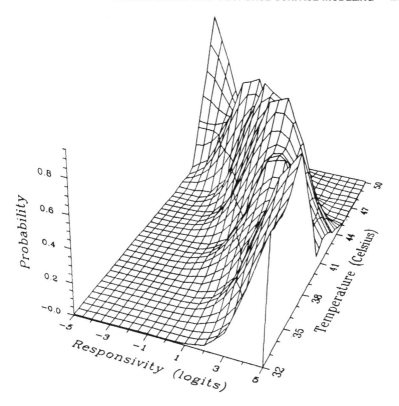

Figure 7.5.   Response surface for "Hot"

RSM yielded $R^2 = 0.763$. This surface is also well-approximated by the same canonical. However, both midrange ratings provide much different pictures: the RSM R^2 values are substantially smaller for both "Warm" (0.294) and "Hot" (0.257), and the visualizations make clear that the more stoic participants behave differently than others in their use of these ratings. The ridge canonical RSM appears to be applicable to only a portion of the response surface; something else must play a significant role in determining the intermediate responses of the stoics.

DISCUSSION

PCM and RSM form a useful methodological pair for studies in which participants give ratings to controlled stimuli. PCM provides every-

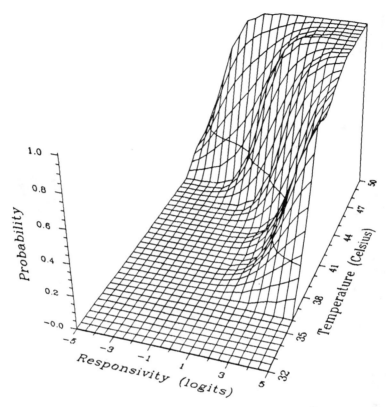

Figure 7.6. **Response surface for "Pain"**

thing necessary for the mathematical evaluation of participants and rating steps, while RSM adds a functional framework for understanding the PCM solution with respect to the stimulus continuum. The RSM approach relies on the fact that each "item" can be considered as a member of a known continuum before the analysis begins. Unlike much of educational testing in which the existence of an item "continuum" is to some degree uncertain, many studies in biobehavioral research are predicated on the use of stimuli controlled to tight tolerances and given in multiple trials: The location of each stimulus on the continuum is unambiguous. In the field of pain research, maintaining control over stimuli is critical to the design of studies of pain perception. In the search for satisfactory clinical explanations of neurological disease or deficit, testing of sensory function depends in no small measure on stimuli that differ from one another by known amounts. Parenthetically, such testing is regarded as "undoubtably the most difficult part of the neurologic examination" (Adams & Victor, 1985, p. 7). The PCM/RSM combination is directly applicable to the task of understanding the results of this testing in both the clinic and the lab.

Despite an obvious debt among pain researchers to pioneering efforts by Stevens (1975), for example, and subsequent attempts to formulate suitable statistical treatments for such approaches (e.g., Thomas, 1984), we believe that the statistical assessment of pain and pain perception has been incomplete. "As yet in the . . . life sciences we do not have underlying laws, but the use of mathematical analysis in such subjects is still in its infancy. We have been applying mathematics to physical problems for 300 years, but to non-physical problems for only at most a few decades" (Burghes & Wood, 1980, p. 18). Traditional methods, using strictly deterministic approaches, have not produced tractable mathematical models which account for differences in stimulus characteristics, inter- and intrasubject variations, and indications of how a particular pain response may be understood in a mathematically calibrated or graduated context. Because it provides immediately useful tests of significance and fit, using strong mathematical principles and minimum numbers of parameters, PCM provides a useful methodology with a strong conceptual basis for analyses of pain perception data. PCM and RSM allow strong predictions of an individual's future pattern of responses to pain stimuli. With the addition of one more design facet reflecting group membership, the PCM/RSM combination also enables detailed statistical comparisons of the responsivities of neurological patients contrasted with nonimpaired controls.

REFERENCES

Adams, R.D., & Victor, M. (1985). *Principles of neurology* (3rd ed.). New York: McGraw-Hill.

BMDP Statistical Software. (1988). *BMDP Statistical Software* [Computer program]. Los Angeles: BMDP Statistical Software, Inc.

Box, G.E.P., & Draper, N.R. (1987). *Empirical model building and response surfaces*. New York: Wiley.

Brena, S.F. (1984). Chronic pain states: A model for classification. *Psychiatric Annals, 14*, 778–782.

Burghes, D.N., & Wood, A.D. (1980). *Mathematical models in the social, management and life sciences*. Chichester: Ellis Horwood.

Chapman, C.R., Casey, K.L., Dubner, R., Foley, K.M., Gracely, R.H., & Reading, A.E. (1985). Pain measurement: An overview. *Pain, 22*, 1–31.

Embretson, S.E. (in press). Implications of a multidimensional latent trait model for measuring change. In J.L. Horn & L. Collins (Eds.), *Best methods for analyzing change*. Washington, DC: APA Books.

Fischer, G.H. (1987). Applying the principles of specific objectivity and generalizability to the measurement of change. *Psychometrika, 52*, 565–587.

Fors, U., Ahlquist, M.L., Skagerwall, R., Edwall, L.G.A., & Haegerstam, G.A.T. (1984). Relation between intradental nerve activity and estimated pain in man—a mathematical model. *Pain, 18*, 397–408.

Fors, U., Edwall, L.G.A., & Haegerstam, G.A.T. (1988). The ability of a mathematical model to evaluate the effects of two pain modulating procedures on pulpal pain in man. *Pain, 33*, 253–264.

Hubert, L.J. (1979). Comparison of sequences. *Psychological Bulletin, 86*, 1098–1106.

Hubert, L.J. (1984). Statistical applications of linear assignment. *Psychometrika, 49*, 449–473.

Khuri, A.I., & Cornell, J.A. (1987). *Response surfaces: Designs and analyses.* New York: Marcel Dekker.

Linacre, J.M. (1989a). *FACETS: Computer program for many-faceted Rasch measurement* [Computer program]. Chicago: Mesa Press.

Linacre, J.M. (1989b). Many-faceted Rasch measurement (Doctoral dissertation, University of Chicago, 1989). *Dissertation Abstracts International, 50*, 2029A.

Masters, G.N. (1982). A Rasch model for partial credit scoring. *Psychometrika, 47*, 149–174.

Ripley, B.D. (1981). *Spatial statistics.* New York: Wiley-Interscience.

Rudy, T.E. (1989). Innovations in pain psychometrics. In C.R. Chapman (Ed.), *The measurement of pain.* New York: Raven.

Stevens, S.S. (1975). *Psychophysics: Introduction to its perceptual, neural and social prospects.* New York: Wiley.

Thomas, H. (1984). Parameter estimation in simple psychophysical methods. *Psychological Bulletin, 93*, 396–403.

Wright, B.D. Rossner, M., & Congden, R.T. (1987). *MSTEPS, a Rasch program for partial credit scoring, person measurement, item step calibration, and person and item fit statistics* [Computer program]. Chicago: University of Chicago, Department of Education.

chapter **8**

Polytomous Rasch Models for Behavioral Assessment: The Tufts Assessment of Motor Performance*

Larry H. Ludlow
School of Education
Boston College

Stephen M. Haley
Tufts University School of Medicine and
New England Medical Center, Medical Rehabilitation
Research and Training

The purpose of this chapter is to describe the psychometric analysis of the Tufts Assessment of Motor Performance (TAMP). The TAMP is a clinical assessment instrument that measures motor performance

*Preparation of this chapter was funded in part by Grants Nos. G00830042 and H133B8009, National Institute on Disability and Rehabilitation Research, U.S. Department of Education.

Appreciation is extended to the following for their assistance with recruitment of patients: Massachusetts Hospital School, Greenery Rehabilitation and Skilled Nursing Center, Shaugnessy Rehabilitation Hospital, Spaulding Rehabilitation Hospital, and the Rehabilitation Institute at New England Medical Center Hospital.

functional skills. Two-item response theory (IRT) models, the Rasch partial-credit and rating-scale models (Andrich, 1978; Masters, 1982; Rasch, 1960; Wright & Masters, 1982) were employed as key elements in the identification and specification of a sequential model of motor performance proficiency. The central tenets of this chapter are that sequential scales of motor performance proficiency can be specified and that these sequential scales provide a basis for the creation of clinically meaningful summary scores.

The TAMP is a diagnosis-independent, criterion-referenced clinical evaluation instrument. The TAMP samples a broad range of physical skills in the areas of mobility, activities of daily living, and physical aspects of communication. Its purpose is to examine motor performance functional skills in sufficient detail to adequately describe and identify current status and subsequent clinical change. The TAMP has been structured to independently assess individual tasks within global functional items.

Our goal for the TAMP was to develop measures for motor performance scales that could be defended from both a conceptual and psychometric perspective. We were acutely aware of the significant limitations in the current status of aggregate score utilization in functional assessment measures in the field of rehabilitation. For example, one problem with many functional and motor performance tests utilized in rehabilitation medicine is the lack of a parsimonious method to describe detailed information about motor performance (Jette, 1985). Difficulties in test interpretation are encountered when items across multiple domains are summed into an aggregate index (Klein & Bell, 1982; Riddick, 1989). Even if items are summed within consistent domains, the same total score may result from many different variations of score components (Feinstein, 1986; Sheikh, 1986). Summary scores often obscure the clinical meaningfulness of the patient's true ability in a particular domain of behavior (Merbitz, Morris, & Grip 1989). Furthermore, with the exception of the Vineland Adaptive Behavior Scales (Sparrow, Balla, & Cicchetti, 1984) and the Scales of Independent Behavior (Bruninks, Woodcock, Hill, & Weatherman, 1985), most current functional test scores are not based on a hierarchical or sequential model, and most have no procedure by which summary scores can be validated against a sequential model. Finally, we needed a quick, easily administered, and easily interpreted clinical instrument.

METHOD

Sample

Two-hundred-and-six patients with muscular, skeletal, and neurological impairments have been scored. They range in age from 6 to 82 years and are evenly distributed across the sexes. The wide range in age is appropriate because the functional problems affecting children (above age 6) and adults who have a disabling disorder are strikingly similar. They were volunteers representative of the diversity of patients at local rehabilitation centers in the greater Boston area. All patients consented to the study in accordance with the requirements of the Human Investigation Review Committee at New England Medical Center Hospitals.

The TAMP was generally administered in less than one hour by one of three trained physical or occupational therapists. All tests were videotaped and analyzed at a later date. Three raters, two physical

---

Name _____ ID_____ Test Date_____ Scoring Date_____

Tester_____ Rater _____ Facility_____ Study_____

Classification:
FM1 Grasp/release
FM2 Stabilization
FM3 Fine manipulation
FM4 Manipulation
FM5 U/E alignment
GM1 Preparatory moves
GM2 Transition
GM3 Upright balance
GM4 LE/trunk alignment
GM5 WC skills
GM6 Ambulation
OM1 Talking
OM2 Drinking

Assistance:
5 Standard cues only
4 Additional cues, demonstration/supervision
3 Stabilization/contact
2 Physical assistance
1 Approximates movement only
Ø No score
Subtract 0.5 if assistive device aids in attempt

Performance Factors:
D = Difficulty
O = Omit
R = Refuse
S = Safety
NA = not applicable

Technique Scoring:
Approach, Movement Pattern:
2 =correct technique used
1 =incorrect technique used
Proficiency:
3 Smooth, error-free single attempt
2 Fumbling or multiple attempts but no errors
1 Task specific error

Measurement Dimensions

# Item	Phase	Task	classification	assistance	performance	approach	pattern	proficiency	time (minutes)
			assistance			**technique**			
1. TALKING	I	Balances, prepares devices	GM 3			■			
	II	Communicates effectively	OM1			■			
	III	Balances, discontinues device	GM3			■			
2. WRITING	Ia	Picks up pen	FM1						
	Ib	Takes cap off pen	FM2						
	II	Writes sentence/shapes, (at least one legible word or shape)	FM3						
	IIIa	Puts cap back on pen	FM2						
	IIIb	Puts pen down	FM1						
3. TYPING	Ia	Places paper in typewriter	FM4			■			
	Ib	Turns typewriter on	FM3						
	II	Types sentence	FM3						
	IIIa	Turns typewriter off	FM3						
	IIIb	Takes paper out of typewriter	FM4			■			

Figure 8.1. Tufts Assessment of Motor Performance Scoresheet

therapists, and one occupational therapist independently rated each videotape. A complete description of the reliability analyses conducted may be found in Gans et al. (1988).

Instrument

Figure 8.1 presents page 1 of the TAMP. There are a total of 32 item sets (like "talking") with a total of 113 scorable tasks. These items may be grouped and scored in a variety of ways. For example, "Classification" (indicated in the upper-left section) essentially groups items into separate fine motor and gross motor groups.

The items are also broken into two "Measurement Dimensions" (the column headings) referred to as "assistance" and "technique." These Measurement Dimension specifications include levels of assistance (person and device) needed to complete the task, approach (general technique used), pattern (movement patterns defined for specific gross and fine motor components), proficiency (movement control and accuracy), and time to complete the task. Level of assistance was scored from 0 to 5 with 0.5 subtracted from a score if an assistive device aided in the attempt (the score of 0.5 itself was not possible because a score of 1 included an assistive device). This scoring system was rescored to a 10-point scale ranging from 0 to 9. Other than the performance domain under the assistance dimension, the remaining domains were scored 0 for a nonstandard attempt, or 1 for a standard attempt.

Finally, the items can be grouped into "mobility," "activities of daily living," and "communication" domains. Obviously, from a measurement and practical perspective, this multitude of grouping and scoring formats for the same set of data constitutes a potentially bewildering task of analysis and summarization.

RESULTS

Analyses

Four steps were undertaken to develop the final sequential model and scoring system for the TAMP. These included: (a) a factor analysis and classical reliability analysis to initially identify the major motor dimensions, (b) exploratory application of the two IRT models to test both the hypothesized structure of the scales and the applicability of the models, (c) modification of the original scoring scheme and elimination of redundant tasks, and (d) application of the Rasch rating-scale model to define the scale structures and reporting systems.

Dimension Identification

The dimension identification analyses sought evidence for the original classifications of fine motor and gross motor skills. Using the assistance scoring strategy, a principal factors analysis was performed on the 113 tasks and 10 factors were initially extracted (74% of the common factor variance was accounted for). A varimax rotation was performed, and after inspecting the factor matrix it was concluded that an eight-factor solution could be interpreted. These factors were labeled: grasp/release, manipulation, fasteners, typing, dynamic balance, mat mobility, ambulation, and wheelchair skills. Factor composition ranged from 5 to 22 tasks. Cronbach alpha reliability coefficients computed for each factor ranged from .79 to .99. There was no additional compelling factor analytic evidence that the data could be reduced to the three originally hypothesized global factors of mobility, activities of daily living, and communication.

Exploratory IRT Analyses

In the present application, the Rasch partial credit and rating scale models provide a mechanism for identifying patient status through their placement of patient measures along latent continua of functional proficiency. The measurement of a patient along a scaled continuum is accomplished by rationally hypothesizing a sequential model for the order of the tasks that define the scale and then statistically estimating the position of each task and patient along the proficiency continuum. The scoring system and its success in identifying proficiency levels is dependent upon the validity and generalizability of the sequential model. For example, a valid scoring profile requires a relatively low score for patients with low proficiency. However, if a patient receives a low score that results from accomplishing only the most difficult tasks while not accomplishing the easier ones, then the summary score does not adequately reflect the patient's true proficiency.

When data (whether academic achievement, attitude, performance, etc.) possess an ordered scoring format such that each successive change in the ordinal values represents either an increase or decrease in the variable of interest, then a Rasch rating-scale or partial-credit analysis of the structure of the variable may be appropriate. In the present application, the tasks were scored 0 to 9 where 0 meant complete dependence and successive increasing integers implied increasing functional independence. The specific psychometric difference between these models that we investigated was whether or not the probability of the patients taking the "step" up between any specific pair of scoring category transitions remained the same across all the tasks. If it was the case that, say, the probability of stepping from response category 4 to 5 was roughly the same across all tasks within a given scale, then the rating-scale model would be the model of choice. If, however, the relative probability of response from one scoring category to the next shifted greatly from task to task, then the partial credit model might likely be more versatile for explaining the observed response patterns. At the outset of this research we could not predict which psychometric model and its respective set of estimated parameters would best explain the data.

Once the respective parameters of either model are estimated they are used to compute the expected (or predicted) behavior for each patient on each task (Andrich, 1978). These expected patterns of behavior are then compared to the observed clinical behaviors. The difference between each pair of observed and predicted behaviors may be expressed as a standardized residual (Wright & Masters, 1982). Each standardized residual has expected value of approximately zero and variance of approximately one.

Residuals provide a check on the reasonableness of task difficulty and patient performance estimates. If a patient performs tasks in a manner consistent with his or her estimated performance level and the difficulty of the tasks, then small residuals result. Otherwise, unexpected failures produce large negative residuals while unexpected successes produce large positive residuals.

Vectors of residuals may be inspected graphically in order to detect patterns of unexpected behaviors (Ludlow, 1985, 1986) or goodness-of-fit statistics that follow an approximate t distribution may be computed from the aggregation of the residuals (Wright & Masters, 1982). A large positive fit statistic (for either patients or tasks) results when either unexpected successes or failures have frequently occurred. A fit statistic of 2.0 is often chosen as the initial critical value to signal unusual behavior patterns. Once a task or patient with a fit greater than 2.0 has been found it usually becomes necessary to inspect the respective vector of residuals in order to pinpoint where the unusual behaviors came from. Then, of course, the analytic problem is to try to explain why those unexpected behaviors occurred.

Initially, a partial-credit solution was assumed appropriate as the IRT model of choice. This was because there was no a priori expectation that the response probability curves between adjacent pairs of scoring categories across all items would be similar enough to qualify as a rating-scale scoring strategy. The eight factors, now being tested for the extent to which they might be labeled scales, were thus subjected to a partial-credit analysis.

An immediate practical problem arose—there were large numbers of scoring categories within each scale with zero frequency counts. From an estimation perspective this is not particularly important because the partial-credit model obtains estimates of the difficulty of proceeding from one nonzero frequency category to the next, that is, the difficulty of taking the next "step" defined as an estimate between any two adjacent scoring categories containing non-zero frequency counts. From an applied perspective, however, this situation caused considerable problems. Ideally, for a task with 10 score categories, 9 steps, and all categories with non-zero counts, step 1 would correspond to the 0/1 transition, step 2 would correspond to the 1/2 transition, step 5 would be the 4/5 transition, and so on. In other words there is a direct relation between step estimation and scoring category transition and interpretation.

Our particular situation, in contrast to the above ideal data matrix, is illustrated by the data distribution for the grasp/release tasks. Out of a total of 90 tasks-by-category data cells, 45 had a zero frequency. As a consequence, the estimation results do not yield an obvious relation between step estimation and scoring category transition. In fact, with a different sample or subsample of patients new steps may appear or disappear. This results in the problem of trying to develop a score equivalence table for the purpose of assigning a proficiency estimate to a new patient based simply on their TAMP raw scores—the patient could score in response categories that were not used in the original calibration study. These situations are exceedingly frustrating when trying to operationally define a scale and its potential invariance.

Although the problem of empty categories and perfectly scoring patients (out of 206, 123 had maximum scores) is characteristic of clinical applications where patients often tend to fall in the extreme categories of complete dependence or complete independence, an effort was made to interpret the scales under this model. A "task-step" map for the grasp/release tasks is illustrated in Figure 8.2.

The vertical line delineates for each task (to the right) and patient (to the left) along the logit continuum the most likely step transition a patient is expected to have taken. At the top are the more difficult tasks and the more able patients. At the bottom are the easiest tasks and the least functionally proficient patients. Each task has its name label and a digit appended to its right-most position. The digit indicates the particular task step to be taken at that point along the continuum. For example, "CUT31" refers to the transition from the "No Score" category to "Additional cues without assistive device" category for the "puts down knife and fork" task. In this case the zero frequency scoring categories yield a first step estimate that represents the transi-

MAP SHOWING POSITIONS OF PEOPLE AND ITEM DIFFICULTY STEPS

```
POSITION          PEOPLE(N= 83)              ITEMS(L= 9)        STEPS= 36

2.63

2.10       XXXXXXXXXXXXXXXXXXXXXXXXXXXXXXXXXXXXXXXXX|   WT3A6       puts cap on pen (8/9)

1.81                                            XX|

1.59                                 XXXXXXXXXXX|   CUT33      puts down knife/fork (8/9)

1.41                                     XXXX|
1.27                                     XXXXXXXX|

1.14                                       XX|   PR3B6      places jar on desk (8/9)
1.03                                     XXXX|
0.86                                     XXXX|
0.78                                        X|
0.71                                        X|
0.58                                        X|   WT1B4 WT3A2 WT3A4   takes cap off pen (8/9)
0.47                                        X|   WT1B2 PR3B4 CUT14   picks up knife/fork (8/9)
0.36
0.26
0.20
0.08                                      XXX|   WT1A4      picks up pen (8/9)
-0.04                                            EN13       picks up edge of paper (8/9)
-0.11
-0.18                                        X|   WT3B3      puts pen down (8/9)
-0.26                                            EN33       puts envelope on desk (8/9)
-0.36                                            EN11       picks up edge of paper (3/7)
-0.46
-0.59

-0.76                                            EN31       puts envelope on desk (0/7)

-0.98                                            CUT31      puts down knife/fork  (0/7)

-1.32

-1.99
```

Figure 8.2. Partial-Credit Solution for Grasp/Release Tasks

tion between scoring categories 0/7, not 0/1 as one might initially expect. Essentially, this map tells us that patients were either completely dependent or fully independent when attempting these tasks.

From this perspective we gain some appreciation for the scale defined by these tasks. The three easiest steps to take—CUT31, EN31, EN11 (put down knife and fork, put envelope on desk, pick up edge of paper)—are steps that require additional cues but no assistive devices. The three hardest steps—PR3B6, CUT33, WT3A6 (place jar on desk, put down knife and fork in specific location, put cap back on pen)—are steps that require standard cues only. The midrange steps are a mixture of tasks requiring additional or standard cues.

From a functional perspective this scale is reasonable and consistent with the expected order of difficulty for these tasks. The reason why this scale was chosen for illustration is because it was the only one of the eight that yielded a readily interpretable solution. At this point a decision had to be made about whether or not this line of psychometric analysis was practical. Furthermore, how were the other scoring domains of "approach," "pattern," "accuracy," and "attempt" to be incorporated in some form of summary assessment?

New Scoring Scheme

Before concluding whether or not partial-credit solutions were the most informative way to explain the data we attempted a series of rating-scale analyses. The problem of empty response categories was immediately encountered. Every scale had at least one response category with a zero frequency count—thus preventing the use of the rating scale model. At this point a decision to rescore the data was reached.

The data were rescored to reflect not only level of assistance required but also the approach, motor pattern, and proficiency domains. For example, if patients required only standard cues and demonstrated standard approach and motor pattern and proficiency, then they received a maximum score of 7. Scores now ranged from 0 to 7. These scoring criteria were now specifically and explicitly defined to represent a rating scale structure. It was intended that progress up the scoring continuum result in response probabilities that would be similar across all tasks within a scale.

The partial-credit and rating-scale solutions were obtained under this scoring format. In these analyses the rating-scale solutions began to appear as a viable representation of functional proficiency. In fact, some useful, but previously unanticipated, information appeared. For example, in the fasteners scale there were six item sets and each one included the same finishing task—"arms down in lap." Each of these six tasks received a large positive fit statistic. An inspection of the underlying residual patterns revealed that numerous higher proficiency patients were unexpectedly failing on these tasks. Although it initially seemed reasonable to score the same task across all six sets of items, these results told us that the patients who should have been able to accomplish the task in one item set, but didn't, usually couldn't do the expected task in any of the other item sets. Thus, even though the task served a useful purpose as a "flag" task for identifying one type of unexpected performance, it certainly did not need to be scored six separate times. Other problems with a few tasks were also noticed and when a solution could not be found they were discarded.

Overall, the partial-credit scales remained quite unwieldy because with the still numerous zero frequency categories on individual tasks within each solution it was confusing, time-consuming, and impractical to labor over what the tasks and steps were defining. The rating-scale model had its problems too. There were two scales with zero frequency counts for all tasks within the third response category and most of the other scales had only a few in that category. As a consequence, all scores from 3 through 7 were reduced by 1 so that the final scoring scheme ranges from 0 to 6. Table 8.1 presents the specific scoring criteria. The final set of scorable tasks was reduced to 91.

Rating-Scale Analyses

Rating-scale solutions were obtained for each of the eight scales. Inspection of the fit statistics and residuals within each solution indicated that there were no longer any tasks with obvious misfit problems. This was a rather remarkable finding given the range in age and disability represented in the sample. The occasional misfitting patient appeared more idiosyncratic than having occurred principally as the result of an age/sex/disability interaction (see next subsection for an example). Overall, the scales were reasonable in their sequential structure and consistent with the original clinical hypotheses.

One solution is briefly discussed. Figure 8.3 contains the fasteners scale. The easiest tasks are those involving reaching for fasteners (at the bottom of the scale). Patients with the least functional proficiency would be expected to succeed on only these easy tasks. Next come those tasks requiring an undoing of fasteners. The most difficult tasks involve the actual fastening. Only the most proficient patients would be expected to succeed on these tasks. Note also that zipper tasks tend to

Table 8.1.   TAMP Proficiency Scoring Scheme

Score	Proficiency	Description
6	Independent/full proficiency	No assistance is needed to complete the item; full proficiency demonstrated.
5	Independent/modified proficiency	No assistance is needed to complete the item; patient demonstrates modified proficiency in completing the item which may involve use of device, altered motor strategy or postural alignment.
4	Minimal Assistance	Patient requires close supervision, contact guard assist, stabilization of item, or minimal help with completing item; proficiency altered only by requirement of minimal assistance.
3	Minimal Assistance/modified proficiency	Patient requires minimal assistance (see #4); patient demonstrates modified proficiency in completing the item which may involve use of device, altered motor strategy, or postural alignment.
2	Moderate Physical Assistance	Patient requires moderate physical assistance; patient does more than half of effort of item.
1	Maximal Physical Assistance	Patient requires maximal physical assistance; patient does less than half of effort of item.
0	Total Dependence	Patient is unable to attempt item due to difficulty.

be easier than button tasks which, in turn, tend to be easier than snap tasks.

The estimates of task difficulty presented in this figure represent the relative overall difficulty of the tasks based on total scores resulting from the 0–6 scoring format. This means that we can compare the tasks to one another and place patients along the continuum relative to the tasks but we don't really know what score or performance a patient's location represents. To obtain this information we have to add each rating scale category threshold estimate to all the task difficulties before we can define what skill a patient's position actually represents.

Figure 8.4 contains one solution to this problem (using the typing scale tasks). The process of labeling tasks is the same as in the previous partial-credit solution but now the last digit corresponds to specific response category transitions. For example, a "3" represents tran-

TAMP: Fasteners

Item Calibrations	Items	Person Location
High	*Ability*	
0.67	Hooks zipper	
0.63	Snaps jacket	
0.54	Zip jacket	
0.25	Buttons jacket	
0.15	Aligns to zip	
0.08	Unsnaps jacket	Person
0.07	Unbutton jacket	Scores
0.05	Unzips jacket	
0.01	Reaches strap/snap	
-0.57	Reaches button	
-0.82	Reaches zipper	
	Low Ability	

Figure 8.3.   Rating-Scale Solution for Fastener Tasks

sition between the 2/3 categories—"physical assistance" to "supervision/minimal assistance; modified technique." A "5" represents transition between the 4/5 categories—"supervision/minimal assistance" to "independent; modified technique." A "6" represents transition between the 5/6 categories—"independent; modified technique" to "independent."

This scale is easily understood when v.e think about how difficult the tasks are for patients with motor dysfunction; it takes one finger to turn on or off the typewriter, a hand grasp is needed to pull out the paper, locating and pressing the correct key is needed for typing a sentence, and both hands may be needed to place and load paper into the machine. Within any particular task it is easier to perform the task with assistance ("3") than to achieve complete independence ("6"). Furthermore, we are also able to compare relative levels of category difficulty across tasks. For example, it is easier to score "5" on turning off the typewriter (TY3A5) than it is to score "3" on putting the paper in the typewriter (TY1A3). (Not all transitions are represented because some response categories were never the most likely response for anyone along the continuum.)

With evidence suggesting that the scales were working as intended we addressed the problem of forming summary scores. All 206 pa-

MAP SHOWING POSITIONS OF PEOPLE AND ITEM DIFFICULTIES+THRESHOLDS

POSITION	PEOPLE(N= 176)	ITEMS(L= 5)	STEPS= 30

```
POSITION
-----------------------------------------------------------------------------
 3.25   XXXXXXXXXX

 2.34   XXXXXXXXXXXXXXXXXXXXXXXX|  TY1A6          paper in typewriter (5/6)
                                   TY26           types sentence (5/6)
 1.78   XXXXXXXXXXXXXXXXXXXXXXXXXXXXXXXXXX|  TY3B6   paper out of typewriter (5/6)

 1.41   XXXXXXXXXXXXX           TY1B6          turns on typewriter (5/6)

 1.16   XXXXXXXXXXXXX           TY3A6          turns off typewriter (5/6)
 0.95   XXXXXXXXXXXXXXXXXX
 0.79   XXXXXXXXXXXXXXXXXX
 0.64   XXXXXXX|               TY1A5
 0.52   XXXXX|                 TY25           "5" = 4/5 transition
 0.40   XXXXXXXXX|
 0.29   XXXXXX|                TY3B5
 0.19   XXX|
 0.09   XXXXX|
-0.01   XXXXX|
-0.10   XX|
-0.20   X|                    TY1B5 TY1A3
-0.29
-0.39   XX|                   TY23  TY3A5
-0.49   XX|
-0.59                         TY3B3
-0.70
-0.81
-0.94   XX|                   TY1B3

-1.07
-1.23                         TY3A3
-1.41

-1.64
```

Figure 8.4. Rating-Scale Solution for Typing Tasks

133

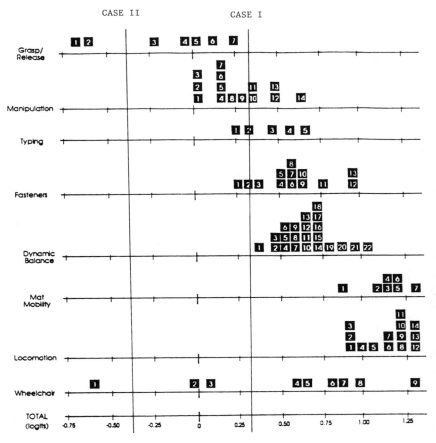

Figure 8.5. TAMP Assessment Report for Case I and Case II

tients' 91 task scores were analyzed together and a practitioners report form was developed. The result is shown in Figure 8.5. The tasks (identified numerically by order of difficulty within each scale) are placed at their respective locations on the logit continuum. Proceeding from the left the tasks increase in the difficulty of a patient scoring a "6" on each task (fully independent). The scales within the fine motor section (grasp/release through fasteners) are ordered by their overall pattern of relative difficulty, as are the gross motor scales (dynamic balance through wheelchair). The fine motor tasks are generally easier than the gross motor tasks. A plot of the distribution of patient logit estimates revealed that most patients demonstrated fairly high functional proficiency across these tasks.

Within the grasp/release scale releasing an envelope was the easiest task while replacing the cap on a felt pen was the most difficult. Pouring a liquid was easiest while cutting thera-putty was most difficult within the manipulation scale. Turning a typewriter off and placing paper into a typewriter were the easiest and most difficult tasks, respectively, within typing. Reaching for a zipper and hooking a zipper were the easiest and hardest tasks within the fasteners scale. Within dynamic balance, static sitting and transferring from supine to long sit were the easiest and hardest tasks, respectively. Simply rolling from supine to prone was the easiest task within mat mobility while getting out of quadruped position with full alignment was hardest. The easiest task within locomotion was transferring from sit to stand while walking up stairs was the hardest task. Finally, within the wheelchair scale, positioning the wheelchair on a level surface was the easiest task while propulsion of the chair up an inclined ramp was the most difficult. These solutions are reasonable and consistent with clinical expectations.

Case Examples

Two case examples are presented to illustrate the clinical usefulness of the model: (a) explicit definition of functional performance status, and (b) identification of a situation in which a summary score is not an appropriate estimate of overall motor performance.

Case I is a 27-year-old female with a left hemiparesis secondary to head trauma. Her overall functional performance estimate translates into a level of expected domain performance represented by the rightmost solid vertical line in Figure 8.5. She was able to accomplish all the grasp release tasks, accomplished many of the manipulation tasks, but had difficulty with most of the fastener and typing tasks. She was able to do some parts of the balance, mat mobility, and locomotion tasks, but was not independent on any of them. She was able to do some wheelchair tasks independently. An analysis of her goodness-of-fit statistics indicated that her observed and estimated performance status were consistent with the theoretical sequential hierarchy of skills. All fit statistics were less than 2.0.

Case II is a 5-year-old boy with dominating athetoid movements resulting from a traumatic brain injury at one year of age (left-most vertical line in Figure 8.5). He demonstrated a pattern of motor abilities that was substantially deviant from the behaviors predicted under the model. This child had severe limitations in fine motor skills but was independent on higher level gross motor skills such as locomotion and going up and down stairs. The total score, however, indicates that a child at his estimated level of performance would not ordinarily have mastered any of the locomotion skills.

The total summary score on the TAMP for him does not adequately reflect his overall ability. His fit statistic of 7.91 for the total TAMP score indicated a very poor congruence between his demonstrated skills and those predicted of him under the model. All the fit statistics of the individual motor performance factors, however, were acceptable. As a consequence the individual motor performance scores are the only valid scores to represent the motor performance status of this child.

SUMMARY

We have described the analysis of a clinical motor performance assessment instrument based on a hypothesized sequential model of proficiency skills. In addition, empirical advantages and disadvantages of the Rasch partial-credit and rating-scale models for the TAMP were discussed. Given the results obtained thus far with the clinical application of our motor performance functional proficiency instrument, we believe that the TAMP, and other functional assessment instruments based on a sequential model can (a) yield valid scoring procedures, (b) enhance the theoretical and clinical understanding of the progression of motor performance changes in functional tasks, and (c) provide sensitive scoring mechanisms to document relevant clinical changes in functional status.

REFERENCES

Andrich, D. (1978). A rating formulation for ordered response categories. *Psychometrika, 43*, 561–573.

Bruninks, R.H., Woodcock, R.W., Hill, B.K., & Weatherman, R.F. (1985). *Development and standardization of the Scales of Independent Behavior*. Allen, TX: DLM Teaching Resources.

Feinstein, A. (1986). Scientific and clinical problems in indexes of functional disability. *Annals of Internal Medicine, 105*, 413–420.

Gans, B.M., Haley, S.M., Hallenborg, S.C., Mann, N., Inacio, C.A., & Fass, R.M. (1988). Description and interobserver reliability of the Tufts Assessment of Motor Performance. *American Journal of Physical Medicine and Rehabilitation, 66*, 202–210.

Jette, A. (1985). State of the art in functional status assessment. In J.M. Rothstein (Ed.), *Measurement in physical therapy*. New York: Livingston.

Klein, R., & Bell, B. (1982). Self-care skills: Behavior measurement with Klein-Bell ADL Scale. *Archives of Physical Medicine and Rehabilitation, 63*, 335–338.

Ludlow, L.H. (1985). A strategy for the graphical representation of Rasch model residuals. *Educational and Psychological Measurement, 45,* 851–859.

Ludlow, L.H. (1986). Graphical analysis of item response theory residuals. *Applied Psychological Measurement, 10,* 217–229.

Masters, G.N. (1982). A Rasch model for partial credit scoring. *Psychometrika, 47,* 149–174.

Merbitz, C., Morris, J., & Grip, J.C. (1989). Ordinal scales and foundations of misinference. *Archives of Physical Medicine and Rehabilitation, 70,* 308–312.

Rasch, G. (1960). *Probabilistic models for some intelligence and attainment tests.* Copenhagen: Danmarks Paedgogiske Institut. (Reprinted by the University of Chicago Press, 1980).

Riddick, L.N. (1989). Quantitative assessments: Their mathematical faults. *WFOT Bulletin, 20,* 11–13.

Sheikh, K. (1986). Disability scales: Assessment of reliability. *Archives of Physical Medicine and Rehabilitation, 67,* 245–249.

Sparrow, S., Balla, D., & Cicchetti, D. (1984). *Interview edition, survey form manual, Vineland behavior scales.* Circle Pines, MN: American Guidance Services, Inc.

Wright, B.D., & Masters, G.N. (1982). *Rating scale analysis.* Chicago: MESA Press.

chapter **9**

Vertically Equating Reading Tests: An Example from Chicago Public Schools

E. Matthew Schulz
National Council of State Boards of Nursing
Chicago, IL

Carole Perlman and William K. Rice, Jr.
Chicago Public Schools
Chicago, IL

Benjamin D. Wright
MESA Psychometric Laboratory
The University of Chicago

School reform legislation in Illinois requires school districts to develop local reading goals that meet or exceed statewide goals, and to report student progress with respect to these goals annually by means of objective assessments (Illinois State Board of Education, 1988). In response, Chicago Public Schools undertook the development of criterion reference tests (CRTs) to assess student progress in reading. Students who fail to get a predetermined percentage of CRT items correct, for a given reading goal, are required to review the material on that goal and to be retested. A student's progress through the curriculum depends on his performance on the CRTs.

The success of this CRT application depends on knowing the relative difficulty of CRTs across grade levels and marking periods. The tests should increase in difficulty at the same rate as student ability. The inconsistencies of retaining a student who could pass a test at a higher grade level, or promoting a student who would fail a test at a lower grade level must be avoided. It is also important to avoid overburdening the system at arbitrary points by retaining a disproportionate number of students because a test is more difficult than intended.

These considerations extend from the CRT tests to the curricular goals. The difficulty of a relevant CRT test is a good index of the difficulty of the corresponding instruction. Knowledge of test difficulty can be used to ensure that curricular goals are sequenced from "easy" to "hard" and that the level of instruction is matched to the level of student achievement. When the difficulty increase of instructional material matches the growth of student achievement, learning can be kept challenging, but not frustrating.

Typically, however, criterion referenced tests are used as though the difficulty of the tests were not only known, but also so perfectly equated that the same score or percent correct can be used as the criterion point for all tests. For example, the Chicago Public Schools uses a criterion of 70 percent correct for all 24 tests covering grades 3 to 8. This fixed criterion presumes that the difficulty of each test is known and, further, that the tests increase in difficulty across marking periods and grades in a way that matches student growth. Empirical evidence to the contrary would challenge policies involving this particular use of the CRTs and even challenge assumptions about the underlying curriculum. The rationale for retaining a student who fails to get 70 percent of CRT items correct is that the student is not ready for instruction at the next, presumably more difficult, level. This rationale would be challenged if any CRT later in the instructional sequence were discovered to be easier than a CRT earlier in the sequence.

The purpose of this chapter is to show how Rasch measurement (Rasch, 1960; Wright & Stone, 1979; Wright & Masters, 1982; Schulz, Junker, Perlman, Rice, & Toles, 1987) can be used to improve the implementation of a locally developed criterion reference test program. The Rasch computer program, MFORMS (Wright & Schulz, 1987), was used to construct a reading scale that spans grade levels 3 to 8. The "vertically equated" measurement scale enables (a) a plot of student growth in reading achievement, (b) a comparison of the difficulties of the CRT tests across marking periods and grade levels, (c) the establishment of criterion passing scores for each test which are consistent with student growth in reading achievement, and (d) an evaluation of the sequential position of instructional goals.

METHOD

Setting and Subjects

The Chicago Public Schools' reading curriculum contains 16 "goals" per grade. These goals are divided equally among the four marking periods of the academic year, four goals per period, so that goals one to four are covered during marking period 1 (September to mid-November), while goals 13 to 16 are covered during marking period 4 (April to June).

Criterion referenced tests are administered four times a year at the end of each marking period. Each CRT consists of 40 items—10 items per goal. There are 24 tests covering grades 3 to 8 reading curriculum: Grade 3, tests 1 to 4; Grade 4, tests 5 to 8; Grade 5, tests 9 to 12; Grade 6, tests 13 to 16; Grade 7, tests 17 to 20; Grade 8, tests 21 to 24. These tests contain 960 items and represent 96 instructional goals.

Design for Linking Tests

Two kinds of linking were needed to connect the 24 CRTs to a common measurement scale: within grade and between grade. The four CRTs within each grade were connected by composing a 40-item linking test made up of 10 items from each. These items represented one goal per marking period. The goals selected for the linking tests were those considered to be least sensitive to instruction. Items insensitive to instruction were desired for linking because their relative difficulty had to be assessed with students who had not received instruction specific to the items immediately prior to taking the linking test. The linking between grades was accomplished by having these linking tests taken by students in the prior, adjacent grade at the end of the year just after their regular, fourth marking period CRT. Thus, six linking tests were constructed to connect these twenty-four tests to a common measurement scale. Linking test "A" connected tests 1 to 4 at the third grade. Linking test "B" connected tests 5 to 8 at the fourth grade, and so on to linking test "F" which connected tests 21 to 24 at the eighth grade.

The linking tests were administered at the end of the fourth marking period of the 1986–87 school year in a random sample of 30

**Table 9.1.   Linking of Reading Tests Covering Grades 3 to 8
(Tests #1 to #24)**

Linking Group	Grade	Tests Taken CRT	Tests Taken LINK	Tests Linked	Number of Items per Test Linked
1	4		A	1, 2, 3, **4**	10, 10, 10, 10
2	3	4 and	B	**4**, 5, 6, 7, **8**	40, 10, 10, 10, 10
3	4	8 and	C	**8**, 9, 10, 11, **12**	40, 10, 10, 10, 10
4	5	12 and	D	**12**, 13, 14, 15, **16**	40, 10, 10, 10, 10
5	6	16 and	E	**16**, 17, 18, 19, **20**	40, 10, 10, 10, 10
6	7	20 and	F	**20**, 21, 22, 23, 24	40, 10, 10, 10, 10

Note: Tests 1 to 24 are regular CRT tests and are administered each marking period (quarterly) to grades 3 to 8. Tests A to F are linking tests and were administered at the end of the fourth marking period to students from an adjacent grade along with their regular fourth marking period CRT. All tests contained 40 items.

schools. The links between tests 1 to 24 are shown in Table 9.1. At the end of the fourth marking period, grade 3 students took linking test B and CRT 4 in separate test sessions two weeks apart. These data were treated as an 80-item test in which CRT 4 from grade 3, and CRTs 5, 6, 7, and 8 from grade 4 were linked. Likewise, CRT 8 from grade 4, and CRTs 9, 10, 11, and 12 from grade 5 were linked by giving fourth-grade students CRT 8 and linking test C. Thus, tests 1 to 24 were linked across grade 3 to 8 through the fourth marking period CRT at each grade. The only exception to the above-level testing in this design was that fourth-grade students were given linking test A, a test containing help students effectively can be overcome by the sheer number of Table 9.1.

Data Analysis

The data were analyzed with the MFORMS computer program (Wright & Schulz, 1987). MFORMS is a derivative of MSTEPS (Wright, Congdon, & Rossner, 1987) and MICROSCALE (Wright & Linacre, 1985) in its ability to accommodate missing values in the data. MFORMS can read records from multiple forms and create an internal data matrix which encompasses the missing values. Missing values arise because no one person takes all of the items in all of the forms and no item is taken by all of the persons. In a traditional test equating exercise using tests linked with common items, the present data would have to be divided into 30 separate data sets—forms 1 to 24, plus six sets of test-linking data corresponding to the six rows of Table 9.1. The item calibrations from these 30 analyses would then have to undergo a secondary data analysis in order to derive the translation constants necessary to link all 30 forms. MFORMS analyzed the data for all 960 items in one step.

Item calibration estimates were supplied to MFORMS using the PRESET option (Schluz, 1988), and the program performed 250 iterations of the UCON estimation procedure to improve the initial estimates. The standard deviation of item calibrations reached 1.4 logits on the 26th iteration, 1.40 on the 131st iteration, 1.396 on the 167th iteration, and remained at 1.396 through the 250th iteration.

The estimates of student ability produced by MFORMS confirmed our expectation that student ability increases across marking periods and grades. There were some random irregularities however. Mean student achievement occasionally declined slightly across marking periods. We attribute these irregularities to the learning goals used for test linking, inconsistent student motivation, and differences in administration conditions between the linking tests and the fourth marking period CRTs.

To correct for these irregularities, we fit a regression line to the Rasch estimates of student achievement. The independent variables in the regression equation were (a) test booklet number (1 to 24), (b) the square of test booklet number, and (c) grade (3 to 8). The resulting regression line represented our expectation that student reading achievement increases monotonically, but in a nonlinear fashion, over time. The regression accounted for .96 of the residual variance in the Rasch measures. This proportion was near the maximum that could be accounted for, given the standard errors of the person measures, but nevertheless resulted in a significant smoothing of the growth curve.

Item calibrations were adjusted to the regression line by subtracting the difference between the observed and predicted measures of students who took the item. For example, if the residual (observed - predicted) achievement of students who took booklet 15 was .25 logits, .25 logits was subtracted from the calibrations of items in booklet 15. Presumably, testing irregularities caused student achievement and item difficulty from booklet 15 to be overestimated by about .25 logits. This procedure distributes random problems with test linking evenly over the range of the tests so that those effects cancel.

RESULTS

Change in Reading Achievement

Figure 9.1 shows the growth in student reading achievement, averaged by grade, after the Rasch estimates were corrected by regression.

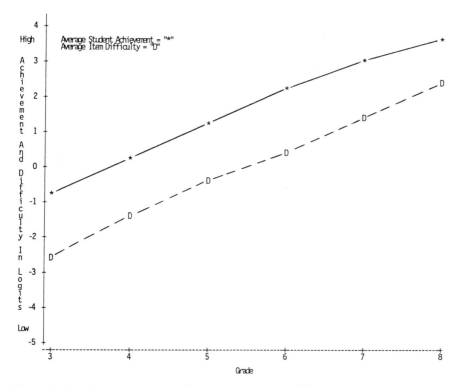

Figure 9.1. Plot of student achievement and item difficulty by grade

Achievement increases 4.4 logits from −0.82 logits at third grade to 3.58 logits at eighth grade. Growth between adjacent grades slows for higher grades. Growth from grade 3 to 4 is 1.08 logits (from −0.82 to 0.26), but only 0.67 logits from grade 7 to 8 (from 2.91 to 3.58). The item difficulties represented in Figure 9.1 are discussed below. A solid, rather than a dashed line, marks student achievement because we will treat these results as given and use them to evaluate the difficulty of the subtests and criterion scores.

Figure 9.2 shows growth in student reading achievement, now averaged by test booklet. The growth shown in this figure is 5.09 logits— from −1.25 logits at the end of marking period 1, grade 3 to 3.84 logits at the end of marking period 4, grade 8. It is clear that student achievement increases during the school year from one marking period to the next. In grade 3 the average achievement of *the same students* (n = 250) increases 0.86 logits from −1.25 logits (marking period 1) to −0.39 logits (marking period 4). In grade 8, repeated measures of students (n = 344) increase 0.56 logits, from 3.28 logits, marking period 1

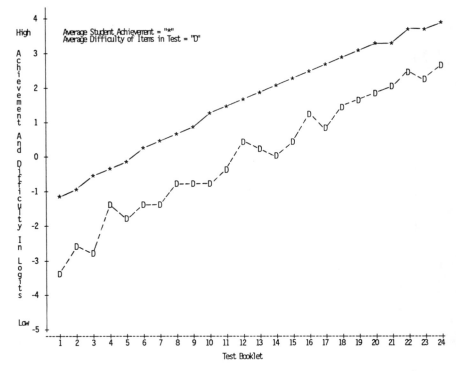

Figure 9.2.   Plot of student achievement and item difficulty by test booklet

to 3.84 logits, marking period 4. The rate of growth declines with increasing grade level.

Change in Test Difficulty

Figure 9.1 shows that item difficulty, averaged by grade, increases parallel with student achievement. At third grade, item difficulty averages −2.51 logits; at eighth grade, item difficulty averages 2.33 logits. The change in difficulty from grade 3 to grade 8 is 4.84 logits. This change is comparable to the 4.4 logit increase in student achievement also illustrated in this figure. The difficulty of the items is about 1.5 logits less than the achievement level of the students on average. This difference reflects the fact that students scored well over 50 percent correct on these tests. If students had scored 50 percent on the tests, item difficulty would equal student achievement. On average, students got more than 70 percent of the items correct. This is the result of a policy decision that students should, in general, experience more success than failure on these tests.

Although the tests increase in difficulty uniformly when averaged by grade, irregularities emerge when the items are averaged by test booklet, as Figure 9.2 shows. Test booklet 1 is 2.05 logits easier than the average achievement level of students taking this test (-3.30 vs. -1.25), while test booklet 4 is only 0.99 logits easier than the achievement level of students for which it is intended (-1.38 vs. -0.39). Also, the relative difficulty of the tests is occasionally out of sequence: Test 3 is easier than test 2; test 5 is easier than test 4; test 14 is easier than tests 12 and 13, even though student achievement increases uniformly over the sequence.

In order to understand and address the variation in test difficulty, we focused on the 10-item subtests. The relative difficulty of the subtests is important because students are evaluated by these subtests, rather than by the test booklet as a whole. Students are expected to get 70 percent of the items, or seven items, correct per subtest. Furthermore, subtests represent goals that are intended to be related through a central idea or skill. Two or more related subtests represent a curriculum strand. For example, there are subtests for the goal "Makes Predictions" at grades 3, 5, 6, 7, and 8. Goals within a substrand presumably represent a unidimensional progression in cognitive development and reading achievement. Therefore, within curriculum strands earlier goals and their subtests should be easier than later goals and their subtests.

Figure 9.3 is a plot of the difficulty of the five subtests for "Makes Predictions." The difficulty of the subtests is shown in three ways: (a) the average difficulty of items in the subtests (bottom line), (b) the level of achievement corresponding to a criterion score of 7 out of 10 correct (middle dashed line), and (c) a level of achievement corresponding to a criterion score targeted on student achievement (middle solid line). Dashed, rather than solid, lines connect points of average item difficulty and achievement for 7 out of 10 items correct because these points show values that turn out to be flawed as criterion reference points. Mean item difficulty and the level of achievement corresponding to a score of 7 out of 10 correct are found *not* to increase in step with student achievement. We discover that an across-the-board decision at 7 out of 10, or 70 percent, does *not* implement the intentions of criterion referencing.

We may also wish to limit the percent of students who fail the CRTs. On average, 29 percent of the students in our sample failed to get 7 out of 10 items correct. We may want to alter this percent for a particular CRT or for all the CRTs averaged together. There are many considera-

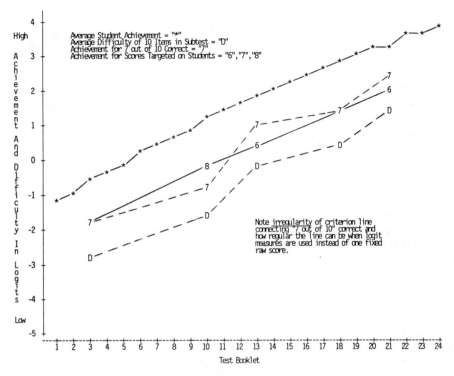

Figure 9.3. Plot of learning goal "Makes Predictions" by position in instructional sequence (test booklet)

tions affecting this percent. The criterion should not be decided only with respect to the desired level of performance. One must also consider whether there are effective means and resources for helping students who fail, and whether students who fail ultimately benefit from remedial instruction. At some point, the ability of the system to help students effectively can be overcome by the sheer number of students who fail. Thus, there may be a limit to the cost-effectiveness of failing students, even with a criterion referenced test.

To illustrate how the percent passing can be used to set criterion scores, we decided on criterion scores that are "targeted on student achievement" so that (a) the achievement standards increase uniformly with student achievement, and (b) 10 percent of the students fail a CRT test on average. These decisions required the criterion scores for the various "Makes Predictions" subtests to range from 6 to 8. The corresponding uniform achievement standards implemented by

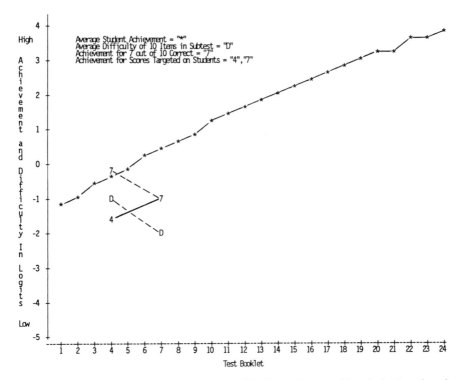

Figure 9.4. Plot of learning goal "Uses a Dictionary" by position in instructional sequence (test booklet)

these criterion scores are illustrated in Figure 9.3 with a solid line. The solid, as opposed to a dashed, line represents the intended effect of the criterion referenced testing program.

Another outcome of Rasch measurement bears on curriculum revision. Figure 9.4 is a plot of the difficulty of subtests for goals in the strand "Uses a Dictionary." This goal is taught in grade 3, marking period 4, and again in grade 4, marking period 3. But the difficulty of the test items is poorly suited to students' reading development. The average difficulty of grade 3 dictionary items is 0.89 logits harder than that of grade 4 dictionary items (−1.08 vs. −1.97 logits). The achievement standard corresponding to 7 out of 10 items correct is 0.79 logits higher at grade 3 (−0.16) than at grade 4 (−0.95). In fact, the "Dictionary" achievement standard at grade 3, −0.16, is higher than the average achievement of students who took the test, indicating that fewer than fifty percent passed. Paradoxically, many of these same third grade students, those with reading achievement above the grade 4 standard of -0.95 logits, would have passed the grade 4 test in the same instructional strand. This topsy-turvy outcome is not useful.

It is often impractical to revise tests between administrations, but one need not accept the impractical result of using the same criterion score, 7, for both of the dictionary tests. The solid line connecting achievement standards in Figure 9.4 is based on the unrevised tests of "Uses a Dictionary," but shows criterion scores targeted on student achievement. The new criterion score on the grade 3 test is 4 rather than 7. The criterion score on the grade 4 test is still 7. These scores set achievement standards that parallel change in general student achievement and which 90 percent of students will pass on average.

Curriculum evaluation

If time and resources permit, one can use the results of Rasch analysis to rewrite tests or to change their curriculum sequence. One of the basic steps in this process is to examine individual test items to see what they are testing, how difficult the tested concept is, and whether the item is invalidated by technical faults. Technical faults and item misfit to the Rasch scale, will not be discussed in this chapter. Item misfit is discussed at length by Masters (1988), Wright and Masters (1982), and Wright and Stone (1979).

An item analysis, aided by Rasch estimates of difficulty, provides direct, objective evidence of the unsuitable placement of goals related to "Uses a Dictionary" in this curriculum sequence. Table 9.2 shows selected items from the outcome "Uses a Dictionary" at grades 3 and 4. Specific skills are called for by these items. The grade 3 dictionary skill is to understand phonic and pronunciation symbols in a dictionary, and to know the correct pronunciation of the words in the item stem. The grade 4 dictionary skill is to find guide words on the dictionary page. The Rasch difficulties of the items show that the skills are inappropriately placed in the curriculum. Grade 3 dictionary items #26 to #30 have difficulties of -1.63 to $+0.37$ logits making them more suited to the achievement level of fourth graders than to third graders (see Figure 9.1). Grade 4 dictionary items #3 and #6 are much easier in comparison, having difficulties of only -2.94 and -3.11, and are more suited to the achievement level of third graders.

With this evidence, one can make a strong case for revising the tests, and/or changing the curriculum. The placement of the two "Uses a Dictionary" goals in the curriculum could be switched so that the current grade 3 goal is taught at grade 4 and vice versa. If this is not

Table 9.2.   Items for Learning Goals "Uses a Dictionary"

Grade 3, Fourth Quarter, Booklet 4		Grade 4, Third Quarter, Booklet 7	
Calibrated Difficulty		Calibrated Difficulty	
−0.52	26. Please be *silent* while I read. A. s ' lənt *B. si' lənt C. si lənt' D. si lent'	−2.94	3. What are the guide words on the sample dictionary page? A. shack and shiver *B. shack and shuttle C. shiver and shuttle D. shrug and shut
−0.37	27. That large machine has a great deal of *power*. A. pow' or B. po' wer C. poiw' er *D. pou' ər	−3.11	6. What are the guide words on the sample dictionary page? A. asterisk and audi-ence B. audience and auburn C. avoid and avenue *D. asterisk and avoid
−1.63	28. A hose can be used to *spray* water. A. spre *B. spra C. sprā D. spra	−2.45	9. Which guide words would appear at the top of the page for the word *name*? A. night/novice B. noon/number *C. name/net D. needle/nine
−0.65	29. Elena pushed the hair off her *fore-head*. *A. for' hed B. four head' C. for' had D. fər hed'	−1.74	10. Which guide words would appear at the top of the page for the word *ready*? A. rhinocerous/rose *B race/ribbon C. rooster/rust D. ruler/rye
−0.96	30. The squirrel ate the *acorns* that fell from the oak tree. A. a' Kərnz B. a' Karnz *C. a' Kornz D. a' Kornz		

acceptable, one can further study the items to see if there are ways of making these items easier or harder without changing the learning objectives. This might involve correcting technical faults in the items, modifying non-content related attributes of the items that affect diffi-

culty, or slightly modifying the content of the item so that it tests an
easier or a more difficult component of the targeted skill. For example,
Table 9.2 shows that one-syllable words are easier than two-syllable
words in the grade 3 subtest. Item #28, a one-syllable word, is calibrated at −1.68, while the easiest two-syllable word (item #30) is
calibrated at −0.96. The third-grade test for "Uses a Dictionary" would
become significantly easier, while still focusing on phonics and pronunciation symbols, if items were based only on one-syllable words.

Selecting Criterion Scores

The achievement level corresponding to criterion scores were obtained
from score equivalency tables, such as Table 9.3. The score equivalency
table lists the Rasch measure and standard error for every raw score
that can be obtained on a test or subtest (except for 0 and a perfect
score). The subtest of Table 9.3 is for the goal "Uses a Dictionary" in
CRT 4, Grade 3. The raw score, 7, is the criterion score that was used to
make pass/fail decisions for this goal during the 1986/87 school year.
The Rasch measure corresponding to the score, 7, is −0.16. This is the
off-target standard illustrated in Figure 9.4. Table 9.3 shows that it is
the lower score of 4, at −1.54 logits, which imposes the criterion actually intended.

A score equivalency table can be built directly from the person
measures put out by a Rasch analysis of test data, or indirectly by
using the item calibrations from the analysis. Frequently, one's data
fails to contain at least one case for each raw score possible on a test, so
one cannot build a complete score equivalency table directly from
person-measure output. In these situations, the UCON procedure can

**Table 9.3. Score-Equivalency Table
for "Uses a Dictionary" at Grade 3**

Raw Score	Estimated Achievement	Std. Error
1	−3.42	1.06
2	−2.58	.81
3	−2.01	.71
4	−1.54	.67
5	−1.09	.66
6	−0.65	.68
7	−0.16	.72
8	.43	.82
9	.30	1.08

always be used to build a complete score equivalency table from the item calibrations, as described by Wright and Stone (1979). In this study, we used the item-calibration output and the UCON procedure to build the score equivalency table.

In order to select criterion scores that were better targeted on student achievement, we calculated the variables listed below, followed by their notation or value:

Mean student achievement for booklet, B .... X(B)
Achievement corresponding to criterion score, S .... Y(S)
Pooled, within booklet standard deviation of measures of student achievement .... (0.97 logits)
The difference between the average student achievement and the achievement standard .... X(B)-Y(S).
The Z-score for achievement corresponding to criterion score, S, within the distribution of student achievement (X(B)-Y(S))/.97

Each subtest yielded nine values of Y(S), one for each score 1 to 9. We chose the criterion score that yielded X(B)-Y(S) closest to a measure of difference of 1.25 logits, which in turn yields a Z-score closest to 1.33. A Z-score of 1.33 has a cumulative normal probability of 0.90, meaning that about ninety percent of students will pass a criterion score so selected, assuming that students are normally distributed on the achievement scale. The particular criterion score necessary to implement this uniform criterion measure varied among subtests according to the difficulty distribution of their items on the common scale.

To check the accuracy of our procedure, we compared the expected percent passing to the actual percent passing in the general sample of students from ten schools, most of which were not used to construct the Rasch scale. There were over 400 students per test booklet in the general sample, of whom fewer than 200 per booklet were in the test-linking sample. We predicted that 71 percent of students would earn a score of at least seven on the subtests. We observed an average of 71 percent of the general sample passing. We predicted that 40.5 percent of grade 3 students would pass the Uses a Dictionary subtest by getting at least 7 items correct. In the general sample ($n = 477$) 40.7 percent passed.

Students in the general sample were classified only with reference to a score of 7 out of 10, since 7 was the criterion score actually used in practice. However, our predictions can be usefully accurate for any criterion score. The accuracy of prediction depends on how well the test-linking sample represents the population for whom the predictions are made. In this case, the sample of students matched the population of all students in the system well.

Finally, the Rasch measurement system is helpful in maximizing the reliability of pass/fail decisions. The reliability of pass/fail decisions depends on the measurement error associated with the criterion score. Measurement error is greatest near the extreme levels of performance on a test and is most precise near the 51 percent correct mark. A Rasch analysis routinely supplies the standard error of measurement for every raw score obtained from the data, except for 0 and a perfect score. Table 9.3 shows the standard error of the Rasch measures corresponding to the scores, 1 to 9, for a 10-item test. As expected, measurement error is least (0.66) with a score of 5 out of 10, and greatest with a non-zero score of 1 (1.06) and a near-perfect score, 9 (1.08). To optimize reliability of pass/fail decisions, one should adjust the difficulty of the test so that a criterion score of 5 (or 50 percent), represents the desired level of achievement on the measurement scale.

SUMMARY AND CONCLUSIONS

Rasch measurement can be an essential tool in a criterion referenced testing program. Criterion referenced tests covering a curriculum strand such as reading are presumed to function together, much as individual items on a unidimensional scale. A students' success or failure on one test is expected to have implications for his chance of success on related tests and instructional material. The use of criterion referenced tests is based on these assumptions. Therefore, to actually accomplish criterion referencing we need to operationalize these assumptions by constructing a measurement scale that spans and connects the entire curriculum sequence. Further, the scale must be based on measures of achievement defined by the probability of success on test items.

Clearly, tests do not always have the level of difficulty they are intended to have. The vertically equated scale shows that (a) the difficulties of some tests are out of order with their position in the instructional sequence, and (b) the match between test difficulty and general student achievement is not uniform among tests. This kind of unknown and uncontrolled variance in the difficulty of tests destroys the meaning of criterion referenced test scores. One *cannot* know the achievement level of the students without knowing the difficulty of the test.

It is not enough that a given criterion score has been "judged" to indicate mastery of the instructional material. Judgments, just like assumptions about test difficulty, are arbitrary to an unknown degree and always subject to errors. Judgments must always be reexamined through objective data on student performance and improved when they do not function fairly and effectively. Second, there is a real need to know whether the material is appropriately positioned in the instructional sequence and also how many students can be expected to meet a criterion. Standards must be relatively consistent so that the system is not overburdened with unnecessary reviewing and retesting at arbitrary points. With a vertically equated scale, the criterion score for a given test can be set in a comprehensive framework within which the general reading achievement of students and the difficulty of material in the curriculum sequence are known from grades 3 to 8.

We have two options for improving the alignment between the difficulty of the local curriculum standards and student achievement in the subject area. We can either (a) revise the tests and/or curriculum, or (b) adjust the scoring standards. The goal in revising the tests is to construct test difficulty so that it parallels growth in student achievement in the subject. This goal is compatible with arriving at a single criterion score, that is, 70 percent correct, on all tests. The goal in revising the scoring standards is to make the relative difficulty of achieving a passing score on the tests be constant across marking periods and grades, given the expected growth in student achievement in the subject. This goal is compatible with a situation in which test difficulty varies considerably relative to the achievement of students taking the test, as seen in Figure 9.2, and when the tests and/or the curriculum cannot be revised. Revision of tests and/or curriculum can be expensive and time-consuming, and might be impossible to do between successive test administrations.

In order to free criterion referenced achievement standards from unintentional variation in test difficulty, the achievement standards should be set first with reference to a vertically equated scale. The standards can then be converted into the particular relevant criterion score for any given test as long as some of the items in the test are calibrated on the common scale. Teachers will be able to score tests and evaluate student performance with reference to criterion scores, but because they are based on equated measures, criterion scores will be fairer, more objective, and less likely to create problems for the educational system.

REFERENCES

Illinois State Board of Education. (1988). *The school code of Illinois*. St. Paul, MN: West Publishing.

Masters, G.N. (1988). Item discrimination: When more is worse. *Journal of Educational Measurement, 25*(1), 15–29.

Rasch, G. (1960). *Probabilistic models for some intelligence and attainment tests.* Copenhagen: Danmarks Paedogogiske Institut. (Reprinted by the University of Chicago Press, 1980)

Schulz, E.M. (1988). *A user's guide to MFORMS* [A computer program manual]. Chicago: Chicago Public Schools (Mimeographed).

Schulz, E.M., Junker, L.K., Perlman, C.L., Rice, W.K., & Toles, R. (1987, April). *Vertical test equating: Procedures and applications with Rasch analysis.* Paper presented at the annual meeting of the American Educational Research Association, Washington DC

Wright, B.D., Congdon, R.T., & Rossner, M. (1987). *MSTEPS* [A FORTRAN computer program for Rasch analysis of dichotomous and partial credit data]. Chicago: MESA Press.

Wright, B.D., & Schulz, E.M. (1987). *MFORMS* [A FORTRAN computer program for one-step item banking of dichotomous and partial credit data from multiple forms]. Chicago: MESA Press.

Wright, B.D., & Linacre, J.M. (1985). *MICROSCALE* [A computer program]. Westport, CT: MEDIAX.

Wright, B.D., & Masters, G.N. (1982). *Rating scale analysis.* Chicago: MESA Press.

Wright, B.D., & Stone, M.H. (1979). *Best test design.* Chicago: MESA Press.

part III

Measurement Theory

chapter **10**

Components of Difficulty in Spatial Ability Test Items

Richard M. Smith
City University of New York
New York, NY

Gene A. Kramer
American Dental Association
Chicago, IL

Anna T. Kubiak
Educational Testing Service
Princeton, NJ

Recent advances in psychometric theory and cognitive psychology have focused attention on research examining the cognitive processes or components that underlie complex tasks. The methods of this research, componential analysis and cognitive components analysis, have successfully used item difficulties as the measure of the complexity of the tasks on a number of item types (Pellegrino & Glaser, 1979; Smith & Green, 1985; Smith & Kramer, 1988; Sternberg, 1977; and Whitely, 1977). Component analysis of the factors that underlie or contribute to the difficulty of test items provides useful information for several purposes. Stenner, Smith, and Burdick (1983) suggest that the regularity and pattern of item-scale-value variation is as important a part of construct definition as person-score variation. This is a different approach to construct validity than is commonly found in the literature. In addition to construct validation, the information available from component analysis can be extremely useful in item development procedures.

Component analysis can be conducted at two levels. First, the analysis can be conducted with regard to the characteristics of the items that can influence the degree to which certain cognitive processes are used in determining the solution. For example, Embretson and Wetzel (1987) examined the relative impact of cognitive variables such as encoding, coherence processing, and text mapping on paragraph comprehension items. Second, the analysis can be conducted for more global processes. Components identified in these types of analyses might be undefined composites of elementary cognitive processes. For example, Smith and Green (1985) examined the components of difficulty in a paper-folding test. Among others, the components examined included horizontal, vertical, and diagonal folds; symmetric and asymmetric folds; and the position of the hole. Component difficulties were estimated using both regression and linear logistic test models. The results of the analyses showed, for example, that global processes such as visually unfolding diagonal folds are more difficult than visually unfolding either horizontal or vertical folds. Spatial ability items, which require visualizing various types of folds, hidden parts, or mental rotations of objects, lend themselves to component analysis because of the relative ease of developing quantifiable indices of these processes, for example, number of hidden figures and degree of rotation.

Several approaches can be used in component analysis (Green & Smith, 1987). In the first, item difficulties (p values) are regressed on the specified components of the problem. With this approach, the components are specified by their presence in the problem or by the frequency with which they occur in the problem. In the second approach, logit item difficulties are estimated, fit of the items to the measurement model is investigated, and then the logit item difficulties are regressed on the component frequencies. The components are specified in the same manner as for the first approach. Finally, component parameters are estimated by the Linear Logistic Test Model (LLTM) directly from the response matrix (Fischer, 1973). Item difficulties can then be calculated from the component difficulties using the specification equation:

$$\delta_i = \sum_{j=1}^{m} q_{ij} \, \eta_j + c$$

where δ_i is the difficulty of item i, q_{ij} is the weight (frequency) of operation j in item i, η_j is the difficulty parameter estimate of cognitive operation j, and c is a centering constant. LLTM assumes a linear relationship between item difficulty and component difficulty as do the previous two regression approaches.

Mislevy (1981) and Green and Smith (1987) suggest that the results of using the regression approach can separate problems of fit of the data to the psychometric model from problems of fit of the data to the component model. In the case of LLTM these two fit issues cannot easily be separated because of the estimation procedure.

This chapter summarizes research that has been performed on a variety of spatial ability item types. The item types are drawn primarily from the Perceptual Ability Test (PAT) contained in the Dental Admission Test (DAT) battery. The item types are well suited to component analysis because they all purport to measure spatial ability, also they are freed from confounding factors—for example, reading difficulty, lexical complexity, item length—that can be factors in determining the difficulty of subject-matter multiple-choice items. And finally, these items generally consist of variations on a relatively small set of underlying constructs. The approach that is taken in these studies is to analyze the items from the point of view of variations in the components which are used in constructing the item rather than from the point of view of the cognitive processes that can be used to solve the items. This approach has several advantages, including the obvious ease in enumerating each type of item component and its frequency, and the freeing of the analysis from the a priori development of a cognitive process model of spatial ability.

METHOD

Instruments

The items used in this study are regular and experimental items types taken from the PAT. This test battery is used for graduate admission to all dental schools in the United States and is taken by approximately 5,500 persons each year. Traditionally, the test has been administered twice each year in October and April. The PAT consists of 90 multiple-choice items that are divided into five or six item types: form development, cube items, apertures, orthographic projections, angle discrimination, and paper folding, an experimental item type. The first five of these item types appear on every test form. The paper-folding items appear only as experimental items included on some test administrations. All of the data used in these studies were taken from test administrations in 1986, 1987, and 1989.

The PAT is designed to assist dental schools in selecting students

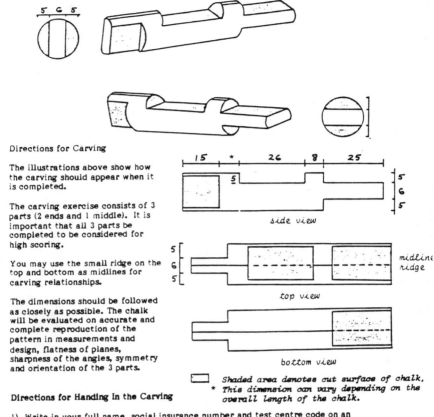

Directions for Carving

The illustrations above show how the carving should appear when it is completed.

The carving exercise consists of 3 parts (2 ends and 1 middle). It is important that all 3 parts be completed to be considered for high scoring.

You may use the small ridge on the top and bottom as midlines for carving relationships.

The dimensions should be followed as closely as possible. The chalk will be evaluated on accurate and complete reproduction of the pattern in measurements and design, flatness of planes, sharpness of the angles, symmetry and orientation of the 3 parts.

side view

top view

bottom view

☐ Shaded area denotes cut surface of chalk.
* This dimension can vary depending on the overall length of the chalk.

Directions for Handing In the Carving

1) Write in your full name, social insurance number and test centre code on an uncut surface of your carving (not on the napkin).

2) Wrap your carving carefully and securely so it may be shipped safely for grading. Fold the napkin in such a way that the carving will not fall out.

3) Hand in your wrapped carving to your examination proctor.

Figure 10.1. Chalk Carving

who would have a higher probability of success in technique courses, which require a high degree of manual dexterity. Between 1950 and 1972 the DAT relied on the Chalk Carving Test (see Figure 10.1) as a measure of perceptual motor ability. In 1972, an earlier form of the PAT, the Perceptual-Motor Ability Test (P-MAT), replaced the chalk carving. This change was undertaken in an effort to improve the reliability of grading the tests, improve the predictive validity, and reduce test administration costs. The P-MAT contained four types of two-dimensional and four types of three-dimensional multiple-choice

Form Development

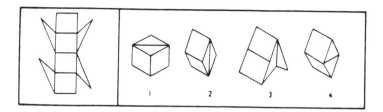

Orthographic Projections

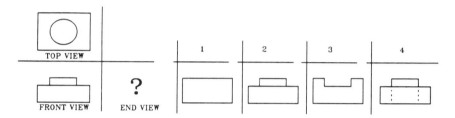

Apertures

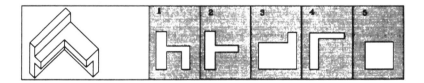

Figure 10.2. **Examples of Perceptual Ability Test Items**

spatial ability test items. In 1981, the P-MAT was condensed to its present format. In that reduction five of the original eight item types were retained. In 1987, the paper-folding items were added to the PAT as an experimental section. (See Figure 10.2 for an example of each item type.)

Eliot and Smith (1983), in their review of spatial tests, divide these tests into 10 basic categories broadly based on item characteristics and cognitive processes used in solving the items. Of the six item types in the current study, three are classified in the Eliot and Smith taxonomy. The form-development items are listed under both surface development and combined tasks. In this case, the combined tasks primarily

Cubes

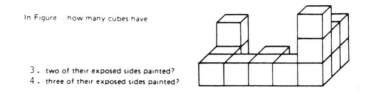

In Figure   how many cubes have

3. two of their exposed sides painted?
4. three of their exposed sides painted?

Angles

A   B   C   D

(1.) A - B - C - D
(2.) B - A - D - C
(3.) A - C - B - D
(4.) C - D - A - B

Paper Folding

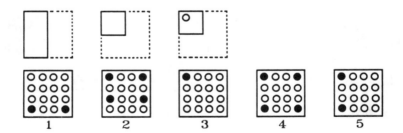

1   2   3   4   5

Figure 10.2. Continued

involve folding the flat surface into a solid figure and rotating the solid figure imaginatively. The cube items are classified under block counting tasks. The paper-folding items are listed under paper-folding tasks. Aperture items, though not specifically listed, can be classified as either block rotation or as a combined task. Specifically, the task includes imaginatively rotating figures and then visualizing a cross section of the rotated object. Angle discrimination items are not listed but appear to be similar to one of the visual memory item types. Orthographic projection items are not listed, and no similar item types can be found.

Interestingly, the classification of the items suggests that five of the item types are classified or are similar to those found in one of the two broad classifications, that is, manipulation division. The remaining item type, angle discrimination appears to be similar to an item type found in the other broad classification, that is, recognition division. Factor analyses of the PAT (Kramer, Kubiak, & Smith, 1989) suggest that the angle items do not load on a factor with the other item types. The uniqueness of these items is also picked up in the item calibration and fit analyses of the PAT, which is discussed later.

Analysis

Although the methods vary slightly from one analysis to another, there is a common thread throughout. After each test administration the items are calibrated to locate the difficulties on a linear metric. The item calibrations were accomplished with the MSCALE program (Wright, Congdon, & Rossner, 1986), which is a PC version of the missing data rating scale estimation algorithm that can be used with dichotomous data. In some instances, there were sufficient items on each form to perform a preliminary analysis without linking to other forms or test administrations. In these cases, a calibration sample of 1,000 to 2,500 persons was chosen from the total examinee population. In the case of paper folding and later cube analyses, it was necessary to link the item difficulties across test forms and administrations to increase the sample of items on the common metric. In these instances, calibration samples of approximately 400 to 600 were used when alternate forms from a single administration were linked. The linking technique used was the common-item approach described by Wright and Stone (1979). Although the five or six item types are administered as a 90-item test, for the purposes of these analyses, each item type was calibrated separately so that the results would not be confounded by possible multidimensionality introduced by the different test item types.

During the calibration process, the fit of the items was assessed using the outfit statistic included in MSCALE, which is the unweighted total item fit statistic (Smith, 1989). At that point a decision was made as to whether to include misfitting items in the analysis.

For each item type analyzed, an attempt was made to conceptualize and quantify the major design factors that are included in each item type. To date, only three of the item types have been analyzed: paper folding, cube items, and form development. The frequency with which each of the item components occurred was used as the independent variable in a multiple regression analysis. Rasch item difficulties

Table 10.1. October 1986 PAT Item Calibration

Item Type	N. of Items	Outfit Mean	Outfit S.D.	Outfit >3.0
Orthographic Projections	15	−1.31	1.97	1
Angle Discrimination	15	5.63	1.54	14
Apertures	18	−1.89	1.94	1
Cubes	12	−0.06	1.63	0
Form Development	30	−1.48	2.06	1

served as the dependent variable. During these analyses, various items were dropped from the analysis to improve the explained variance in the item difficulties due to the variance in component frequencies.

RESULTS

Table 10.1 shows a summary of the outfit statistics from an MSCALE analysis of the entire 90-item PAT. The unusually high mean outfit for the angle items (approximate expected value for outfit is 0.0 with an approximate standard deviation of 1.0 when the data fit the model) and the unusually high proportion of items with an outfit statistic greater than 3.0 suggest that the entire set of angle items is measuring something quite different from the remaining four item types. The conclusion drawn from these data is further supported by the average subtest intercorrelations for two forms of the PAT (October 1986 and October 1987), which are shown in Tables 10.2 and 10.3. In both cases, there is a low correlation between the angle item subscore and the subscores on the other sections of the test. In both administrations, there are high correlations among the orthographic projection, aperture, form development, and cube items. In the October 1987 administration, there are low correlations among the paper-folding subscore and the other five subtest scores. These data are supported by the

Table 10.2. October 1986 PAT Median Subtest Correlations

Item Type	Angles	Others
Orthographic Projections	0.24	0.48
Angle Discrimination	—	0.22
Apertures	0.26	0.53
Cubes	0.20	0.45
Form Development	0.18	0.49

Table 10.3.   October 1987 PAT Median Subtest Correlations

Item Type	Angles	Paper Folding	Others
Orthographic Projections	0.21	0.37	0.48
Angle Discrimination	—	0.13	0.18
Apertures	0.24	0.28	0.55
Cubes	0.16	0.05	0.46
Form Development	0.15	0.07	0.51
Paper Folding	0.13	—	0.19

factor analysis results reported in Kramer, Kubiak, and Smith (1989) and suggest that these six item types are not unidimensional. Further, these data support the decision to calibrate each item set separately before component analysis.

The paper-folding items require an examinee to mentally unfold a square of paper that has been folded up to three times and then punched in one of 16 predetermined positions. The examinee must determine the number and location of the holes in the original (unfolded) square. Three examples of this item type are shown in Figure 10.3. The original analysis of these data reported in Smith and Green (1985) identified three primary factors that influence the difficulty of these items: the number of folds, the position of the punched hole, and the type of fold. This analysis indicated that the greater the number of folds the higher the difficulty; this appears to be a complexity factor. With the position of the punched hole, locating the hole in a position other than the outside corner or the inside square made the items more difficult. This appears to result from the ease in identifying the corner or center holes in the unfolding process. The other holes had less of a structural anchor to assist in the positioning during unfolding. The type of fold that contributed most to the difficulty was the diagonal fold and the hidden asymmetric fold. The diagonal fold was particularly difficult in that it introduced a shift in the orientation of the holes where a horizontal pair of holes will become vertical on unfolding. Hidden asymmetric folds appear to be difficult because they require the visualization of the hidden piece.

Table 10.4 lists the correlations of the identified components of difficulty in an experimental administration of 23 paper-folding items in multiple-choice format to 156 examinees. Table 10.5 lists the regression weights for a multiple regression conducted on the component frequencies and the item difficulties. The multiple R resulting from this analysis was .935 ($R^2 = .874$). This indicated that these 12 components of the item accounted for a large portion of the variance in the item difficulties.

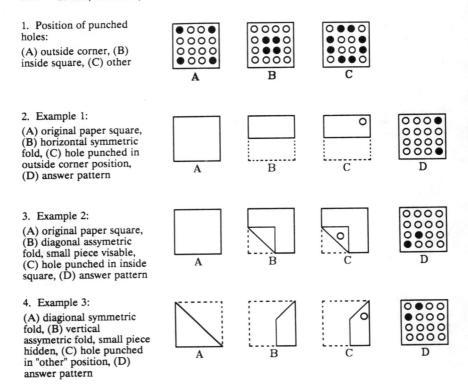

1. Position of punched holes:

(A) outside corner, (B) inside square, (C) other

2. Example 1:

(A) original paper square, (B) horizontal symmetric fold, (C) hole punched in outside corner position, (D) answer pattern

3. Example 2:

(A) original paper square, (B) diagonal assymetric fold, small piece visable, (C) hole punched in inside square, (D) answer pattern

4. Example 3:

(A) diagonal symmetric fold, (B) vertical assymetric fold, small piece hidden, (C) hole punched in "other" position, (D) answer pattern

Figure 10.3.   Examples of Paper-Folding Items and Difficulty Dimensions

Table 10.4.   Pearson Correlations between Experimental Test Item Difficulty and Redefined Independent Variables Paper-Folding Items

Variable	Definition	Number of Occurrences	Correlation
1	Position of hole: outside corner	3	−.19
2	Position of hole: inside square	10	−.36
3	Position of hole: other	10	.49
4	Vertical symmetric fold	6	−.03
5	Horizontal symmetric fold	7	.23
6	Diagonal symmetric fold	8	.02
7	Vertical asymmetric visible fold	4	−.16
8	Horizontal asymmetric visible fold	4	.09
9	Diagonal asymmetric visible fold	18	−.51
10	Vertical asymmetric hidden fold	1	−.01
11	Horizontal asymmetric hidden fold	2	.27
12	Diagonal asymmetric hidden fold	5	.69

Table 10.5.   Multiple Regression Weights for Experimental Test Paper-Folding Items

Variable	Definition	Regression Weight	(SE)
1	Position of hole: other	1.63	(0.66)
2	Vertical symmetric fold	1.63	(0.73)
3	Horizontal symmetric fold	1.33	(0.60)
4	Diagonal symmetric fold	1.96	(0.78)
5	Vertical asymmetric visible fold	0.20	(0.97)
6	Horizontal asymmetric visible fold	2.24	(0.91)
7	Diagonal asymmetric visible fold	1.41	(0.60)
8	Vertical asymmetric hidden fold	3.68	(1.28)
9	Horizontal asymmetric hidden fold	3.66	(1.09)
10	Diagonal asymmetric hidden fold	5.28	(0.79)
	Constant	−5.38	(1.36)

On the basis of these results, 45 new paper-folding items were constructed and administered in six forms containing 15 items each. These items were included on the October 1987 PAT, which was administered to approximately 2,600 examinees. The items were equated and placed on a common scale. The results of the multiple regression analysis are shown in Table 10.6. The resulting multiple R of .926 is almost identical to that found in the preliminary analysis. There was some variation in the regression weights for the 10 variables. However, the factors that contributed most to determining the difficulty of the items remained the three types of asymmetric hidden folds, which must be

Table 10.6.   Component Analysis of Paper-Folding Items, October 1987

Variables in Multiple Regression	R^2
1. No. of diagonal asymmetric hidden folds	.49
2. No. of horizontal asymmetric hidden folds	.59
3. No. of vertical asymmetric hidden folds	.71
4. No. of diagonal symmetric folds	.78
5. No. of horizontal asymmetric visible folds	.81
6. No. of vertical asymmetric visible folds	.83
7. Position of hole	.83
8. No. of diagonal asymmetric visible folds	.84
9. No. of vertical symmetric folds	.85
10. No. of horizontal symmetric folds	.85

Multiple R = 0.93

Number of items = 45

Example:
PROBLEM Z

In Figure Z how many cubes have

702. only two of their sides painted?
703. only four of their sides painted?
704. all five of their sides painted?

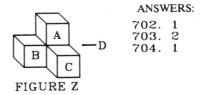

ANSWERS:
702. 1
703. 2
704. 1

FIGURE Z

Figure 10.4.   Examples of Cube Items

visualized to solve the item, and the diagonal symmetric fold, which changed the orientation of the holes, that is, shifting horizontal patterns to vertical and vice versa. The regression weights for the horizontal and vertical folds were similar within the three types: symmetric, asymmetric visible, and asymmetric hidden. This supports the hypothesis that there is no difference conceptually between vertical and horizontal folds.

The correlation between the predicted item difficulty and the observed item difficulty for the 45 new items, which were generated for this study, was 0.852. Thus, it would appear that the multiple regression equation, developed from the limited item set administered under the experimental conditions, did a very accurate job in predicting the difficulty of the new items in the regular testing condition.

The analysis of the cube items is taken from two sources: Smith and Kramer (1988), and Kramer, Smith, and Kubiak (1989). An example of this item type is found in Figure 10.4. The results of the preliminary analysis are found in Table 10.7. In both of these cases there were a limited number of items (12) in relation to the number of components (6). The components identified in this analysis are similar to those found in the paper-folding example. The number of cubes is a complexity variable as is the number of blocks in the answer. The number of fully hidden blocks and the number of hidden blocks in the answer reflect the degree that imagination of unseen surfaces is required. Unlike the paper-folding items there is no variable that shifts the orientation of the figure.

The results of the analysis of the April 1987 set of 12 items yield a multiple R of .94 (R^2 = .89). The multiple R for the October 1986 analysis, which involved a different set of 12 items, was much lower than expected. However, four of the items in that set had an unusual angle of presentation. When those four items were dropped, the multiple R increased significantly.

As a result of these analysis, a new set of 48 cube items was created and added to the previous set of items. This resulted in a total of 79

Table 10.7.   Preliminary Component Analysis of Cube Items

April 1987

Variables in Multiple Regression	R^2
1. No. of blocks	.60
2. No. of fully hidden blocks	.75
3. No. of hidden blocks in answer	.78
4. No. of blocks in answer	.79
5. No. of painted sides hidden in answer	.85
6. No. of partially hidden blocks	.89

Multiple R = 0.92
Number of items = 12

October 1986
Total Item set
Multiple R = 0.36 R^2 = 0.13
Number of items = 12

Reduced Item Set

Variables in Multiple Regression	R^2
1. No. of blocks	.26
2. No. of painted sides hidden in answer	.42
	.55
3. No. of fully hidden blocks	.72
4. No. of hidden blocks in answer	.76
5. No. of blocks in answer	

Multiple R = 0.87
Number of items = 8

cube items. These new items were used on four experimental versions administered as part of the April 1988 PAT. Through common item equating, all 79 items were placed on a common scale. The ranges of the frequency of the components of difficulty in the new item set are shown in Table 10.8.

The results of the regression analyses for the complete set of cube items are summarized in Table 10.9. The first analysis was designed to replicate the analysis of the April 1986 item set reported in Smith and Kramer (1988). The results of this analysis indicate that the R^2 value for the six components increased from 0.69 in the April 1986 administration to .71 in the April 1988 administration. The order of entry into the regression changed slightly, that is, component four dropped from first to third but the number of cubes remained the last component entered.

Table 10.8.   Frequency of Components in Cube Items

Component	Range
1. No. of cubes in figure	6–17
2. No. of partially hidden cubes in figure (less than 2 full sides visible)	0– 6
3. No. of fully hidden cubes	0– 6
4. No. of painted sides hidden in answer	0–11
5. No. of hidden cubes in answer	0– 3
6. No. of cubes in answer	1– 8

Number of items = 79

The next analysis was based on all previously administered items in the complete set of cube items ($n = 31$). The results of the multiple regression show a multiple R^2 of 0.55. The change in the entry order of the components, that is, number of cubes going from last entered to first entered, suggests that there might be a difference between the October 1986 set and the set of all previously administered items.

The next analysis included all new items, that is, those specially constructed for this analysis, which featured the same cube figure shown in three different orientations. The R^2 for these 48 items was 0.60. To test the effect of misfitting items on the component analysis, all items with outfit statistics such that $|t| > 3$ were removed from the analysis and then all items with $|t| > 2$ were removed. Removing the four items with $|t| > 3$ reduced the R^2 to 0.50. This appears to be due largely to the fact that these four items included the easiest and the hardest items in the 48-item set. Eliminating the remaining 12 items with absolute t values between 3 and 2 increased the R^2 to 0.52.

Table 10.9.   Component Analysis of Cube Items

Analysis	No. of Items	R^2	Component Entry Order
April 1986 items	12	0.71	5,6,2,4,3,1
All previously administered items	31	0.55	1,5,6,2,4,3
All new items	48	0.60	1,3,2,4,6,5
All new items less 4 misfit	44	0.50	1,3,2,4,6,5
All new items less 16 misfit	32	0.52	1,3,4,6,5,2
Center items	17	0.58	1,2,3,4,6,5
Left items	32	0.46	1,5,6,2,4,3
Right items	30	0.41	1,4,2,5,6,3
Total	79	0.45	1,2,5,6,4,3

Example:

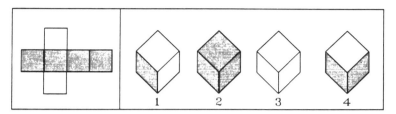

One of the above figures (1,2,3,4,) can be formed from the flat pattern given at the left. The only figure that corresponds to the pattern is 4. If the shaded surfaces are looked at as the sides of the box, then all four sides must be shaded, while the top and bottom are white.

Figure 10.5.   Examples of Form Development Items

The next three analyses investigated items with regard to the mode of presentation (left, center, and right). The center items were predominately from the new item set while approximately one-half of the left and right items were new items. The common element is that the number of cubes in the figures is the first component entered in each analysis.

Finally, the analysis of the total 79-item set resulted in a R^2 value of 0.45. Again, the first component added was the number of cubes in the item followed by the number of partially hidden cubes. The number of hidden cubes in the answer entered third. These results suggest that, across the analyses, the number of cubes in the problem is the most important factor in predicting difficulty. The number of partially hidden cubes in the figure is the second most important factor, and the number of hidden cubes in the answer is the third most important.

The final analysis is based on the form development items. An example of this item type is shown in Figure 10.5. The item type is more complex than the previous two because it allows an infinite variety of figure shapes and two major variations in item format, that is, complex shapes with uncolored surfaces, such as the item shown in Figure 10.2, and simple shapes with colored surfaces, such as the item shown in Figure 10.5. The development of the components of the item that contribute to the difficulty of the item is less trivial in this case because of the complexity and the two basic variations. These two basic variations might actually constitute two different item types. The preliminary analysis of these data have focused on components such as the number of irregular panels in the flat object, number of panels with regular shading, and number of regular folds. The number of

Table 10.10.   Component Analysis of Form Development Items, October 1986

Variables in Multiple Regression	R^2
1. No. of irregular panels	.16
2. No. of panels	.25
3. No. of panels with regular shading	.32
4. No. of regular folds	.33
5. No. of different panels	.34
6. No. of irregular folds	.35
7. No. of regular panels	.37
8. No. of complex panels	.38
9. No. of panels with irregular shading	.39
Multiple R = 0.62	

Number of items set = 30

panels and the number of folds seem to represent the same complexity variable as identified in the previous two analyses. With almost all of the items, there appears to be a shift in the orientation of the item so that components that change orientation, such as the diagonal fold in paper folding, do not seem to be easily quantified here. Finally, because the answers to all items are presented as isometric views of the solid object, each answer appears to have the same amount of surface hidden from view. The only difference might be how regular is the hidden part of the solid figure. This component might be captured by counting the number of irregular panels.

The results of the analysis of a sample of 2,400 examinees who took the 30 items in the October 1986 administration are presented in Table 10.10. The multiple R for the nine identified components is lower than that found for the paper-folding items, but certainly in the range of values found in the analysis of the equated cube item set. The first three components in the multiple regression were number of irregular panels, number of panels, and number of panels with regular shading. Again, the pattern seems consistent with the two previous analyses. The number of panels appears to be the complexity factor. The number of irregular panels appears to be a measure of the amount of information that has to be visualized as does the number of panels with regular shading.

The preceding only represents a preliminary analysis of the form development items. A total of approximately 80 of these items have been administered and will be equated for further analysis. This analysis has suggested that the form development items are comprised of two major item types or major variations within one item type, that is, items with surface shading and items without. Future analyses will investigate these two item types separately.

CONCLUSIONS

These three analyses show the applicability of the component analysis to spatial ability items. In all three cases, simple counts of item features account for substantial portions of the variance in the observed item difficulties. This technique facilitates the design of items that have predictable difficulties. This would be important in defining a variable with items evenly spaced across the range of the variable or to target new items on populations with narrow ranges of ability. As the technique is applied to less restricted item types, there is a potential utility in the test development cycle. It allows item writers to follow prescriptions to arrive at appropriate difficulty ranges for new items.

The component analysis of items will also be of assistance in the study of the construct validity of items sets from rather divergent item formats such as those found for spatial ability tests. If, as has been observed in these analyses, it is possible to identify common factors that contribute to item difficulty across divergent item types, then this technique can be used to validate theories regarding the constructs that underlie the different item types or the cognitive processes necessary for the solution of those item types.

The understanding of the aspects of an item that contribute to the item's difficulty is of far greater importance to the advancement of measurement and the development of calibrated metrics for measurement than the knowledge that a particular item had a particular difficulty for a particular population.

REFERENCES

Eliot, J., & Smith, I.M. (1983). *An international directory of spatial tests.* Windsor, Berks, England: NFER-Nelson.

Embretson, S.E., & Wetzel, C.D. (1987). Component latent trait models for paragraph comprehension tests. *Applied Psychological Measurement, 11,* 175–193.

Fischer, G.H. (1973). The linear logistic test model as an instrument in educational research. *Acta Psychologica, 37,* 359–374.

Green, K.E., & Smith, R.M. (1987). A comparison of two methods of decomposing item difficulties. *Journal of Educational Statistics, 12,* 369–381.

Kramer, G.A., Kubiak, A.T., & Smith, R.M. (1989). Construct and predictive validity of the Perceptual Ability Test. *Journal of Dental Education, 53,* 119–125.

Kramer, G.A., Smith, R.M., & Kubiak, A.K. (1989). *A cross-validation of components influencing the difficulty of cube items.* Paper presented at the annual meeting of the National Council on Measurement in Education, San Francisco, CA.

Mislevy, R. (1981). *A general linear model for the analysis of Rasch item threshold estimates.* Unpublished dissertation. University of Chicago, IL.

Pellegrino, J.W., & Glaser, R. (1979). Cognitive components and correlates in the analysis of individual differences. *Intelligence, 3,* 187–214.

Smith, R.M. (1989). *Item and person fit in the Rasch model.* Paper presented at the annual meeting of the American Educational Research Association, San Francisco, CA.

Smith, R.M., & Green, K.E. (1985). *Components of difficulty in paper folding items.* Paper presented at the annual meeting of the American Educational Research Association, Chicago, IL.

Smith, R.M., & Kramer, G.A. (1988). *Component analysis of factors influencing the difficulty of perceptual ability items.* Paper presented at the annual meeting of the National Council on Measurement in Education, New Orleans, LA.

Stenner, A.J., Smith, M., & Burdick, D.S. (1983). Toward a theory of construct definition. *Journal of Educational Measurement, 20,* 305–316.

Sternberg, R.J. (1977). *Intelligence, information processing, and analogical reasoning.* Hillsdale, NJ: Erlbaum.

Whiteley, S.E. (1977). Some information processing components of intelligence test items. *Applied Psychological Measurement, 1,* 465–476.

Wright, B.D., Congdon, R.T., & Rossner, M. (1986). *MSCALE: A Rasch program for rating scale analysis.* Chicago: MESA Press.

Wright, B.D., & Stone, M. (1979). *Best test design.* Chicago: MESA Press.

chapter **11**

Test Anxiety and Item Order: New Concerns for Item Response Theory*

Richard C. Gershon
Johnson O'Connor Research Foundation
and Northwestern University

> An examinee's response pattern on a test can be viewed as a product of a three-way interaction between the characteristics of the individual, of the test, and of the situation in which the test is given. (Birnbaum, 1986)

Ability testing has become an increasingly important feature in the lives of children attending school, adolescents applying to colleges, and adults seeking employment. Modern test construction uses Item Response Theory (IRT) to decrease test length and increase reliability in all of these milieus. The theory is used to compute item parameters to predict the likelihood of a person answering a given item correctly. The model presumes fixed parameters, and that the likelihood of the person answering the item correctly is based only on ability relative to the item's difficulty. However, contemporary psychometricians have not addressed the impact of individual differences other than ability on

*The research in this chapter was conducted in partial fulfillment for the M.S. at Northwestern University. A more complete version of the material was also presented at the 20th meeting of the American Educational Research Association (Gershon, 1989).

test behavior, a mistake earlier discovered in implementing classical test theory. Personality researchers have demonstrated that test performance is affected by test anxiety as well as changes in item order. If this is true, a major assumption of IRT is incorrect, and the adequacy of a limited set of fixed parameters placed in question.

While there are major theoretical differences between the application of conventional test theory and item response theory, both models should produce similar estimates of ability for the same person. However, proponents of IRT have yet to address the effects of individual differences other than ability on performance. Anxiety serves as an example of a personality variable which has been shown to affect performance.

The first section of this chapter reviews theories of test anxiety, discusses the underlying mechanisms that cause test anxiety, and examines how varying levels of test anxiety differentially affect performance. This is followed by the presentation of a study to examine the effects of anxiety, item difficulty order, and ability on performance. Finally, new testing strategies are proposed that allow tests to be manipulated in various ways to maximize performance.

TEST ANXIETY

Test anxiety was first presented by Mandler and Sarason as the mechanism underlying their Test Anxiety Questionnaire (TAQ). Previous measures of anxiety had looked only at general measures of anxiety, while the TAQ was implemented to look at a singular anxiety state (Wine, 1971).

Sarason defined test anxiety "as a form of self-preoccupation—characterized by self-awareness, self-doubt, and self-depreciation—that influences overt behavior and psychological reactivity" (Sarason & Stoops, 1978, p. 103). For Sarason, performance decrements due to test anxiety are caused by a situationally induced cognitive style that interferes with normal performance.

Differential Effects of Test Anxiety

Test anxiety has differential effects dependent upon the level of anxiety and varying situational elements commonly found in testing situations. These conditions can be loosely grouped into (a) environmental factors, and (b) test characteristics. Environmental factors are those elements of testing situations that are dependent upon the testing situation. These factors include externally introduced stresses (evaluation emphasis and time pressures), the presence of observes, the presentation of feedback (Anastasi, 1982; Meunier & Rule, 1969; Sarason, 1958), or the level of aspiration (Mandler & Sarason, 1952; Trapp & Kausler, 1958). Test characteristics refer to those elements of the testing situation which are found within the testing protocol itself including: test difficulty, the order of test items, the associative values of those items, the effect of repeated trials within a given testing situation, and the effects of tests which contain initial failure items.

Test characteristics. Overall test difficulty is perhaps the most obvious test characteristic known to differentially affect anxious individuals. Many of the first research attempts in this area used the Taylor Manifest Anxiety Scale. Highly anxious subjects were found to exhibit better performance than their less anxious counterparts on classical conditioning tasks. It was assumed that level of anxiety was related to a state of "reactivity" or "excitability" that affected drive, which in turn was necessary for increased performance (Farber & Spence, 1953). When Sarason and Palola (1960) compared trait anxiety ratings with test anxiety ratings, the test anxiety ratings were found to be more accurate in predicting level of performance, especially when difficulty was taken into consideration.

There is overwhelming evidence for an interaction effect between test difficulty and level of anxiety (Child, 1954; Farber & Spence, 1953; Nicholls, 1984; Sarason, 1960). When high-anxious (HA) students are given difficult problems, they are faced with a situation which they are unprepared to handle, and thus they are unable to complete the task at hand. But when the same individuals are faced with less difficult items, they can solve them with ease. The reverse is true for low-anxious (LA) examinees. These persons are prepared to handle complex situations, and actually excel at them. However, should they be faced with test items of low difficulty, they will skim over them too quickly, and consequently their level of performance will decline.

Test anxiety has also been found to influence person fit measures (Birnbaum, 1986; Schmitt & Crocker, 1984). Some subjects missed easier items, and correctly answered more difficult items. A good test should give equal results regardless of the order of the items on the test. However, Doris and Sarason (1955) found this not to be the case when comparing high- and low-anxious groups. They found patterns of success and failure differentially based upon level of anxiety on two forms of a test in which only the item orders differed (also see Galassi, Frierson, & Sharer, 1981).

Initial failure experiences also interact with level of anxiety. It is interesting to note that early studies of anxiety and performance used failure experiences to increase the level of anxiety. Later research continued to treat failure experiences as an independent variable. It was hypothesized that failure would elicit responses too strong for HA subjects to handle, and thus performance would decline. For LA individuals, some degree of failure should serve to increase motivational drive and subsequently improve overall performance (Child, 1954).

Perhaps test examiners would do well to take the advice of a researcher not even concerned with the effects of anxiety, but who clearly understood the possible negative effects of failure experiences. Hutt (1947) asserts that we do all individuals a disservice by having them encounter a series of failure experiences at the end of subtests within intelligence tests. Subsequent performance is likely to decrease in quality and animosity could develop towards the test administrator. HA subjects are likely to be overwhelmed and thus perform more poorly on subsequent subtests and LA subjects are likely to decline even more rapidly than usual as they are experiencing a series of related failure tasks, the failure of each one increasing the probability of failure on the next.

HYPOTHESES

This study examined the varying effects of test anxiety on tests with different item orders. In this regard the following hypotheses were made: (a) The method of item administration can be manipulated so as to increase or decrease performance depending upon the individual's level of test anxiety, and (b) person fit statistics will deteriorate for conditions where there is an anxiety by difficulty-order interaction.

Both hypotheses predict a difficulty order by anxiety interaction. When subjects are initially presented with items which are easy for them, LA subjects are predicted to perform more poorly overall, as they do when presented with easy items in general. This effect is probably due to an insufficient level of effort caused by the appearance of lessened task importance, decreased stress, or a change in direction of attention. For HA subjects in the same condition, the converse is thought to be the case. Easier items result in less stress and fewer of the avoidance responses which ordinarily limit performance.

When subjects are initially presented with difficult items, the resultant effect on performance is predicted to be reversed for both anxiety groups. LA subjects will excel in the presence of items which challenge their ability level, resulting in on-task behaviors which increase their overall performance. However, when HA subjects are continually administered items beyond their ability level, the level of stress will rise above their coping level, and dysfunctional thought processes will overwhelm the task-relevant responding necessary for good test performance.

The first hypothesis can also be substantiated by comparing performance on a conventional test with performance on a test where item difficulty order has been manipulated. In this way a direct comparison can be made of the difference in performance which can be attributed to the effects of test anxiety and difficulty order versus the overall performance which is likely to be demonstrated in conventional test situations. Holding ability constant, the performance of LA persons should be better on a test in which difficult items are initially presented as compared to HA individuals, whose performance should be worse in this situation.

Performance can also be evaluated on a within-test level. On a test where easy items are administered first, LA subjects are likely to perform more poorly on the easy items than had they been presented later in the test, but performance should still improve once the test becomes more challenging. For HA subjects in this situation, initial performance should be quite strong in the presence of easy items which are less stress inducing, but stress should increase, and performance deteriorate, once they begin to encounter the more difficult items. These effects should be further aggravated for individuals based upon their ability level. The performance of low-ability, HA subjects is more likely to deteriorate when they encounter the difficult section of the test than is the performance of high-ability subjects.

These within-test effects can also be conceived of in terms of the effect of time. The performance of HA subjects should improve over time, as they get used to the test and their level of confidence begins to grow. But this effect will be moderated by item difficulty order and ability, which serve to impede or hasten the building of confidence. The performance of LA subjects should deteriorate over time, as concentration for this group diminishes. But this effect will also be moderated by difficulty order and ability. Time will have less of an impact on LA subjects encountering more difficult items later in the test, as interest will be increased by the new level of item difficulty. The LA subjects encountering easy items at the end of the test will be affected by both the decreased interest associated with easier items as well as the negative influence of time. These effects will be further compounded by person ability. On a test where item difficulty decreases later in the test, low-ability subjects will encounter easier items later in the test than will more able subjects, who may find the test items in the middle of the test to be easier for them.

When difficulty order is manipulated, person-fit statistics sometimes will indicate that a problem exists, particularly in the case of LA subjects who miss items which should be easy for them, and in the case of HA subjects whose performance deteriorates following the administration of items which are too difficult for them. Fit is also likely to be affected by the influence of ability. Low-ability subjects are likely to guess at more items as compared to high-ability subjects, resulting in poorer fit statistics for all low-ability subjects.

METHOD

Subjects

Subjects were drawn from the regular testing pool of the Johnson O'Connor Human Research Foundation. The population tested at Johnson O'Connor ranges in age from 14 to 60. The 1,233 subjects for this study were drawn from the regularly scheduled appointments in 15 testing laboratories across the United States.

Materials

The vocabulary tests were administered in three parts. The first part was a 20-item pretest. The results of this pretest were used to select the appropriate form of the Foundation's standard vocabulary test, which has reliabilities in the range of .95–.97 depending upon the form (Bowker, 1981). Following the conventional test administration, subjects were given one of the experimental tests. None of the vocabulary tests were timed, nor were they supervised.

The 100 experimental items were selected from the Foundation's vocabulary item bank (see Gershon, 1988). Using Rasch modeling (Wright & Stone, 1979), many of the items had been placed on a common scale, providing a broad-band pool from which to draw items. The item parameters for this test as well as for many of the items in the item bank were computed using MSCALE (Wright, Rossner, & Congdon, 1985). Only items which met rigorous inclusion criteria based upon Rasch fit have been retained in the item bank.

Three experimental tests were constructed. The items from the first experimental test (Easy-Hard) were administered in increasing difficulty fashion, easy items first, most difficult items last. The other two tests differed from the first only in terms of difficulty order. In the second form (Hard-Easy), the more difficult items were administered initially, followed by the easier items. In the third form (Random) the items were distributed in random difficulty order. The same 100 items were used in all three cases.

Mandler and Sarason's Test Anxiety Scale (TAS) was administered in paper and pencil form. The test consists of a series of True-False items.

Procedure

Three primary factors were included in the analyses: level of test ANXIETY, difficulty ORDER, and a pretest measure of ABILITY. The dependent variables included: the person MEASURE obtained at different points on the experimental test, a measure of person fit—INFIT, and the LOGIT CHANGE SCORE.

Anxiety. The anxiety variable was computed as the raw score obtained on the Test Anxiety Scale. Statistical analyses were conducted using the continuous data, but, for the purpose of presenting data in tables, anxiety scores of all of those participating in the study were placed into categories with those scoring above .8 standard deviations from the sample mean labeled as HIGH anxious, those within the range ± .8 standard deviations of the sample mean as MEDIUM anxious, and those in the bottom group as LOW anxious.

Ability. The ability measure for the conventional test is expressed in terms of a Vocabulary Scale Score (VSS) (Bowker, 1981). The VSS score was designed by the Johnson O'Connor Research Foundation to act as a linear vocabulary scale which could be used to equate all vocabulary words and tests, regardless of difficulty.

Measure. The person measure obtained on the experimental test was computed using MSCALE. This program centers items at zero, computes item difficulties, and estimates person abilities according to their performance relative to the item difficulties. The measure obtained is expressed in logits.

In order to analyze performance at the within-test level, ability measures were also computed for three different parts of each test: the first 30 items, the 40 middle items and the last 30 items. These three ability measures for each person were constructed by using the average item difficulties from all three test forms (effectively controlling for test length). A raw-score to logit conversion table was then generated for each group of items, within each test form, using a series of UCON iterations to compute the estimated measure given each possible raw score for that particular group of items (see Wright & Stone, 1979). The measure values for each section thus controlled for the difficulty of the items in that section.

Infit. Person-fit measures were also obtained using MSCALE. MSCALE calculates a statistic to assess person fit called INFIT which is comparable across subjects. This statistic will remain small for those individuals whose response pattern is well predicted by ability. However, the statistic will increase when numerous items are missed which are easier than the person's ability level, or when questions are answered correctly beyond the person's obtained ability score.

Logit change score. The logit change score was computed as the difference between the score obtained on the conventional test (the VSS score expressed in its logit equivalent) and the score obtained on the experimental test where:

LOGIT CHANGE SCORE = Experimental Test Performance - Conventional Performance

Poorer performance on the experimental test yields a negative logit change score, and better performance on the experimental test yields a positive logit change score.

RESULTS

The major independent variables included in the analyses were all found to have some effect on performance, often interacting with the other variables in ways which had not been predicted. In general: (a) test anxiety was found to be a factor in overall performance, logit change score, within-test performance, and person fit; (b) item difficulty order was not a factor in person fit, but did play a role in overall performance, logit change score and within-test performance; and (c) person ability was also a factor in within-test performance and person fit.

Predicting Overall Performance

The performance measures were analyzed by SYSTAT (Wilkinson, 1988) using a repeated measures analysis of variance design (see Table 11.1). The dependent variable was the logit score obtained on the first 30 items, the middle 40 items, and the last 30 items on the experimen-

Table 11.1. Analysis of Variance

Source	SS	df	MS	F
Between Subjects				
Ability (pre-Test)	393.30	1	393.30	774.94***
TAS (Anxiety)	2.97	1	2.97	5.86*
(Item) Order	3.13	2	1.57	3.08*
Order × Ability	2.61	2	1.31	2.57
Order × TAS	2.72	2	1.36	2.68
Ability × TAS	2.84	1	2.84	5.60*
Order × Ability × TAS	2.65	2	1.33	2.61
Error	597.36	1177	0.51	
Within Subjects				
Pos (Position), lin	0.20	1	0.23	0.55
Pos, quad	2.62	1	2.62	10.96***
Ability × Pos, lin	0.21	1	0.21	0.56
Ability × Pos, quad	2.48	1	2.48	10.36***
Order × Pos, lin	5.79	2	2.90	7.84***
Order × Pos, quad	0.53	2	0.27	1.11
TAS × Pos, lin	0.00	1	0.00	0.01
TAS × Pos, quad	0.44	1	0.44	1.83
Order × Ability × Pos, lin	6.71	2	3.35	9.07***
Order × Ability × Pos, quad	0.22	2	0.11	0.47
Order × TAS × Pos, lin	0.61	2	0.30	0.82
Order × TAS × Pos, quad	1.59	2	0.79	3.32*
Ability × TAS × Pos, lin	0.00	1	0.00	0.01
Ability × TAS × Pos, quad	0.66	1	0.66	2.76
Order × TAS × Able × Pos, lin	0.59	2	0.30	0.80
Order × TAS × Able × Pos, quad	1.02	2	0.51	2.12
Error, lin	435.23	1177	0.37	
Error, quad	281.81	1177	0.24	

Pos = Position   *$p < .05$
TAS = Anxiety   **$p < .01$
Lin = Linear effect for Position   ***$p < .001$
Quad = Quadratic effect for Position

tal test. Difficulty order was entered as a fixed factor with three levels and analyzed along with the continuous variables test anxiety (TAS) and ability (pretest measure).

As one would expect, ability has an extremely strong relationship with the experimental test forms. However, there was also an indication that if one used a total score approach, there would be a significant item order by ability interaction (see Table 11.2) such that medium ability persons perform better on the Easy-Hard form, while low- and high-ability persons demonstrate no overall preference.

As expected, there was a significant main effect for TAS (see Table 11.1 and Figure 11.1), showing that performance decreases for the

Table 11.2. Average Person Measures Based on Total Scores for Different Item Orders and Different Pretest Ability Groups

Order	Low Ability	Medium Ability	High Ability
Easy-Hard	−.50	.54	1.64
Hard-Easy	−.53	.39	1.51
Random	−.54	.48	1.60

more anxious persons (Pearson correlation of overall measure with anxiety, $r = -.27$). The main effect for difficulty order was also significant (see Table 11.1 and Figure 11.2) such that persons who took the items in the Easy-Hard order performed significantly better than did persons who took the items in the Hard-Easy or Random conditions. While the interaction of Item Order by TAS was not significant using a repeated measures design, there are indications that a total score approach, rather than using repeated measures, would show otherwise (see Table 11.2).

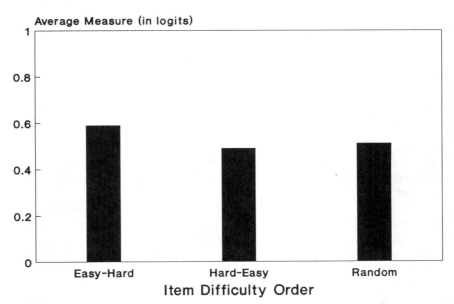

Figure 11.1. The Main Effect of Anxiety

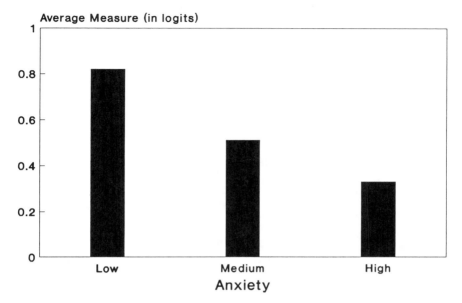

Figure 11.2.   The Main Effect of Item Order

Within-Subjects Effects

While most of the main effects and interactions of the factors were significant, the interesting information was found in the higher order interactions involving performance at different points within the test. In general, performance declined over time for the Easy-Hard form, improved for the Hard-Easy forms, and was unaffected on the random form. Test anxiety further moderated performance at different positions in the test, particularly for the Easy-Hard form. Finally, the greatest variance in performance was in terms of item position effects related to differences in ability level.

Table 11.3.   Average Person Measures for Different Item Orders and Different Anxiety Groups

Order	Low Anxious	Medium Anxious	High Anxious
Easy-Hard	.88	.57	.27
Hard-Easy	.71	.43	.31
Random	.82	.44	.22

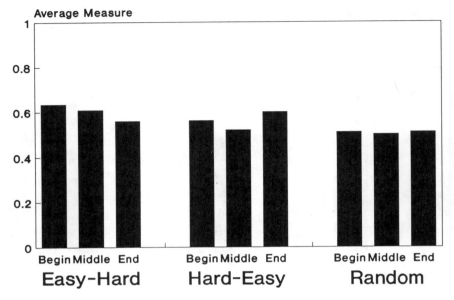

Figure 11.3.   Item Order X Position

Test performance across the test varied for only two of the three forms, when one examines the item order by position relationship (see Figure 11.3). Performance decreased over time on the Easy-Hard form, and improved on the Hard-Easy form, indicating a distinct preference for the easy items regardless of their position on the test. There were no effects for item position in the random order. While the easy items were more likely to be answered correctly on the Easy-Hard form, performance on the difficult items was the same on both the Easy-Hard and the Hard-Easy forms.

Test anxiety was found to differentially affect within-test performance depending on the item order. On the Easy-Hard form, low-anxious subjects peaked in performance in the middle of the test, as opposed to the high-anxious individuals, who showed their worst performance during the middle of the test (see Figure 11.4). Item position was not a factor in within-test performance for the medium anxious group. In addition, performance over time on the Hard-Easy and Random forms was not affected by test anxiety, regardless of its intensity.

Persons of low ability were found to perform worse during the middle of the test, as contrasted with persons of high ability whose performance peaks in the middle (see Figure 11.5). Performance of the medium-able group did not vary over time.

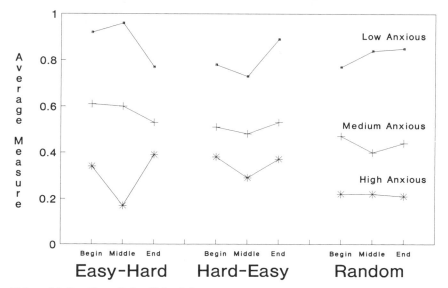

Figure 11.4.   Item Order X Anxiety

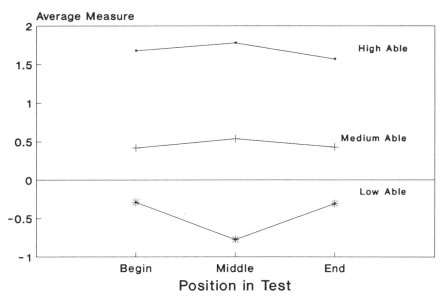

Figure 11.5.   Position X Pretested Ability

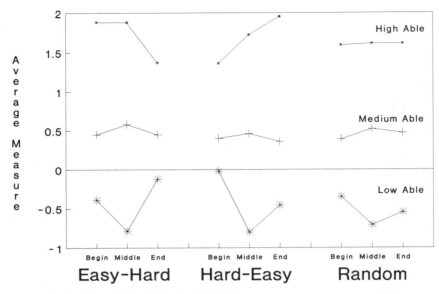

Figure 11.6. **Item Order X Pretested Ability**

Item position was also a factor in a three-way interaction with difficulty order and ability (see Figure 11.6). The opposing performance which appeared for the high- and low-anxious groups on the Easy-Hard form was also apparent when looking at the low- and high-ability groups with close to a .75 logit difference between performance in the middle versus end of the form for the low able group. Also, the high-able group demonstrated a distinct preference for the easy items regardless of item position.

Logit Change Score

The logit change score data were analyzed using multiple regression with the dependent variable Logit Change Score, defined as the experimental test measure minus the conventional test measure.

Measured ability on the experimental test was greater for people taking the Easy-Hard version of the experimental test, while it was less for those taking the Hard-Easy form (see Figure 11.7, $F = 6.8, p <$ .001). Test anxiety also played a role in predicting the Logit Change Score (see Figure 11.8, $F = 15.7, p < .001$). Low test anxious subjects received negative logit change scores. Performance was worse on their second test, as compared to high test anxious subjects, whose perfor-

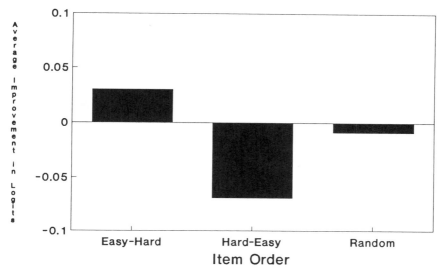

Figure 11.7.   Comparing Differences Between Pretest and Experimental Test

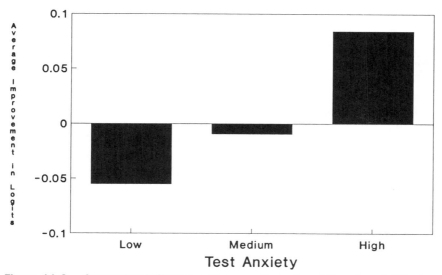

Figure 11.8.   Comparing Differences Between Pretest and Experimental Test

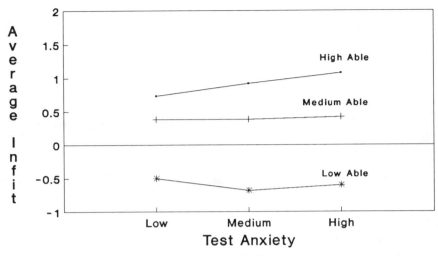

Figure 11.9. Average Infit Test Anxiety by Ability

mance was better the second time around. The interaction effect of Order by Test Anxiety was not significant.

Person Fit

Person fit was analyzed using analysis of variance along with the independent variables of item order, test anxiety and person ability. Person fit was not affected by difficulty order, but was modified by the effects of test anxiety and person ability. Increases in test anxiety lead to proportionately higher values of INFIT, $F = 11.8, p < .001; r = .11$. However, since a higher INFIT actually indicates worse fit, the lower test anxious subjects were the best fitting. The main effect for Order and the Order by TAS interaction were not significant.

When ability was added as a factor the main effect of test anxiety continued to be significant, $F = 14.7, p < .001$. Ability, $F = 11.8, p < .001$, and the interaction of test anxiety with vocabulary ability (TAS × VSS), $F = 16.4, p < .001$, were also found to be significant. Correlational analysis confirmed the existence of a negative relationship, $r = -.45$, between vocabulary ability and INFIT (see Figure 11.9). Low-ability persons are least likely to fit the item response theory model. This relationship seems to worsen even further for those with high test anxiety. However, there appears to be little or no difference in person fit due to test anxiety for those of medium or high ability.

DISCUSSION

Item response theory assumes that performance can be predicted based solely upon the fixed parameters of the items within a test (and person abilities). Contemporary proponents of the theory have neglected to consider that there is more to performance than just ability. Factors such as test anxiety and item order have been shown to affect performance. These variables cause test scores and within-test performance to increase for some persons and decrease for others.

The predictions set forth in this study regarding person fit were confirmed, but only with regards to anxiety, and without regard to the item difficulty order. Further analysis also revealed that INFIT is related to ability—fit worsens as ability declines. This may be due to guessing effects such that persons of low ability are able to correctly guess the answers of difficult items.

As predicted, test anxiety affected overall performance; low test anxious subjects performed better overall than those with higher levels of anxiety. Anxiety also affects performance when repeated tests are administered. In comparison with the conventional test, scores for low-anxious subjects on the experimental test were worse, while scores for high-anxious examinees were better. It appears that low test anxious individuals lost some of their competitive edge when facing their second test, resulting in poorer performance. In contrast, high-anxious individuals built confidence during the initial testing session and receive higher scores on the second test. This may also be an indication that the effects of a pretest diminish the differential effects of test anxiety.

The difficulty order was a significant factor for predicting total test score and in determining part of the difference in performance between the conventional and experimental test administrations. Subjects had better performance relative to the conventional test when given the Easy-Hard form; however, their performance was worse on the Hard-Easy form, when the most difficult items were administered at the beginning of the test. This finding substantiates the predictions of Hutt that failure experiences decrease performance.

Within-test analyses revealed that while difficulty order is a significant factor in overall performance, performance at different points in time is also affected by the item order, level of anxiety, and ability. These effects seem to decrease when items are administered in a random order. The Easy-Hard form is the most greatly affected by individual differences. Low test anxious individuals improve in performance during the middle of the test, when the performance of high test anxious individuals declines. Within-test performance is further moderated by ability. Persons of high-ability peak in their performance on the easy items, while low-ability persons actually peak on the most difficult items.

It is clear that items can no longer be viewed in a vacuum without regard for individual differences other than ability. The fundamental assumption of IRT that ability may be used to predict performance on any one item is insufficient. Within-test performance, and performance on individual items, is subject to the effects of item order, test anxiety and ability, all interacting together.

The issue of changes in performance over time also has a major impact in determining test length. Adaptive testing is a commonly used method of shortening test length. Items are usually administered alternating between being above and below the examinee's ability level. This administration pattern is likely to produce performance similar to that found in the random difficulty order form. If this is the case, test anxiety is unlikely to affect within-test performance. Unfortunately, random presentation will not offset the within-test effects of differences in ability.

Test length appears to affect persons of differing abilities in unique ways. Depending on the interaction of item order, anxiety and ability, some individuals seem to improve towards the end of the test, and others decline, at least up until a certain point when the trend reverses. In such a situation, there should be a test length where performance stabilizes regardless of ability level. Unfortunately, it is the goal of most testing programs to decrease test length, regardless of the needs of the examinee. In order to maximize measured performance, test length could be individually tailored to the testing situation and to unique characteristics of the test taker.

This study demonstrated that the understanding of test performance can be enhanced by knowledge of personality factors and test characteristics. These results may be used by some to prove the nonutility of IRT-based operations such as adaptive testing procedures. However, the findings could also be interpreted as demonstrating that particular individuals are better suited to unique test formats. Individual differences should be taken into consideration, and difficulty order and test length included as test variables. The appropriate manipulation of these variables within an adaptive testing situation will then maximize measured performance for all persons.

REFERENCES

Anastasi, A. (1982). *Psychological testing*. New York: MacMillan.
Birnbaum, M. (1986). Effect of dissimulation motivation and anxiety on re-

sponse pattern appropriateness measures. *Applied Psychological Measurement, 10* (2), 167–174.

Bowker, R. (1981). *English vocabulary manual*. Chicago: Johnson O'Connor Research Foundation.

Child, I.L. (1954). Personality. *Annual Review of Psychology, 5,* 149–171.

Doris, J., & Sarason, S. (1955). Test anxiety and blame assignment in a failure situation. *Journal of Abnormal and Social Psychology, 50,* 335–338.

Farber, I., & Spence, K. (1953). Complex learning and conditioning as a function of anxiety. *Journal of Experimental Psychology, 45,* 120–125.

Galassi, J.P., Frierson, H.T., & Sharer, R. (1981). Behavior of high, moderate and low test anxious students during an actual test situation. *Journal of Consulting and Clinical Psychology, 51,* 51–62.

Gershon, R. (1989, April). *Test anxiety and item order: New parameters for item response theory.* Paper presented at the annual meeting of the American Educational Research Association Annual Meeting in San Francisco and at The Fifth International Objective Measurement Workshop in Berkeley, CA. (ERIC Document Reproduction Service No. TM013441).

Gershon, R. (1988). *Index of words in the Johnson O'Connor Research Foundation, Inc. vocabulary item bank* (Tech. Rep. 1988–3). New York: Johnson O'Connor Research Foundation—Human Engineering Laboratory.

Hutt, M.L. (1947). A Clinical study of "consecutive" and "adaptive" testing with the revised Stanford-Binet. *Journal of Consulting Psychology, 11,* 93–103.

Mandler, G., & Sarason, S.B. (1952). A study of anxiety and learning. *Journal of Abnormal and Social Psychology, 47,* 166–173.

Meunier, C., & Rule, B.G. (1969). Anxiety, confidence and conformity. *Journal of Personality, 35,* 498–504.

Nicholls, J.G. (1984). Achievement motivation: Conceptions of ability, subjective experience, task choice, and performance. *Psychological Review, 91,* 328.

Rasch, G. (1966). An item analysis which takes individual differences into account. *British Journal of Mathematical and Statistical Psychology, 19,* 49–57.

Sarason, I.G. (1958). The effects of anxiety, reassurance, and meaningfulness of material to be learned in verbal learning. *Journal of Experimental Psychology, 56,* 472–477.

Sarason, I.G. (1960). Empirical findings and theoretical problems in the use of anxiety scales. *Psychological Bulletin, 57,* 403–415.

Sarason, I.G., & Palola, E.G. (1960). The relationship of test and general anxiety, difficulty of task, and experimental instructions to performance. *Journal of Experimental Psychology, 59,* 185–191.

Sarason, S.B., & Stoops, R. (1978). Test anxiety and the passage of time. *Journal of Consulting and Clinical Psychology, 46,* 102–109.

Schmitt, A.P., & Crocker, L. (1984). *The relationship between test anxiety and person fit measures.* Paper presented at the annual meeting of the American Educational Research Association, New Orleans, LA.

Trapp, E., & Kausler, D. (1958). Test anxiety and goal setting behavior. *Journal of Consulting Psychology, 22,* 31-34.

Wilkinson, L. (1988). *SYSTAT: The system for statistics.* Evanston, IL: SYS-TAT, Inc.

Wine, J. (1971). Test anxiety and direction of attention. *Psychological Bulletin, 76,* 92–104.

Wright, B.D., Rossner, M., & Congdon, R. (1985). *MSCALE.* Chicago: Statistical Laboratory, Department of Education, University of Chicago, IL.

Wright, B.D., & Stone, M.H. (1979). *Best test design.* Chicago: MESA Press.

chapter **12**

Objective Measurement of Rank-Ordered Objects

John M. Linacre
Department of Education
University of Chicago

THE UTILITY OF RANK ORDERING

"Examiners who are asked to place answer books in rank order, or order of merit, are asked to do a task which is far simpler for human judgment than is the assigning of absolute marks" (Harper & Misra, 1976, p. 255). The use of judge rankings of the performance of examinees on each test item, instead of judged scores or ratings, frees test analysis from the effects of variations in the severities of the judges, the difficulties of the test items, and the arbitrary definition and idiosyncratic utilization characteristic of rating scales.

Ranking, however, would also appear to remove the foundational component identified by Rasch for measurement models in psychology: "The possible behavior of a pupil is described by means of a probability that he solves the task" (Rasch, 1960, p. 11). A ranking of examinees contains no indication of what level of success the examinees attained on the particular item on which they were judged. It does, however, contain information about their relative success.

It has been observed that judges differ considerably in the rankings they assign: "The [examinee's performance with] the highest degree of agreement still covered nearly one-third of the range of ranks, while the average [range of ranking a performance] included nearly two-thirds of the available ranks" (Harper & Misra, 1976, p. 14). Thurstone perceived that "it is possible to use the proportion of readers or judges who agree about the rank order of any two statements as a basis for actual measurement" (Thurstone & Chave, 1929, p. 18). Indeed, it is the variation in orderings across judges which provides the stochastic element necessary for Rasch measurement.

Consider the situation in which a number of independent judges have each compiled a rank ordering of two or more objects, such as examinees, teams, models of car, or attributes of a good vacation spot. These rank orderings are compiled by each judge based on that judge's perception of the relative standing of each of the objects on a variable, such as writing ability, or on a given item representing the variable, such as the quality of an essay.

Independence of the judges requires that there be no consultation between them about the objects to be ranked while they compile their rankings. Before the ranking begins, judges do need instruction about the ranking process and some general guidance on issues relating to the item or variable that is to form the basis for the ranking, but, once they start compiling their rankings, each judge must act independently as though he were the only judge.

The conceptual basis and intention of the ranking can be thought of in broad terms as a latent variable such as musical ability, or more precisely as the response to a particular test item or task, such as the quality of performance of a Chopin Etude. When the intention is to rank examinees on the latent variable, rather than just on some single item bearing on it, there are usually a number of similar items which can be considered functionally identical in terms of their representation of that latent variable, so that one of these items is just as useful as another as a basis for ranking. Then rankings based on any one such functionally identical item are directly comparable with rankings based on any other such item, even though the items themselves may represent different levels of challenge. For example, if the latent variable is "performing skill," the rankings compiled by one group of judges, who independently rate examinees on their performance of one Etude, can be combined with the rankings compiled by another group of judges, who independently rate the same examinees on their performance of another Etude, perhaps requiring a different level of skill.

Every judge need not rank every object. All that is required is that there be sufficient overlap in the objects ranked, across the rankings, to allow one joint ranking to be constructed unambiguously. Indeterminate situations are those in which the judges in one panel rank only the boys while the judges in another panel rank only the girls. It is then not possible to compare the relative standings of the boys with the girls. Apart from such general considerations, the overlap between rankings can be arranged to meet the exigencies of the judging situation and the convenience of the judges. Thus supervisors need only rank those trainees of whom they have knowledge, provided that in each supervisor's ranking are included some trainees who are also ranked by other supervisors, and that these supervisor-trainee connections form a complete network. Obviously the more supervisors rank a trainee, the more precise the resulting measures will be. Exact judging plans, such as balanced incomplete block designs, are unnecessary.

THE MEASUREMENT MODEL
FOR PAIRED OBJECTS

A record of the relative performance of two objects, O_m and O_n, (e.g., examinees) across numerous replications of a given item (e.g., a spelling test) representing a variable (e.g., spelling ability) would contain counts of the three possible outcomes:

1. F_{mn}, the count of successes when O_m outperforms O_n.
2. F_{nm}, the count of successes when O_n outperforms O_m.
3. T_{mn}, the count of ties when O_m and O_n are observed to perform at the same level.

The possibility of tied rankings raises the issue of the usefulness of identical outcomes to measurement. In Rasch's comparison of two items based on the performance of one person (Rasch, 1960, p. 171), the relative difficulty of the items is determined solely by consideration of the probabilities of those instances in which the person succeeds on one item and fails on the other. Instances of identical outcomes, in which the person either succeeds or fails on both items, do not compare the difficulty of the two items. In the extreme, if a person always succeeds on both items, the conclusion is that the person performs at a higher level than the difficulty level of either item, but no conclusion at all can be drawn about the relative difficulty of the two items. From this argument, it would appear that tied rankings are not informative for making a comparison between two ranked objects, and that the relative measures of two ranked objects can be estimated only from a comparison of their different relative rankings, F_{mn}/F_{nm}.

Tied rankings, however, are qualitatively different from identical outcomes in Rasch's two item test. Tied rankings are not a manifestation of an infinite range of relative performance, but rather represent performance at levels that are so similar that the judge cannot discriminate between them. If every judge were to award tied rankings to two objects, the conclusion would be that the two objects perform at statistically equivalent levels, not that their relative performance might fall anywhere within an infinite range.

If the two objects, O_m and O_n, are observed to perform at the same level, then, from the judge's viewpoint, the credit to be given to O_m for outperforming O_n is the same as the credit to be given to O_n for outperforming O_m. Thus, since credit is being determined by counting successes, a tie is equivalent to increasing the success counts for both objects, F_{mn} and F_{nm}, by 0.5. Alternatively, tied rankings may be conceptualized as two rankings, each given half weight, in one of which O_m outperforms O_n, and in the other of which the reverse occurs. In any case, the count for tied performances is combined with the counts of successes with the resulting comparison of the performance levels of the two objects becoming $[F_{mn} + (T_{mn}/2)]/[F_{nm} + (T_{mn}/2)]$. This ratio becomes P_{mn}/P_{nm}, in the stochastic limit, where P_{mn} is the probability that O_m outperforms O_n and P_{nm} is similarly defined.

We must choose some convenient reference object O_0, whose performance level can be used to locate a local origin for the measurement scale. The comparison of the performance of O_m with O_0 is, in the limit, P_{m0}/P_{0m}, and similarly the comparison of O_n with O_0 is P_{n0}/P_{0n}. Rasch states:

> If a relationship between two or more variables is to be considered really important, as more than an *ad hoc* description of a very limited set of data—if a more or less general interdependence may be considered in force—the relationship should be found in several sets of data which differ materially in some relevant respects. (Rasch, 1960, p. 9)

In our case, this implies that the results of a direct comparison of O_m and O_n lead to the same conclusion as a comparison of O_m with O_n via O_0. This requirement for generalizability can be modeled as

$$P_{mn}/P_{nm} = (P_{m0}/P_{0m}) / (P_{n0}/P_{0n}) \tag{1}$$

but P_{m0}/P_{0m} is the performance of O_m relative to a measure set at the origin of the scale, and so is a constant, A_m. Similarly P_{n0}/P_{0n} is a constant, A_n. Then,

$$P_{mn}/P_{nm} = A_m/A_n \tag{2}$$

which is a multiplicative measurement model for paired objects. Taking logarithms and reparameterizing gives an additive measurement model:

$$\log(P_{mn}/P_{nm}) = B_m - B_n \qquad (3)$$

where

P_{mn} is the probability that object O_m outperforms object O_n,
P_{nm} is the probability that object O_n outperforms object O_m,
B_m is the measure of object O_m in logits (log-odds units),
B_n is the measure of object O_n.

The relevant statistic for estimating $(B_m - B_n)$ is $[F_{mn} + (T_{mn}/2)]/[F_{nm} + (T_{mn}/2)]$.

If the objects were examinees and the item of measurement a spelling item, then B_m would be a measure of the spelling ability of examinee O_m. In some psychometric models, B_m is required to be sampled randomly from a population of standard or known distribution, in which case the unsubscripted parameter θ may be employed. For this model, however, no distributional requirements need be imposed on the parameters. Indeed it is exactly the object parameter estimates which are of interest. Accordingly, this model is similar to Thurstone's Law of Comparative Judgment, Case V (Thurstone 1927), though with a different method of scaling.

This measurement model is independent of the severity of the judges who are compiling the orderings and also of the difficulty of whatever item or task is the basis of the comparison. Consequently, these facets need not and, in fact, cannot be parameterized in this measurement model. Nevertheless, fit statistics can be constructed not only for each object, indicating the extent of agreement as to its performance across the orderings, but also for each judge's ordering, indicating the extent to which it is in accord with a consensus of all the orderings.

EXTENDING THE MODEL TO RANKINGS

If a ranking is of only two objects, then the measurement model for paired objects applies directly. Thus the probability, R_{mn}, of observing object O_m ranked higher than object O_n is given by

$$R_{mn} = P_{mn} / (P_{mn} + P_{nm}) \qquad (4)$$

where the denominator contains $2! = 2$ terms, comprising all possible valid numerators for ordering two objects.

The ranking of three objects, O_m, O_n, O_c, can be regarded as a set of three paired rankings, but with the transitivity constraint that if O_m is

Table 12.1.   Probabilities of All Possible Paired Comparisons of Three Objects

Probability of Independent Pairing	Representation as Rank Order
$P_{mn}P_{mc}P_{nc}$	$R(O_m,O_n,O_c)$
$P_{mn}P_{mc}P_{cn}$	$R(O_m,O_c,O_n)$
$P_{mn}P_{cm}P_{cn}$	$R(O_c,O_m,O_n)$
$P_{nm}P_{mc}P_{nc}$	$R(O_n,O_m,O_c)$
$P_{nm}P_{cm}P_{nc}$	$R(O_n,O_c,O_m)$
$P_{nm}P_{cm}P_{cn}$	$R(O_c,O_n,O_m)$
$P_{mn}P_{cm}P_{nc}$	inconsistent
$P_{nm}P_{mc}P_{cn}$	inconsistent

Note: The contents of R( ) represent the ordering of the objects.

ranked higher than O_n, and O_n is ranked higher than O_c, then O_m must be ranked higher than O_c. The probabilities of their eight conceivable paired relationships are shown in Table 12.1.

The effect of the constraint imposed on the pairings by ranking is that two of the eight conceivable paired combinations of three objects are inconsistent and cannot be observed. Apart from this constraint, the probability of observing any particular rank ordering is required to depend only on the paired comparison of the objects, in response to the provocation of a particular item, and not to involve any other characteristics of the sample of objects or of the judges compiling the rankings. This is equivalent to the "local independence" axiom of other Rasch models. Thus the comparison of the objects manifested in the ranking is asymptotically "judge-free." Moreover, when orderings are produced for the objects on a number of different items, such as spelling questions, all of which are realizations of the same underlying variable, then this measurement model is also asymptotically "test-free." Since, for any observed set of rankings, local independence is never completely realized, the practical validity of the measures obtained by means of the measurement model must be verified through examination of the fit of the rankings to the model.

Considering the possible rankings of three objects, and using R_{mnc} to denote the probability of observing the ranking $R(O_m,O_n,O_c)$, in which Om is ranked higher than On and On is ranked higher than Oc, and referring to Table 12.1,

$$R_{mnc} = \frac{P_{mn}P_{mc}P_{nc}}{1 - P_{mn}P_{cm}P_{nc} - P_{nm}P_{mc}P_{cn}} \tag{5}$$

where

$$1 - P_{mn}P_{cm}P_{nc} - P_{nm}P_{mc}P_{cn} = P_{mn}P_{mc}P_{nc} + P_{mn}P_{mc}P_{cn}$$
$$+ P_{mn}P_{cm}P_{cn} + P_{nm}P_{mc}P_{nc}$$
$$+ P_{nm}P_{cm}P_{nc} + P_{nm}P_{cm}P_{cn} \qquad (6)$$

When the objects are numbered, O_1, O_2, O_3, then the probability R_r of any particular rank ordering of the three objects, labeled r, is

$$R_r = \frac{\prod\limits_{j=1}^{2} \prod\limits_{k=j+1}^{3} (X_{rjk}P_{rjk} + X_{rkj}P_{rkj})}{\sum\limits_{s=1}^{3!} Q_s} \qquad (7)$$

where

R_r is the probability of a particular ranking, r, of the 3 objects,
X_{rjk} = 1 if O_j is ranked higher than O_k in rank ordering r,
    = 0 otherwise.
X_{rkj} = $1 - X_{rjk}$, so that, if O_j is ranked higher than O_k, $(X_{rjk}P_{rjk} + X_{rkj}P_{rkj})$ = P_{rjk}, but if O_j is ranked lower, $(X_{rjk}P_{rjk} + X_{rkj}P_{rkj})$ = P_{rkj}.
$\sum\limits_{s=1}^{3!} Q_s$ is the normalizing sum of numerators corresponding to all possible rank orderings of the three objects. It contains one term for every permutation of 3 objects, that is, 3! = 6 terms, one of which is Q_r, the numerator of this equation.

INDEPENDENT RANK ORDERINGS OF n OBJECTS

For convenience of generalization, let us number the objects O_1, O_2, . . . , O_n and their corresponding parameters B_1, B_2, . . , B_n. Then, for any particular rank ordering of the n objects, R_r, equation (7) generalizes to

$$R_r = \frac{\prod\limits_{j=1}^{n-1} \prod\limits_{k=j+1}^{n} (X_{rjk}P_{rjk} + X_{rkj}P_{rkj})}{\sum\limits_{s=1}^{n!} Q_s} \qquad (8)$$

where

R$_r$ is the probability of a particular ranking, r, of the n objects,
X$_{rjk}$ = 1 if O$_j$ is ranked higher than O$_k$ in rank ordering r,
  = 0 otherwise,
X$_{rkj}$ = 1 − X$_{rjk}$,

$\sum\limits_{s=1}^{n!}$ is the normalizing sum of numerators corresponding to all possible rank orderings of the n objects. It contains one term for every permutation of n objects, that is, n! terms.

When T independent rank orderings of the same n objects have been compiled, the likelihood of the data set of T rankings, Λ, is

$$\Lambda = \prod_{r=1}^{T} R_r \tag{9}$$

The log-likelihood of a set of T rank orderings of n objects is, expressing log(Λ) by λ,

$$\lambda = \sum_{r=1}^{T} \log(R_r) \tag{10}$$

ESTIMATION EQUATIONS FOR RANK-ORDERED OBJECTS

The estimation equations for these parameters can be obtained using first and second partial derivatives of the log-likelihood function, equation (10). Thus, to estimate B$_m$, partially differentiate the log-likelihood with respect to B$_m$, giving

$$\frac{\partial \lambda}{\partial B_m} = \left[\sum_{r=1}^{T} \sum_{j=1, \neq m}^{n} X_{rmj} \right] - T\left[\sum_{r=1}^{n!} \sum_{j=1, \neq m}^{n} X_{rmj}R_r \right] \tag{11}$$

The first term in equation (11) represents the observed raw score and is a count of the number of objects higher than which O$_m$ is ranked in all the observed rank orderings. The second term represents the expected score and is the sum, across all possible rank orderings, of the number of objects higher than which O$_m$ is ranked in each rank ordering multiplied by the probability of that rank ordering, all weighted by the number of rank orderings in the observed data.

Differentiating the log-likelihood again with respect to B_m,

$$\frac{\partial^2 \lambda}{\partial B_m^2} = T \left[\sum_{r=1}^{n!} \sum_{j=1, \neq m}^{n} X_{rmj} R_r \right]^2 - T \left[\sum_{r=1}^{n!} \left(\sum_{j=1, \neq m}^{n} X_{rmj} \right)^2 R_r \right] \quad (12)$$

and also with respect to any other parameter, B_a,

$$\frac{\partial^2 \lambda}{\partial B_m B_a} = T \left[\sum_{r=1}^{n!} \sum_{j=1, \neq m}^{n} X_{rmj} R_r \right] \left[\sum_{r=1}^{n!} \sum_{j=1, \neq a}^{n} X_{raj} R_r \right]$$

$$- T \left[\sum_{r=1}^{n!} \left(\sum_{j=1, \neq m}^{n} X_{rmj} \right) \left(\sum_{j=1, \neq a}^{n} X_{raj} \right) R_r \right] \quad (13)$$

provides the terms of the information matrix which can be used to obtain an improved estimate of B_m, the measure corresponding to object O_m.

Maximum likelihood estimates are obtained when the observed and expected rank score for each object coincide, at which point all the partial first derivatives go to zero simultaneously. From these derivatives, asymptotic standard errors as well as standard Rasch model fit statistics can be calculated (Wright & Masters, 1982, p. 100).

For estimability of all parameters in one frame of reference, it is required that the orderings of the objects overlap in such a way that every object can be compared to every other object, either directly or indirectly, in terms of *both* relative successes and relative failures. If, for instance, one object is always ranked highest, then its parameter is inestimable. A more subtle example of inestimability is a set of orderings in which the objects form two groups, the high group and the low group, and no object in the high group is ever ranked below any object in the low group.

If all objects do not participate in every rank ordering, the overall likelihood becomes the product of the likelihood of several homogeneous subgroups, in each of which the same set of objects has been ranked at least once. The log-likelihood for the entire data set is the sum of the log-likelihoods of each subgroup, from which can be derived estimation equations similar to those obtained here. For unique estimates to be obtained, there must be some overlap of objects across subgroups. This facility for analyzing rankings of overlapping subsets of objects greatly aids the application of measurement based on rank ordering, since it is not necessary for every judge to rank every object in order to obtain comparable measures for all objects.

The linear scale of the object measures obtained from rank ordering is a generalization of the rankings but is local to the sample of objects. This scale can be equated with another scale by means of the measures of objects common to the two scales. For instance, if the performances to be ranked are on video tape, a few performances from last year can be ranked with this year's performances in order to establish a common frame of reference across the years.

TIED RANKINGS

In some judging situations, two or more objects may be given the same ranking. The implications of this have been discussed for measurement based on paired comparisons. The same argument applies to orderings containing more than two objects. If two objects O_j and O_k are given the same ranking, then this is equivalent to the statement that, as far as the judge is concerned, orderings (O_j, O_k) and (O_k, O_j) are equally reasonable as representations of the ordering of these two objects on the latent variable. Consequently, if two orderings, one containing (O_j, O_k) and the other (O_k, O_j), but otherwise identical, are each given a weight of one-half, then the sum is equivalent to the tied ordering. Considered in this way, allowing tied rankings does not add any orderings into the scheme of all possible rank orderings. The weighting of one half can be achieved by incorporating the values $X_{jk} = 0.5$ and $X_{kj} = 0.5$ into the computation of the empirical rank scores when O_j and O_k are tied in the ordering.

AN APPLICATION OF THE MODEL FOR RANK-ORDERED OBJECTS

In Polskin (1988), and reproduced in Table 12.2, are rankings of seven baseball announcers on six specific items of broadcasting appeal. For this analysis, the six rankings are considered to be locally independent reflections of the same latent appeal in announcers, so that they can be employed equally to estimate a single set of appeal parameters for the announcers. The requirement for local independence implies that there is no local covariance between pairs of rankings either due to the nature of the items which form the basis of the rankings or to the judges who compiled the rankings. Fit statistics will indicate where this requirement is challenged.

Table 12.2.   Rankings of Baseball Announcers

Calling the Game	Broadcasting Ability	Quality of Anecdotes
1. Vin Scully	1. Vin Scully	1. Vin Scully
2. Bob Costas	2. Al Michaels	2. Bob Costas
3. Al Michaels	3. Bob Costas	3. Al Michaels
4. Skip Caray	4. Skip Caray	4. Skip Caray
5. Harry Caray	5. Harry Caray	5. Ralph Kiner
6. Steve Zabriskie	6. Steve Zabriskie	6. Harry Caray
7. Ralph Kiner	7. Ralph Kiner	7. Steve Zabriskie
Working with Analyst	**Knowledge of baseball**	**Enthusiasm level**
1. Bob Costas	1. Vin Scully	1. Harry Caray
2. Al Michaels	2. Ralph Kiner	2. Al Michaels
3. Vin Scully	3. Bob Costas	3. Bob Costas
4. Skip Caray	4. Al Michaels	4. Vin Scully
5. Steve Zabriskie	5. Harry Caray	5. Steve Zabriskie
6. Ralph Kiner	6. Skip Caray	6. Skip Caray
7. Harry Caray	7. Steve Zabriskie	7. Ralph Kiner

Note: Reproduced from Polskin (1988).
Reprinted with permission from TV Guide® Magazine. Copyright© 1988 by News America Publications Inc., Radnor, PA.

The Rasch rank-order measurement model can be used to answer such questions as "Do the items cooperate to define one latent variable?" "Which announcers have the most consistent level of appeal?" and "How much more appealing is one announcer than another?"

In answer to the question, "How much more appealing is one announcer than another?" Table 12.3 lists the estimates of the measures obtained for this data set using the computer program FRANK (Linacre, 1989). As can be seen by inspection of Figure 12.1, the relationship between the sum of each announcer's ranks and his measure, while necessarily ogival in the extreme, is close to linear here because only the central section of the ogive is manifested in these data.

Consistency of performance can be examined by means of the fit statistics. The expectation of the mean-square statistic is 1.0. The most consistently ranked announcer is Al Michaels with a mean-square fit statistic of 0.34, and the most inconsistently ranked is Ralph Kiner with a fit of 2.12. Polskin, according to the analysis given in the text of his article, had the impression that Harry Caray was the least consistently ranked announcer, due to his first place on "Enthusiasm". This is an indication of how difficult it is to determine overall misfit in rank order listings by eye.

A basic question concerning the success of any measurement opera-

Table 12.3. Appeal of Baseball Announcers

Appeal Order	Sum of Rankings	Logit Measure	S.E.	Mean Square Fit Statistic	Announcer
		MOST			
1	11	0.98	0.41	1.51	Vin Scully
2	14	0.67	0.35	0.40	Bob Costas
3	16	0.50	0.32	0.34	Al Michaels
4	28	−0.26	0.28	0.43	Skip Caray
5	29	−0.33	0.29	1.73	Harry Caray
6	34	−0.69	0.33	2.12	Ralph Kiner
7	36	−0.87	0.37	0.54	Steve Zabriskie
		LEAST			
	Mean:	0.00		1.01	

tion is the extent to which the unidimensionality implied by the latent variable has been realized. Is it reasonable to use these six orderings as though they were independent manifestations of one latent variable? Table 12.4 summarizes the degree of fit within each ordering. The fit statistics indicate the extent to which these items are acting in a coherent manner to define a single variable. The low values of the fit statistics for "Calling the game" and "Broadcasting ability" indicate a redundancy in these data which suggests that these two items are used more synonymously and hence less independently than the other items. "Enthusiasm" displays the most misfit and may, in fact, invoke a different dimension. According to Polskin, this could be because it is easier to announce for "home-team fans" as Harry Caray does.

Since an ordering provides no information about the relative difficulty of the items used as a basis of the ordering, it is not possible from these data to determine how difficult it is to, say "call the game."

Table 12.4. Fit Statistics for Items as Disclosed by the Rank Orders

Mean Square Fit Statistic	Name of Ordering Item
LEAST DISORDERED	
0.32	Calling the game
0.39	Broadcasting ability
0.41	Quality of anecdotes
0.91	Working with analyst
1.80	Knowledge of baseball
2.22	Enthusiasm level
MOST DISORDERED	

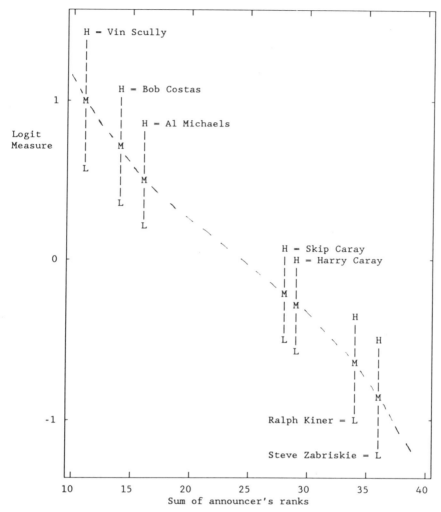

Figure 12.1. Announcers' measures plotted against sum of rankings. (M = estimated measure of the announcer, H = M + standard error, L = M − standard error.)

Consequently, no difficulty calibrations for the items are shown. Similarly, were the rankings produced by individual judges, there would be no means to determine the relative severity of those judges.

Table 12.5 shows the particular observed ranks which were the least expected. For each announcer on each item, his observed rank is compared with his expected rank. The numerical difference is divided by

Table 12.5. Most Unexpected Rankings of Announcers

Ordering	Announcer	Rank	Expected	Difference	S.E.	Z-Score
		Ranked unexpectedly high:				
Knowledge	Ralph Kiner	2	5.7	3.67	1.23	2.97
Enthusiasm	Harry Caray	1	4.8	3.83	1.42	2.71
Working	Bob Costas	1	2.3	1.33	1.18	1.13
		Ranked unexpectedly low:				
Enthusiasm	Vin Scully	4	1.8	−2.17	0.99	−2.19
Working	Harry Caray	7	4.8	−2.17	1.42	−1.53
Working	Vin Scully	3	1.8	−1.17	0.99	−1.18
Mean for all ranks:				0.0		0.00
Variance for all ranks:						1.00

the estimated standard error of the observed rank given the expected rank. This yields a diagnostic fit statistic, a Z-score, which approximates a unit normal distribution asymptotically. The identification of the most unexpected rankings, in Table 12.5, aids the discovery and diagnosis of aberrations in the measuring process. This is a potentially productive feature which Polskin's analysis apparently lacked, since he failed to comment on the most unexpected ranking, that of Ralph Kiner on "Knowledge."

CONCLUSION

The application of the principles of objective measurement to rank ordered data has provided a means to convert rankings into linear measures of latent abilities. Moreover, fit statistics for each object and for each ordering enable a determination of the success of the ranking process as a basis for the construction of measurement.

REFERENCES

Harper, A.E., Jr., & Misra, V.S. (1976). *Research on examinations in India.* New Delhi, India: National Council of Educational Research and Training, New Delhi.

Linacre, J.M. (1989). *FRANK Rasch analysis computer program for rank-ordered data.* Chicago: MESA Press.

Polskin, H. (1988, July 30). The best sportscasters in baseball. *TV Guide,* pp. 31–35.

Rasch, G. (1960). *Probabilistic models for some intelligence and attainment tests*. Copenhagen: Danmarks Paedogogiske Institut. (Reprinted by University of Chicago Press, 1980)

Thurstone, L.L. (1927). A law of comparative judgment. *Psychological Review, 3*, 273–286.

Thurstone, L.L., & Chave, E.J. (1929). *The measurement of attitude.* Chicago: University of Chicago Press.

Wright, B.D., & Masters, G.N. (1982). *Rating scale analysis: Rasch measurement.* Chicago: MESA Press.

chapter 13

Conjunctive Measurement Theory: Cognitive Research Prospects*

Robert J. Jannarone
University of South Carolina

INTRODUCTION

Scope. Cognitive theories have shown an increasing complexity trend throughout their history. Notable examples are the early trend from single to multiple ability traits (Guilford, 1967; Spearman, 1904; Thurstone, 1938), the analysis of analogical reasoning tasks into component subtasks (Embretson, 1984; Sternberg, 1977); and recent new advances in test design (Embretson, 1985). In reaction to this trend in *cognitive* theory, *psychometric* theorists have proposed increasingly detailed test models. Notable examples include the advent of multiple factor analysis (Jöreskog, 1978; Thurstone, 1932); and multivariate item response theory (Andersen, 1980; Embretson, 1985; Fischer, 1973). Cognitive and psychometric theories have thus shown increasing trends in generality, resulting in increased mutual alignment.

---

* Approved for public release; distribution unlimited. Reproduction in whole or in part is permitted for any purpose of the United States Government. This research was sponsored by Personnel and Training Research Programs, Psychological Sciences Division, Office of Naval Research Contract No. N00014-86-K00817, Authority Identification Number, NR 4421-544. This is an abridged version of a detailed report, which is available from the author upon request.

The recent development of conjunctive item response theory (Jannarone, 1986, 1987, 1989; Jannarone, Yu, & Laughlin, forthcoming) suggests new areas for psychometric model expansion. The conjunctive modeling development has partly been in reaction to the componential analogical reasoning movement—both involve component abilities that are individually necessary for solving a composite task, hence *conjunctively* related. Conjunctive measurement theory has not yet influenced cognitive modeling, however, because it is rather new and has so far only been presented in mathematical form. Yet the structures that conjunctive measurement reflects are both closely related to modern cognitive work and clearly distinct from more traditional psychometric structures. Some interesting related prospects for cognitive research thus seem to be emerging.

This report is an attempt to describe conjunctive test theory, to contrast it with other test theories, and to encourage related psychometric and cognitive future developments. As will be shown with a variety of examples, conjunctive measurement has the potential for uncovering conjunctive cognitive structures; measuring different problem-solving styles; measuring person's abilities to learn information at one point and successfully apply it at a later point; evaluating persons' uses of alternative learning styles; and providing realistic models for computer-aided instruction settings.

Several distinctions between conjunctive and traditional test items will also be described. The most theoretically important distinction is that conjunctive measurement allows persons to change as a part of the measurement process. As a result conjunctive measurement permits traits such as learning styles to be measured, but it also marks a basic (axiomatic) departure from traditional test theory.

Purpose. One goal of this report is to describe the major distinctions between conjunctive and traditional measurement theories. A second goal is to show how conjunctive measurement can be useful, by describing its key features within ability assessment settings.

In the following sections I first give some examples of conjunctive ability settings, structural models, and procedural guidelines. I follow with some theoretical perspectives and finish with some future directions for psychometric and cognitive research.

CONJUNCTIVE MEASUREMENT OVERVIEW

Some examples. I give three examples next—one involving two component abilities that have conjunctive effects on a composite abili-

```
Total Item              ┌─────────────────────────────────────────
                        │ Fist:Clench::Teeth:_____
                        │
                        │ 1) Pull  2) Brush  3) Grit  4) Gnaw  5) Jaw
                        └


Rule Construction       ┌─────────────────────────────────────────
                        │ Fist:Clench::Teeth:_____ __
         Subtask        │
                        │ Rule:_____
                        └


Response Evaluation     ┌─────────────────────────────────────────
                        │ Fist:Clench::Teeth:_____
         Subtask        │
                        │ Rule:  Angry reaction done with "teeth"
                        │
                        │ 1) Pull  2) Brush  3) Grit  4) Gnaw  5) Jaw
                        │
                        │ Circle answer that best fulfills the given rule
                        └
```

Figure 13.1.   Information component subtasks for verbal analogies.

ty; one based on a chain of items that are linked by sequential learning effects; and one involving replicated tests that have conjunctively linked pretest and posttest items. For now, the common elements to look for in these examples are that (a) each involves component items that are linked together by underlying cognitive tasks, (b) each measures individual differences in item linkages, and (c) each leads to measures of item linkages that are nonadditive functions of item cross-product scores, rather than additive functions of item scores.

The first example involves measuring component abilities and evaluating their joint effects on analogical reasoning. Figure 13.1 contains three items that are designed to reflect analogical reasoning abilities (kindly provided by Susan Embretson—see Embretson (Whitely), 1984). Such items are presented to subjects in triplets like that in Figure 13.1. The Total Item represents overall analogical reasoning ability, whereas the Rule Construction and the Response Evaluation items represent two component subtest abilities. Tests made up of such item triplets have been studied in the past (Embretson (Whitely), 1984; Pellegrino & Glaser, 1979; Pellegrino, Mumaw, & Shute, 1985; Sternberg, 1977) to show how subtask skills are used in solving analogies. I focus on how persons' responses might indicate whether (a) both subtask skills are necessary for passing a Total Item; or (b) only one of the subtask skills may be sufficient for passing the Total Item.

Suppose that scores were available from a group of persons who were tested on N such item triplets. Traditional test construction methods would suggest that three subscales be formed, each being based on n out of the $3n$ items. In their simplest form the subscales would combine their item scores additively and equally, yielding,

$$s^{(C)} = \sum_{n=1}^{N} x_n^{(C)}, \, s^{(E)} = \sum_{n=1}^{N} x_n^{(E)}, \, s^{(T)} = \sum_{n=1}^{N} x_n^{(T)}, \tag{1}$$

where the three sums indicate the number of correct Rule Construction (R), Response Evaluation (E), and Total (T) items, respectively. (The items are meant to be coded in the usual binary way, *i.e.*, $x_n^{(C)}$, $x_n^{(E)}$, $x_n^{(T)} = 1$ for PASS, 0 for FAIL.)

The traditional additive scoring formulas shown in (1) could be useful, up to a point. The relative additive impacts of each subtask ability on total ability could be evaluated separately as well as stepwise. The effects of the three subscales on external criteria could also be assessed by using standard factor analysis and regression methods.

Some interesting response pattern differences could not be reflected by additive subscales, however. For example two viable strategies could exist for passing a Total Item. One strategy might require that both the Rule Construction skill and the Response Evaluation skill be available for passing each Total Item. However, the other strategy might require only one of the subtask skills, perhaps along with other unmeasured skills. Suppose that 18 item triplets were presented to a group of people and that a subgroup responded correctly to exactly 6 items of each type. Thus, each person in the subgroup would earn number-correct scores of 6, 6, and 6 out of 18 $s^{(C)}$, $s^{(E)}$, and $s^{(T)}$ items, respectively. Any analysis based only on those scores alone could not distinguish the responses among any persons in the subgroup. Yet, different subsample members might use different strategies consistently in ways that were measurably distinct. In the extreme, the scores on each item triplet for some persons would be 1 if and only if their Total Item score on the triplet were 1. Such response patterns would clearly indicate the use of a strategy that required *both* subtask skills. For other persons, passing Total items would always coincide with passing only one of the two subtask items, indicating another strategy.

These kinds of distinct strategies could not be reflected by additive scales, but could be represented by nonadditive subscales of the form,

$$s^{(CE)} = \sum_{n=1}^{N} x_n^{(C)} x_n^{(E)}. \tag{2}$$

For example, in the subsample of persons who had additive scores of 6, 6, and 6 on the 18-item test, those requiring both subtasks would have $s^{(CE)}$ values of 6. By contrast, those requiring only one subskill would have lower $s^{(CE)}$ values. Formal logic can also be used to contrast different types of measurement in such cases. In logical terms, distinct strategies would be reflected by distinct *conjuncts* among the component item events (PASS = TRUE, FAIL = FALSE). For example, those having many TRUE values for three-way conjuncts among item triplets would reflect one strategy; whereas those having few TRUE values would reflect another. This is my basis for referring to the models based on expressions like (2) and on similar measures as *conjunctive*.

More complex subscales could be used that were based on all possible conjuncts among the three subscale items, for example by going beyond item triplet boundaries. However, these would be difficult to deal with, both statistically and conceptually. Similar concerns hold for the two examples to follow.

The second example is a test made up of items that are linked into a chain by adjacent interitem dependencies. The first three items in one such chain are given in Figure 13.2. (The key words for these items were kindly suggested by Chris McCormick and Gloria Miller—see McCormick & Miller, 1986.) Item 1 tests for word comprehension in the usual way by first introducing a word (PADLE) and then testing whether or not the word's meaning was correctly learned. Item 2 is unusual, however, because passing it requires that both among two words be learned—one word (KAVA) that is introduced in Item 2, but another word (PADLE) that is introduced in Item 1. Likewise, Item 3 tests whether or not both the word introduced in Item 2 and the word introduced in Item 3 are learned. Other items in the test similarly evaluate whether both the word from an item and the word from the immediately preceding item are learned. The resulting structure of such a test is a chain made up of adjacent items that are linked together semantically.

The dependencies among items for such a test link adjacent items so that persons' abilities to *effectively learn* may be measured. By effective learning, I mean learning something new as well as successfully applying it later. Measuring effective learning ability would be potentially useful in selecting training programs, studying learning skills, and diagnosing learning impairments.

The most direct way to solve the items in Figure 13.2 would be to learn both the meaning of the new concept for one item and the concept from the preceding item. The most direct way to measure this item-solving style, in turn, would be to evaluate the following *adjacent cross-product* score for an M-item test:

1. PADLE

For gardening, the most common earth-moving tasks are digging, smoothing, breaking clods, and furrowing. Therefore, a gardener's tools should include a shovel, a rake and a padle.

What is a padle?

    (a) a spade

    (b) a pickaxe

    (c) a hoe

    (d) a mower

2. PADLE ∩ KAVA

The term 'root beer' may be misleading, unless the beverage happens to be made from kava.

How can a padle be instrumental to having a good time?

    (a) through distilling kava

    (b) through harvesting kava

    (c) through transporting kava

    (d) through weaving kava

3. KAVA ∩ CANGUE

In medieval Asia, using a cangue on a prisoner would often result in a quick confession, unless perhaps the guards had provided him with kava.

How could the kava intervene?

    (a) by poisoning the prisoner

    (b) by arming the prisoner

    (c) by intoxicating the prisoner

    (d) by befriending the prisoner

4. CANGUE ∩ ____

.
.
.

Figure 13.2.   Three possible linked learning items.

$$s^{(d)} = \sum_{m=1}^{M-1} x_m x_{m+1}. \tag{3}$$

As in the previous example, alternative item passing styles might also be possible. For example some people might tend to learn the correct word meaning for an item only after having thought about its usage in the next item. In that case more items might be passed than the value of d in (3) might indicate. Also as in the previous example, useful information could be obtained by only using the additive alternatives to (3), such as persons' usual number-correct scores,

$$s^{(g)} = \sum_{m=1}^{M} x_m. \tag{4}$$

Table 13.1. Contingencies among Test Score Patterns Yielding Distinct Joint and Marginal g,d Values ($M = 15$)*

	d															Marginal g Frequencies
g	0	1	2	3	4	5	6	7	8	9	10	11	12	13	14	
0	1	0	0	0	0	0	0	0	0	0	0	0	0	0	0	1
1	15	0	0	0	0	0	0	0	0	0	0	0	0	0	0	15
2	91	14	0	0	0	0	0	0	0	0	0	0	0	0	0	105
3	286	156	13	0	0	0	0	0	0	0	0	0	0	0	0	455
4	495	660	198	12	0	0	0	0	0	0	0	0	0	0	0	1365
5	462	1320	990	220	11	0	0	0	0	0	0	0	0	0	0	3003
6	210	1260	2100	1200	225	10	0	0	0	0	0	0	0	0	0	5005
7	36	504	1890	2520	1260	216	9	0	0	0	0	0	0	0	0	6435
8	1	56	588	1960	2450	1176	196	8	0	0	0	0	0	0	0	6435
9	0	0	28	392	1470	1960	980	168	7	0	0	0	0	0	0	5005
10	0	0	0	0	126	756	1260	720	135	6	0	0	0	0	0	3003
11	0	0	0	0	0	0	210	600	450	100	5	0	0	0	0	1365
12	0	0	0	0	0	0	0	0	165	220	66	4	0	0	0	455
13	0	0	0	0	0	0	0	0	0	0	66	36	3	0	0	105
14	0	0	0	0	0	0	0	0	0	0	0	0	13	2	0	15
15	0	0	0	0	0	0	0	0	0	0	0	0	0	0	1	1
Marginal d Frequencies	1597	3970	5807	6304	5542	4118	2655	1496	757	326	137	40	16	2	1	Total 32,768

*Each entry is the number of distinct test patterns from a 15-item test that could yield the indicated joint and marginal g and d values.

For example, additive scores would provide the best single measures of overall test performance.

A key issue for conjunctive modeling is the extent that nonadditive scoring adds information to traditional additive scoring. Table 13.1 illustrates the extra potential for nonadditive information in the item chain learning case. The row margins in Table 13.1 give the number of test patterns that could lead to number-correct scores from 0 to 15 on a 15-item test. (They also give the expected number of persons out of 32,768 who would get different g values if all such patterns were equally likely.) Each row in Table 13.1 breaks down its g contingency into possible $(s^{(g)}, s^{(d)})$ contingencies. For example, if g were 6 then d could have possible values between 0 and 5, as indicated by the corresponding row in the table.

The potential for added information shown in Table 13.1 is similar to that for cross-product scores from the previous analogy example. Suppose that possible associations were of interest between some external measure and performance on a test having this kind of item chain structure. An analysis based on g alone from a 15-item test would allow 16 groups of people to be compared on the external measure. Including d in the analysis as well, however, could lead to a much finer breakdown. For example, among the subgroup having g values of 6, five smaller subgroups could be compared on the external criterion, and so on for the other possible g values. Using d along with g could also be substantively interesting, insofar as different d values might reflect distinct strategies and skills.

Tests having serially dependent item structures can reflect other traits that traditional models cannot. These include (a) settings where some persons may have positive learning transfer (for example, learning on one item that improves the likelihood of passing later items) but others may have negative learning transfer; (b) cases where students perform worse after some training than they did at the outset—for example when people knew inferior techniques prior to training; and (c) cases where clearly brighter persons perform worse than less bright persons, because they "think themselves into a jam"—for example, from being distracted by some incorrect item choices. The power of conjunctive models for reflecting such traits is illustrated in Figure 13.3. The figure contains passing probabilities as functions of ability for one item from a test that follows a certain item chain structure (Jannarone, 1987). Three probability functions for the item are shown: one that is conditional on the previous item having been failed, one that is conditional on the previous item having been passed, and the third that is unconditional. The two conditional graphs show that for all ability levels the probability of passing item 5 is always higher if

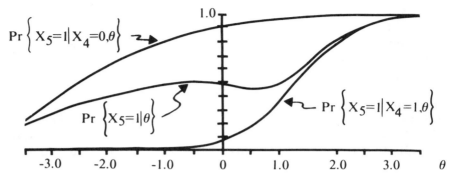

Figure 13.3. Response probabilities for one item, given a particular univariate Rasch Markov model.

item 4 was passed than if it was failed. The two conditional graphs thus indicate positive transfer for all persons, reflecting a trait like that suggested in (a) above. The unconditional graph indicates that along part of the ability range the probability of passing the item *goes down* as ability increases. It thus permits traits to impact upon items as in (b) and (c).

This conjunctive modeling potential for reflecting traits like (a) through (c) is notable because no traditional test models have the same potential (but see Wilson, 1989, for a recent related development). By contrast, traditional models require performance to be an increasing function of ability, thus ruling out settings like (b) and (c). They also require that persons' item passing probabilities be independent of their other item scores. This rules out the possibility for reflecting learning transfer effects as in (a).

The third example concerns settings where the same test or test battery is given on different occasions. Figure 13.4 shows some possible responses from a battery of 10 subtests taken on two different dates (pretest and posttest). Each of the five graphs in Figure 13.4 is a possible scatterplot *for a given person,* with that person's 10 pretest, posttest scores each marked by an "x" in the graph. The five graphs are similar in that they share the same 10 pretest scores. Also, all five of the graphs show the same average improvement of the 10 posttest scores over the 10 pretest scores. The five graphs differ, however, in the ways that the pretest and posttest scores are correlated. The Figure 13.4c graph shows a person whose posttest scores and pretest scores are uncorrelated. The other four graphs show persons having pretest and posttest scores that are correlated, but in different ways.

The graphs in Figure 13.4 might indicate different strategies that

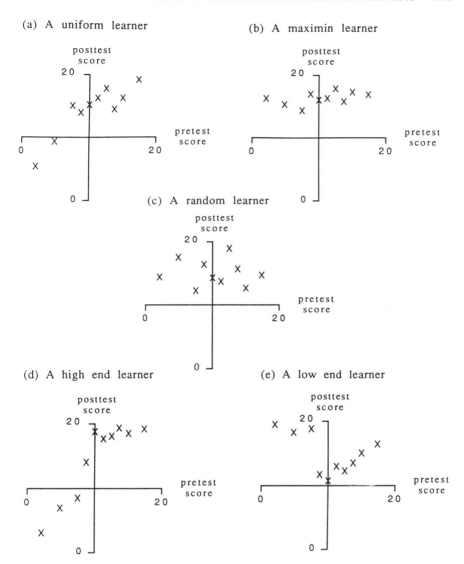

Figure 13.4.   Some hypothetical learning styles.

people might use. For example, suppose that five persons were given a diagnostic test battery and then allowed to study before retaking the test battery. Figure 13.4a shows a person who would decide to improve on each topic uniformly; Figure 13.4b shows a person who would choose to maximize his or her minimum posttest score; Figure 13.4d shows a person who would decide to excel on her or his best pretest scores; and Figure 13.4e shows a person who would choose to excel on her or his worst pretest scores.

As in the previous examples, additive measurement can be useful in the pretest-posttest case, up to a point. The most popular way to analyze such scores is to construct additive pretest scores and additive posttest scores of the form,

$$s^{(pre)} = \sum_{k=1}^{K} x_k^{(pre)}, \ s^{(post)} = \sum_{k=1}^{K} x_k^{(post)} \tag{5}$$

Given such scores, individual differences can be explored in pretest scores, posttest scores, and change scores of the form, $s^{(post)} - s^{(pre)}$. Moreover, individual differences in such change scores can be quite informative (Rogosa & Willett, 1983). However, the additive statistics in (5) may not reflect some interesting data features. For example, all of the five graphs in Figure 13.4 have been constructed to each have the same pretest and posttest scores, hence the same change scores. Yet the different patterns among the graphs point toward some distinct strategies and styles, as stated earlier.

One way to capture the distinctions among the Figure 13.4 graphs is to evaluate nonadditive statistics of the form,

$$s^{(pre, \ post)} = \sum_{k=1}^{K} x_k^{(pre)} x_k^{(post)}. \tag{6}$$

For example, Pearson correlation coefficients based on the cross-product statistic in (6) could be computed among the 10 pretest and posttest items for each graph. The correlation coefficients would have distinct values for the five graphs, thus providing a means for reflecting the five different styles.

The Figure 13.4 graphs show how standard pretest/posttest formats may be used for measuring something novel—a kind of learning style. The graphs also reflect an interesting psychometric property. They all violate what is often called the fundamental axiom of test theory—the (local independence) requirement that for a given person no item/subtest measures can depend on any others. This important distinction will be discussed later.

These examples have been presented with an emphasis on three distinct features: (a) tests can be formed within standard binary item formats, yet with substantively interesting item response dependencies; (b) individual differences in these dependencies may be of interest; and (c) measuring such individual differences requires nonadditive rather than traditional additive scoring formulas. All three examples focus on different strategies that persons might use, which are based on and reflected by conjunctive item information. Indeed, this potential for reflecting how persons can *react to*—rather than simply be measured by—items separates conjunctive from additive measurement.

Procedural guidelines. In this section I first outline a simple model assessment method for the item-chain-learning case. Detailed descriptions of efficient—but far more complicated—procedures are available elsewhere (Jannarone, 1986, 1987, 1989; Jannarone, Yu, & Laughlin, forthcoming).

The additive version of the item-chain-learning model is simply a Rasch model, leading to persons' scores that can only take on the values of the row margins in Table 13.1, as was pointed out earlier. If evaluating associations between the learning test scores and scores on an external variable were of interest, the simplest way to evaluate the conjunctive model over and above the Rasch model would be to test for subgroup differences within each row of Table 13.1. If the external criterion were binary, tests for equality of binomial proportions (Fleiss, 1981) could be used; if the external criterion were continuous, one-way analyses-of-variances (*ANOVAs*) could be used, multivariate *ANOVAs* could be used for multiple continuous criteria; and so on.

For the analog example, Total Item scores may be regarded as criterion variables and the two subtask scores as predictor variables. Appropriate conjunctive versus additive model comparisons may then be based on the corresponding statistics that appear in (1) and (2). As in the Table 13.1 case, subgroups would be first obtained by breaking down equal additive groups according to conjunctive statistic values. Tests for association between subgroups and the Total scores could then be performed (perhaps with a nonparametric version of a one-way *ANOVA* test—see Lehmann, 1975). If the correct model were additive, the subgroups would be expected to have the same mean Total scores; otherwise they would not. Other conjunctive versus additive cases would be treated similarly.

I will end this section by discussing the process of aligning cognitive individual differences work with psychometric individual differences efforts and pointing out its importance. Both fields seem to have developed together, in alternating cycles of increased generality and improved alignment. Thurstone's remarkable success at jointly developing both his psychometric (multiple factor analysis) model and his cognitive (primary mental abilities) model is an excellent example. The *psychometric* side of Thurstone's alignment process included the sublime introduction of factorial rotation as an alignment device (Meredith, 1977; Thurstone, 1947). His *cognitive* work, which was more subtle and perhaps more important, focused on selecting items that fit his model. The following excerpt from Thurstone's (1938) monograph describes the cognitive side of the process.

> In the exploratory study that we are reporting in this monograph we did not have the advantage of orientation about any known landmarks. Consequently, the tests in the present study were often more complex as to factorial composition than we had anticipated. The tests have been constructed for the subsequent studies as more nearly pure in that some of them could be designed so as to feature one factor with little admixture of others. This process will continue for some time until we shall be able to prepare psychological tests that involve only one or two factors instead of three, four, or five, as is the case with most of the tests in current use.

The most productive development of conjunctive models would entail an alignment process much like the one that Thurstone used. For a given cognitive domain, items would first be constructed with a particular conjunctive model in mind. The items would then be empirically evaluated against the model, with well-fitting items being retained and others being discarded. Still other items would be introduced into the process that were similar to those that had been retained, and so on. The *psychometric* part, by contrast, would entail fitting slightly different models to reflect the slightly different nature of the retained items, and so on.

The potential gains from such an alignment process are much greater than those would be from simply testing conjunctive models against existing additive measures. The reason is that most existing measures have come from a long process of selecting items to fit additive models. It would thus be surprising to find that conjunctive models added much to additive model explanatory power in such cases.

SOME THEORETICAL ISSUES

Conjunctive versus compensatory structure. The term "compensatory" was introduced (Sympson, 1977) to describe cases where an individual's deficiency in one component trait can be overcome by superiority in another. For example, factor analysis and *LISREL* (Jörekog & Sörbom, 1984) models are compensatory in that persons' factor values have additive effects on their component item/subtest scores. As a consequence of additivity, high levels of one factor can compensate for low levels of another. Compensatory and additive models are thus equivalent on the one hand, whereas conjunctive and nonadditive models are equivalent on the other hand. Compensatory models clearly dominate both early psychometric history and current psychometric practice. Most notably, the classical-test, Spearman, Thurstone, general-linear, Rasch, and logistic models are all compensatory.

The compensatory tradition has been largely unchallenged over the years, perhaps for three main reasons: (a) additive systems explain scientific data well as a rule, and psychometric modeling is no exception; (b) estimation and hypothesis testing procedures based on additive psychometric models are relatively simple; and (c) established additive models tend to reify themselves by encouraging researchers to retain only additive data. For these reasons compensatory models will remain prominent in psychometric modeling, even after compelling alternative models and methods become established.

With all of its virtues, compensatory psychometric modeling carries certain liabilities. First, cognitive psychologists have become increasingly interested in certain *conjunctive* (noncompensatory) tasks (Embretson, 1985; Pellegrino & Glaser, 1979; Pellegrino, Mumaw, & Shute, 1985; Sternberg, 1977). Second, all of the examples that I presented earlier are conjunctive rather than compensatory, as are many related instances. Finally, compensatory measurement only reflects how persons perform, not how they *react* to items. This subtle but important distinction will be described next.

Noninvasive versus reactive measurement. The concept of noninvasive measurement is closely tied to the local independence axiom of mental test theory. Given a (possibly multivariate) latent trait value for a person, local independence assumes that all item (or subtest) scores for that person will be mutually independent. Local independence is considered to be test theory's principal axiom (Lazarsfeld, 1958; Lord & Novick, 1968) for several reasons. First, local independence leads to simple mathematics: If items are independent then their joint probabilities are products of their marginal probabilities. Second, local independence brings focus to the test score analysis process. Given that all item dependencies can be explained by person parameters, evaluating person parameters will be sufficient for describing all elements that the items have in common (Lord & Novick, 1968).

The main substantive feature of local independence is its noninvasive measurement property. No matter how a person responds to an item, local independence guarantees that the person's responses to future items will be unaffected. The item measurement process itself is thus assumed to have no measurable effects on the person's future behavior. (That future item scores will not depend on *whether or not an item was presented* is also assumed insofar as binary item non-responses are scored as FAILs.) The noninvasive feature implies that the testing process yields independently distributed (*ID*) item scores for each person. The availability of *ID* item scores, in turn, leads to simple and effective procedures for estimating latent traits, evaluating reliability and validity, and so on. In addition, local independence implies that observed individual and treatment differences cannot be caused by the measurement process itself, thus removing a cumbersome confound from the inference process.

Noninvasive measurement has its drawbacks, however, especially in certain developmental settings. Suppose that a person were presented a sequence of information by a tutor in a way that at once evaluated the person, taught the person, and governed how future information was to be presented. Any reasonable explanatory model of such a sequence would necessarily allow the person to change during the process. That is, a reasonable model would allow for local *dependence*. Moreover, by permitting local dependence, such a model would allow persons to *react* to items, thus making them measurably different after taking an item than before. Such might be the case in other repeated measurement settings, as in the replicated test and item chain learning examples that were given earlier.

One way to reflect change and yet preserve local independence is to allow persons' latent traits to change over time. Some of the additive models that I presented earlier allow for such changes. For example, pretest-posttest Rasch and classical models allow for two different traits to be measured at two different time points. Other more detailed models also permit change but preserve local independence (Bieber & Meredith, 1986; Jöreskog & Sörbom, 1977). Such models also can be quite useful in reflecting change (Rogosa & Willett, 1982). For example, a variety of people could have pretest-posttest scatterplots that were similar to the one in Figure 13.4c, but distinct from each other in terms of pretest, posttest differences. Measuring such differences could be useful, especially if they were related to other interesting variables.

However, merely allowing distinct traits to govern different item responses is not enough in some cases. For example, no such model could reflect the individual differences that appear among the Figure 13.4 graphs, because all five change scores are the same. The strategies indicated in the other two examples likewise cannot be reflected by merely assigning distinct traits to each item.

The fact that both local dependence and multidimensionality can reflect change has led some authors to conclude that the two are related (Andrich, 1984; Goldstein, 1980; Hambleton, Swaminathan, Cook, Eignor, & Gifford, 1978). Some have speculated that locally dependent models are necessarily multidimensional, although I have been able to construct viable counterexamples (Jannarone, 1987). A more complementary relationship between the two exists, however, in that local dependence can perhaps be explained away by introducing additional traits. In the pretest-posttest case, for example, all of the graphs in Figure 13.4 might be explained by providing for: (a) one distinct trait for each subtask, and (b) other distinct traits that would somehow describe how different persons might have different strategies, even if they had the same prescore patterns. (Indeed, any locally dependent model can always be replaced by a multivariate, locally independent alternative proposed by Suppes & Zanotti, 1981—the locally independent version is unsatisfactory, however—see Jannarone, in revision.)

Locally dependent and multivariate test models could represent two alternatives, then. The multivariate alternative would provide for predicting each person's performance even in learning settings, provided that the person's latent traits were known. The locally dependent alternative, in turn, could allow for measuring item dependencies that could not be reflected by existing multivariate models.

One major practical problem separates the two, however. Satisfactory locally independent alternatives to conjunctive measurement are simply not yet available. In addition, the prospects for such models may not be good. For example, no viable multivariate models for reflecting the kinds of strategies in the pretest-posttest example come to mind. Moreover, even if such models could be formulated their resulting statistical procedures might not be sound for certain technical reasons (see below). Therefore, locally dependent measurement procedures may remain useful, at least until viable locally independent alternatives have been worked out.

I will end this argument for considering locally dependent alternatives with a physical measurement analogy. The reaction of persons to items somewhat resembles the reaction of particles to measurement in quantum physics. Physicists have found that certain particle measurements are always invasive. Moreover, such measurements of one property tend to change values of other properties in uncertain ways. It seems like physicists are saying that (a) particles always "notice" when they are being observed and "decide to" react by changing their nature; and (b) modern models are unable to predict how they will react. (A more basic question is whether or not models *could* be formed that would completely describe their reactions—see Suppes, 1976). In terms of the previous discussion, some measurements *always* cause particles to react unpredictably, like persons do in learning settings. Most psychologists seem to believe that human dynamics are far more complex than those of atomic particles. It would be ironic, then, if psychologists were to assume that humans *never* react to solving test items. Yet, this is precisely the assumption behind test theory's local independence axiom.

I have chosen the term *reactive* rather than *interactive*, because locally dependent reactions are distinct from item-by-person *ANOVA* interactions. One distinction is only semantic: Strictly speaking, when an item is taken no interaction is possible—the person can react to the item but not the item to the person. The second distinction is between the role assigned to interactions in statistics and the role of locally dependent measures. Typical *ANOVA* interaction formulations treat underlying data as both replicable and *ID*. (This also appears to be the case with interactive item response models, e.g., Spada & McGaw, 1985.) By sharp contrast, locally dependent models cannot permit replicable, *ID* observations. Not only can the person change while taking an item, but item scores can be statistically dependent as well. (The interaction, reaction distinction also seems related to the frequentist versus Bayesian debate in statistics (Savage, 1954; Neyman, 1977)— for example, making frequentist inferences about a person being measured reactively would seem to be much more awkward than making Bayesian inferences.)

So far several terms have been used to describe models that are equivalent. It may be useful to group them together at this point for clarity. With minor technical exceptions, additive, traditional, compensatory, noninvasive, and locally independent models represent one alternative, whereas nonadditive, conjunctive, reactive, and locally dependent models represent the other. Except where noted, such terms will be used interchangeably in the sequel.

Sound versus ad hoc measurement. So far I have only contrasted conjunctive with compensatory ability measurement. However, conjunctive as well as compensatory versions of several different models are possible, including factor analysis, logistic, Rasch, and binomial models. As a result, the prospects for conjunctive versions of these different models are worth noting. Although I have introduced conjunctive versions for all four models (Jannarone, 1986), I have focused on developing only conjunctive Rasch versions so far. In this section I indicate the main advantage as well as some disadvantages of conjunctive Rasch extensions, relative to other possibilities.

Several bases could be considered for evaluating competing models, but I focus on two: axiomatic soundness or *substantive validity* and statistical soundness or *procedural viability*. From an axiomatic viewpoint a mathematical model can range from being very specific to very general. Very specific models are also called strong models (Lord & Novick, 1968), because they make restrictive and falsifiable assumptions about nature. Conversely, more general models are called weak, but they can reflect a broader array of natural events. Ideally, a family of test models would be available with members ranging from very specific to very general. Procedures for selecting the best family members for particular situations would also ideally be available. The family of test models does not line up according to such a neat generality ordering, however. Instead, the family tree branches off in a few axiomatic directions, each having the following relative strengths and weaknesses. (The references in the next four paragraphs are primary—more refined descriptions appear in Gulliksen, 1950; Lord & Novick, 1968; Thissen & Steinberg, 1986.)

Beginning with test models for continuous component scores, the oldest and strongest is the classical test model (Spearman, 1904). The classical model's axioms provide for independently and identically distributed (*IID*) as well as unidimensional item scores. Spearman's (1904, 1927) factor analysis model is more general than the classical model, because it relaxes the assumption of equal item weighting. Spearman's model also allows component measures to have unequal difficulties, because it is based on standardized rather than raw component measures. Thurstone's (1932) factor analysis model is still more general than Spearman's, because it relaxes the unidimensionality assumption. Recent conjunctive extensions of multivariate normality (Jannarone, 1986) point toward conjunctive versions of all three continuous test models. No continuous conjunctive versions have yet been refined, however.

Applications of continuous models to binary data have historically resulted in serious violations of the *IID* error assumption. Item response theory for binary items has been developed as a result. Item response (*IR*) models make up a distinct branch of test theory, because they reflect binary rather than continuous responses and they have their own generality ordering.

The strongest *IR* model, called the binomial model (Keats & Lord, 1962), requires that all items have the same characteristics, much like the classical test model. The Rasch model (Rasch, 1980) allows items to have different difficulties, and still weaker *IR* models allow items to vary in discriminating power as well. (An item's discriminating power evaluates its change-in-difficulty to change-in-ability ratio.) One of these is called the normal ogive model (Ferguson, 1942; Lawley, 1943), and the other is called the two-parameter logistic model (Birnbaum, 1958, 1968). The Rasch and binomial models are like the classical model in that they yield ability estimates that are unweighted sums of item scores. By contrast, the two-parameter logistic model yields weighted sums of item scores as ability estimates, like Spearman's model for continuous measures. Still weaker *IR* models allow different items to have different wild guessing probabilities. The most popular among these is the three-parameter logistic model (Birnbaum, 1958, 1968).

Multidimensional versions of Rasch models (Fischer, 1973; Whitely, 1980) and logistic models (McKinley & Reckase, 1983) have also been introduced. Categorical versions of *IR* models have appeared as well (Andrich, 1978; Bock, 1972; Samejima, 1969). Finally, conjunctive versions of binomial, Rasch, logistic, and multidimensional IR models have all been introduced (Andrich, 1985; Fischer & Formann, 1982; Embretson, 1984; Jannarone, 1986, 1987; Kempf, 1977; Lord, 1984; Spray & Ackerman, 1986). However only the conjunctive Rasch versions have been successfully developed (Embretson, 1984; Jannarone, 1987).

From an axiomatic viewpoint, it would be best to develop conjunctive versions of the most general models available. The most general versions could reflect the broadest array of test responses, and they could also identify simpler versions as special cases. Thus, multivariate logistic models and factor analysis models would be the soundest choices for conjunctive development, on purely axiomatic/substantive validity grounds.

From the viewpoint of statistical/procedural viability, however, both factor analysis and logistic models are not as sound. Statistical problems may exist for factor analysis and logistic models, because they do not belong to a very sound and broad family of statistical models called the natural *multiparameter exponential family* (Anderson, 1980; Lehmann, 1983). Exponential family likelihoods are easy to use because their exponents are additive functions of parameters. Exponential family members have maximum likelihood estimates that are unique; iterative estimation procedures that always converge; and hypotheses test statistics that have known asymptotic distributions (Andersen, 1980; Lehmann, 1983). Useful Bayes estimates (Jannarone, Yu, & Laughlin, forthcoming) are also easy to derive for exponential family models. Multiparameter exponential family members also have some useful conditional probability properties, including (a) easy provisions for statistical control—the effects of nuisance parameters can be removed simply by conditioning on the nuisance variables' sufficient statistics; and (b) provisions for conditional maximum likelihood (*CML*) estimation—*CML* estimates can sometimes be obtained much more quickly and simply than maximum likelihood estimates.

The Rasch model's exponential family membership has led to simple estimation procedures, relative to those for weaker models. For example, no local maximum, nonconvergence, or nonidentifiability problems have occurred with Rasch models. The Rasch model has another feature—stemming from the exponential family's statistical control properties—that is very attractive for testing applications. Item parameters and individual parameters for the Rasch model can be estimated completely separately from each other (Rasch, 1980). The conjunctive Rasch models that I have developed (Jannarone, 1986, 1987) are not only exponential family members but they share the same sound estimation properties as well.

By contrast, nonexponential family members have potentially serious estimation problems. For example, factor analysis/*LISREL* models are not exponential family members, because their likelihoods involve cross-products among parameters. Such models are known to have identifiability, local solution, and nonconvergence properties (Long, 1983). Logistic item response models are also potentially problematic, because they too have products of parameters in their likelihoods. Thus, no guarantee exists that logistic parameter estimates are indeed optimal or even unique.

(I should point out that equating soundness with exponential family membership is a bit simplistic. For example, some nonexponential family members such as the principal components model have very sound least squares properties (Eckard & Young, 1936). Also, exponential model estimates are not perfect—they tend to be biased in ways that persist even in large samples, for example (Anderson, 1982). In addition, existing factor analysis and logistic model procedures must be sound for the most part, or else they would have long since been abandoned. However, debugging complex test model estimation algorithms is much easier when they carry an unconditional guarantee of correct convergence—otherwise it is hard to identify when model problems begin and programming mistakes end.

In this section I have described two criteria for evaluating the soundness of test models: substantive validity and procedural viability. In terms of substantive validity, multivariate factor analysis and logistic models would be ideal for conjunctive model development, because they are the most general. In terms of procedural viability, however, Rasch type models are much preferred. So far I have decided to develop

Rasch conjunctive models because of their sound statistical properties. Other conjunctive approaches may also prove to be reasonable, however.

Online versus offline measurement. This section describes some prospects for estimating parameters nearly instantly. Such prospects point toward developing both conjunctive and additive models in settings that require *online* rather than *offline* measurement. For example, traditional educational testing allows tests to be taken at one point but abilities and item difficulties to be estimated offline at some later point. By contrast tailored testing or computer aided instruction would require parameter estimates to be updated each time a person reacted to an item. Neural and machine learning models must also require fast parameter updating (i.e., internal representation updating) in order to be practical (Jannarone, Yu, & Takefuji, 1988). Online test parameter estimation prospects thus point toward a much broader substantive base for test models than merely traditional testing.

In their present form, procedures for estimating parameters based on the *CRF*, including the Rasch model, have limited potential because they are iterative. Using such procedures for interactive modeling is not practical, because they may take many seconds to converge. Also, the possibility that humans use such iterative procedures to update their learning states is simply out of the question (given that neurons take about 10^5 times longer to function than computer processing units). Thus, iterative procedures are limited as either vehicles for real time measurement or models of human thought.

Far better possibilities for fast estimation now exist, because of some recent developments in computer technology and statistical parameter estimation. These will only be mentioned here—for details see Jannarone, Yu, and Takefuji (1988), Takefuji and Jannarone (1987), and Yu (1987). Briefly, *CML* estimation allows useful estimates for a parameter to be expressed as functions of only three variables: the sufficient statistic for that parameter, along with the lowest and highest values that the statistic can take given the other sufficient statistics' values. Also, for members of the Rasch conjunctive family those three variables may be rescaled so as to always fall between 0 and 1. Consider a $100 \times 100 \times 100$ array representing a million equally spaced points on a cube, having boundaries at 0 and 1 along all three dimensions. Current very large scale integration (*VLSI*) technology allows for such an array to exist on a single chip in the form of a read-only memory. Moreover, each address in the array could be rapidly accessed (in about 100 nanoseconds). Now consider such a chip with each of its elements containing the known *CML* estimate corresponding to its three independent statistic values. Given such availability online estimation would be feasible, since after each person's (or learning machine's) item response sufficient statistics could be quickly updated and their corresponding updated *CML* parameter estimates could be quickly accessed. Prototypes of massively parallel computing modules that implement such estimation procedures in about one microsecond are currently being fabricated (Takefuji, Jannarone, Cho, & Chen, 1988).

In sum, recent developments in statistical estimation theory and VLSI technology are pointing toward online versus offline measurement capabilities for Rasch conjunctive models. Given such capabilities, some new media for conjunctive as well as additive test models—including tailored testing, computer-aided instruction, and neural/machine learning—may become feasible.

FUTURE DIRECTIONS

Beginning with some necessary psychometric work, the need for several added statistical procedures has been indicated earlier. Besides that need, developing conjunctive models for categorical rather than strictly binary items seems necessary. Multiple-category extensions of conjunctive models would be useful for at least three reasons. First, scoring multiple choice items as only correct or incorrect can lead to distorted results due to wild guessing. Second, a good deal of useful information may be obtainable from multiple category items. Indeed, much more cognitively interesting multiple-choice formats than PASS-FAIL could be considered if more general categorical item response models were available. Such formats could become useful in the analysis of choice and attitude structures as well. The prospects for categorical extensions seems promising (Andrich, 1985; Laughlin & Jannarone, 1986), but some procedural details still need to be worked out.

At a more foundational level, reexamining Luce's (1959) choice axiom in terms of noninvasive versus reactive measurement might be useful. It seems that the choice axiom could be described in terms of whether or not current choices depend on previous choices. With that connection to the previous discussion in mind, perhaps categorical extensions of conjunctive models could lead to useful extensions of Luce's logistic choice model as well.

A third prospect is the potential for evaluating conjunctive functions of response speed and response accuracy measures. It seems clear (e.g., Bloxom, 1985) that since response latencies can be easily measured in computer aided testing settings, procedures based on such measures should also be developed. I would add that since many parametric models based on latencies belong in the exponential family, viable models based on latency/correctness conjunctions may easily be worked out by using conjunctive models. For example, scoring an item differently if it was answered correctly *and* quickly rather than correctly *and* slowly could be useful. Also, focusing only on latencies in experimental studies rather than including accuracy measures as well has been rightly criticized (Whitely & Barnes, 1979). Simple conjunctive approaches may be useful in such experimental settings as well.

A fourth prospect involves tailored item selection. When the choice of items to be administered depends on previous item performance, item scores will necessarily be locally dependent. For this reason it seems not only natural but essential to model local dependence into tailored testing.

Finally, the necessary framework for aligning of psychometric models to conjunctive settings is now available. However, identifying suitable settings, screening suitable items, and shaping corresponding models will all be necessary efforts toward making conjunctive measurement work. Such efforts may not be easy.

REFERENCES

Andersen, E.B. (1980). *Discrete statistical models with social science applications.* Amsterdam: North-Holland.

Andrich, D. (1978). A rating formulation for ordered response categories. *Psychometrika, 43,* 561–573.

Andrich, D. (1984, April). *The attenuation paradox of traditionalist test theory as a breakdown of local independence in person item response theory.* Paper presented at the National Conference of Measurement in Education, New Orleans, LA.

Andrich, D. (1985). A latent trait model for items with response dependencies: implications for test construction and analysis. In S.E. Embretson (Ed.), *Test design: development in psychology and psychometrics* (pp. 245–275). Orlando, FL: Academic Press.

Bieber, S.L., & Meredith, W. (1986). Transformation to achieve a longitudinally stationary data matrix. *Psychometrika, 51,* 535–547.

Bloxom, B. (1985). Considerations in psychometric modeling of response time. *Psychometrika, 50,* 383–398.

Birnbaum, A. (1958). Statistical theory of tests of a mental ability. *Annals of Mathematical Statistics, 29,* 1285 (abstract).

Birnbaum, A. (1968). Some latent trait models and their use in inferring an examinee's ability. In F.M. Lord & M.R. Novick (Eds.), *Statistical theories of mental test scores.* Reading, MA: Addison-Wesley.

Bock, R.D. (1972). Estimating item parameters and latent ability when responses are scored in two or more numerical categories. *Psychometrika, 37*, 29–51.

Eckard, C., & Young, G. (1936). The approximation of one matrix by another of lower rank. *Psychometrika, 1*, 211–218.

Embretson (Whitely), S. (1984). A general latent trait model for response processes. *Psychometrika, 49*, 175–186.

Embretson, S.E. (1985). Multicomponent latent trait models for test design. In S.E. Embretson (Ed.), *Test design: Developments in psychology and psychometrics* (pp. 195–218). Orlando, FL: Academic Press.

Ferguson, G.A. (1942). Item selection by the constant process. *Psychometrika, 7*, 19–29.

Fischer, G. (1973). The linear logistic test model as an instrument in educational research. *Acta Psychologica, 37*, 359–374.

Fischer, G., & Formann, A.K. (1982). Some applications of logistic latent trait models with linear constraints on the parameters. *Applied Psychological Measurement, 6*, 397–416.

Fleiss, J.L. (1981). *Statistical methods for rates and proportions* (2nd ed.). New York: Wiley.

Goldstein, H. (1980). Dimensionality, bias, independence and measurement scale problems in latent trait test score models. *British Journal of Mathematical and Statistical Psychology, 33*, 234–246.

Guilford, J.P. (1967). *The nature of human intelligence.* New York: McGraw Hill.

Gulliksen, H. (1950). *Theory of mental tests.* New York: John Wiley & Sons.

Hambleton, R.K., Swaminathan, H., Cook, L.L., Eignor, D.E., & Gifford, J.A. (1978). Developments in latent trait theory: Models, technical issues, and applications. *Review of Educational Research, 48*, 467–510.

Jannarone, R.J. (1986). Conjunctive item response theory kernels. *Psychometrika, 51*, 357–373.

Jannarone, R.J. (1987). *Locally dependent models for reflecting learning abilities* (Center for Machine Intelligence Tech. Rep. #87-64). Columbia, SC: University of South Carolina.

Jannarone, R.J. (1989). *Locally dependent models for Embretson analogy items.* Unpublished manuscript.

Jannarone, R.J. (in revision). Some conjunctive/traditional IRT connections. *Psychometrika.*

Jannarone, R.J., Yu, K.F., & Takefuji, Y. (1988). Conjunctoids: Statistical learning models for binary events. *Neural Networks, 1*, 325–337.

Jöreskog, K.G. (1978). Statistical analysis of covariance and correlation matrices. *Psychometrika, 43*, 443–477.

Jöreskog, K., & Sörbom, D. (1984). *LISREL VI users' guide.* Chicago: International Educational Resources.

Jöreskog, K.G., & Sörbom, K. (1977). Statistical models and methods for analysis of longitudinal data. In D.V. Aigner & A.S. Goldberger (Eds.), *Latent variables in sociometric models.* Amsterdam: North-Holland.

Keats, J.A., & Lord, F.M. (1962). A theoretical distribution for mental test scores. *Psychometrika, 27*, 59–72.

Kempf, W.F. (1977). A dynamic test model and its use in the microevaluation of instructional material. In H. Spada & W.F. Kempf (Eds.), *Structural models for thinking and learning.* Vienna: Hans Huber.

Laughlin, J.E., & Jannarone, R.J. (1985). *Latent trait items in choice settings.* Paper presented at the annual Psychometric Society Meetings, Nashville, TN.

Lawley, D.N. (1943). On problems connected with item selection and test construction. *Proceedings of the Royal society of Edinburgh, 61,* 273–287.

Lazarsfeld, P.F. (1958). Latent structure analysis. In S. Koch (Ed.), *Psychology: A study of a science* (Vol. III). New York: McGraw-Hill.

Lehmann, E.L. (1975). *Nonparametrics: Statistical methods based on ranks.* San Francisco: Holden-Day.

Lehmann, E.L. (1983). *Theory of point estimation.* New York: Wiley.

Long, J.S. (1983). *Covariance structure models: An introduction to LISREL.* Beverly Hills, CA: Sage.

Lord, F.M., & Novick, M.R. (1968). *Statistical theories of mental test scores.* Reading, MA: Addison-Wesley.

Lord, F.M. (1984). *Conjunctive and disjunctive item response functions* (Educational Testing Service Tech. Rep. No. 84-45-ONR). Princeton, NJ: Educational Testing Service.

Luce, R.P. (1959). *Individual choice behavior.* New York: John Wiley & Sons.

McCormick, C., & Miller, G.E. (1986). *A comparison of mnemonic approaches to learning English vocabulary.* Unpublished manuscript, University of South Carolina College of Education, Columbia, SC.

McKinley, R.L., & Reckase, M.D. (1983). *An extension of the two-parameter logistic model to the multidimensional latent space* (Research Rep. No. R83-2). Iowa City: American College Testing Program.

Meredith, W. (1977). On weighted procrustes and hyperplane fitting in factor analytic rotation. *Psychometrika, 42,* 491–522.

Pellegrino, J.W., & Glaser, R. (1979). Cognitive components and correlates in the analysis of individual differences. *Intelligence, 3,* 187–214.

Pellegrino, J.W., & Mumaw, R.J., & Shute, V.J. (1985). Analysis of spatial aptitude and expertise. In S.E. Embretson (Ed), *Test design: Developments in psychology and psychometrics* (pp. 45–76). Orlando, FL: Academic Press.

Rasch, G. (1980). *Probabilistic models for some intelligence and attainment tests.* Chicago: University of Chicago Press.

Rogosa, D.R., & Willett, J.B. (1983). Demonstrating the reliability of the difference score in the measurement of change. *Journal of Educational Measurement, 20,* 335–343.

Samejima, F. (1969). Estimation of latent ability using a response pattern of graded scores. *Psychometric Monograph, No. 17.*

Savage, L.J. (1954). *The foundations of statistics.* New York: Wiley.

Spada, H., & McGaw, B. (1985). The assessment of learning effects with linear logistic test models. In S.E. Embretson, (Ed.), *Test design: Developments in psychology and psychometrics* (pp. 169–194). Orlando, FL: Academic Press.

Spearman, C. (1904). The proof and measurement of association between two things. *American Journal of Psychology, 15*, 72–101.

Spearman, C. (1927). *The abilities of man.* New York: Macmillan.

Spray, J.A., & Ackerman, T.A. (1986, June). *The effects of item response dependency on trait or ability dimensionality.* Paper presented at the annual Psychometric Society Meetings, Toronto, Canada.

Sternberg, R.S. (1977). *Intelligence, information processing and analogical reasoning: The componential analysis of human abilities.* Hillsdale, NJ: Erlbaum.

Suppes, P. (Ed.). (1976). *Logic and probability in quantum mechanics.* Dordrecht, Holland: Reidel.

Suppes, P., & Zanotti, M. (1981). When are probabilistic explanations possible? *Synthese, 48*, 191–199.

Sympson, J.B. (1977, July). *A model for testing with multidimensional items.* Paper presented at the Adaptive Testing Conference, Minneapolis, MN.

Takefuji, Y., Jannarone, R.J., Cho, Y.B., & Chen, T. (1988). Multinomial conjuctoid statistical learning machines. *Proceedings of the 15th Annual IEEE International Symposium on Computer Architecture.*

Thissen, D., & Steinberg, L. (1986). A taxonomy of item response models. *Psychometrika, 51*, 567–577.

Thurstone, L.L. (1932). *The theory of multiple factors.* Ann Arbor, MI: Edwards Brothers.

Thurstone, L.L. (1938). *Primary mental abilities.* Chicago: University of Chicago Press.

Thurstone, L.L. (1947). *Multiple factor analysis: A development and expansion of the vectors of mind.* Chicago: University of Chicago Press.

Whitely, S.E., & Barnes, G.M. (1979). The implications of processing event sequences for theories of analogical reasoning. *Memory and Cognition, 7*, 323–331.

Wilson, M. (1989). Saltus: A psychometric model of discontinuity in cognitive development. *Psychological Bulletin, 105*, 276–289.

Yu, K.F. (1987). *Conditional maximum likelihood estimate consistency.* Unpublished manuscript, University of South Carolina Center for Machine Intelligence, Columbia, SC.

chapter **14**

A Rasch Model with a Multivariate Distribution of Ability

C.A.W. Glas
National Institute for Educational Measurement (CITO)
Arnhem, the Netherlands

INTRODUCTION

This first section will be devoted to studying item response models that apply to polytomous ability items. Within this framework dichotomous ability items will be a special case. Consider the response of a person, indexed by n, to an item, indexed i, which has $m_i + 1$ response categories with index $j = 0, 1, \ldots, m_i$. The response of person n will be represented by a m_i-dimensional vector of stochastic variables χ_{ni} with elements

$$\chi_{nij} = \begin{cases} 1 & \text{if person n scores in category j on item i,} \\ 0 & \text{if this is not the case,} \end{cases} \tag{1}$$

for $j = 1, \ldots, m_i$. So if the respondent scores in category $j = 0$, $\chi_{ni} = \mathbf{o}$. Notice that if $m_i = 1$, the item is dichotomously scored, and the vector χ_{ni} has only one element. In ability measurement, the category indices can be seen as appreciation marks, and scoring in category j of the ith item is the same as obtaining the mark j for item i. One of the interesting things about item response models is that they do not come out of

236

the blue, but they can be derived from a set of assumptions. The most important assumption concerns the adoption of a scoring rule, or, to be more exact, of a sufficient statistic for the ability of a respondent. As an example, one may think of the Rasch model for dichotomous items (Rasch, 1960), where Andersen (1973) and Fischer (1974) have shown that it is the only model compatible with (a) a unidimensional representation of ability, (b) using the unweighted sum score as a sufficient statistic for a respondent's ability, and (c) some technical requirements, the most important being local stochastic independence. An important consequence of this derivation is that workers in the field of educational measurement who use the sum score for evaluating proficiencies should adopt the model or reject it and take the consequence, which is adopting a multidimensional model and a vector-valued sufficient statistic.

Also, for the more general case of polytomous items, derivations of item response models exist. For instance, Andersen (1973) has shown that, if there exists a vector-valued minimal sufficient statistic $R_n(\chi_{ni}, \ldots, \chi_{ni}, \ldots, \chi_{nk})$ for some vector-valued person parameter ϑ_n, which is symmetric in its arguments, the multidimensional Rasch model (Rasch, 1961) must necessarily follow. Suppose that for all items $m_i = m$, let $\eta'_i \stackrel{d}{=} (\eta_{i1}, \ldots, \eta_{ij}, \ldots, \eta_{im})$ and $\vartheta'_n \stackrel{d}{=} (\vartheta_{n1}, \ldots, \vartheta_{nj}, \ldots, \vartheta_{nm})$. The main result derived by Andersen can be summarized by saying that if, for $j = 1, \ldots, m$, $\Sigma_i \chi_{nij}$ is sufficient for ϑ_{nj}, the model must have the form

$$\Pr(\chi_{ni} = \mathbf{x}_{ni} | \vartheta_n, \eta_i) = \frac{\exp\left(\sum_{j=1}^{m} x_{nij}(\vartheta_{nj} - \eta_{ij}) \right)}{1 + \sum_{h=1}^{m} \exp(\vartheta_{nh} - \eta_{ih})}. \tag{2}$$

Inspection of (2), however, shows that the multidimensional Rasch model is little suited for analyzing ability items, since every score j is associated with a distinct ability ϑ_{nj}. This means that, for all items, the response category j must be related to the same response tendency ϑ_{nj}, and that this response tendency must be distinguishable from the other response tendencies. Therefore, the model is especially suited for analyzing choice behavior. One could, for instance, think of an experiment where every item consists of the choice between a Coke, a lime, and a root beer, and different items are constructed by varying the makes of the beverages. More in line with the practice in educational measurement of using a sum score for evaluating a respondents performance is the unidimensional version of the model (Rasch, 1961). Andersen (1977) has shown that if R_n is a scalar-valued minimal sufficient statistic for a scalar-valued ability parameter ϑ_n, which is symmetric in its arguments, the model is necessarily given by

$$\Pr(\chi_{ni} = \mathbf{x}_{ni}|\vartheta_n, \boldsymbol{\eta}_i) = \frac{\exp\left(\sum_{j=1}^{m} x_{nij}(j\vartheta_n - \eta_{ij})\right)}{1 + \sum_{h=1}^{m} \exp(h\vartheta_n - \eta_{ih})}. \tag{3}$$

Further, it turns out that the sufficient statistic is given by $R_n \overset{\text{d}}{=} \Sigma_i \, jx_{nij}$. Notice that (3) is a specialization of (2), with ϑ_{nj} replaced with $j\vartheta_n$ and ϑ_{nh} replaced with $h\vartheta_n$.

A different derivation of the unidimensional Rasch model for polytomous items is given by Masters (1982). Masters derives an alternative formulation of the model, which is known as the partial-credit model, from the assumption that every category j ($j > 0$) of an item can be seen as a step which is either taken or not taken by the respondent. It is assumed that the probability of a person scoring in category j rather than scoring in category $j - 1$ is a logistic function of a person parameter ϑ_n and a parameter δ_{ij} associated with category j of item i. Thus if $j > 0$

$$\Pr(\chi_{nij} = 1|\chi_{nij} = 1 \text{ or } \chi_{nij-1} = 1, \vartheta_n, \delta_{ij}) = \frac{\exp(\vartheta_n - \delta_{ij})}{1 + \exp(\vartheta_n - \delta_{ij})}. \tag{4}$$

Masters (1982) shows that it follows from (4) that the probability of a person with parameter ϑ_n scoring in category j, $j = 1, \ldots, m_i$, on an item with parameter δ_i, $\delta_i' \overset{\text{d}}{=} (\delta_{i1}, \ldots, \delta_{ij}, \ldots, \delta_{im_i})$ is given by

$$\Pr(\chi_{ni} = \mathbf{x}_{ni}|\vartheta_n, \delta_i) = \frac{\exp\left(\sum_{j=1}^{m_i} x_{nij}\left(\sum_{p=1}^{j} (\vartheta_n - \delta_{ip})\right)\right)}{1 + \sum_{h=1}^{m_i} \exp\left(\sum_{p=1}^{h} (\vartheta_n - \delta_{ip})\right)}. \tag{5}$$

Notice that if $m_i = m$ for $i = 1, \ldots, k$ and the reparameterization $\eta_{ij} = \Sigma_{p=1}^{j} \delta_{ip}$ is applied, the models defined by (2) and (3) are equivalent. The fact that Andersen (1977) only considers items with the same number of response categories, where Masters (1982) allows for different numbers of categories, has to do with the following. Andersen's derivation, which, disregarding reparameterizations, identifies (2) as the only model compatible with the sufficient statistic R_n, rests entirely on the assumption that R_n is symmetric in its arguments. This does, however, not mean that no minimal sufficient statistics exist if the assumption of symmetry is dropped (see, for instance, Masters, 1985; Glas & Verhelst, 1989). Only in this case, the proof of the uniqueness of the model is lacking. Generalizing Andersen's results to the broader class of response formats, however, is beyond the scope of the present chapter.

One of the main motivations for studying Master's parameterization of the model is an interpretation of the parameters which is not possible for Andersen's version. Before turning to the correct interpretation, a faulty one, which has been pinpointed by Molenaar (1983) will be studied. From (5) it follows that the model is linear in the log-odds of scoring categories j and $j - 1$:

$$\ln\{\Pr(\chi_{nij} = 1|\vartheta_n,\delta_i)/\Pr(\chi_{nij-1} = 1|\vartheta_n,\delta_i)\} = \vartheta_n - \delta_{ij}. \tag{6}$$

So, unlike the case of the Rasch model for dichotomous items, where the item parameter can be interpreted as the difficulty of the item, δ_{ij} cannot be interpreted as the difficulty parameter of category j alone, since the probability of completing the item in category $j - 1$ must also be taken into account.

A correct interpretation of the item parameters, however, can be derived from the model for dichotomous items, where the item parameter can be viewed as the point on the latent scale where the probability of a correct response and the probability of an incorrect response are equal. This interpretation can also be applied to the model for polytomous items. For every item a set of $m_i + 1$ item characteristic functions are defined by

$$\psi_{ij}(\vartheta_n) \stackrel{d}{=} \Pr(\chi_{nij} = 1|\vartheta_n,\delta_i) = \frac{\exp\left(\sum_{h=1}^{j} (\vartheta_n - \delta_{ih})\right)}{1 + \sum_{h=1}^{m_i} \exp\left(\sum_{p=1}^{h} (\vartheta_n - \delta_{ip})\right)}, \tag{7}$$

for $j = 1, \ldots, m_i$ and

$$\psi_{i0}(\vartheta_n) \stackrel{d}{=} \Pr(\chi_{ni} = 0|\vartheta_n,\delta_i) = \frac{1}{1 + \sum_{h=1}^{m_i} \exp\left(\sum_{p=1}^{h} (\vartheta_n - \delta_{ip})\right)}. \tag{8}$$

It can be easily verified that, for $j = 1, \ldots, m_i$,

$$\psi_{ij-1}(\vartheta) = \psi_{ij}(\vartheta) \Leftrightarrow \vartheta = \delta_{ij}. \tag{9}$$

So δ_{ij} is the boundary value where the probability of scoring in category j and the probability of scoring in category $j - 1$ are equal.

In this chapter, an extension of the unidimensional Rasch model, or Partial Credit model, will be studied, that may be appropriate if the usual model does not hold for the complete test. The essence of the idea is to postulate the hypothesis, that the test is made up of number of subtests, where every subtest follows the Rasch model for polytomous items. So it is assumed that the subtests relate to (slightly) different proficiencies. To formalize this notion, let the response pattern χ on a test with polytomous items (and dichotomous items as a special case) be partitioned $\chi' = (\chi^{(1)\prime}, \ldots, \chi^{(q)\prime}, \ldots, \chi^{(Q)\prime})$, where, for $q = 1, \ldots, Q$, $\chi^{(q)}$ stands for the response pattern on a subtest relating to ability $\vartheta^{(q)}$. Let $\vartheta' \underline{d}(\vartheta^{(1)}, \ldots, \vartheta^{(Q)})$ have a Q-variate normal distribution. For every subtest, a restriction must be imposed to fix the scale. It will prove convenient to assume that the mean of the distribution of ability is the zero vector, and, as a consequence, the density of ϑ can be denoted by $g(\vartheta|\Sigma)$, where Σ is the variance-covariance matrix of the latent abilities underlying the subtests. The probability of observing response pattern $\mathbf{x}$ is given by

$$\Pr(\chi = \mathbf{x}|\boldsymbol{\eta},\Sigma) = \int, \ldots, \int \Pr(\chi = \mathbf{x}|\vartheta,\boldsymbol{\eta}) \, g(\vartheta|\Sigma) \, d\vartheta$$

$$= \int, \ldots, \int \prod_{q=1}^{Q} \Pr(\chi^{(q)} = \mathbf{x}^{(q)}|\vartheta^{(q)},\boldsymbol{\eta}^{(q)}) \, g(\vartheta|\Sigma) \, d\,\vartheta^{(1)}, \ldots, d\vartheta^{(Q)}, \tag{10}$$

with $\boldsymbol{\eta}^{(q)}$ the item parameters of test q, for $q = 1, \ldots, Q$. In the sequel, it will prove convenient to use Andersen's parameterization. Since the partial-credit model is a reparametrization of Andersen's version, the results which will be presented also hold for Master's model. The most important reason for studying this model is that it provides a multi-dimensional representation of ability. Studying the model, however, is also motivated by the following observation.

Consider a test with dichotomous items, where the first $k^{(1)}$ items relate to $\vartheta^{(1)}$ and the remaining $k^{(2)}$ items relate to $\vartheta^{(2)}$. Using the shorthand notation $\Pr(\mathbf{x}|. \, .)$ for $\Pr(\chi = \mathbf{x}|. \, .)$, (10) specializes to

$$\Pr(\mathbf{x}|\boldsymbol{\eta},\Sigma) = \int\int \Pr(\mathbf{x}^{(1)}|\vartheta^{(1)},\boldsymbol{\eta}^{(1)})\Pr(\mathbf{x}^{(2)}|\vartheta^{(2)},\boldsymbol{\eta}^{(2)})g(\vartheta|\Sigma)d\vartheta^{(1)}d\vartheta^{(2)}. \tag{11}$$

Consider the change of variables $\vartheta^{*(1)} = \vartheta^{(1)}/\sigma_1$ and $\vartheta^{*(2)} = \vartheta^{(2)}/\sigma_2$, with σ_1 and σ_2 the standard deviation of, respectively, $\vartheta^{(1)}$ and $\vartheta^{(2)}$. Notice that if $C \underline{d} \text{diag}(\sigma_1^{-1},\sigma_2^{-1})$ and $\vartheta^{*\prime} \underline{d} (\vartheta^{*(1)},\vartheta^{*(2)})$, the change of variables can also be written as $\vartheta^* = C\vartheta$. Using $\Sigma^* = C\Sigma C'$, (11) becomes

$$\Pr(\mathbf{x}|\boldsymbol{\eta},\Sigma^*) = \int\int \Pr(\mathbf{x}^{(1)}|\vartheta^{*(1)},\boldsymbol{\eta}^{(1)})\Pr(\mathbf{x}^{(2)}|\vartheta^{*(2)},\boldsymbol{\eta}^{(2)})g(\vartheta^*|\Sigma^*)d\vartheta^{*(1)}d\vartheta^{*(2)}. \quad (12)$$

The probabilities of observing the partial response patterns $\mathbf{x}^{(1)}$ and $\mathbf{x}^{(2)}$ as a function of the relevant abilities is now given by

$$\Pr(\mathbf{x}^{(1)}|\vartheta^{*(1)},\boldsymbol{\eta}^{(1)}) = \prod_{i\in I_1} \frac{\exp(x_i\sigma_1(\vartheta^{*(1)} - \eta_{i1}/\sigma_1))}{1 + \exp(\sigma_1(\vartheta^{*(1)} - \eta_{i1}/\sigma_1))} \quad (13)$$

and

$$\Pr(\mathbf{x}^{(2)}|\vartheta^{*(2)},\boldsymbol{\eta}^{(2)}) = \prod_{i\in I_2} \frac{\exp(x_i\sigma_2(\vartheta^{*(2)} - \eta_{i1}/\sigma_2))}{1 + \exp(\sigma_2(\vartheta^{*(2)} - \eta_{i1}/\sigma_2))}, \quad (14)$$

where I_1 and I_2 are the set of the indices of the first and second test.

Comparing (13) and (14) with the Birnbaum model (1968), it can be seen that, if $\vartheta^{*(1)} = \vartheta^{*(2)}$, the standard deviations σ_1 and σ_2 play a role, which can be compared with the role of the discrimination parameters in the Birnbaum model; that is, σ_1 and σ_2 are related to differences in the slopes of the item characteristic curves of the items of both tests. If the usual Rasch model does not fit, this suggests the following strategy. First a number of subtests have to be found where the item characteristic curves have approximately the same slopes. This can, for instance, be done by inspecting the scaled deviates that come with the R_{1m} or R_{1c} statistic (see Glas, 1988). Another suggestion might be to use the relationship between item/test correlations and the discrimination indices (see Lord, 1980), and group together items with approximately the same item/test correlations. With the subtests identified, one may impose the general model, where Σ is an unrestricted covariance matrix, or special versions of the general model. One can think of the special case where rank(Σ) = 1, which is equivalent with a Birnbaum model where subgroups of items have item characteristic curves with the same slope.

Summing up, adoption of the model defined by (10) is motivated by the multidimensional representation of ability and by the fact that, in contrast to the usual Rasch model, not all the slopes of the item characteristic curves have to be equal.

Before turning to estimating and testing the model, it must be remarked that the model proposed here is identical with a model proposed by Andersen (1985). Andersen's motivation for studying the model, however, was different from the one in this chapter, since he adopted it for modeling a pretest/posttest situation. In this framework $\chi^{(1)}$ stands for the response to the pretest and $\chi^{(2)}$ for the response to the posttest. Andersen (1985) reports some difficulties with estimation of the model. Since the present author did not encounter any serious difficulties (apart from the computer time-consuming nature of the procedure), some numerical aspects of the estimation procedure will also be studied.

A GENERAL FRAMEWORK FOR MML ESTIMATION

The next section is devoted to developing a general framework for the derivation of estimation equations for marginal item response models, that is, item response models with the assumption that the ability parameters are sampled from some distribution. The reason for including this section, where so many excellent introductions have already been written (see Bock & Aitkin, 1981, Mislevy, 1984, 1986; Rigdon & Tsutakawa, 1983, 1987; Thissen, 1982), is to introduce a general framework for MML estimation, which simplifies the derivation of the likelihood equations for future marginal item response models. Generally speaking, an item response model is a stochastic model relating to the responses of persons to items, where the persons and items are characterized by separate sets of parameters. Let the K-dimensional vector $\mathbf{x}_n$ be the response pattern of a person indexed n on a test of k items. The range of the responses need not be specified. Let person n be characterized by a Q-dimensional parameter vector ϑ_n and let the test be characterized by a R-dimensional vector δ. Further, $\{\mathbf{x}\}$ stands for the set of all possible response patterns. Then an item response model is defined by specifying the probability

$$\Pr(\chi_n = \mathbf{x}_n | \vartheta_n, \delta) \tag{15}$$

for $\vartheta_n \in \mathbb{R}^Q$, $\delta \in \mathbb{R}^R$ and all possible $\mathbf{x}_n \in \{\mathbf{x}\}$. To avoid an unnecessary clumsy notation, $\Pr(\chi_n = \mathbf{x}_n | \vartheta_n, \delta)$ is abbreviated to $\Pr(\mathbf{x}_n | \vartheta_n, \delta)$.

Suppose that the response patterns of N persons are observed and that these observations are collected in a $N \times K$ matrix X, which has rows $\mathbf{x}_n'$. Further, Θ is a $N \times Q$ matrix with rows ϑ_n'. The likelihood function of δ and Θ is given by

$$L(\delta,\Theta,X) = \prod_{n=1}^{N} \Pr(\mathbf{x}_n|\boldsymbol{\vartheta}_n,\delta). \tag{16}$$

Maximizing (16) with respect to δ and Θ will generally not produce consistent estimates, since the number of parameters in Θ goes to infinity if the sample size goes to infinity (see Neyman & Scott, 1948). Therefore, let the person parameters have a common distribution with a probability density function $g(.|\tau)$, where τ stands for the vector of parameters characterizing this density. Then the likelihood function of δ and τ given Θ and X can be written as

$$L(\delta,\tau|\Theta,X) = \prod_{n=1}^{N} \Pr(\mathbf{x}_n|\boldsymbol{\vartheta}_n,\delta)\, g(\boldsymbol{\vartheta}_n|\tau). \tag{17}$$

Notice that it is irrelevant whether every respondent has a fixed person parameter and the person parameters have a density $g(.|\tau)$ in the population, or every respondent's ability is a stochastic variable with the density $g(.|\tau)$.

Obviously (17) cannot be used for deriving maximum likelihood estimation equations, because Θ is not observed. Therefore the so-called marginal likelihood function $L(\delta,\tau|X)$ is introduced. This function is defined as

$$
\begin{aligned}
L(\delta,\tau|X) &= \int \ldots \int L(\delta,\tau|\Theta,X)\, d\vartheta_{11}, \ldots, d\vartheta_{NQ} \\
&= \int \ldots \int \prod_{n=1}^{N} \Pr(\mathbf{x}_n|\boldsymbol{\vartheta}_n,\delta)\, g(\boldsymbol{\vartheta}_n|\tau)\, d\vartheta_{n1}, \ldots, d\vartheta_{NQ} \\
&= \prod_{n=1}^{N} \int \ldots \int \Pr(\mathbf{x}_n|\boldsymbol{\vartheta}_n,\delta)\, g(\boldsymbol{\vartheta}_n|\tau)\, d\vartheta_{n1}, \ldots, d\vartheta_{nQ}, \tag{18}
\end{aligned}
$$

where it is assumed that the range of each integration is $\mathbb{R}$. The MML estimation equations are now given by

$$\Delta(\delta) \stackrel{d}{=} \partial \ln L(\delta,\tau|X)/\partial \delta = \mathbf{o} \tag{19}$$

and

$$\Delta(\tau) \stackrel{d}{=} \partial \ln L(\delta,\tau|X)/\partial \tau = \mathbf{o}\cdot \tag{20}$$

The derivation of explicit expressions for the $\Delta(\delta)$ and $\Delta(\tau)$ is greatly simplified by using an identity derived by Louis (1982) in the context of the EM algorithm. If $\mathbf{b}(\delta) \overset{\mathrm{d}}{=} \partial \ln L(\delta,\tau|\Theta,X)/\partial \delta$ and $\mathbf{b}(\tau) \overset{\mathrm{d}}{=} \partial \ln L(\delta,\tau|\Theta,X)/\partial \tau$, $\Delta(\delta)$ and $\Delta(\tau)$ can also be written as

$$\Delta(\delta) = E(\mathbf{b}(\delta)|X,\delta,\tau) \tag{21}$$

and

$$\Delta(\tau) = E(\mathbf{b}(\tau)|X,\delta,\tau). \tag{22}$$

The expectations on the right-hand side of (21) and (22) are with respect to the density of the ability parameters Θ given the data X, so if

$$f(\vartheta_n|\mathbf{x}_n,\delta,\tau) \overset{\mathrm{d}}{=} \frac{\Pr(\mathbf{x}_n|\vartheta_n,\delta)\, g(\vartheta_n|\tau)}{\int \ldots \int \Pr(\mathbf{x}_n|\vartheta_n,\delta)\, g(\vartheta_n|\tau)\, d\vartheta_{n1} \ldots d\vartheta_{nQ}} \tag{23}$$

is the density of ϑ_n given $\mathbf{x}_n$, it follows that

$$\Delta(\delta) = \sum_{n=1}^{N} \int \ldots \int [\partial \Pr(\mathbf{x}_n|\vartheta_n,\delta)/\partial \delta]\, f(\vartheta_n|\mathbf{x}_n,\delta,\tau)\, d\vartheta_{n1}, \ldots, d\vartheta_{nQ} \tag{24}$$

and

$$\Delta(\tau) = \sum_{n=1}^{N} \int \ldots \int [\partial \Pr(\mathbf{x}_n|\vartheta_n,\tau)/\partial \tau]\, f(\vartheta_n|\mathbf{x}_n,\delta,\tau)\, d\vartheta_{n1}, \ldots, d\vartheta_{nQ}. \tag{25}$$

As will become clear in the next section, the importance of (21) and (22) is due to the fact that $\mathbf{b}(\delta)$ and $\mathbf{b}(\tau)$ are usually very easy to derive.

The obvious way to solve the MML estimation equations (19) and (20) is to use the Newton-Raphson algorithm. In much literature on marginal item response theory (Bock & Aitkin, 1981; Mislevy, 1984, 1986; Rigdon & Tsutakawa, 1983, 1987; Thissen, 1982), however, the EM algorithm (expectation maximization algorithm) is used. Using a notation adapted to the present problem, the algorithm, which was described by Dempster, Laird, and Rubin (1977), can be characterized as follows. Let $\delta^{(p)}$ and $\tau^{(p)}$ be estimates of δ and τ. Then these estimates can be improved by maximizing the function

$$Q(\delta,\tau|\delta^{(p)},\tau^{(p)}) \overset{\mathrm{d}}{=} E(\ln L(\delta,\tau|\Theta,X)|X,\delta^{(p)},\tau^{(p)}) \tag{26}$$

with respect to δ and τ. Let $\delta^{(p+1)}$ and $\tau^{(p+1)}$ be the solution. Dempster et al. have shown that if this iteration is repeated for $p = 1, 2, 3, \ldots ,$ the process converges to a stationary point of $L(\delta,\tau|X)$. Depending on the properties of $L(\delta,\tau|X)$, this stationary point may be the maximum of the function. The general proof of this assertion is rather involved (see Dempster et al., 1977), in the present case, however, the equivalence of the EM algorithm and the common method of obtaining maximum likelihood estimations can easily be demonstrated. The maximum of (26) can be found by solving $\partial Q(\delta,\tau|\delta^{(p)},\tau^{(p)})/\partial(\delta,\tau) = o$, that is, by setting the first-order derivatives of $Q(\delta,\tau|\delta^{(p)},\tau^{(p)})$ with respect to δ and τ equal to zero. But

$$\partial Q(\delta,\tau|\delta^{(p)},\tau^{(p)})/\partial(\delta,\tau) = E(\partial \ln L(\delta,\tau|\Theta,X)/\partial(\delta,\tau)|X,\delta^{(p)},\tau^{(p)}) =$$
$$E(b(\delta)|X,\delta^{(p)},\tau^{(p)}) + E(b(\tau)|X,\delta^{(p)},\tau^{(p)}) . \tag{27}$$

So if the algorithm converges, $\Delta(\delta) = o$, and $\Delta(\tau) = o$, and a stationary point of $L(\delta,\tau|X)$ is found. In the next section all this is adopted to the Rasch model with a multivariate ability distribution.

MML ESTIMATION FOR THE RASCH MODEL WITH A MULTIVARIATE NORMAL DISTRIBUTION

The theory for the derivation of MML estimation equations developed in the previous section, will now be applied to the present model. The derivation consists of two steps. In the first step the likelihood function, given the response patterns and the ability parameters, is considered and the derivative of this function with respect to the item and population parameters, which, for the present model, are denoted by η and Σ, are identified. Let $b(\eta)$ and $b(\Sigma)$ be the vectors of these derivatives. The second step consists of applying (21) and (22), that is, deriving the expectation of $b(\eta)$ and $b(\Sigma)$ with respect to the joint density of the ability parameters given the response patterns. Putting these expectations equal to zero results in the estimation equations. Applying this to the present model proceeds as follows.

First, the expression for the density of ϑ given x has to be derived. Let k be the total number of items in the test. It will prove convenient to define $o(i)$, for $i = 1, \ldots , k,$ as the index of the subtest to which item i belongs. Further, let the Q-dimensional vector $r(x)$ be defined by $r(x)' \overset{d}{=} (r_1(x^{(1)}), \ldots ,r_q(x^{(q)}), \ldots , r_Q(x^{(Q)}))$, where $r_q(x^{(q)})$ is the sum score of the partial response vector $x^{(q)}$, for $q = 1, \ldots , Q$. The vector $r(x)$, which will usually be abbreviated to r, will be called a score pattern. Using these definitions, the density of ϑ given $\mathbf{x}$ is given by

$$f(\vartheta|\mathbf{x},\boldsymbol{\eta},\Sigma) = \frac{\Pr(\mathbf{x}|\vartheta,\boldsymbol{\eta})\, g(\vartheta|\Sigma)}{\int,\ldots,\int \Pr(\mathbf{x}|\vartheta,\boldsymbol{\eta})\, g(\vartheta|\Sigma)\, d\vartheta}$$

$$= \frac{\exp(-\mathbf{x}'\boldsymbol{\eta})\,\exp(\mathbf{r}(\mathbf{x})'\vartheta)p_0(\vartheta)g(\vartheta|\Sigma)}{\int,\ldots,\int \exp(-\mathbf{x}'\boldsymbol{\eta})\,\exp(\mathbf{r}(\mathbf{x})'\vartheta)p_0(\vartheta)g(\vartheta|\Sigma)\, d\vartheta}, \qquad (28)$$

where $p_0(\vartheta)$ is defined by

$$p_0(\vartheta) \stackrel{d}{=} \prod_{i=1}^{k} \left(1 + \sum_{h=1}^{m_i} \exp(h\vartheta^{(o(i))} - \eta_{ih})\right)^{-1}. \qquad (29)$$

Notice that the factor $\exp(-\mathbf{x}'\boldsymbol{\eta})$ in (28) cancels, and so $f(\vartheta|\chi,\boldsymbol{\eta},\Sigma)$ only depends on χ via score pattern $\mathbf{r}(\mathbf{x})$. Therefore it is convenient to introduce the densities

$$f(\vartheta|\mathbf{r},\boldsymbol{\eta},\Sigma) = \frac{\exp(\mathbf{r}'\vartheta)P_0(\vartheta)g(\vartheta|\Sigma)}{\int,\ldots,\int \exp(\mathbf{r}'\vartheta)P_0(\vartheta)g(\vartheta|\Sigma)\, d\vartheta}, \qquad (30)$$

for all score patterns $\mathbf{r}' \stackrel{d}{=} (r_1, \ldots, r_q, \ldots, r_Q)$ which are possible given the partitioning in subtests. Next, the estimation equations for the parameters $\boldsymbol{\eta}$ and Σ will be derived under the assumption that the person parameters are known constants.

Suppose that the response patterns of N persons are observed. The data are collected in a $N \times K$ matrix X which has rows $\mathbf{x}_n$, for $n = 1, \ldots, N$. Suppose further that Θ stands for the set of fixed person parameters $\vartheta_1, \ldots, \vartheta_n, \ldots, \vartheta_N$. Then the likelihood function of $\boldsymbol{\eta}$ given X and Θ is given by

$$L(\boldsymbol{\eta}|X,\Theta) = \exp\left(\sum_{n=1}^{N} \mathbf{r}_n'\vartheta_n\right)\exp\left(-\sum_{i,j} s_{ij}\eta_{ij}\right)\prod_{n=1}^{N} p_0(\vartheta_n), \qquad (31)$$

where $\mathbf{r}_n$ is the score pattern of person n and s_{ij} is the number of respondents responding in category j of item i. Notice that if the person parameters are seen as fixed constants, the likelihood function belongs to an exponential family (see, for instance, Andersen, 1980, or Barndorff-Nielsen, 1978). As a consequence, the vector of first-order derivatives of the likelihood function with respect to the parameters has as elements the differences between the sufficient statistics and their expected values. So for $i = 1, \ldots, k$ and $j = 1, \ldots, m_i$, $\mathbf{b}(\boldsymbol{\eta})$ has elements

$$-s_{ij} + \sum_{n=1}^{N} \psi_{ij}(\vartheta_n^{o(i)}), \tag{32}$$

with

$$\psi_{ij}(\vartheta_n^{o(i)}) = \Pr(\chi_{nij} = 1 \mid \vartheta_n^{o(i)}, \boldsymbol{\eta}_i) = \frac{\exp(j\vartheta_n^{o(i)} - \eta_{ij})}{1 + \sum_{h=1}^{m_i} \exp(h\,\vartheta_n^{o(i)} - \eta_{ih})}. \tag{33}$$

Combination of (32) with (21) results in the estimation equations

$$s_{ij} = \sum_{\{r\}} n_r E(\psi_{ij}(\vartheta^{(o(i))}) \mid \mathbf{r}, \boldsymbol{\eta}, \Sigma) \tag{34}$$

for $i = 1, \ldots, k$ and $j = 1, \ldots, m_i$, where $\{r\}$ is the set of all possible score patterns $\mathbf{r}$. The MML estimates for the elements of Σ can be derived noticing that

$$\partial \left[\sum_n \ln g(\vartheta_n \mid \Sigma) \right] \Big/ \partial \sigma_q = c_q(\Sigma) \left[N\sigma_q^2 - \sum_n \vartheta_n^{(q)2} \right],$$

where σ_q is the standard deviation of $\vartheta^{(q)}$, and $c_q(\Sigma)$ is a function depending only on Σ and not on $\boldsymbol{\vartheta}$ (see, for instance, Morrison, 1967, pp. 95–96). Further, if σ_{qq} stands for the covariation between $\vartheta^{(q)}$ and $\vartheta^{(q')}$

$$\partial \left[\sum_n \ln g(\vartheta_n \mid \Sigma) \right] \Big/ \partial \sigma_{qq'} = c_{qq'}(\Sigma) \left[N\sigma_{qq'} - \sum_n \vartheta_n^{(q)} \vartheta_n^{(q')} \right]$$

where $c_{qq'}(\Sigma)$ is also a function depending only on Σ and not on $\boldsymbol{\vartheta}$. Combining this with (22) results in the estimation equations

$$\sigma_q^2 = N^{-1} \sum_{\{r\}} n_r E(\vartheta^{(q)2} \mid \mathbf{r}, \boldsymbol{\eta}, \Sigma) \tag{35}$$

for $q = 1, \ldots, Q$, and

$$\sigma_{qq'} = N^{-1} \sum_{\{r\}} n_r E(\vartheta^{(q)} \vartheta^{(q')} \mid \mathbf{r}, \boldsymbol{\eta}, \Sigma) \tag{36}$$

for $q = 1, \ldots, Q$ and $q' = 1, \ldots, Q$.

Also, on the present case, it is possible to solve the MML estimation equations using the EM algorithm. Using the theory stated earlier, an iteration step boils down to solving (34), (35), and (36) with respect to η and Σ, where (33) is evaluated using the solution of the previous iteration. In the next section some additional numerical aspects of computing the MML estimates are discussed.

SOME REMARKS WITH RESPECT TO THE COMPUTATION OF THE MML ESTIMATES

For the computation of MML estimates and test statistics for unidimensional Rasch models, integrals of the form

$$\int f(\vartheta)g(\vartheta\,|\,\mu,\sigma)d\vartheta = \pi^{-1/2} \int f(\vartheta) \frac{\exp\left(-\left(\frac{\vartheta - \mu}{\sigma\sqrt{2}}\right)^2\right)}{\sigma\sqrt{2}}\,d\vartheta, \qquad (37)$$

with $f(.)$ some function of ϑ, have to be evaluated (see, for instance, Thissen, 1982). This is accomplished by using the Gauss-Hermite quadrature formula, which has the form

$$\int h(x)\exp(-x^2)dx \approx \sum_p h(a_p)E_p, \qquad (38)$$

where a_p are quadrature points and E_p the associated weights (see, for instance, Ralston & Rabinowitz, 1978, pp. 105–108).

Applying the change of variable $x = \frac{\vartheta - \mu}{\sigma\sqrt{2}}$, or equivalently $\vartheta = x\sigma\sqrt{2} + \mu$, to (37) results in

$$\int f(\vartheta)g(\vartheta\,|\,\mu,\sigma)d\vartheta = \pi^{-1/2} \int f(x\sigma\sqrt{2} + \mu)\exp(-x^2)dx$$
$$\approx \pi^{-1/2} \sum_p f(a_p\sigma\sqrt{2} + \mu)E_p. \qquad (39)$$

In a multidimensional Rasch model, such as the one proposed in the present section, many integrals take the form

$$(2\pi)^{-Q/2}|\Sigma|^{-1/2} \int, \ldots, \int f(\vartheta) \exp(1/2\vartheta'\Sigma^{-1}\vartheta)\,d\vartheta. \qquad (40)$$

Evaluation of these integrals by Gauss-Hermite quadrature is accomplished as follows. Consider the decomposition $\Sigma = A\Lambda A'$, where Λ is the diagonal matrix of the eigenvalues of Σ, and A has, as columns, the normalized eigenvectors of Σ. Since A is an orthogonal matrix, $\Sigma^{-1} = A\Lambda^{-1}A'$. It proves convenient to introduce the change of variables $v = \Lambda^{-1/2}A\vartheta/\sqrt{2}$, and so $\vartheta = A'\Lambda^{1/2}v\sqrt{2}$. Applying this to (40) results in

$$\pi^{-Q/2} \int, \ldots, \int f(A'\Lambda^{1/2}v\sqrt{2})\exp(-v'v)\, dv =$$

$$\pi^{-Q/2} \int, \ldots, \int h(\nu_1, \ldots, \nu_Q)\exp(-\sum_q \nu_q^2)\, d\nu_1, \ldots, d\nu_Q \approx$$

$$\pi^{-Q/2} \sum_{p_1}, \ldots, \sum_{p_Q} h(a_{p_1}, \ldots, a_{p_Q})E_{p_1} \ldots E_{p_Q}. \tag{41}$$

It can be seen that the computational effort grows exponentially with the dimensionality of ϑ, since the summation in (41) runs over all combinations of the quadrature points $(a_{p_1}, \ldots, a_{p_Q})$. The fact that every iteration of the estimation algorithms need the eigenvalue decomposition of the current estimate of Σ is less dramatic, because fast algorithms for this purpose exist and the order of Σ cannot be too large anyway.

AN APPLICATION OF THE MODEL

In the Dutch schooling system, students can complete lower general secondary education at two levels, which are labeled MAVO-C and MAVO-D. The courses leading to these two levels of certification are the same, and the pupils make the decision at which level the examinations are entered a couple of months before the examination date. In the Dutch schooling system, the existence of two levels of certification can only be justified if both the levels of the two populations taking the examinations and the levels of the two examinations themselves are essentially different.

To evaluate the differences in the levels of the two populations and the differences in the levels of the two examinations, the two examinations did have a number of common items which were attempted by both groups of students. This resulted in a design which is shown in Figure 14.1, in the form of a persons-by-items matrix.

One of the relevant questions is what percentage of students passing an examination at the MAVO-C level would also have passed the examination at the MAVO-D level. For answering this question, the confounding of item difficulty and level of proficiency suggests applying an IRT model, while the fact that the students' papers are marked using sum scores suggests applying the Rasch model.

The example to be presented here concerns the 1988 examinations

items

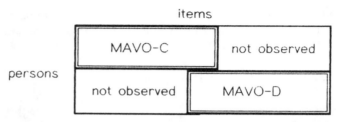

Figure 14.1. Administration design for the MAVO-C and MAVO-D examinations.

in reading comprehension in English. Both the MAVO-C and MAVO-D examination consisted of 50 multiple-choice items, the common part of the two examinations consisted of 10 items. For both examinations, a random sample of 2,000 pupils was drawn from the entire examination population.

The analysis of these data consisted of three steps:

1. Searching for a number of unidimensional Rasch-homogeneous subscales,
2. Combining the subscales by applying the Rasch model with a multivariate ability distribution and testing the fit of this model,
3. Applying the latter model to estimate the frequency distribution of the MAVO-C population (MAVO-D population) on the MAVO-D examination (MAVO-C examination).

Searching for Rasch homogeneous subscales and testing model fit for these subscales were done by applying test statistics and diagnostic techniques introduced by Glas (1988, 1989) and Glas and Verhelst (1989). These techniques can be applied in the framework of conditional maximum likelihood estimation (CML) and marginal maximum likelihood estimation (MML). For the test statistic for the CML framework, the R_{1c} statistic, the score continuum is partitioned into a number of sections, labeled $g = 1, \ldots, G$. The test is based on the differences d_{gi} between the observed and expected number of respondents scoring in section g and making item i correct. If M_{gi} stands for the number of respondents who score in section g and make item i correct, m_{gi} stands for its realization, and $E(M_{gi}|\mathbf{n},\hat{\boldsymbol{\delta}})$ stands for the expected value of M_{gi}, given the frequency distribution of sum scores $\mathbf{n}$ and the CML estimate of the item parameters in the Rasch model for dichotomous items $\hat{\boldsymbol{\delta}}$, $d_{gi} \stackrel{d}{=} m_{gi} - E(M_{gi}|\mathbf{n},\hat{\boldsymbol{\delta}})$. The vector of the differences d, with elements $d_{gi}, g = 1, \ldots, G$ and $i = 1, \ldots, k$, is combined into a quadratic form $R_{1c} = d'W^{-1}d$, where W is an approximation of the covariance matrix of d. It can be shown (see Glas 1988, 1989; Glas

& Verhelst, 1989) that R_{1c} has an asymtotic χ^2 distribution. The R_{1m} statistic, which is defined in the MML framework, follows the same lines, only here $d_{gi} = m_{gi} - E(M_{gi}|\hat{\delta},\hat{\mu},\hat{\sigma})$, where $\hat{\delta}$ is the MML estimate of the item parameters and $\hat{\mu}$, and $\hat{\sigma}$ are the MML estimates of the mean and the variance of a normal ability distribution. The R_{1c} and R_{1m} tests have power against violation of the assumption with respect to equal item discrimination indices. To test the validity of the assumption with respect to the ability distribution in the MML framework, Glas (1989) and Glas and Verhelst (1989) have introduced the R_0 statistic, which is based on the differences $d_r = n_r - E(N_r|\hat{\delta},\hat{\mu},\hat{\sigma})$, for $r = 0, \ldots, k$, where n_r is the observed number of respondents attaining sum score r and $E(N_r|\hat{\delta},\hat{\mu},\hat{\sigma})$ is its expectation. As with the other two statistics, the differences are combined into a quadratic form which has an asymptotic χ^2 distribution.

The results from the initial analyses are shown in the first column of Table 14.1. In the row labeled "k," the total number of items in the design is given, in the rows labeled "$k^{(1)}$" and "$k^{(2)}$" the numbers of items of the examinations are given, and the row labeled "$k^{(1,2)}$" gives the number of items common to both examinations. The remaining rows give the value of the various test statistics. The row labeled "$R_{0(1)}$" gives the value of the R_0 statistic, computed using the assump-

Table 14.1. Evaluation of Model Fit for Examinations in Reading Comprehension of English

	Examination	Subscale 1	Subscale 2	Subscale 3
k	90	41	30	13
$k^{(1)}$	50	21	16	8
$k^{(2)}$	50	22	16	7
$k^{(1,2)}$	10	2	2	2
$R_{0(1)}$	267.21	124.29	65.85	24.37
df	98	41	30	13
prob	0.00	0.00	0.00	0.03
$R_{0(2)}$	106.39	46.47	36.54	6.45
df	96	39	28	11
prob	0.22	0.19	0.13	0.84
R_{1m}	3619.43	232.57	165.91	92.64
df	595	204	149	77
prob	0.00	0.08	0.16	0.11
R_{1c}	3274.74	185.38	128.18	81.17
df	499	165	121	66
prob	0.00	0.13	0.31	0.10

tion that all respondents are sampled from the same normal ability distribution. It can be seen that this assumption results in rejection of the model. The row labeled "$R_{0(2)}$" gives the value of the R_0 statistic computed using the assumption that the MAVO-C and MAVO-D populations have distinct normal ability distributions. With this assumption, the model is not rejected. Finally, the rows labeled "R_{1m}" and "R_{1c}" give the value of the statistics of the same name, the former computed using the assumption of two distinct normal distributions. Both statistics were highly significant, and the hypothesis that the Rasch model holds for the complete data set had to be rejected.

The second phase of the data analyses consisted of searching for Rasch homogeneous subsets of items. These subsets of items shall be referred to as subscales. For equating the two examinations, the restriction was imposed that every subscale had to have at least one item belonging to the common part of the examinations. Further, the other items of a subscale should be about evenly distributed over the two examinations, that is, it should not be the case that a subset consisted of, say, 20 items for one and three items from the other examination.

The process used for identifying the subscales can best be characterized by the phrase trial and error; the heuristic used for identifying subscales consisted of three steps. Firstly, ML estimates of the parameters in the Birnbaum model were computed on the complete data set, to identify items with approximately the same discrimination indices. It was attempted to form subscales with, respectively, high-, medium-, and low-discrimination indices. Secondly, given a partitioning of the items that met the two restrictions above, for each subscale CML and MML, estimates and the associated test statistics were computed. Thirdly, the relative contributions of individual items to the value of the R_{1c} and R_{1m} statistics were assessed by inspecting the values of d_{gi}. For every item, the pattern of the signs of $d_{gi}, g = 1, \ldots, G$ is informative with respect to the cause of the lack of item fit. For instance, if the signs are negative for the lower and positive for the higher sections of the score continuum, the discrimination index of the item is too large compared to the ones of the other items. In the present example this pattern was used to determine whether it was worth trying to assign an item to a subscale characterized by higher- or lower-discrimination indices. Finally, the last two steps were repeated until an acceptable degree of model fit was obtained. The results of this process are shown in the last three columns of Table 14.1. The column labeled "subscale 1" relates to a subscale that mainly consisted of items which had medium discrimination indices in the initial analysis, the columns labeled "subscale 2" and "subscale 3" relate to, respectively, subscales which mainly consisted of items with low- and high-discrimination indices in the initial analysis. Using the restriction that the mean discrimination index of subscale 1 equaled 1.000, the mean discrimination index of the other two subscales was equal to 0.882 and 1.259. The rows labeled "k", "$k^{(1)}$", "$k^{(2)}$", and "$k^{(1,2)}$" give the total number of items in a subscale, the number of items belonging to the first and second examination and the number of items belonging to both examinations. Notice that 6 out of 90 items could not be categorized in one of the three subscales. Neither was it possible to construct a fourth subscale from these remaining items. The fact that not all items could be categorized with one of the subscales was dealt with as follows. On the MAVO-C examination, the original cut-off point was 24/25, where 24 is the highest score resulting in failing and 25 the lowest score resulting in passing the examination. With this cut-off point, 23.2 percent of the students failed. For the MAVO-C examination without the 6 misfitting items, the adjusted cut-off point was chosen such that the percentage of failing students remained the same, which resulted in an adjusted cut-off point 21/22. The percentage of students passing with the original cut-off point and failing with the adjusted one was 1.1 percent, the reversed change in final result applied to 3.6 percent of the students. The same procedure resulted in adjusting the MAVO-D cut-off point from 29/30 to 24/25, in this case the percentage of reverses from passing to failing, and failing to passing were, respectively, 2.3 and 4.2 percent.

The second step of the analysis consisted of combining the subscales by applying the Rasch model with a multivariate ability distribution, and testing the fit of this model. Using this partitioning of the two examinations into subscales, three models were tested. In Model 1, it was assumed that the ability of a MAVO-C examinee had a trivariate normal distribution with mean o and covariance matrix Σ_C. Let $L(\delta, \Sigma_C | X_C)$ be the likelihood given the MAVO-C data matrix X_C. Further, it was assumed that the ability of a MAVO-D examinee had a trivariate normal distribution with mean μ_D and covariance matrix Σ_D. The likelihood given the MAVO-D data matrix is denoted by $L(\delta, \mu_D, \Sigma_D | X_D)$. Due to experimental independence,

$$L(\delta, \Sigma_C, \mu_D, \Sigma_D | X_C, X_D) = L(\delta, \Sigma_C | X_C)\, L(\delta, \mu_D, \Sigma_D | X_D). \tag{42}$$

For maximizing the left-hand side of (42), the estimation equations given in section 3 must be generalized to an incomplete design. This generalization will not be worked out in detail, only the principle will be given. Since

$$\ln L(\delta, \Sigma_C, \mu_D, \Sigma_D | X_C, X_D) = \ln L(\delta, \Sigma_C | X_C) + \ln L(\delta, \mu_D, \Sigma_D | X_D), \tag{43}$$

the derivation boils down to considering the estimation equations for the design groups, and summing both sides of these equations over design groups to obtain the estimation equations for the complete model.

In Model 2, which is a special case of Model 1, it was assumed that the correlations between the three subscales are the same for both groups of examinees. So if P_C is the correlation matrix for MAVO-C and P_D the correlation matrix for MAVO-D, $P = P_C = P_D$. On the other hand, the standard deviations of the ability distributions of MAVO-C and MAVO-D, say σ_C and σ_D, are left unrestricted. The likelihood of this model is given by

$$L(\delta,\sigma_C,\mu_D,\sigma_D,P|X_C,X_D) = L(\delta,\sigma_C,P|X_C) \, L(\delta,\mu_D,\sigma_D,P|X_D). \tag{44}$$

Finally, Model 3 is the special case of both Model 1 and Model 2, where it is assumed that the ability distributions of both populations have the same covariance matrix Σ. The likelihood of this model is given by

$$L(\delta,\Sigma,\mu_D|X_C,X_D) = L(\delta,\Sigma|X_C) \, L(\delta,\mu_D,\Sigma|X_D). \tag{45}$$

Testing the validity of these models proceeds as follows. Let L_0 be the likelihood function of a model which is a special case of some more general model with likelihood function L_1. It is assumed that L_0 has s' parameters and L_1 has s parameters, $s' < s$. The validity of the special model can be tested against the more general alternative using the likelihood ratio statistic $\lambda = -2ln(L_0/L_1)$, which has an asymptotic χ^2 distribution with $s - s'$ degrees of freedom (Lehmann, 1986).

In the first two rows of Table 14.2, the values λ for testing Model 3 against Model 2 and testing Model 2 against Model 1 are given. It can be seen that in both cases, the special model had to be rejected.

To test the validity of Model 1, a more general model had to be constructed. Let δ_C be the vector of all parameters in the MAVO-C examination, and let δ_D be the vector of all parameters in the MAVO-D examination. Notice that δ_C and δ_D have parameters of items which figure in both examinations to be in common. Since only items that

Table 14.2. Sequential Hypothesis Testing Using the Likelihood Ratio Statistic

Test	L_0	L_1	λ	df	prob.
Model 3 versus *Model 2*	(45)	(44)	19.25	3	0.000
Model 2 versus *Model 1*	(44)	(42)	16.52	3	0.000
Model 1 versus *Model 0*	(42)	(46)	5.35	3	0.148

could be categorized in the subscales are considered, δ_C and δ_D have 6 items in common. The likelihood of Model 0 is given by

$$L(\delta_C, \delta_D, \Sigma_C, \Sigma_D | X_C, X_D) = L(\delta_C, \Sigma_C | X_C)\, L(\delta_D, \Sigma_D | X_D), \qquad (46)$$

where it is assumed that the parameters of the common items are different for both subgroups. For the present model the restriction $\mu_D = o$ has to be imposed, since the models for MAVO-C and MAVO-D are no longer linked, and every subscale now needs a separate normalization. Obviously, Model 0 cannot be used for equating. Testing Model 1 against Model 0 boils down to testing whether introducing separate estimates of the parameters of the common items for both examinations results in a significant improvement of model fit. The result of the test is given in the last row of Table 14.2; Model 1 was not rejected.

With respect to testing this hypothesis, a short remark is in order. When using a likelihood ratio statistic, the restricted model must be a special case of the general model. However, to identify model (46) the additional restriction $\mu_D = o$ is imposed on the general model, while in the restricted model (42) μ_D is free. This, however, does not invalidate the procedure. Consider a reparametrization of both the models (42) and (46), where μ_C and μ_D are free. Further, every subscale in (42) is fixed by putting an item of the common part of both examinations equal to zero. The subscales in (46) are identified putting the two parameters of the same items, which are fixed to identify (42), equal to zero. With this parametrization it can be easily seen that (42) is indeed a special case of (46), and the likelihood ratio procedure is properly applied.

The last step of the analysis consisted of estimating the frequency distribution of the MAVO-C population on the MAVO-D examination and the frequency distribution of the MAVO-D population on the MAVO-C examination. The former distribution was estimated by computing $E(N_r | \delta_D, \Sigma_C)$, for $r = 0, \ldots, k_D$, where k_D is the maximum score that could be obtained on the MAVO-D examination, the latter by computing $E(N_r | \delta_C, \mu_D, \Sigma_D)$, for $r = 0, \ldots, k_C$, where k_C is the maximum score that could be obtained on the MAVO-C examination. The parameters were estimated using Model 1, that is, the model given by (42). Details of the computation of these expectations are beyond the scope of this chapter, but can be found in Glas (1989).

An analogous procedure was carried out for computing the percentage of MAVO-D students passing or failing the MAVO-C examination. The results are summarized in Table 14.3.

The outcome clearly shows that both the examinations and the populations are of distinctly different levels: 0.5 percent of the MAVO-D

Table 14.3. Percentage of Students Passing and Failing

Population		Examination	
		MAVO-C	MAVO-D
MAVO-C	passed	76.2%	16.3%
	failed	23.8%	83.7%
MAVO-D	passed	99.5%	82.4%
	failed	0.5%	17.6%

students failed the MAVO-C examination, and 17.6% of the MAVO-C students passed the MAVO-D examination.

DISCUSSION

In this chapter a generalization of the Rasch model is presented where it is assumed that a test consists of a number of Rasch homogeneous subscales and the ability parameters associated with the various subscales have a multivariate normal distribution. It is shown that introduction of the model can be motivated, not only from its multidimensional representation of ability, but also from the fact that it can be viewed as an alternative for the Birnbaum model that does not suffer from the well-known estimation and testing problem associated with the latter model (see, for instance, Fischer, 1974).

In the application setting, the model is utilized to solve a problem that essentially boils down to test equating. The analysis presented consists of three steps. First, the items are partitioned into a number of Rasch-homogeneous subscales using data analysis techniques developed for the usual unidimensional Rasch model. Next, the fit of the Rasch model with a multivariate ability distribution is evaluated using a number of hierarchical likelihood ratio tests. Finally, various examinations are equated by estimating the score distributions of the various populations under consideration.

REFERENCES

Andersen, E.B. (1973). Conditional inference for multiple-choice questionnaires. *British Journal of Mathematical and Statistical Psychology, 26,* 31–44.

Andersen, E.B. (1977). Sufficient statistics and latent trait models. *Psychometrika, 42,* 69–81.

Andersen, E.B. (1980). *Discrete statistical models with social science applications.* Amsterdam: North-Holland.

Andersen, E.B. (1985). Estimating latent correlations between repeated testings. *Psychometrika, 50,* 3–16.

Barndorff-Nielsen, O. (1978). *Information and exponential families in statistical theory.* New York: John Wiley & Sons.

Birnbaum, A. (1968). Some latent trait models and their use in inferring an examinee's ability. In F.M. Lord & M.R. Novick (Eds.), *Statistical theories of mental test scores* (pp. 397–479). Reading, MA: Addison-Wesley.

Bock, R.D., & Aitkin, M. (1981). Marginal maximum likelihood estimation of item parameters: An application of an EM algorithm. *Psychometrika, 46,* 443–459.

Dempster, A.P., Laird, N.M., & Rubin, D.B. (1977). Maximum likelihood from incomplete data via the EM algorithm (with discussion). *Journal of the Royal Statistical Society, Series B, 39,* 1–38.

Fischer, G.H. (1974). *Einführung in die theorie psychologischer tests.* Wien: Verlag Hans Huber.

Glas, C.A.W. (1988). The derivation of some tests for the Rasch model from the multinomial distribution. *Psychometrika, 53,* 525–546.

Glas, C.A.W. (1989). *Contributions to estimating and testing Rasch models.* Master's Thesis, University of Twente.

Glas, C.A.W., & Verhelst, N.D. (1989). Extensions of the partial credit model. *Psychometrika, 54,* 635–659.

Lehmann, E.L. (1986). *Testing statistical hypotheses* (2nd ed.). New York: John Wiley & Sons.

Lord, F.M. (1980). *Applications of item response theory to practical testing problems.* Hillsdale, NJ: Lawrence Erlbaum.

Louis, T.A. (1982). Finding the observed information matrix when using the EM algorithm. *Journal of the Royal Statistical Society, Series B, 44,* 226–233.

Masters, G.N. (1982). A Rasch model for partial credit scoring. *Psychometrika, 47,* 149–174.

Masters, G.N. (1985). Comparing latent trait and latent class analysis of Likert type data. *Psychometrika, 50,* 69–82.

Mislevy, R.J. (1984). Estimating latent distributions. *Psychometrika, 49,* 359–381.

Mislevy, R.J. (1986). Bayes modal estimation in item response models. *Psychometrika, 51,* 177–195.

Molenaar, I.W. (1983). Item steps. *Heymans Bulletins* (Report No. HB-83-630-EX). Rijks Universiteit Groningen.

Morrison, D.F. (1967). *Multivariate statistical methods.* New York: McGraw-Hill.

Neyman, J., & Scott, E.L. (1948). Consistent estimates based on partially consistent observations. *Econometrika, 16,* 1–32.

Ralston, A., & Rabinowitz, P. (1978). *A first course in numerical analysis* (2nd ed.). Tokyo: McGraw-Hill.

Rasch, G. (1960). *Probabilistic models for some intelligence and attainment tests.* Kopenhagen: Danish Institute for Educational Research.

Rasch, G. (1961). On the general laws and the meaning of measurement in psychology. *Proceedings of the Fourth Berkeley Symposium on Mathematical Statistics and Probability* (pp. 321–333). Berkeley: University of California Press.

Rigdon, S.E., & Tsutakawa, R.K. (1983). Parameter estimation in latent trait models. *Psychometrika, 48,* 567–574.

Rigdon, S.E., & Tsutakawa, R.K. (1987). Estimation for the Rasch model when both ability and difficulty parameters are random. *Journal of Educational Statistics, 12,* 76–86.

Thissen, D. (1982). Marginal maximum likelihood estimation for the one-parameter logistic model. *Psychometrika, 47,* 175–186.

part IV

Mathematical and Statistical Applications to Measurement

Chapter 15

Computerized Test Construction

Jos J. Adema
Ellen Boekkooi-Timminga
Department of Education
University of Twente, The Netherlands

A.J.R.M. (Noud) Gademann
Department of Applied Mathematics
University of Twente, The Netherlands

Lately, item banking has become a very popular topic in the practice of testing (e.g., Hambleton, 1986; van der Linden, 1986). It assumes the availability of large collections of items stored with their characteristics in a computer. Two major conditions for this development were the progress made in item response theory (Hambleton & Swaminathan, 1985; Lord, 1980; Rasch, 1960) and the availability of computers. In item banking one can distinguish three main stages: (a) building an item bank (including item writing, item pretesting, and calibration; see, for example, Chapters 16 and 17, respectively), (b) test item selection, and (c) analyzing and reporting scores.

This paper considers the problem of test item selection (Stage b). The purpose is to select tests from item banks that fit the desires of the test constructor best. In practice, items are often selected by spreading out item cards on the floor (Bejar, 1985). Numerous revision stages are needed to delete and add test items, considering all kinds of criteria. It is clear that this is a subjective process that may conceal many sources of invalidity. The two major problems with this approach are the time-consuming aspect and the possibility of a bad test quality, especially in a psychometric sense. In view of these problems many authors have recommended the development of computerized test construction systems (e.g., Bejar, 1985; Lippey, 1974; van Thiel & Zwarts, 1986).

At the moment most testing institutes are interested in or already developing a test construction system, for instance: Educational Testing Service (ETS), American College Testing Program (ACT), and the National Institute of Educational Measurement in The Netherlands (CITO). The design of an integrated system that includes the greater part of the stages denoted above is discussed by van Thiel and Zwarts (1986).

In this chapter test construction is approached from a linear programming perspective. Algorithms for solving linear programming problems can be implemented in a computerized test construction system. Two advantages of approaching test construction problems this way are: (a) Good quality tests can be constructed meeting a series of practical test requirements, and (b) computer packages are available for solving these kinds of problems. The linear programming models that are discussed do not depend on the particular item response model used. In the remainder of this chapter, however, only a special item response model is considered namely the Rasch model (Rasch, 1960). As the linear programming models for test item selection are based on the use of item and test information functions, first, an introduction to the Rasch model and information functions is given. Then, two basic linear programming models for test construction are described, that can be expanded by all kinds of practical constraints of interest. Next, some examples for one of the two models are given. The chapter ends with some conclusions and a discussion.

INFORMATION FUNCTIONS FOR THE RASCH MODEL

In this section the notion of information functions is introduced for the Rasch model. In general an item response model specifies "a relationship between the observable examinee's test performance and the unobservable traits or abilities assumed to underlie performance on the test" (Hambleton & Swaminathan, 1985). An important feature of item response theory with respect to item banking is that ability and item parameter estimates are not population-dependent. Here the

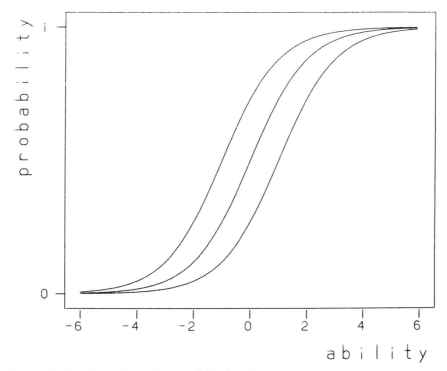

Figure 15.1.   Three item-characteristic functions

Rasch model is considered because it is a simple, computationally attractive item response model for dichotomously (right-wrong) scored responses.

In the Rasch model it is assumed that the probability of a correct response on an item i is a function of the ability of the examinee, θ, and the difficulty of the item:

$$P_i(\theta) = \exp(\theta - b_i)/[1 + \exp(\theta - b_i)], \tag{1}$$

where b_i is the difficulty parameter of item i. $P_i(\theta)$ is called the item characteristic function. In Figure 15.1 three item-characteristic functions are displayed, for items with item difficulties -1, 0, and 1, respectively. The Rasch model assumes a single underlying latent ability (unidimensionality) and statistical independence among the examinee's reponses to different items in the test (local independence).

For the Rasch model the information function of an item i is formulated as follows:

$$I_i(\theta) = P_i(\theta) [1 - P_i(\theta)]. \qquad (2)$$

The item information function is important in test construction, because it gives an indication of the accuracy of measurement: The greater the information at ability level θ, the smaller the standard error of measurement. The information function of a test is found by adding up the item information functions of the items in the test:

$$I_t(\theta) = \sum_{i=1}^{n} I_i(\theta), \qquad (3)$$

where $I_t(\theta)$ is the test information function and n is the number of items in the test. In Figure 15.2 the item information functions of the three items in Figure 15.1 and their test information function are graphed.

In this chapter it is assumed that item banks with known item parameters b_i are available. From these item parameters information

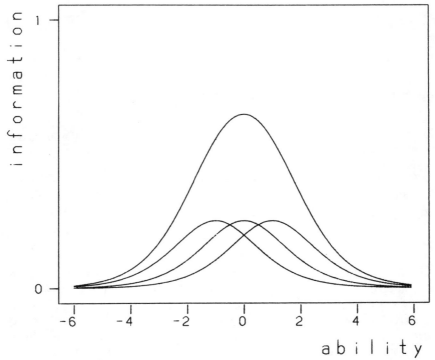

Figure 15.2. Three item-information functions and their test-information function.

functions of the items can be computed. The linear programming models in the next section are formulated such that items with relatively greater information are selected.

TEST CONSTRUCTION MODELS

The problem of selecting items from an item bank for a test can be formulated as a linear programming model. A linear programming model consists of an objective function and a number of constraints, which are both linear in the decision variables. The objective function is the part of the model that should be optimized under the restrictions as formulated in the constraints. Some references to linear programming are Daellenbach, George, and McNickle (1983) and Wagner (1975).

Two linear programming models with 0–1 variables for test construction will be given. The decision variables x_i are defined as follows:

$$x_i = \begin{cases} 0 & \text{if item i is not selected for the test} \\ 1 & \text{if item i is selected for the test,} \end{cases} \quad i = 1, \ldots, I$$

where I is the number of items in the item bank.

Target Information Function

In both models it is assumed that the test constructor specifies a target information function at some well-chosen ability levels. It is not necessary to specify the target for the whole ability continuum for two reasons. First, the item information function values hardly differ at nearby ability levels. Second, one is often only interested in the amount of information in the test at some specific ability levels, for instance, at the level where the cut-off point in a certain decision procedure is located.

Eliciting target information function values from a test constructor is not a simple task. A possible procedure for determining the exact heights of the target information function is described by Kelderman (1987). In this procedure the test constructor has to specify the acceptable probabilities of a wrong order of the ability estimates of several pairs of subjects. From these probabilities the information values can be computed. Another procedure that assumes the use of the maximin model to be described later in this section, is discussed by van der Linden and Boekkooi-Timminga (1989). Using this method the desired shape and not the exact height of the target information function can be obtained. However, it is expected that this method will only be suited for test constructors with a fair amount of knowledge of information functions.

In case the maximin model is used, the shape of the target information function can also be derived from the type of decision one wants to take with the test. This will be attractive to test constructors without knowledge of information functions. For a discussion of types of decisions that can be made using tests the reader is referred to van der Linden (1985). Whenever a selective test has to be constructed the cut-off point at the ability continuum needs to be indicated, next the test information is maximized at this point. For a diagnostic test a flat target information function will be desired. In this case the test constructor can be asked to specify the interval of the ability continuum that he or she is interested in, next the test information in this interval is maximized. For a classification test, two or more cut-off points have to be given by the test constructor, next the information at these points is maximized. Experiments have shown that the latter approach can be fruitful (Boekkooi-Timminga, 1989).

Model 1: Minimum Test Length

The first linear programming model for test construction was proposed by Theunissen (1985). Theunissen minimized the number of items in the test under the constraints that the obtained test information values at some specified ability levels θ_k, $k = 1, \ldots, K$ had to be at least as high as the corresponding required target values. The ability levels θ_k, $k = 1, \ldots, K$ and the target information values at these levels were chosen by the test constructor. The resulting linear programming model is formulated as follows:

$$\text{minimize} \sum_{i=1}^{I} x_i \tag{4}$$

subject to

$$\sum_{i=1}^{I} I_i(\theta_k)x_i \geq T(\theta_k), \qquad k = 1, \ldots, K, \tag{5}$$

$$x_i \in \{0,1\}, \qquad i = 1, \ldots, I, \tag{6}$$

where $T(\theta_k)$ is the target for the value of the test information function at ability level θ_k, $k = 1, \ldots, K$. The objective function of the model is given in (4), and (5) and (6) are the constraints of the model.

Model 2: Maximin Model

The second linear programming model was proposed by van der Linden and Boekkooi-Timminga (1989). In this model the test length is fixed and the targets are specified in relative instead of absolute values. So, the test constructor has to specify the number of items in the test and the shape of the target test information function. The advantage of the latter compared to specifying absolute values is that the test constructor does not have to be able to specify the target test information function in the required metric. The corresponding linear programming model can be formulated as a maximin model:

$$\text{maximize } z, \tag{7}$$

subject to

$$\sum_{i=1}^{I} I_i(\theta_k)x_i - r_k z \geq 0, \qquad k = 1, \ldots, K, \tag{8}$$

$$\sum_{i=1}^{I} x_i = n, \tag{9}$$

$$x_i \in \{0,1\}, \qquad i = 1, \ldots, I, \tag{10}$$

$$z \geq 0, \tag{11}$$

where the test constructor specifies the shape of the target test information function by choosing values for r_k, $k = 1, \ldots, K$. The r_k's specify a particular target shape for the information, but not the vertical location of the information. By maximizing the additional decision variable z in (7) the constraints in (8) imply that the obtained test information at each of the ability levels θ_k will be greater than or equal to $r_k z$. Thus, the test information function has at least the shape as required by the test constructor. The number of items in the test is fixed to n by constraint (9). The difference between the model of Theunissen and the maximin model is that in the former the target test information function is controlled and the test length is optimized, while in the latter the test length is controlled and the test information function is maximized.

Additional Practical Constraints

The test construction models as presented here are basic models which can be extended by all kinds of linear constraints with respect to the properties of the test. For instance, in case of model (7)–(11) a test constructor can control the composition of the test by imposing the constraints:

$$\sum_{i \in V_j} x_i = n_j, \qquad j = 1, \ldots, J, \tag{12}$$

where $V_j, j = 1, \ldots, J$ are subsets of items from which the test constructor wants to select $n_j \leq n$ items. In the same way it is possible to extend the test construction models with constraints regarding administration time, dependencies between items, and so on (e.g., van der Linden & Boekkooi-Timminga, 1989).

SOME NUMERICAL EXAMPLES

In this section some examples of tests are given that can be constructed using the model that minimizes the test length. In some examples there are additional practical conditions involved.

For the numerical examples a simulated item bank of 200 items that fit the Rasch model is used. The item difficulty parameter values are sampled randomly from an $N(0,1)$-distribution. The items in the bank are sorted in order of increasing item difficulty. So item 1 is the easiest item and item 200 is the most difficult item in the bank. The target information function is specified for three ability levels and is given by:

$$T(-1) = 3.50,$$

$$T(0) = 4.00,$$

$$T(1) = 3.50.$$

Here the only goal is to reach the target information by selecting as few items as possible in the test. The associated 0–1 programming problem is solved using an linear programming method, which gives a fractional solution ($0 \leq x_i \leq 1$). Next a rounding procedure is applied which converts the fractional solution into a feasible 0–1 solution. In this case the following test is constructed:

Test 1

Selected items:	86, 87, . . . , 103 (18 items).
Test information:	$I_t(-1) = 3.55$,
	$I_t(0) = 4.48$,
	$I_t(1) = 3.51$.

It is seen that at least 18 items are needed to reach the target information values. Looking at the item numbers of the items that are selected, it is observed that the selected items have about the same item difficulty parameter values. This is a typical result when no additional constraints are imposed and the objective is to minimize the test length. Due to this fact one could prefer to add a condition, namely that a certain spread in the item difficulty parameter values of the selected items is reached. If, for example, a condition is added requiring that a group of easier items as well as a group of more difficult items is to be selected, the following test is constructed:

Test 2

Selected items:	57, 58, . . . , 65,
	126, 127, . . . ,135 (19 items).
Test information:	$I_t(-1) = 3.55$,
	$I_t(0) = 4.30$,
	$I_t(1) = 3.63$.

Again the target information is reached, but it is seen that also a somewhat larger (and perhaps more preferable) spread in the item difficulty parameter values of the selected items is achieved. However, it is noticed that 19 items were needed instead of 18 in the first example. This is a typical property of test construction problems, that is intuitively clear. When the number of constraints is increased, the number of tests fulfilling these conditions decreases. For example, the first test (of 18 items) does not fulfil the extended set of conditions for the second test, and neither does any other test of 18 items. One should take these properties into account when specifying a set of test requirements.

The last example including another practical constraint is given next. Suppose the two tests of the previous examples were already used, and a third test is desired that does not contain any of the items that were used in the first or the second test, but that also fulfils the set of conditions as specified for test 2. Then the following test is constructed:

Test 3

Selected items: 42, 43, . . . , 51,
                   144, 145, . . . , 153 (20 items).

Test information: $I_t(-1) = 3.57$,
                   $I_t(0) = 4.00$,
                   $I_t(1) = 3.58$.

The same tendency is observed: To fulfil the extended set of conditions (now consisting of target information, spread of the item difficulties of the selected items, and no items from previous tests) again an additional item is needed.

Of course it is not always the case that additional conditions result in tests with more items, but these examples were just meant to illustrate some of the possibilities to use linear programming for solving test construction problems, and to illustrate some properties of these problems. It has to be noted that the above problems were solved in about 20 seconds each, on an Olivetti M24 with mathematical coprocessor.

CONCLUSIONS AND DISCUSSION

In this chapter it was shown how practical test construction problems can be formulated as linear programming problems. Two different linear programming models for test construction were given. The first minimizes the test length subject to constraints that at least a specified level of information is obtained at certain ability levels. The second assumes that only the shape of the target test information function is specified. Then, the total amount of test information at certain ability levels is maximized considering the desired shape and test length.

Other models are also possible. Different objective functions can be considered and all kinds of practical constraints can be added (e.g., van der Linden & Boekkooi-Timminga, 1989). Furthermore, research has been carried out on typical test construction problems: The construction of tests from an IRT-based item bank using classical item parameters (Adema & van der Linden, 1989); interitem dependencies (Theunissen, 1986, 1989; Verstralen, 1989); two-stage and multistage test construction (Adema, 1990); simultaneous construction of a number of related tests (Boekkooi-Timminga, 1987); and parallel test construction (Boekkooi-Timminga, 1990).

Algorithms for solving 0–1 linear programming problems are available (e.g., Land & Doig, 1960) and have been implemented in computer code, for instance, MPSX370 (IBM) and Lindo (Lindo Systems, Inc.). However, determining the best solution might take a very large amount of time. In the previous section the continuous solution was rounded, however, this will not always be practical. Further research is being carried out on speeding up the algorithms (e.g., Adema, 1988; Kester, 1988; Razoux Schulz, 1987; van der Linden & Boekkooi-Timminga, 1989), and on formulating new models that probably can be solved more easily (Baas & Gademann, 1989; Boekkooi-Timminga, in press; Gademann, 1987).

Before the linear programming models presented in this chapter can be applied successfully in real life, they have to be implemented in a computerized test construction system. Test constructors not familiar with item response theory (in particular, information functions) and linear programming should be able to use such a system. Six major procedures should be implemented: (a) item and test bank processing, in particular composing an item bank, changing item bank charac-teristics, and saving selected tests in a test bank; (b) model bank pro-cessing, in particular changing and adding test construction models; (c) eliciting test specifications; (d) test item selection; (e) reviewing the selected test; and (f) test editing and printing. Several standard linear programming models for test construction are included in the model bank. Only specialists should be able to view, add, or change linear programming models. After a test is selected the test constructor should be able to fix items for the test, exclude others, and restart the selection process. A more complete description of a computerized test construction system including linear programming models is given by Boekkooi-Timminga (1989).

In the introduction, three stages of item banking were distinguished of which stage b (test item selection) formed the main subject of this paper. Next, the other stages are briefly considered. The process of item writing that is part of the first stage takes a lot of time, and has many sources of possible invalidity. Rikers (1988) gives a description of the design of a computerized item construction system that should reduce the invalidity and should structure the process of item writing. With respect to the other aspects of testing it is noted that procedures for calibration, scoring, and reporting have been implemented in com-puter code for several years now.

REFERENCES

Adema, J.J. (1988). *A note on solving large-scale zero-one programming prob-lems* (Research Rep. 88–4). Enschede, The Netherlands: University of Twente, Department of Education.

Adema, J.J. (1990). The construction of customized two-stage tests. *Journal of Educational Measurement, 27,* 241–253.

Adema, J.J., & van der Linden, W.J. (1989). Algorithms for computerized test construction using classical item parameters. *Journal of Educational Statistics, 14,* 279–290.

Baas, S.M., & Gademann, A.J.R.M. (1989, March). *Multi-objective test design with mathematical programming.* Paper presented at the Annual Meeting of the American Educational Research Association, San Francisco, CA.

Bejar, I.I. (1985). Speculations on the future of test design. In S.E. Embretson (Ed.), *Test design: Developments in psychology and psychometrics* (pp. 279–294). New York: Academic Press.

Boekkooi-Timminga, E. (1987). Simultaneous test construction by zero-one programming. *Methodika, 1,* 101–112.

Boekkooi-Timminga, E. (1989). *Models for computerized test construction* (Doctoral dissertation, University of Twente). De Lier: Academisch Boeken Centrum.

Boekkooi-Timminga, E. (1990). The construction of parallel tests from IRT-based item banks. *Journal of Educational Statistics, 15,* 129–145.

Boekkooi-Timminga, E. (in press). A cluster-based method for test construction. *Applied Psychological Measurement.*

Daellenbach, H.G., George, J.A., & McNickle, D.C. (1983). *Introduction to operations research techniques* (2nd ed.). London: Allyn and Bacon, Inc.

Gademann, A.J.R.M. (1987). *Item selection using multi-objective programming* (OIS-project Report No. 01). Arnhem: National Institute for Educational Measurement (Cito).

Hambleton, R.K. (1986). The changing conception of measurement: A commentary. *Applied Psychological Measurement, 10,* 415–421.

Hambleton, R.K., & Swaminathan, H. (1985). *Item response theory: Principles and applications.* Boston: Kluwer-Nijhoff.

Kelderman, H. (1987). Some procedures to assess target information functions. In W.J. van der Linden (Ed.), *IRT-based test construction* (Research Rep. 87–2). Enschede: University of Twente, Department of Education.

Kester, J.G. (1988). *Various mathematical programming approaches toward item selection* (OIS-project Rep. No. 03). Arnhem: National Institute for Educational Measurement (Cito).

Land, A.H., & Doig, A.G. (1960). An automated method for solving discrete programming problems. *Econometrica, 28,* 497–520.

Lippey, G. (1974). Overview. In G. Lippey (Ed.), *Computer-assisted test construction* (pp. 3–27). Englewood Cliffs, NJ: Educational Technology Publications.

Lord, F.M. (1980). *Applications of item response theory to practical testing problems.* Hillsdale, NJ: Erlbaum.

Rasch, G. (1960). *Probabilistic models for some intelligence and attainment tests.* Copenhagen: Nielsen and Lydiche.

Razoux Schultz, A.F. (1987). *Item selection using heuristics* (OIS-project Report

No. 02). Arnhem: National Institute for Educational Measurement (Cito).

Rikers, J.H.A.N. (1988). *Towards an authoring system for item construction* (Research Rep. 88–7). Enschede, The Netherlands: University of Twente, Department of Education.

Theunissen, T.J.J.M. (1985). Binary programming and test design. *Psychometrika, 50,* 411–420.

Theunissen, T.J.J.M. (1986). Optimization algorithms in test design. *Applied Psychological Measurement, 10,* 381–390.

Theunissen, T.J.J.M. (1989, March). *Boolean expressions in item banking.* Paper presented at the Annual Meeting of the American Educational Research Association, San Francisco, CA.

van der Linden, W.J. (1985). Decision theory in educational research and testing. In T. Husen & T.N. Postlethwaite (Eds.), *International encyclopedia of education: Research and studies* (Vol. 3, pp. 1320–1333). Oxford: Pergamon Press.

van der Linden, W.J. (1986). The changing conception of measurement in education and psychology. *Applied Psychological Measurement, 10,* 325–332.

van der Linden, W.J., & Boekkooi-Timminga, E. (1989). A maximin model for test design with practical constraints. *Psychometrika, 54,* 237–247.

van Thiel, C.C., & Zwarts, M.A. (1986). Development of a testing service system. *Applied Psychological Measurement, 10,* 391–403.

Verstralen, H.H.F.M. (1989, March). *Test specification with constraints at item level: Algorithms.* Paper presented at the Annual Meeting of the American Educational Research Association, San Francisco, CA.

Wagner, H.M. (1975). *Principles of operations research: With applications to managerial decisions.* London: Prentice-Hall International, Inc.

Chapter **16**

Optimality of Sampling Designs in Item Response Theory Models

Martijn P.F. Berger
Wim J. van der Linden
Department of Education
University of Twente, The Netherlands

Item response theory (IRT) models have been used in many applications where test construction and item selection play a central role. For example, Theunissen (1985), van der Linden (1987,1988) and van der Linden and Boekkooi-Timminga (1989) used information about the ability parameters to optimally design tests. Samejima (1977) used this information for tailored testing and Lord (1974), Lord and Wingersky (1985), Wingersky and Lord (1985), Thissen and Wainer (1982), and de Gruijter (1985, 1988) used the asymptotic standard errors of the parameters to compare the relative efficiency of different tests and IRT models. See Lord (1980) and Hambleton and Swaminathan (1985) for applications of these procedures in various fields of measurement.

Lord (1962) and Pandey and Carlson (1976) investigated the precision of the estimation of population means for an item domain and showed that the mean performance of a population for an item domain is estimated most reliably when each item is taken by a different sample of persons. This result stresses the importance of multiple-matrix sampling designs to increase efficiency. Berger (1989) investigated the efficiency of some sampling designs for IRT models and Vale (1986) applied sampling designs to minimize equating errors.

The purpose of this chapter is to review some concepts of optimal design research and to emphasize that the same concepts and measures can be applied to the design problem in test situations. In the next sections a review of criteria for optimal designs in linear and in nonlinear models will be given and the application of these criteria to IRT modeling will be discussed.

REVIEW OF OPTIMAL DESIGN RESEARCH

The problem of designing experiments has been encountered in various fields of research. In agriculture and in the biological sciences, for example, so-called bioassay experiments often demand a special structure for the sampling of experimental units. In experiments in the technical and social sciences the structure of the treatments is often rather complicated and a wide variety of combinations of treatments and experimental units can be encountered. Research on optimal design started with emphasis on the practical demands for the design of experiments. Later on the development of a theory of optimal designs has grown out of the need for more precise statistical inference. The work of R.A. Fisher was crucial for the initial development of a mathematical theory on optimal designs, and over the years a huge amount of literature has been devoted to various aspects of the optimality of designs (see Kiefer, 1959; Kiefer & Wolfowitz, 1959; Federov, 1972; and Silvey, 1980, among others). Reviews of the developments in the design of experiments are given by Atkinson (1982) and Steinberg and Hunter (1984).

To decide whether one design should be preferred over another, a criterion is needed. If the design has to be optimal with respect to maximum-likelihood estimation of the parameters in the model for the data, all criteria in the literature are some function of Fisher's well-known measure for information in the sample. Let the model for data Y be defined as a probability (density) function $f(y;\xi)$ with parameter ξ, and let $L(\xi;y)$ denote the likelihood function associated with $Y = y$. Then Fisher's information is defined as

$$E\left[\frac{\partial}{\partial \xi} \ln L(\xi;y)\right]^2 \tag{1}$$

where E denotes the expected value operator and ∂ is the derivative sign.

Generally, Fisher's measure shows the extent to which the observation has reduced our prior uncertainty regarding the parameter (Rao, 1973, sect. 5a.5). When ξ is a vector of parameters, the measure takes the general form of an information matrix with elements

$$E\left[\frac{\partial}{\partial \xi_i} \ln L(\xi;y) \frac{\partial}{\partial \xi_j} \ln L(\xi;y)\right] \tag{2}$$

where ξ_i and ξ_j are individual parameters in ξ. For $i = j$ the two measures can be shown to reduce to each other (Lindgren, 1976, sect. 4.5.4). For maximum-likelihood estimation of ξ it holds that (2) is equal to the inverse of the asymptotic variance-covariance matrix of the estimator, a property which motivates the interest in (2) as a relevant measure.

In general, a distinction must be made between optimal design problems for linear and nonlinear models. An easy way of checking whether a model, $f(y;\xi)$, is nonlinear is to examine the derivatives of the function with respect to each of its parameters. If the derivatives do not depend on the parameters, then the model is linear. Since $f(y;\xi) = L(\xi;y)$, it follows for a nonlinear model that the derivatives in (2), and hence any function of it, still depend on the (unknown) parameter ξ. Therefore, unlike linear models, optimal design criteria for nonlinear models usually depend on the parameters to be estimated. The problems involved in this feature will be amply discussed below.

Linear Models

Kiefer (1959) formulated the problem of selecting an optimal design for the estimation of p parameters in a linear model:

$$E(Y) = X\xi, \tag{3}$$

where Y is an $n \times 1$ vector of responses on n trials, X is an $n \times p$ design matrix with n fixed values x_i for the independent variable, and ξ is a $p \times 1$ vector of unknown parameters. For example, if we assume a polynomial function of degree $p - 1$, then the matrix X is given by:

$$X = \begin{bmatrix} 1 & x_1 & x_1^2 & \dots & x_1^{p-1} \\ 1 & x_2 & x_2^2 & \dots & x_2^{p-1} \\ 1 & x_3 & x_3^2 & \dots & x_3^{p-1} \\ . & . & . & & . \\ . & . & . & & . \\ . & . & . & & . \\ 1 & x_n & x_n^2 & \dots & x_n^{p-1} \end{bmatrix} \tag{4}$$

The elements of X must be specified such that rank $(X) = p \leq n$. If it is assumed that the variances and covariances of the errors are given by $\sigma^2\Omega$, where Ω is a known $n \times n$ symmetric positive definite matrix and σ^2 is an unknown constant, then the generalized least-squares estimator is $\hat{\xi} = (X'\Omega^{-1}X)^{-1}X'\Omega^{-1}Y$ with mean ξ and variance

$$\mathrm{Var}(\hat{\xi}) = \sigma^2(X'\Omega^{-1}X)^{-1}. \tag{5}$$

Thus, the variance of the estimator $\hat{\xi}$ is inversely related to Fisher's information matrix, which for the model in (3) is equal to $X'\Omega^{-1}X$. Note that for independent errors Ω reduces to an identity matrix.

Research on optimal designs in linear models has mainly been concerned with the question of how the elements of X can be chosen in order to select a "best" experimental design. The question what design is best can be approached from various points of view, and a number of optimality measures have been proposed (see Kiefer, 1959). These criteria will be reviewed now.

Suppose that we have a joint normal probability density for the parameter estimator $\hat{\xi}$ (Graybill, 1969):

$$p(\hat{\xi}) = (2\pi)^{-p/2}|\mathrm{Var}(\hat{\xi})|^{-1/2}\exp[-1/2(\xi-\hat{\xi})'\{\mathrm{Var}(\hat{\xi})\}^{-1}(\xi - \hat{\xi})]. \tag{6}$$

Shannon (1948) proposed a measure of uncertainty h{.} about the parameters in $p(\hat{\xi})$, which is defined as:

$$h\{p(\hat{\xi})\} \equiv -E[\ln(p(\hat{\xi}))]. \tag{7}$$

In (7) uncertainty (left-hand side) is inversely related to the expected log of the probability density (right-hand side). Note that the second-order derivative of the latter is Fisher's information in (2). Substitution of (6) into (7) yields

$$h(p(\hat{\xi})) = \text{constant} + \ln|\mathrm{Var}(\hat{\xi})|. \tag{8}$$

Thus, apart from the constant term, $\ln|\mathrm{Var}(\hat{\xi})|$ reflects the amount of uncertainty about the parameters. Minimizing this function is equivalent to minimizing $|\mathrm{Var}(\hat{\xi})|$. This criterion, that is, the determinant of the variance-covariance matrix of the estimated parameters, is often referred to as the generalized variance (Anderson, 1984) or D-optimality criterion.

Apart from the D-optimality criterion, several other criteria have also been proposed. However, each criterion is a function of the variance-covariance matrix of the estimated parameters. The relation between these criteria can be expressed in terms of the eigenvalues λ_i of $\text{Var}(\hat{\xi})$. The following criteria are the most familiar ones:

D-optimality criterion: $\Phi_D\{\text{Var}(\hat{\xi})\} = |\text{Var}(\hat{\xi})| = \Pi \, \lambda_i$
A-optimality criterion: $\Phi_A\{\text{Var}(\hat{\xi})\} = \text{Trace}[\text{Var}(\hat{\xi})] = \Sigma \, \lambda_i$
E-optimality criterion: $\Phi_E\{\text{Var}(\hat{\xi})\} = \max_i \, (\lambda_i)$.

Each of these measures may have advantages in specific situations; arguments in favor of these criteria have been given by Kiefer (1959), Kiefer and Wolfowitz (1959, 1960), and Federov (1972).

It should be remarked, however, that there are also disadvantages connected with these criteria. If, for example, a design is set up under the assumption that a model with, say, p parameters is correct, but in fact a model with $p + 1$ parameters would be more appropriate, then the resulting design is likely to have little power to detect departures from this model. Another problem with the Φ_A and Φ_E criteria is that they depend upon the scale of the independent variable X. In this they differ from the Φ_D criterion. Although this problem can be diminished by only comparing results based on identical scalings of the independent variable, the problem still remains when different scalings are encountered.

The problem of actually finding (nearly) optimal designs is a problem of numerical optimalization, and much research has been done in this area. A simple algorithm has been given by Mitchell (1974); Welch (1982) proposed a branch-and-bound algorithm for D-optimal designs. See Cook and Nachtsheim (1980) for a comparison of algorithms for exact D-optimal designs.

Nonlinear Models

Although in fact the optimality criteria proposed for linear models can also be applied to designs for nonlinear models, the latter is a more complicated problem than the former. As noted earlier, the main problem is that Fisher's information matrix is generally not independent of the values of the parameters in the model. This means that we should know the values of the parameters before we can select an optimal design based on one of the above mentioned criteria. This is why such designs are often called locally optimal designs. There are, however, several strategies to go around this difficulty.

Sequential designs. One way to avoid the problem of unknown parameter values is to set up a sequence of experiments, where the next experiment is designed using the estimated parameters from a previous experiment. Thus, in each stage the estimates of the parameters are updated. A similar procedure in educational and psychological testing is the two-stage or the multistage procedure. In this form of testing, each student first takes a pretest on the same subject matter area. The pretest is scored and the appropriate second-stage test form is then assigned. At each stage a design is selected that matches the ability level of an examinee with the (difficulty) level of the items in some optimal way. Initial estimates of ability and item difficulty are updated at each step.

Approximation of parameter values. For nonlinear models the usefulness of the optimality criteria will depend on the accuracy of the estimates of the parameters in them. The impact of poor estimates has not received much attention in the literature. In some situations a good approximation of the parameter values may be available from other (pilot) studies. For some models the range of the parameter values is limited. In IRT models, for example, the effective range of the item difficulties and abilities usually is -3 to $+3$, and a very good overall picture of the efficiency of a design can be obtain by considering combinations of parameter values.

A similar approach has been suggested by Fisher (1966). For some models it may be possible to perform experiments with restrictions on the values of the independent variable for which the total information is (approximately) constant, whatever the parameter values are. Another strategy is choosing the worst possible value for a parameter and optimalizing the information for that value. Such a strategy is often referred to as the maximin strategy (Silvey, 1980, p. 59; van der Linden, 1989).

Bayes methods. Another often used method to solve the problem of unknown parameter values is to use a prior distribution for the parameters. Suppose that the prior covariance matrix of the estimated parameters is Σ_1 and that the Fisher information matrix is Inf, then the posterior covariance matrix is:

$$\Sigma_2 = (\Sigma_1^{-1} + \text{Inf})^{-1}. \tag{9}$$

The posterior covariance matrix Σ_2 can be used to formulate the optimality criteria. Zacks (1977) and Tsutakawa (1980) solved the problem of unknown parameters by preposterior analysis, taking expectations with respect to the prior distribution. The effectiveness of this procedure, however, will depend on the quality of the prior distribution.

A combination of this approach with a sequential approach is also possible. In a so-called empirical Bayes approach values for the independent variable are determined by maximizing the expected information on the parameters with respect to the posterior distribution of the parameters given the data from the previous design (see Zacks, 1977, and Tsutakawa, 1980).

OPTIMALITY CRITERIA APPLIED TO IRT MODELS

Consider the three-parameter logistic model, which gives the probability of a correct response to item i ($i = 1, \ldots, n$) as a function of the ability parameter $\theta_j \in \langle -\infty, +\infty \rangle$ for examinee j ($j = 1, \ldots, N$):

$$P_i(\theta_j) = c_i + (1 - c_i)\{1 + \exp[-a_i(\theta_j - b_i)]\}^{-1} \tag{10}$$

where $b_i \in \langle -\infty, +\infty \rangle$ and $a_i \in \langle 0, +\infty \rangle$ are the item difficulty and discrimination parameters, respectively, and $c_i \in \langle 0,1 \rangle$ is the guessing parameter. If we assume that joint estimation yields consistent estimates if the number of examinees and the number of items becomes large simultaneously, then it seems reasonable to write the information on the m parameters in model (10) as in (2). To avoid indeterminacy of the model, two parameters must be fixed, that is, $m = 3n + N - 2$. $\xi = \{\xi_i\} = \{\mu, \theta\}$, where $\theta = \{\theta_1, \theta_2, \ldots, \xi_{N-2}\}$ and $\mu = \{a_1, b_1, c_1, a_2, b_2, c_2, \ldots, a_n, b_n, c_n\}$.

Lord and Wingersky (1985) proposed to gather the information on the m parameters in the following partitioned matrix:

$$\text{Inf}_3 = \begin{bmatrix} I_1 & & & & & K_{11} & K_{12} & \cdots & K_{1(N-2)} \\ & & & 0 & & K_{21} & K_{22} & \cdots & K_{2(N-2)} \\ & I_2 & \cdot & & & \cdot & & & \cdot \\ & & \cdot & & & \cdot & & & \\ & & \cdot & & & \cdot & & & \\ & 0 & & I_n & & K_{n1} & K_{n2} & \cdots & K_{n(N-2)} \\ \hline K'_{11} & K'_{21} & \cdots & K'_{n1} & & J_1 & & & \\ K'_{12} & K'_{22} & \cdots & K'_{n2} & & & J_2 & & 0 \\ \cdot & \cdot & & \cdot & & & & \cdot & \\ \cdot & \cdot & & \cdot & & & 0 & & \cdot \\ \cdot & & & \cdot & & & & & \\ K'_{1(N-2)} & K'_{2(N-2)} & \cdots & K'_{n(N-2)} & & & & & J_{(N-2)} \end{bmatrix} = \begin{bmatrix} I & K \\ \hline K' & J \end{bmatrix} . \tag{11}$$

The $3n \times 3n$ super diagonal matrix I contains the 3×3 item informa-tion matrices I_1 through I_n for the parameters a_i, b_i, and c_i, respec-tively. The $(N - 2) \times (N - 2)$ diagonal matrix J contains Fisher's information J_1 through J_{N-2} for the ability parameters θ_j and K_{ij} is the 3×1 joint Fisher information vector for item i and person j. It should be noted that the information matrices Inf_1 and Inf_2 for the one- and two-parameter model can be obtained from Inf_3 by deleting the appropriate rows and columns of I_1 through I_n and the correspond-ing elements of K_{ij}.

As has been noted above, the question of efficient estimation of the parameters in IRT models is more difficult than for linear models, the difficulty being that the information depends on the value of the un-known parameters. Each of the above mentioned optimality criteria Φ may be applied to parts of the information matrix Inf_3. The formula-tion of optimality criteria on the full information matrix Inf_3 leads to a problem. The order of Inf_3 increases with the sample size N (ability parameters are incidental), and computations will become unwieldy for large samples. Unless some sort of grouping of the ability parame-ters is applied, this procedure is not generally recommended.

For efficient estimation of the item parameters the following two cases can be distinguished:

1. The criteria $\Phi_D\{I^{-1}\}, \Phi_A\{I^{-1}\}$ and $\Phi_E\{I^{-1}\}$ are applied to matrix I^{-1}, or to parts of it. This will be appropriate when the item parameters are of primary interest and the ability parameters are assumed fixed and known.
2. The criteria $\Phi_D\{I^{*-1}\}, \Phi_A\{I^{*-1}\}$ and $\Phi_E\{I^{*-1}\}$ are based on matrix $I^{*-1} = [I - K J^{-1} K']^{-1}$, or parts of it. This procedure is appropri-ate when the item parameters are of primary interest and the ability parameters are assumed to be fixed but unknown (see Berger, 1989).

The relative efficiency RE_D of a particular design, based on the Φ_D criterion, can be formulated as follows. Let μ_k be a subset of the item-parameter set μ, and let $\text{Inf}(\mu_k)$ be the corresponding information matrix. A design $D(\mu_k)$ can be characterized by the sampling procedure used to select examinees from a population and by the selection of items from an item domain. The relative efficiency of a particular design $D_1(\mu_k)$ relative to another design $D_2(\mu_k)$, both used to estimate the same parameter set μ_k, is:

$$RE_D\{D_1(\mu_k), D_2(\mu_k)\} = \frac{\Phi_D\{\text{Inf}^1(\mu_k)^{-1}\}}{\Phi_D\{\text{Inf}^2(\mu_k)^{-1}\}}, \qquad (12)$$

where the superscripts 1 and 2 on the information matrix refer to design 1 and 2, respectively. If RE_D is less than one, the item parameters in the design $D_2(\mu_k)$ are estimated less efficiently than in $D_1(\mu_k)$, and if RE_D is greater than one, the converse is true. A similar formulation of the relative efficiencies can be given for the E- and A-optimality criteria.

Choice of An Optimality Criterion

As has been discussed in the literature, the criteria Φ_D, Φ_A, and Φ_E usually imply each other. There are, however, exceptions and each of the criteria may have advantages in specific situations.

Criterion Φ_E is only based on the largest eigenvalue of the variance-covariance matrix of estimated parameters and therefore does not use all available information on the parameters. Intuitively, it may be inferred that Φ_E would only be appropriate when the variances of the estimated parameters are mainly located on one canonical variate, that is, when the largest eigenvalue explains most of the variance of the estimated parameters.

Both criteria Φ_D and Φ_A use information from all the eigenvalues of the variance-covariance matrix of estimated parameters. From experience in linear models it may be inferred that the trace criterion Φ_A is somewhat less sensitive to variables with a relatively large or small variance than the Φ_D criterion. Criterion Φ_D not only depends on the variances of the estimated parameters, but also on the covariances. If, for example, two parameters μ_1 and μ_2 are estimated, and Σ is the variance-covariance matrix of $\hat{\mu}_1$ and $\hat{\mu}_2$:

$$\Sigma = \begin{bmatrix} \sigma_1^2 & \rho\sigma_1\sigma_2 \\ \rho\sigma_1\sigma_2 & \sigma_2^2 \end{bmatrix}, \tag{13}$$

then $|\Sigma| = \sigma_1^2\sigma_2^2(1 - \rho^2)$. This shows that $|\Sigma|$ may be small, not only because the variances are small, but also because the correlation ρ is large.

For the logistic IRT model it is well known that, when the discrimination parameter a_i is fixed and when $c_i = 0$, the information on b_i is $I_b = a_i^2\{\Sigma \, P_i(\theta_j)[1 - P_i(\theta_j)]\}$ and that it is maximal for $P_i(\theta_j) = 0.5$, that is, when $\theta_j = b_i$. In this situation a sample of examinees with abilities all equal to the item difficulties would give optimal information (van der Linden, 1988). This is not generally true for the case of simultaneous estimation of two or three item parameters.

In Figure 16.1 the relative efficiencies RE_D and RE_A are given for the one-, two- and three-parameter model as a function of the standard

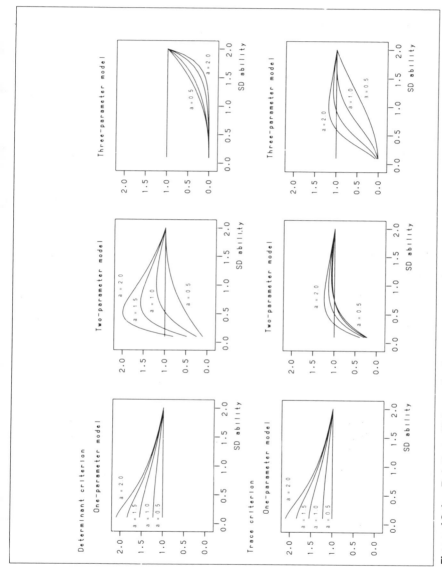

Figure 16.1. Relative efficiency for D- and A-optimality criteria of designs with standard deviations for ability $0.1 < SD_\theta < 2.0$

deviation of the abilities SD_θ. Several designs with examinees sampled from normal populations with mean abilities $\theta = b = 0$ and SD_θ ranging from 0.1 to 2 are considered. Each of these designs is related to a design where the examinees are also sampled from a normal population with the same mean and $SD_\theta = 2$. It is assumed that $c_i = 0$. The ability parameters are assumed to be fixed and known.

As expected, the relative efficiencies for the one-parameter model increase when SD_θ decreases. Note that the results of RE_D and RE_A for the one-parameter model are identical.

For the two-parameter model, a decrease of SD_θ will not always lead to an increase of efficiency. First, the relative efficiency increases, but eventually it decreases as SD_θ becomes much smaller. This result can be explained by the fact that a decrease of SD_θ generally results in an increase of the variance of the discrimination or slope parameter. This phenomenon dominates the outcome, as SD_θ becomes much smaller. Note that in linear regression analysis a similar effect can be found, since the variance of the estimated slope is inversely related to the variance of the independent variable x_i.

For the three-parameter model the results seem somewhat confusing. The pattern of the relative efficiency for Φ_D is reverse to the one for the one-parameter model, while for Φ_A it resembles the one for the two-parameter model.

It may be concluded that the D-optimal design for the three-parameter model is a design with examinees sampled from a population with the largest possible SD_θ. This can be explained by the problems connected with the estimation of the lower asymptote c_i (Thissen & Wainer, 1982). A sample with a large SD_θ will contain relatively many examinees with a low-ability level. For efficient estimation of c_i such a sample would be more appropriate than a sample with relatively few examinees at a low-ability level, that is, with a small SD_θ. From Figure 16.1 it can also be concluded that the Φ_A criterion is less sensitive to this effect than the Φ_D criterion.

The RE_E pattern will not be given here, because not much information will be lost for these models, when only the largest eigenvalue is taken into account and the RE_E pattern generally resembles that of RE_A.

Another problem in selecting an optimality criterion is the sensitivity of a criterion to the situation where the ability parameters are known or unknown. The results of a comparison of efficiencies of designs for known and unknown abilities are given in Figure 16.2. The criteria $\Phi_D(I^{*-1})$ and $\Phi_A(I^{*-1})$ are related to $\Phi_D(I^{-1})$ and $\Phi_A(I^{-1})$ for samples drawn from normal populations with SD_θ ranging from 0.1 to 2. The results show that the relative efficiencies are less than one for

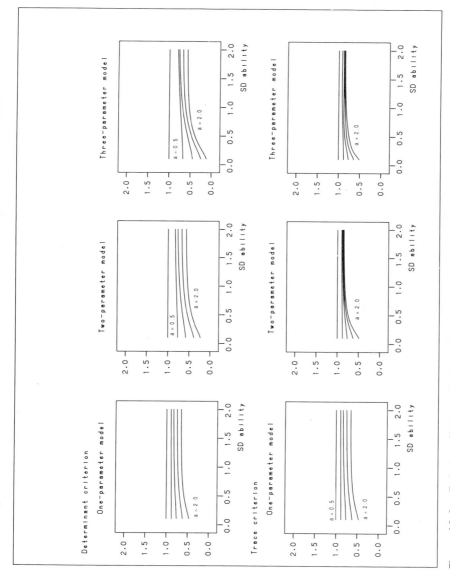

Figure 16.2. Relative efficiency for D- and A-optimality criteria of designs for unknown and known ability parameters with $0.1 < SD_\theta < 2.0$

the whole SD_θ range. This means that item parameters are always estimated more efficiently when the abilities are known than when the abilities are unknown. Both criteria lead to this conclusion.

CONCLUSION

As the sampling concept from survey analysis gained currency in educational measurement, the interest in alternative sampling designs increased. In this chapter it is shown that the ideas from optimal design research can easily be applied to IRT modeling in educational and psychological testing. The main advantage of using optimality criteria is that design efficiency can be expressed by a single measure. Although there may be situations where it will be better to just look at the standard errors of a particular IRT parameter, these optimality criteria enable a researcher to compare the efficient estimation of a whole set of parameters for different designs. The results in this chapter indicate that the pattern of the criteria generally lead to the same conclusions. Because the D-optimality criterion also take into account the covariances of the parameter estimates, this criterion is recommended for the selection of an efficient design.

Finally, it should be observed that the preceding conclusions hold for the case of a complete design, that is the case in which all items are administered to each examinee. For results on optimal incomplete design for IRT parameters, which are needed for such applications as calibrating test item banks or equating different versions of the same test, the reader is referred to Berger (1989) and van der Linden (1988, 1989).

REFERENCES

Atkinson, A.C. (1982). Developments in the design of experiments. *International Statistical Review*, *50*, 161–177.

Anderson, T.W. (1984). *An introduction to multivariate statistical analysis* (2nd ed.). New York: John Wiley & Sons.

Berger, M.P.F. (1989). *On the efficiency of IRT models when applied to different sampling designs* (Research Rep. 89–4). Enschede, The Netherlands: University of Twente.

Cook, R.D., & Nachtsheim, C.J. (1980). A comparison of algorithms for constructing exact D-optimal designs. *Technometrics*, *22*, 315–324.

de Gruijter, D.N.M. (1985). A note on the asymptotic variance-covariance matrix of item parameter estimates in the Rasch model. *Psychometrika*, *50*, 247–249.

de Gruijter, D.N.M. (1988). Standard errors of item parameter estimates in incomplete designs. *Applied Psychological Measurement, 12,* 109–116.

Federov, V.V. (1972). *Theory of optimal experiments.* New York: Academic Press.

Fisher, R.A. (1966). *The design of experiments.* Edinburgh: Oliver & Boyd.

Graybill, F.A. (1969) *Introduction to matrices with applications in statistics.* Belmont, CA: Wadsworth.

Hambleton, R.K., & Swaminathan, H. (1985). *Item response theory.* Boston: Kluwer-Nijhoff.

Kiefer, J. (1959). Optimum experimental designs (with discussion). *Journal of the Royal Statistical Society, Series B, 21,* 271–319.

Kiefer, J., & Wolfowitz, J. (1959) Optimum designs in regression problems. *The Annals of Mathematical Statistics, 30,* 271–292.

Kiefer, J., & Wolfowitz, J. (1960) The equivalence of two extremum problems. *Canadian Journal of Mathematics, 12,* 363–366.

Lindgren, B.W. (1976). *Statistical theory.* New York: Macmillan.

Lord, F.M. (1962). Estimating norms by item-sampling. *Educational and Psychological Measurement, 22,* 259–267.

Lord, F.M. (1974). The relative efficiency of two tests as a function of ability. *Psychometrika, 39,* 351–358.

Lord, F.M. (1980). *Applications of item response theory to practical testing problems.* Hillsdale, NJ: Lawrence Erlbaum Associates, Inc.

Lord, F.M., & Wingersky, M.S. (1985). Sampling variances and covariances of parameter estimates in item response theory. In D.J. Weiss (Ed.), *Proceedings of the 1982 item response theory and computerized adaptive testing conference* (pp. 69–88). Minneapolis: University of Minnesota.

Michell, T.J. (1974). An algorithm for the construction of "D-optimal" experimental designs. *Technometrics, 16,* 203–210.

Pandey, T.N., & Carlson, D. (1976). Assessing payoffs in the estimation of the mean using multiple matrix sampling designs. In D.N.M. de Gruijter & L.J. van der Kamp (Eds.), *Advances in psychological and educational measurement.* London: John Wiley & Sons.

Rao, C.R. (1973). *Linear statistical inference and its applications.* New York: John Wiley & Sons.

Samejima, F. (1977). A use of the information function in tailored testing. *Applied Psychological Measurement, 1,* 233–247.

Shannon, C.E. (1948). A mathematical theory of communication. *Bell System Technical Journal, 27,* 379–423, 623–656.

Silvey, S.D. (1980). *Optimal design.* London: Chapman & Hall.

Steinberg, D.M., & Hunter, W.G. (1984). Experimental design: Review and comment. *Technometrics, 26,* 71–130.

Theunissen, T.J.J.M. (1985). Binary programming and test design. *Psychometrika, 50,* 411–420.

Thissen, D., & Wainer, H. (1982). Some standard errors in item response theory. *Psychometrika, 47,* 397–412.

Tsutakawa, R.K. (1980). Selection of dose levels for estimating a percentage point of a logistic quantal response curve. *Applied Statistics, 29,* 25–33.

Vale, C.D. (1986). Linking item parameters onto a common scale. *Applied Psychological Measurement, 10*, 333–344.

van der Linden, W.J. (1987). *IRT-based test construction* (Research Rep. 87–2) Enschede, The Netherlands: University of Twente.

van der Linden, W.J. (1988). *Optimizing incomplete sampling designs for item response model parameters* (Research Rep. 88–5). Enschede, The Netherlands: University of Twente.

van der Linden, W.J. (1989). *Optimizing item calibration designs.* Paper presented at the Annual Meeting of the American Educational Research Association, San Francisco, CA.

van der Linden, W.J., & Boekkooi-Timminga, E. (1989). A maximin model for test design with practical constraints. *Psychometrika, 54*, 237–247.

Welch, W.J. (1982). Branch-and-bound search for experimental designs based on D optimality and other criteria. *Technometrics, 24*, 41–48.

Wingersky, M.S., & Lord, F.M. (1985). An investigation of methods for reducing sampling error in certain IRT procedures. *Applied Psychological Measurement, 8*, 347–364.

Zacks, S. (1977). Problems and approaches in design of experiments for estimation and testing in non-linear models. In P.R. Krisknaiah (Ed.), *Multivariate analysis IV* (pp. 209–223.) Amsterdam: North-Holland.

chapter 17

Constraint Optimization: A Perspective of IRT Parameter Estimation

Hoi K. Suen
Pennsylvania State University

Patrick S.C. Lee
LaSalle University

AN OPTIMIZATION PERSPECTIVE OF IRT PARAMETER ESTIMATION

Despite many of the apparent differences among major Item Response Theory (IRT) models and estimation procedures in existence today, these models and estimation procedures can be viewed in a unified manner from the perspective of nonlinear optimization. Specifically, differences among existing IRT models and parameter estimation procedures can be viewed as differences in the types and amount of constraints imposed on the optimization process.

From an optimization view, the problem of deriving the maximum likelihood estimates of the vector of person ability parameters Θ, and the vectors of the item parameters in the 3-parameter model **a, b,** and **c** (Lord, 1980) from a K-item by N-subject data matrix has an objective function of:

$$\text{Maximizing} \quad L(\mathbf{U}|\boldsymbol{\theta},\mathbf{a},\mathbf{b},\mathbf{c}) = \prod_{i=1}^{N} \prod_{j=1}^{K} P_{ij}^{u_i} Q_{ij}^{1-u_i} \tag{1}$$

with respect to $\boldsymbol{\Theta}$, $\mathbf{a}$, $\mathbf{b}$, and $\mathbf{c}$, where L is the likelihood and P_{ij} and Q_{ij} are probabilities of success and failure, respectively, for the ith subject on the jth item. That is, the objective is to maximize the IRT likelihood function. With the indeterminacy of the Θ scale, the solution for this problem is theoretically unidentifiable (Lord, 1980). Unique solutions to this optimization problem become possible if constraints are imposed. As new constraints are added to the optimization process, the size of the feasibility region is reduced, and the probability of a unique solution is increased.

A common solution to the indeterminacy of Θ is to scale Θ along the z scale. When expressed as an optimization problem, the properties of the Θ scale can be expressed as constraints. Thus, the estimation problem becomes:

$$\text{Maximize objective function L with respect to } \boldsymbol{\Theta}, \mathbf{a}, \mathbf{b}, \text{ and } \mathbf{c}, \tag{2}$$

$$\text{Subject to: a)} \sum_{i=1}^{N} \theta_i = 0, \tag{3}$$

$$\text{and b)} \left(\sum_{i=1}^{N} \theta_i^2 \right)/N = 1. \tag{4}$$

With constraints 3 and 4, the Θ scale has a mean of 0 and a variance of 1; that is, a z scale. A nonlinear optimization of the likelihood function with constraints 3 and 4 based on this formulation would essentially lead to results equivalent to those from a Joint Maximum Likelihood Estimation of a 3-parameter model (Wingersky, 1983). This is an IRT optimization problem with the least amount of constraints.

When desired or theoretically justifiable, an additional constraint that the guessing parameter vector $c = 0$ can be imposed. Using abbreviations, the optimization problem becomes:

$$\text{Max. L w/r to } \boldsymbol{\Theta}, \mathbf{a}, \mathbf{b}, \text{ and } \mathbf{c}, \tag{5}$$

$$\text{S. t.: a)} \sum_{i=1}^{N} \theta_i = 0, \tag{6}$$

$$\text{b) } \left(\sum_{i=1}^{N} \theta_i^2 \right) / N = 1. \tag{7}$$

$$\text{and c) } c = 0. \tag{8}$$

The results of such an optimization formulation is tantamount to those of a Joint Maximum Likelihood Estimation of a 2-parameter model. Similarly,

$$\text{Max. L w/r to } \Theta, \text{ a, b, and c,} \tag{9}$$

$$\text{S. t.: a) } \sum_{i=1}^{N} \theta_i = 0, \tag{10}$$

$$\text{b) } \left(\sum_{i=1}^{N} \theta_i^2 \right) / N = 1, \tag{11}$$

$$\text{c) } c = 0, \tag{12}$$

$$\text{and d) } a_i = a_j \text{ for all i and j,} \tag{13}$$

is tantamount to a Joint Maximum Likelihood Estimation of a Rasch model. Extending this scheme, prior distributions $F(\Theta_i)$, $f(a_j)$, $g(b_j)$, and $h(c_j)$ for each ith subject and each jth item can be imposed as a constraint and constraints 12 and 13 in the Joint Maximum Likelihood Estimate of the Rasch model removed. In this case, the optimization problem becomes:

$$\text{Max. L. w/r to } \Theta, \text{ a, b, and c,} \tag{14}$$

$$\text{S. t.: a) } \sum_{i=1}^{N} \theta_i = 0, \tag{15}$$

$$\text{b) } \left(\sum_{i=1}^{N} \theta_i^2 \right) / N = 1. \tag{16}$$

$$\text{c) prior } F(\Theta_i), \text{ i} = 1, \ldots, N; \tag{17}$$

$$\text{d) prior } f(a_j), \text{ j} = 1, \ldots, K; \tag{18}$$

$$\text{e) prior } g(b_j), \text{ j} = 1, \ldots, K; \tag{19}$$

f) prior $h(c_j)$, $j = 1, \ldots, K$; $\qquad\qquad$ (20)

For this optimization problem, Constrains 17 through 20 (i.e., the prior distributions) can be incorporated as implicit constraints into the objective function to produce a new objective function of posterior likelihood. The resulting optimization problem then becomes:

$$\text{Max. } g(\theta,a,b,c\,|\,U) \propto L\left[\prod_{j=1}^{K} f(a_j)g(b_j)h(c_j)\right] \prod_{i=1}^{N} F(\theta_i),$$

w/r to **θ, a, b,** and **c,** $\qquad\qquad$ (21)

$$\text{S. t.: a) } \sum_{i=1}^{N} \theta_i = 0, \qquad\qquad (22)$$

$$\text{and b) } \left(\sum_{i=1}^{N} \theta_i^2\right)/N = 1. \qquad\qquad (23)$$

The results of this optimization is then tantamount to a Bayesian Modal Estimation of a 3-parameter model (Swaminathan & Gifford, 1986). Similarly, a marginal distribution $h_m(\Theta)$ can be imposed in place of the prior functions of Θ, a, b, and c, resulting in the following optimization problem:

$$\text{Max. L w/r to } \boldsymbol{\Theta}, \mathbf{a}, \mathbf{b}, \text{ and } \mathbf{c}, \qquad\qquad (24)$$

$$\text{S. t.: a) } \sum_{i=1}^{N} \theta_i = 0, \qquad\qquad (25)$$

$$\text{b) } \left(\sum_{i=1}^{N} \theta_i^2\right)/N = 1. \qquad\qquad (26)$$

$$\text{and c) marginal } h_m(\theta). \qquad\qquad (27)$$

Again, the $h(\theta)$ can be incorporated into the objective function as an implicit constraint:

$$\text{Let } P(U\,|\,\mathbf{a},\mathbf{b},\mathbf{c}) = \int \prod_{i=1}^{K} P_i^{u_i} Q_i^{1-u_i} h_m(\theta)d\theta \qquad\qquad (28)$$

$$\text{and } L \propto \prod_{j=1}^{2^K} P(U|\theta,a,b,c)^{r_j}, \tag{29}$$

where r is the number of subjects with a response vector of u_j. The optimization problem becomes one of maximizing L with respect to **a, b,** and **c.** The result is a Marginal Maximum Likelihood Estimation of a 3-parameter model (Bock & Aitkin, 1981).

By viewing IRT from a nonlinear optimization perspective, major models and estimation procedures can be unified within a single formulation. The differences among models and estimation procedures can then be viewed as a difference in constraints. An immediate advantage of this perspective is that various combinations of IRT models and estimation procedures can be produced as desired by imposing appropriate constraints in the optimization process in a mix-and-match fashion. For example:

$$\text{Max. L w/r to } \Theta, \mathbf{a}, \mathbf{b}, \text{ and } \mathbf{c}, \tag{30}$$

$$\text{S. t.: a)} \sum_{i=1}^{N} \theta_i = 0, \tag{31}$$

$$\text{b) } \left(\sum_{i=1}^{N} \theta_i^2 \right)/N = 1. \tag{32}$$

$$\text{c) } c = 0, \tag{33}$$

$$\text{d) } a_i = a_j \text{ for all i and j,} \tag{34}$$

$$\text{e) prior } F(\Theta_i), \tag{35}$$

$$\text{f) prior } f(a_j), \tag{36}$$

$$\text{g) prior } g(b_j), \tag{37}$$

$$\text{h) prior } h(c_j), \tag{38}$$

would lead to a Bayesian Modal Estimation of a Rasch model.

STRUCTURAL CONSTRAINTS

Another major advantage of viewing IRT from an optimization perspective is its flexibility to accommodate new constraints. Problems of convergence in existing estimation procedures can be minimized with additions of new constraints. Within IRT, there is a set of inherent and relatively incontrovertible constraints which has not been incorporated into the estimation procedures. These are structural constraints fundamental to IRT as defined today. Seven such structural constraints are identified as follows:

1. $0 \leq P(\Theta_i) \leq 1$ for the ith subject.
2. $0 \leq c_m \leq 1$ for the mth item.
3. If the ith subject has a perfect raw score and the response vector $\mathbf{u}_j \neq \mathbf{u}_i$, then $\Theta_i \geq \Theta_j$.
4. If the kth subject has a zero raw score and $u_j \neq u_k$, then $\Theta_j \geq \Theta_k$.
5. If the test is unidimensional and data are fully crossed, then classical difficulties $p_m < p_n$ for the mth and n^{th} items imply that $b_m \geq b_n$.
6. If the response vector for the ith subject $\mathbf{u}_i$ is dominant over that of the jth subject $\mathbf{u}_j$, then $\Theta_i \geq \Theta_j$ [e.g., $\mathbf{u}_i = (101011)$ and $\mathbf{u}_j = (101010)$].
7. If $\mathbf{u}_i = \mathbf{u}_j$, then $\Theta_i = \Theta_j$.

These structural constraints can be added to the optimization process in the manner described earlier. With these constraints and other model and/or estimation constraints mentioned above, the probability of attaining a unique solution should greatly increase beyond those of existing methods.

NONLINEAR OPTIMIZATION ALGORITHMS

When approached from a perspective of a constrained optimization problem, IRT parameter estimation can gain considerable flexibility in that, for the same measurement data, various existing models and estimation procedures can be simulated through the addition of appropriate constraints. Moreover, this approach enables the use of structural constraints, which are fundamental to the characteristics of IRT parameters, to further increase the probability of a unique solution. The constraints implied by various existing models and estimation procedures (e.g., $\mathbf{c} = 0$, prior $F(\Theta_i)$) are not inherent in IRT but are imposed externally. Structural constraints, however, are inherent in IRT as defined today. While the inclusion/exclusion of specific constraints in existing methods would amount to a change in theoretical orientation (e.g., from 3-parameter to Rasch or from maximum likelihood to Bayesian), the exclusion of structural constraints would render the estimation process a mathematical exercise with results that may or may not be IRT parameters.

It is, therefore, suggested that IRT parameter estimations can be more effectively accomplished through a unified approach of nonlinear optimization with respect to Θ, **a, b,** and **c,** minimally subject to the structural constraints identified in this chapter, and subject to additional constraints as appropriate or desired, to yield estimates for various models and theoretic orientations. The nonlinear optimization approach can also be viewed as an elegant alternative to a Lagrange multiplier approach or a Kuhn-Tucker multiplier approach (cf. Mangasarian, 1967).

This approach can guarantee a local maximum. If the global maximum is outside of the feasibility region, this approach will not obtain the global estimator. It can be argued that, for the purpose of IRT parameter estimation, a global maximum outside of the feasibility region is not an IRT parameter but a mathematical entity of no interest.

There are several constrained nonlinear optimization algorithms available today. Two algorithms in particular may be appropriate. These are the GRG-II algorithm (Liebman, Lasdon, Shrage, & Waren, 1986) and the MINOS algorithm (Murtagh & Saunders, 1987) in GAMS (Brooke, Kendrick, & Meeraus, 1988). An additional advantage of using these algorithms is that the estimators are guaranteed to be maxima and not minima or inflexion points. A common numerical procedure used in current IRT estimation today is the iterative Newton-Raphson method (Kale, 1962) or a method based on Newton-Raphson (e.g., Mislevy & Bock, 1984). With Newton-Raphson or other similar methods that are dependent on the second derivatives of the likelihood function, the estimator may be at the maximum, minimum, or inflexion point, depending on whether the likelihood function is concave or convex. This problem does not exist with GRG-II or MINOS in that the results are dependent on the first derivative only and are guaranteed to be maxima.

The current limitation of GRG-II and MINOS is availability of RAM in today's mainframe computers and microcomputers. These algorithms can only be used for a very small number of subjects with a short test. It is expected that the forthcoming new version of MINOS will expand the utility of this algorithm for psychometric analysis. Additionally, if these algorithms are adopted specifically for psychometric analysis, the structural constraints can be generated by the computer internally, hence minimizing the amount of declared constraints. This would improve the efficiency of these algorithms and expand the number of subjects and items that can be analyzed.

APPLICATION

Because of the limitation of computer memory for existing nonlinear optimization programs, for common testing problems, the advantage of the nonlinear optimization perspective is primarily conceptual. However, when the number of subjects and number of items are both extremely small such that they are within the memory limitations of GRG-II or MINOS, the advantage of nonlinear optimization can be demonstrated.

With existing IRT estimation algorithms, the rule of thumb is that the number of items should be greater than 20 (Lord, 1980; Wright & Stone, 1979). Hulin, Lissak, and Drasgow (1982) recommended that 30 items and 500 subjects are the minimum numbers for a 2-parameter model, and 60 items and 1,000 subjects the minimum numbers for a 3-parameter model. When both the number of items and the number of subjects are extremely small, existing methods will most probably not converge, except for the Rasch model. For tests with less than 20 items, Lord (1986) found that marginal maximum likelihood estimation provides better estimates.

Within the severe memory limitations of existing nonlinear optimization algorithms when applied to IRT problems, we compared the results of the GRG-II algorithm against BILOG-II (Mislevy & Bock, 1984) for an unrealistically small sample. The choice of BILOG-II among existing software is based on Lord's finding that marginal maximum likelihood is suitable for small samples. Specifically, a situation in which four subjects took a 3-item test was used. The unrealistically small sample is intended to illustrate the feasibility of GRG-II within existing computer limitations. It is expected that new computer programs currently under development will expand the application of the nonlinear optimization approach.

Four subjects took a 3-item test and obtained the following response vectors: $u_1 = (000)$, $u_2 = (110)$, $u_3 = (011)$, and $u_4 = (111)$. This particular set of data should be particularly problematic for existing methods in two respects. First, both the number of subjects and the number of items are extremely small. Convergence is unlikely to take place. Second, subjects 1 and 4 had zero and perfect raw scores. If these two subjects were deleted, the sample of subjects would be reduced to two. Some form of Bayesian prior would be needed in existing methods in order to retain these two subjects.

When these data were submitted to a marginal maximum likelihood estimation procedure for 1-, 2-, and 3-parameter models through BILOG-II with the default prior distributions of Θ, a, b, and c as appro-

GIVEN DATA: $u_1 = (000)$, $u_2 = (110)$, $u_3 = (011)$, $u_4 = (111)$

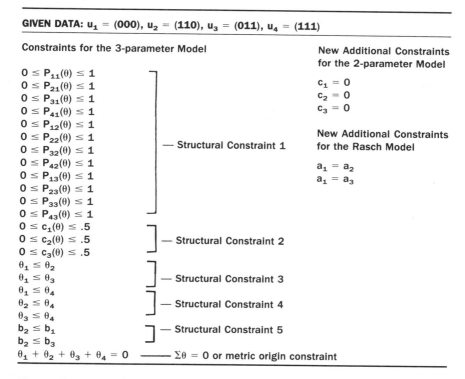

Constraints for the 3-parameter Model

$0 \le P_{11}(\theta) \le 1$
$0 \le P_{21}(\theta) \le 1$
$0 \le P_{31}(\theta) \le 1$
$0 \le P_{41}(\theta) \le 1$
$0 \le P_{12}(\theta) \le 1$
$0 \le P_{22}(\theta) \le 1$
$0 \le P_{32}(\theta) \le 1$ — Structural Constraint 1
$0 \le P_{42}(\theta) \le 1$
$0 \le P_{13}(\theta) \le 1$
$0 \le P_{23}(\theta) \le 1$
$0 \le P_{33}(\theta) \le 1$
$0 \le P_{43}(\theta) \le 1$
$0 \le c_1(\theta) \le .5$
$0 \le c_2(\theta) \le .5$ — Structural Constraint 2
$0 \le c_3(\theta) \le .5$
$\theta_1 \le \theta_2$
$\theta_1 \le \theta_3$ — Structural Constraint 3
$\theta_1 \le \theta_4$
$\theta_2 \le \theta_4$ — Structural Constraint 4
$\theta_3 \le \theta_4$
$b_2 \le b_1$ — Structural Constraint 5
$b_2 \le b_3$
$\theta_1 + \theta_2 + \theta_3 + \theta_4 = 0$ ———— $\Sigma\theta = 0$ or metric origin constraint

New Additional Constraints
for the 2-parameter Model

$c_1 = 0$
$c_2 = 0$
$c_3 = 0$

New Additional Constraints
for the Rasch Model

$a_1 = a_2$
$a_1 = a_3$

Figure 17.1.   Detailed Listing of Structural and Other Constraints Used in the GRG-II Analyses

priate, both the 1- and 2-parameter models failed to converge within 10 EM cycles as expected and the general trend within the 10 EM cycles was one of divergence. Although the 3-parameter model converged quickly at a criterion of .01 within 4 cycles, the parameter estimates diverged beyond the 4 cycles. In other words, for this extreme example, the most appropriate existing method (i.e., BILOG with Bayesian priors) was unable to provide estimates.

These data were also formulated as a 1-, 2-, and 3-parameter nonlinear optimization problems without prior distributions (conceptually more problematic than Bayesian because of the perfect and zero raw scores) and were submitted separately to three analyses through the GRG-II procedure in GINO (Liebman et al., 1986). The structural con-

Table 17.1. Results of BILOG and GRG Estimations

	Ability (θ)					Item Difficulty (b)			
	BILOG	GRG-II				BILOG	GRG-II		
Subject	(3-P)	Rasch	2-P	3-P	Item	(3-P)	Rasch	2-P	3-P
1	−4.000	−.046	−.046	−.051	1	.054	2.602	2.602	1.485
2	.275	−.009	−.009	−.010	2	−.275	.089	.089	.600
3	.275	.015	.015	.017	3	.054	1.494	1.494	1.015
4	4.000	.040	.040	.043					

	Item Discrimination (a)					Pseudo-chance (c)			
	BILOG	GRG-II				BILOG	GRG-II		
Item	(3-P)	Rasch	2-P	3-P	Item	(3-P)	Rasch	2-P	3-P
1	.646	1.481	1.259	1.265	1	0.000	0.000	0.000	0.000
2	4.419	1.481	1.395	1.370	2	0.000	0.000	0.000	.015
3	.646	1.481	1.481	1.425	3	0.000	0.000	0.000	.006

straints described earlier, however, were used as appropriate. Figure 17.1 provides a detailed listing of the structural constraints used for this problem. As expected, solutions were attainable in all cases. Results of the GRG-II analyses as well as those from the 3-parameter BILOG analysis (the only one that converged) are presented in Table 17.1.

Note in Table 17.1 that GRG-II not only consistently converged under all three models, the Θ estimates are consistent across all three models, which is a critically desirable property. The item parameters are quite consistent across all three models. It can be observed that the discrimination parameters are quite similar across the three items for all three models. Similarly, the guessing parameters are practically zero for all three items for all three models. Given these parameters, it is reasonable that the Θ estimates should be similar across the three models. In other words, the most appropriate model is a Rasch model. However, using the 2- and 3-parameter models posed no problem in that GRG-II yielded a and c parameters consistent with a Rasch model. Additionally, given that Θ is on a z-scale, $\Sigma\Theta$ should be zero. In Table 17.1, Θ estimates for all three models do sum to zero. This is, however, not true with the BILOG Bayesian estimate of a 3-parameter model. It is also important to note the BILOG did not converge for the Rasch and 2-parameter models.

DISCUSSION

The above illustration is not intended to demonstrate problems with existing methods. Rather, it is to demonstrate the potential applicability of the nonlinear optimization perspective. The extremely small sample is used due to severe memory limitation of existing nonlinear optimization programs. Until more efficient programs are available, the practicality of the nonlinear optimization approach, despite its conceptual advantages, is unknown. However, for an extremely small sample as the one illustrated, the theoretical and practical advantages of nonlinear optimization is clear.

REFERENCES

Bock, R.D., & Aitkin, M. (1981). Marginal maximum likelihood estimation of item parameters: An application of an EM algorithm. *Psychometrika, 35*, 179–197.

Brooke, A., Kendrick, D., & Meeraus, A. (1988). *GAMS: A user's guide*. Redwood City, CA: Scientific Press.

Hulin, C.L., Lissak, R.I., & Drasgow, F. (1982). Recovery of two- and three-parameter logistic item characteristic curves: A Monte Carlo study. *Applied Psychological Measurement, 6*, 249–260.

Kale, B.K. (1962). On the solution of likelihood equation by iteration processes: The multiparameter case. *Biometrika, 49*, 479–486.

Liebman, J., Lasdon, L., Shrage, L., & Waren, A. (1986). *Modeling and optimization with GINO*. Palo Alto, CA: Scientific Press.

Lord, F.M. (1980). *Application of item response theory to practical testing problems*. Hillsdale, NJ: Erlbaum.

Lord, F.M. (1986). Maximum likelihood and Bayesian parameter estimation in item response theory. *Journal of Educational Measurement, 23*, 157–162.

Mangasarian, O.L. (1967). *Nonlinear programming*. New York: John Wiley & Sons.

Mislevy, R.J., & Bock, R.D. (1984). *BILOG-II: Item analysis and test scoring with binary logistic models*. Mooresville, IN: Scientific Software.

Murtagh, B.A., & Saunders, M.A. (1987). *MINOS 5.1 user's guide* (Report SOL 83-20R). Palo Alto, CA: Stanford University.

Swaminathan, H., & Gifford, J.A. (1986). Bayesian estimation in the three-parameter logistic model. *Psychometrika, 51*, 589–601.

Wingersky, M.S. (1983). LOGIST: A program for computing maximum likelihood procedures for logistic test models. In R.K. Hambleton (Ed.), *Application of item response theory* (pp. 45–56). Vancouver, BC: Educational Research Institute of British Columbia.

Wright, B.D., & Stone, M.H. (1979). *Best test design*. Chicago: MESA.

chapter 18

The Optimization of Decision Studies

P.F. Sanders and T.J.J.M. Theunissen
National Institute for Educational
Measurement (Cito)
Arnhem, The Netherlands

S.M. Baas
Twente University
Enschede, The Netherlands

INTRODUCTION

In generalizability theory (Cronbach, Gleser, Nanda, & Rajaratnam, 1972) a distinction is made between a generalizability (G) study and a decision (D) study. In a G-study, estimates of variance components are obtained which can be used by investigators in D-studies to make decisions about the composition of the measurement instrument. One of the major decisions an investigator has to make is how many observations per subject or another object of measurement are necessary in order to control the principal sources of random sampling error to achieve a given generalizability coefficient (cf. Cardinet & Allal, 1983, p. 42).

For one-facet designs the minimum number of observations per subject can be determined as follows. The coefficient of reliability for the one-facet random-model crossed design, ρ^2, may be expressed as:

$$\rho^2 = \frac{\sigma_p^2}{\sigma_p^2 + \sigma_{res}^2/n_1} \tag{1}$$

where σ_p^2 is the variance component for persons, σ_{res}^2 is the variance component for the $p \times$ facet 1 interaction plus the error, and n_1 is the number of observations, that is, conditions of facet 1, in the D-study. Rewriting (1) and letting ρ^2 be a specific reliability coefficient, the minimum number of observations per subject is equal to:

$$n_1 = \frac{\rho^2 \sigma_{res}^2}{\sigma_p^2 - \rho^2 \sigma_p^2} \tag{2}$$

Equations (1) and (2) both exemplify the Spearman-Brown Prophecy Formula from classical test theory: increase/decrease of the number of observations, for example, items, results in an increase/decrease of the reliability coefficient. This correspondence between number of observations and reliability, however, does not extend to designs with more than one facet. Increasing the number of conditions of a facet with a large error variance component, for example, will have a greater impact on the generalizability coefficient than increasing the number of conditions of a facet with a small error variance component. With multifacet designs it is therefore possible to increase the generalizability coefficient while decreasing the number of observations. The multidimensional nature of error variance is the reason for this paradoxical result, which is inconsistent with assumptions in classical test theory but not with assumptions in generalizability theory (cf. Brennan, 1983, p. 67).

Because of the multidimensional nature of error variance in generalizability theory, the determination of the minimum number of observations is much more complex for multifacet designs than for one-facet designs. Woodward and Joe (1973) presented a method for solving this problem. Their method, however, has a number of shortcomings (Sanders, Theunissen, & Baas, 1989). The method proposed here consists of an algorithm based on the concept of enumeration, using a branch-and-bound algorithm, the principles of which are well known in integer programming (e.g., Salkin, 1975). The method is presented in three parts. First, the structure of a branch-and-bound algorithm is described. Next, an algorithm for a two-facet random-model crossed design is presented. Finally, the algorithm for the two-facet design is generalized for multifacet designs.

BRANCH-AND-BOUND ALGORITHM

The term branch-and-bound algorithm does not refer to one specific algorithm but to a class of algorithms. Papadimitriou and Steiglitz (1982, p. 433) describe the branch-and-bound approach as the construction of a proof that a solution is optimal based on successive partitioning of the solution space. The parts branch and bound refer to rules which reduce the amount of search to be conducted for the optimal solution. A branch-and-bound algorithm is usually represented by a tree composed of branches and nodes, with the nodes organized in levels. In the tree as it is organized for the problem considered here, level $l, l = 1, 2, \ldots, t$, corresponds with variable n_1. Each node at level l represents a partial solution in which variables $n_1, n_2, \ldots, n_l$ have fixed values, say $n_i = \hat{n}_i$, $i = 1, 2, \ldots, l$, whereas the remaining $t - l$ variables are said to be free, to indicate that their values still need to be determined in the further course of the search-process. The root of the full search-tree consists of a single node at level 0 in which all variables are free. The nodes at the highest level (level t) correspond with complete solutions of the problem and may therefore all be regarded as candidates for the optimal solution. A node at level $l \leq t - 1$, with partial solution $\hat{n}_1, \hat{n}_2, \ldots, \hat{n}_l$, is connected by branches with all nodes at level $l + 1$ in which the associated partial solution is different only in the fixed value of variable n_{l+1}, which was free before. Starting from the root of the tree, a complete solution can gradually be developed by passing through individual nodes, one at each level, until level t is reached. In this way any specific node at level t is reachable along a unique path from the root. On the other hand, from any node at an intermediate level $l < t$ several nodes at level t may be attained. In general the tree and thus the number of complete solutions will increase rapidly as the number of variables increases. What is needed, therefore, are additional rules that will allow a significant reduction of the full search-tree by cutting off those parts which are irrelevant regarding an optimal solution.

BRANCH AND BOUND FOR THE TWO-FACET DESIGN PROBLEM

The generalizability coefficient for a two-facet design may be expressed as:

$$\rho^2(n_1, n_2) = \frac{\sigma_p^2}{\sigma_p^2 + \sigma_{p1/n_1}^2 + \sigma_{p2/n_2}^2 + \sigma_{res/n_1 n_2}^2} \qquad (3)$$

where σ_p^2 is the variance component for persons, σ_{p1}^2 is the variance component for the person by facet 1 interaction, σ_{p2}^2 is the variance component for the person by facet 2 interaction, σ_{res}^2 is the variance component for the $p \times$ facet 1 $\times$ facet 2 interaction plus error, n_1 and n_2 are the number of conditions of facet 1 and facet 2 in the D-study. For example, facet 1 could be items or questions, and facet 2 could be raters. Denoting the total number of observations for this design by $L = n_1 n_2$, the problem of determining the minimum number of observations can be stated in terms of mathematical optimization as:

Minimize	$L = n_1 n_2$	(objective-function),	(4)
subject to	$\rho^2(n_1,n_2) \geq g$	(threshold constraint),	(5)
	$n_1 \geq n_2 \geq 1$	(monotonicity constraints),	(6)
	n_1 and n_2 integer	(integer constraint).	(7)

In the minimization statement (4) of this optimization problem, L refers to the value of the objective-function which results when different numbers of conditions, n_1 and n_2, for facet 1 and 2 are used.

In the threshold constraint (5), $\rho^2(n_1,n_2)$ stands for the generalizability coefficient of a two-facet random-model crossed design and g for the lowest acceptable value of a generalizability coefficient. The function $\rho^2(n_1,n_2)$ is strictly increasing with respect to both variables.

The monotonicity constraint (6) $n_1 \geq n_2$ employed here is but one of many linear inequality constraints that could be employed. Note that an optimal solution for the two-facet design problem can also be obtained without this constraint. However, an algorithm employing this constraint will exclude an irrelevant part of the decision-space and consequently reduce the number of branchings in the branch-and-bound process described hereafter.

The integer constraint (7) states that feasible values for n_1 and n_2 have to be integer values.

After the problem has been formulated as an optimization problem, bounding rules are constructed which effectively reduce the search-process. A distinction can be made between feasibility bounds, that is, bounds on the values that n_1 and n_2 can assume without violating the constraints, and optimality bounds, bounds that use a comparison of objective-function values to ascertain whether a given partial solution can lead to an optimal solution. Both types of bounds will be derived in this chapter.

To fix the number of relevant branches emanating from the root of the search-tree, a lower-bound lb_1 and an upper-bound ub_1 on the values that n_1 can assume in an optimal solution can be derived as follows. Regarding the threshold constraint, it can easily be seen that $\rho^2(n_1,n_2)$ is strictly increasing both in n_1 and n_2 so that if $n_1 \geq n_1^*$ and $n_2 \geq n_2^*$, then $\rho^2(n_1,n_2) \geq \rho^2(n_1^*,n_2^*)$, while strict inequality holds whenever $n_1 > n_1^*$ or $n_2 > n_2^*$. Hence, for a given value $\hat{n}_1$ of n_1, there either exists a least-integer value $\hat{n}_2 \leq \hat{n}_1$ so that the threshold constraint is satisfied, or for all $n_2 \leq \hat{n}_1$ this constraint is violated. This observation implies the existence of a value n^- such that $\rho^2(n_1 = n^-, n_2 = n^-) \geq g$, whereas for all $n_1 < n^-$ no value $n_2 \leq n_1$ exists that satisfies the threshold constraint. This means that n^- should be taken as the lower bound for facet 1. For instance, with (3) it can be calculated for Woodward and Joe's example, with $\hat{\sigma}_p^2 = 5.435$, $\hat{\sigma}_{p1}^2 = 3.421$, $\hat{\sigma}_{p2}^2 = 1.140$ and $\hat{\sigma}_{res}^2 = 11.850$, $n_1 = 6$ is the lowest-integer value such that $\rho^2(6,6) \geq .80$. For $n_1 \leq 5$ and for each value $n_2 \leq n_1$ one finds $\rho^2(n_1,n_2) < .80$. Consequently, in this case $lb_1 = n^- = 6$. Note that without the integer constraint $n_1 = n_2 = n^- = 5.08$.

To find an initial solution, let $L^- = (n^-)^2$ be the value of the objective-function associated with the solution $n_1 = n_2 = n^+$. Then $ub_1 = L^-$ is an obvious upper bound on the values of n_1, because any value $n_1 > ub_1$ produces a solution that has a value $n_1 n_2 > ub_1 = L^-$ and is therefore irrelevant for optimality. While initially ub_1 may thus be intractably high, its value can be adapted throughout the search-process whenever a new and better solution is found. The current best solution is called the incumbent. So $n_1 = n_2 = n^-$ as defined above is the initial incumbent. As soon as a complete solution (n_1^*, n_2^*) with value $L^* = n_1^* n_2^* < L^-$ is derived, this becomes the new incumbent and $ub_1 = L^*$ replaces the initial upper bound. This process with repeated successive adaptations of both the incumbent and ub_1 is continued until the whole search-tree has been explored. The then operative incumbent is designated as the optimal solution.

In the example, $ub_1 = n^- n^- = 36$ becomes the first upper bound for n_1. With $lb_1 = 6$ and $ub_1 = 36$ the total number of nodes at level 1 becomes $ub_1 - lb_1 + 1 = 31$. Any such node represents a partial solution with a fixed value for n_1 and n_2 free (see Figure 18.1). Now, for any node at level 1 corresponding with a fixed value $\hat{n}_1$ for n_1 there is a least integer value $\hat{n}_2$ for n_2 such that $\rho^2(\hat{n}_1,\hat{n}_2) \geq g$. Since this value minimizes $L = \hat{n}_1 n_2$ subject to the constraints $\rho^2(\hat{n}_1,n_2) \geq g$ and $\hat{n}_1 > n_2 \geq 1$, it suffices to consider a tree in which each node at level 1 corresponds with precisely one node at level 2. For instance, with (3) the unique feasible value for n_2 that minimizes $\hat{n}_1 n_2$ given $\hat{n}_1 = 8$ is found to be $\hat{n}_2 = 3$.

By convention, the branch associated with the lower bound is fur-

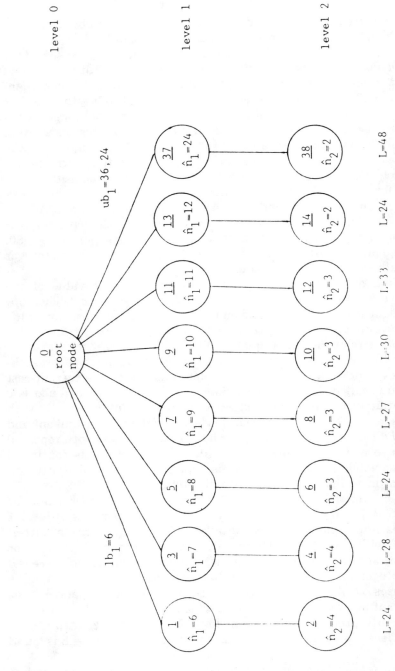

Figure 18.1. Search-tree for the two-facet example

ther referred to as "left-most" branch and the one associated with the upper bound as "right-most" branch. All branches between level 0 (the root) and level 1 are further ordered according to increasing values of n_1. The search-tree for the two-facet problem is now traversed as follows. Starting at the root of the tree, the left-most branch to level 1 is considered first, immediately followed by the unique branch that connects the node with partial solution $\hat{n}_1 = lb_1$ to the corresponding node at level 2 with complete solution $n_1 = \hat{n}_1 = lb_1$, $n_2 = \hat{n}_2$. Next the process returns to the root, which for the two-facet problem is the most recent node from which not all branches to the next level have been considered yet. This is represented by saying that the root is "not fathomed". Note that each node at level 1 is fathomed as soon as the search-process has passed through it once, due to the fact that there is only one branch leading to level 2.

The two nodes regarded next are the one at level 1 with partial solution $\hat{n}_1 = lb_1 + 1$, and its corresponding node at level 2. The full search process as it is conducted for the example with $g \geq .80$ is shown in Figure 1. In this figure the nodes are numbered in their order of appearance. The initial incumbent, whose value is 36, is replaced in node 2 by $(\hat{n}_1, \hat{n}_2) = (6,4)$, giving the new incumbent the value 24. Further exploration of the search tree renders two more solutions, producing the same value for the objective function as node 2: $(\hat{n}_1, \hat{n}_2) = (8,3)$ in node 6 and $(\hat{n}_1, \hat{n}_2) = (12,2)$ in node 14. The search process ends in node 38 with solution $(\hat{n}_1, \hat{n}_2) = (24,2)$, yielding the objective function value 48 which is higher than the incumbent. The results for the two-facet example are presented in Table 18.1.

At the end of the search process there appear to be three candidates for an optimal solution: $(\hat{n}_1, \hat{n}_2) = (6,4)$, $(\hat{n}_1, \hat{n}_2) = (8,3)$, and $(\hat{n}_1, \hat{n}_2) = (12,2)$. Solution $(\hat{n}_1, \hat{n}_2) = (8,3)$ could be considered the "most optimal" solution because it results in a higher generalizability coefficient than

Table 18.1. Various Values of n_1, n_2, L with Resulting Variance Components and ρ^2

n_1	n_2	L	$\hat{\sigma}_p^2$	$\dfrac{\hat{\sigma}_{p1}^2}{n_1}$	$\dfrac{\hat{\sigma}_{p2}^2}{n_2}$	$\dfrac{\hat{\sigma}_{res}^2}{n_1 n_2}$	ρ^2
6	4	24	5.4	.57017	.285	.49375	.80166
7	4	28	5.4	.48871	.285	.42321	.81952
8	3	24	5.4	.42763	.380	.49375	.80681
9	3	27	5.4	.38011	.380	.43889	.81926
10	3	30	5.4	.34210	.380	.39500	.82951
11	3	33	5.4	.31100	.380	.35909	.83808
12	2	24	5.4	.28508	.570	.49375	.80117
24	2	48	5.4	.14254	.570	.24688	.84996

the other two solutions. However, considerations other than obtaining a specific generalizability coefficient can and often will play a role when constructing a measurement instrument. If in this example facet 1 had been items and facet 2 raters, there could have been considerable differences in the costs per condition of these two facets. Raters probably being more expensive than items, an investigator could for economic reasons prefer to increase the number of items rather than to increase the number of raters. This should be indicated by employing an economic constraint such as $n_1 \geq 5n_2$ instead of constraint $n_1 \geq n_2$ which is a psychometric constraint. Using the above specification $g \geq .80$ and employing the economic constraint mentioned, the optimal solution appears to be $(\hat{n}_1, \hat{n}_2) = (12,2)$.

BRANCH AND BOUND FOR THE MULTIFACET DESIGN PROBLEM

How the branch-and-bound method for the two-facet design can be generalized to branch-and-bound methods for multifacet designs can be found in Sanders, Theunissen, and Baas (1989). The presentation here consists of a branch-and bound method for an example of a three-facet design described in Cronbach et al. (1972, p. 171ff.). In this example the aphasic symptoms of 30 patients are rated by 4 raters (facet 2) on 6 graphic subtests (facet 3) using the same 10 objects (facet 1).

The generalizability coefficient for the three-facet random-model crossed design may be expressed as:

$$\rho^2(n_1,n_2,n_3) = \frac{\sigma_p^2}{\sigma_p^2 + \sigma_{p1/n_1}^2 + \sigma_{p2/n_2}^2 + \sigma_{p3/n_3}^2 + \sigma_{p12/n_1n_2}^2 + \sigma_{p13/n_1n_3}^2 + \sigma_{p23/n_2n_3}^2 + \sigma_{res/n_1n_2n_3}^2}$$

(8)

where σ_p^2 is the variance component for patients and the other components are the interaction components divided by the number of conditions being used in the D-study.

The problem for the three-facet design is stated as:

Minimize	$L = n_1n_2n_3$	(objective-function),	(9)
subject to	$\rho^2(n_1,n_2,n_3) \geq g$	(threshold constraint),	(10)
	$n_3 \geq n_1 \geq n_2 \geq 1$	(monotonicity constraints),	(11)
	n_1, n_2 and n_3 integer	(integer constraint).	(12)

Table 18.2. Three Different Constraints with Resulting Values for n_1, n_2, n_3, L, Variance Components and ρ^2

n_1	n_2	n_3	L	$\hat{\sigma}_p^2$	$\dfrac{\hat{\sigma}_{p1}^2}{n_1}$	$\dfrac{\hat{\sigma}_{p2}^2}{n_2}$	$\dfrac{\hat{\sigma}_{p3}^2}{n_3}$	$\dfrac{\hat{\sigma}_{p12}^2}{n_1 n_2}$	$\dfrac{\hat{\sigma}_{p13}^2}{n_1 n_3}$	$\dfrac{\hat{\sigma}_{p23}^2}{n_2 n_3}$	$\dfrac{\hat{\sigma}_{p123}^2}{n_1 n_2 n_3}$	ρ^2
$n_3 \geq n_1 \geq n_2 \geq 1$												
5	3	5	75	5.3	.08200	.05000	.34200	.01000	.08040	.00467	.01320	.90101
4	3	6	72	5.3	.10250	.05000	.28500	.01250	.08375	.00389	.01375	.90577
5	2	6	60	5.3	.08200	.07500	.28500	.01500	.06700	.00583	.01650	.90655
4	2	7	56	5.3	.10250	.07500	.24429	.01875	.07179	.00500	.01768	.90831
6	1	7	42	5.3	.06800	.15000	.24429	.02500	.04786	.01000	.02357	.90301
5	1	8	40	5.3	.08200	.15000	.21375	.03000	.05025	.00875	.02475	.90451
4	1	9	36	5.3	.10250	.15000	.19000	.03750	.05583	.00778	.02750	.90275
3	1	12	36	5.3	.13666	.15000	.14250	.05000	.05583	.00583	.02750	.90315
$n_1 \geq n_3 \geq n_2 \geq 1$												
5	3	5	75	5.3	.08200	.05000	.34200	.01000	.08040	.00467	.01320	.90101
6	2	5	60	5.3	.06800	.07500	.34200	.01250	.06700	.00700	.01650	.90014
7	1	7	49	5.3	.05857	.15000	.24429	.02143	.04102	.01000	.02020	.90668
8	1	6	48	5.3	.05125	.15000	.28500	.01875	.04187	.01167	.02062	.90149
$n_1 \geq n_2 \geq n_3 \geq 1$												
5	5	5	125	5.3	.08200	.03000	.34200	.00600	.08040	.00280	.00792	.90581

309

Note that the remarks made on the monotonicity constraints employed in the two-facet example also apply for the monotonicity constraints employed in the three-facet example.

The results for this example (using Cronbach's values with $\hat{\sigma}_p^2 = 5.3$, $\hat{\sigma}_{p1}^2 = .41, \hat{\sigma}_{p2}^2 = .15, \hat{\sigma}_{p3}^2 = 1.71, \hat{\sigma}_{p12}^2 = .15, \hat{\sigma}_{p13}^2 = 2.01, \hat{\sigma}_{p23}^2 = .07,$ and $\hat{\sigma}_{res}^2 = .99$ and $g \geq .90$) are presented in Table 18.2.

To illustrate our method, three different constraints were employed. The solutions in Table 18.2 show that the psychometric constraint $n_3 \geq n_1 \geq n_2 \geq 1$ results in $L = 36$ observations. This number of observations corresponds with solutions $(\hat{n}_1, \hat{n}_2, \hat{n}_3) = (4,1,9)$ and $(\hat{n}_1, \hat{n}_2, \hat{n}_3) = (3,1,12)$. However, these solutions are also the most expensive solutions since they involve the construction of new tests. An investigator who will therefore probably want to use the six tests that are already available should add constraint $n_3 \leq 6$ to this constraint, obtaining as an optimal solution $(\hat{n}_1, \hat{n}_2, \hat{n}_3) = (5,2,6)$ with $L = 60$. A more economical instrument would be one composed of as many objects and as few raters as possible and using no more tests than are available. Employing the corresponding economic constraints $n_1 \geq n_3 \geq n_2 \geq 1$ and $n_3 \leq 6$ would result in the optimal solution $(\hat{n}_1, \hat{n}_2, \hat{n}_3) = (8,1,6)$ with $L = 48$. Employing another economic constraint $n_1 \geq n_2 \geq n_3 \geq 1$ would result in the optimal solution $(\hat{n}_1, \hat{n}_2, \hat{n}_3) = (5,5,5)$ with $L = 125$ observations.

CONCLUSIONS AND DISCUSSION

The method proposed in this chapter enables an investigator to specify an acceptable threshold for generalizability coefficients. The employment of the threshold constraint together with the integer constraint necessarily results in values for the objective function and values for the number of conditions of facets that are integer.

It has been shown that various constraints can be employed with the method proposed here. In general, methods which employ equality constraints are discouraged because they will often lead to noninteger and/or nonoptimal solutions. Woodward and Joe's method is an example where an equality constraint is used to specify an acceptable generalizability coefficient. With our method, employing in the two-facet example equality constraint $n_1 = n_2$ as an economic constraint and specifying $g \geq .80$ will result in solution $(\hat{n}_1, \hat{n}_2) = (12,3)$ with $L = 36$ observations. However, $g \geq .80$ is also satisfied by solution $(\hat{n}_1, \hat{n}_2) = (8,3)$ with $L = 24$ observations. The latter solution is of course to be preferred because it needs four fewer conditions for facet 1. Employing more than one equality constraint will often even result in no integer solution at all, as for the two equality constraints $n_1 = 4n_2$ and $g = .80$

in the two-facet example. With respect to the number of constraints employed, it should be clear that adding constraints will reduce the set of feasible solutions.

The versatility of our method makes it extremely useful for investigators planning generalizability studies and practitioners involved with making decisions about the composition of measurement instruments. A computer program for the designs discussed here as well as other designs has been developed and can be obtained from the first author. Using as input G-study estimates of variance components obtainable from existing computer programs for generalizability studies, for example, GENOVA (Crick & Brennan, 1982), computation time is no more than a few seconds.

The foregoing presentation has emphasized the practical aspects of the method proposed here. The method does however have important theoretical aspects as well. It can easily be seen that (2), the Spearman-Brown Prophecy formula from classical test theory, can be stated as a noninteger optimization problem with $L = n_1$ and $\rho^2(\hat{n}_1) = g$. By employing a threshold constraint and an integer constraint, this formula can be stated as an integer optimization problem. The search-tree of this problem consists of a root-node with one branch going down to one node at level 1, which is associated with the only feasible value that minimizes L. The method proposed in this article generalizes the Spearman-Brown formula for measurement instruments with one facet to measurement instruments with more than one facet. As generalizability theory is the theoretical framework for these instruments, this method is a theoretical contribution to this framework.

Thus far the number of applications of integer optimization techniques to solve problems in psychometrics has been limited. Theunissen (1985) was the first to show how integer optimization techniques could be used to solve problems in latent trait theory. A computer program (OTD) for test construction using Rasch scaled item parameters can be purchased from Cito. For generalizability theory optimization techniques also appear ultimately suited to handle a broad range of practical problems. More fruitful applications of these techniques are being developed (e.g., Sanders, Theunissen, & Baas, 1991).

REFERENCES

Brennan, R.L. (1983). *Elements of generalizability theory.* Iowa City: ACT Publications.

Cardinet, J., & Allal, L. (1983). Estimation of generalizability parameters. In

L.J. Fyans (Ed.), *Generalizability theory: Inferences and practical applications* (pp. 17–48). San Francisco: Jossey-Bass.

Crick, J.E., & Brennan, R.L. (1982). *GENOVA: A generalized analysis of variance system* (FORTRAN IV computer program and manual). Iowa City: ACT.

Cronbach, L.J., Gleser, G.C., Nanda, H., & Rajaratnam, N. (1972). *The dependability of behavioral measurements*. New York: John Wiley & Sons.

Papadimitriou, Ch.H., & Steiglitz, K. (1982). *Combinatorial optimization: Algorithms and complexity*. Englewood Cliffs, NJ: Prentice-Hall.

Salkin, H.M. (1975). *Integer programming*. Reading, MA: Addison-Wesley.

Sanders, P.F., Theunissen, T.J.J.M., & Baas, S.M. (1989). Minimizing the number of observations: a generalization of the Spearman-Brown formula. *Psychometrika, 54,* 587–598.

Sanders, P.F., Theunissen, T.J.J.M., & Baas, S.M. Maximizing the coefficient of generalizability under the constraint of limited resources. *Psychometrika*. Accepted for publication.

Theunissen, T.J.J.M. (1985). Binary programming and test design. *Psychometrika, 50,* 411–420.

Woodward, J.A., & Joe, G.W. (1973). Maximizing the coefficient of generalizability in multi-facet decision studies. *Psychometrika, 38,* 173–181.

chapter 19

Simultaneous Optimization of the Aptitude Treatment Interaction Decision Problem with Mastery Scores*

Hans J. Vos
Department of Education
University of Twente, The Netherlands

INTRODUCTION

Statistical decision problems arise when a decision maker is faced with the need to choose a preferred action that is optimal in some sense. Moreover, one decision problem often leads to another, which, in turn, leads to a next one, and so on. An example is test-based decision making in an Individualized Study System (ISS), which can be conceived of as an instructional network consisting of various types of decisions as nodes (Vos, 1990; Vos & van der Linden, 1987). How should we model and analyze such sequences of decision problems within a Bayesian

_____

* The author wishes to thank Wim J. van der Linden, Sebie J. Oosterloo, and Paul Westers for their helpful comments and Jan Gulmans for providing the data for the illustration. The computer programs NEWTON and UTILITY are available on request from the author. Research Reports can be obtained at costs from Bibliotheek, Department of Education, University of Twente, P.O. Box 217, 7500 AE Enschede, The Netherlands.

decision-theoretic approach (e.g., DeGroot, 1970; Ferguson, 1967; Keeney & Raiffa, 1976; Lindgren, 1976)? In general, two main approaches can be distinguished: either each decision can be optimized separately or all decisions simultaneously. In the former approach, the expected utility of each separate decision is maximized sequentially while in the latter the overall expected utility of all decisions is maximized simultaneously.

It is the purpose of this chapter to demonstrate how rules for the simultaneous optimization of sequences of decisions can be found. Compared with the separate optimization of decisions, two main advantages can be identified. First, in optimizing combined decision rules, decisions to be made later in the decision network can already be taken into account. As a result of this approach, rules can be found that make more efficient use of the data in the decision network. Also, the overall expected utility will be increased. Second, more realistic utility structures can be handled by the simultaneous approach.

Van der Linden (1985, 1988) has given an elegant typology of decision problems in educational and psychological testing. Each decision problem from this typology can be viewed as a specific configuration of three basic elements—namely a test, a treatment, and a criterion. With the aid of these elements, the following four different types of decision problems can be identified: selection, mastery, placement, and classification.

Well-known examples of the four types of decision making in the field of education are admission of students to educational programs (selection), pass-fail decisions (mastery), the aptitude-treatment-interaction paradigm in instructional psychology where students are allowed to reach the same educational objectives via different instructional treatments (placement), and vocational-guidance situations where, for instance, most appropriate continuation-schools must be identified (classification).

Each of the four elementary decision problems can be formalized as a problem of (empirical) Bayesian decision making. In Hambleton and Novick (1973), Huynh (1976, 1977), Mellenbergh and van der Linden (1981), Novick and Petersen (1976), Petersen (1976), Petersen and Novick (1976), van der Linden (1980, 1981, 1987), and Vos (1988), it is indicated how optimal decision rules can be found for these problems (analytically or numerically).

In this chapter, the emphasis is on deriving simultaneous optimal decision rules for combinations of the elementary decisions. To illustrate the approach, a placement and a mastery decision will be combined into a simple decision network (see also Figure 19.1). The difference between the separate and the simultaneous approach can be

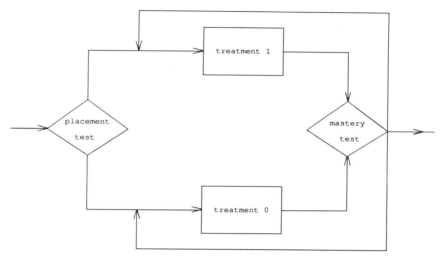

Figure 19.1.   A system of one placement and one mastery decision (Case of two treatments)

demonstrated by the combined placement-mastery decision of Figure 19.1. In the separate approach, first optimal placement rules are found by maximizing the expected utility for the separate placement decision (e.g., van der Linden, 1981). Next, optimal mastery rules are found by maximizing the overall expected utility for the separate mastery decision (e.g., Hambleton & Novick, 1973). In the simultaneous approach, however, the optimal placement as well as the optimal mastery rules are found by maximizing the overall expected utility of both decisions simultaneously. This implies that, in optimizing treatment-assignment rules, pass-fail decisions to be made later can already be taken into account; hence, the first advantage of the simultaneous approach is nicely demonstrated by Figure 19.1.

Besides the pure forms and combinations with each other, further generalizations within each elementary decision are possible, for instance, by accepting only a fixed number of students to some treatments due to shortage of resources or distinguishing between several culturally biased subpopulations, which may create the problem of culture-fair decision-making. In this chapter, only the presence of multiple populations reacting differently to the test items will be assumed.

First, we elaborate the decision-theoretic aspects of culture-fair decision making for a quota-free placement-mastery problem. For a linear utility function we then give the decision rule that optimizes simultaneously the treatment assignments and the pass-fail decisions to be taken after the treatments. Next, optimal rules will be derived for the separate decisions by imposing certain restrictions on the overall expected utility for the simultaneous approach. Finally, optimal cutting scores for quota-free combined decisions will be presented for an empirical application to instructional decision making in an ISS. In the numerical example, it is further assumed that the students can be separated into two subpopulations referred to as the disadvantaged and the advantaged populations.

With respect to the applicability of the approach presented in this chapter, the following should be regarded. Although the area of individualized instruction is a useful application of simultaneous decision making, it should be emphasized that the procedures advocated in this chapter have a larger scope. For instance, the simple placement-mastery decision problem may be important in such areas as psychotherapy in which it can be expected that patients react differentially to a certain kind of therapy and the most promising therapy is followed by an end-of-therapy test.

THE PLACEMENT-MASTERY DECISION PROBLEM

In placement decisions several alternative treatments are available and it is the decision maker's task to assign individuals to the most promising treatment on the basis of their test scores. All subjects are administered the same test and the success of each treatment is measured by the same criterion. Figure 19.1 shows a flowchart of an ISS for the case of two instructional treatments in which the treatment assignment is followed by a mastery test. Using this test, it will be decided whether the student has mastered the instructional treatment sufficiently so that he or she may proceed with the next treatment, or has to relearn the treatment and prepare him(her)self for a new test.

In the following, we suppose that in the placement-mastery decision problem the total population can be separated into g ($g \geq 2$) subpopulations reacting differently to the test items. Let X be the placement test score variable, Y the mastery test score variable, and let the true score variable T underlying Y denote the criterion common to the treatments j ($j = 0,1$), respectively. The variables X, Y, and T will be considered to be continuous.

We consider a hypothetical experiment consisting of a population of students being exposed to each of both possible treatments but where the students are "brainwashed" so that the effects of one treatment do not interfere with those of another. (The actual experiment needed for parameter estimation and in which different samples of students are randomly assigned to the treatments will be described later on.)

Furthermore, it is supposed that the relation between the measurements X, the measurements Y after treatment j, and the criterion T, can be represented for each population i $(i = 1, 2, \ldots, g)$ by a joint probability function $\Omega_{ji}(x,y,t)$. Since the treatment is between the placement and the mastery test, it will influence the relation between X, Y, and T, and this relation can be expected to assume a different shape for each treatment. This is indicated by the index j in $\Omega_{ji}(x,y,t)$. However, because the placement test is administered prior to the treatments, the marginal probability function of X in subpopulation i is the same for both treatments and will be denoted by $q_i(x)$.

The presence of populations reacting differently to test items imply also different cutoff scores for each population (Gross & Su, 1975; Petersen & Novick, 1976). Therefore, let x_{ci} and y_{ci} denote the cutoff scores for subpopulation i on the observed test score variables X and Y, respectively. However, the cutoff score t_c on the criterion score T separating "true masters" from "true nonmasters" is assumed to be equal for each population. Note that, also due to the presence of different populations reacting differently to the test items, different probability functions for each population should be assumed (Gross & Su, 1975; Petersen & Novick, 1976).

The hypothetical experiment being executed, the placement-mastery decision problem now consists of setting simultaneously cutoff scores x_{ci} and y_{ci} such that, given the value of t_c, the overall expected utility is maximized. It should be stressed that, although the nature of the decisions shown in Figure 19.1 is sequential, the cutoff scores x_{ci} and y_{ci} are optimized simultaneously using data coming from the above experiment.

In this chapter, linking up with common practice in criterion-referenced testing, we consider only monotone decision rules δ: students are admitted to a treatment if their test score is above a certain cutting point and rejected otherwise. For the decision network of Figure 19.1 the decision rule can be defined in the following way:

$$\delta(X, Y) = \begin{cases} a_{00} & \text{for } X < x_{ci}, Y < y_{ci} \\ a_{01} & \text{for } X < x_{ci}, Y \geq y_{ci} \\ a_{10} & \text{for } X \geq x_{ci}, Y < y_{ci} \\ a_{11} & \text{for } X \geq x_{ci}, Y \geq y_{ci}, \end{cases} \tag{1}$$

where a_{jh} stands for the action either to retain $(h = 0)$ or advance $(h = 1)$ a student who is assigned to treatment j $(j = 0,1)$. The problem of setting optimal cutting scores x_{ci} and y_{ci}, given the value of t_c, now amounts to selecting a monotone decision rule which maximizes the overall expected utility.

AN ADDITIVE REPRESENTATION OF THE COMBINED UTILITY FUNCTION

Formally, a utility function $u_{jhi}(t)$ describes all costs and benefits involved when action a_{jh} ($j,h = 0,1$) is taken for the student from subpopulation i whose true score is t. The decision maker may have different utilities associated with different populations (Gross & Su, 1975; Petersen & Novick, 1976). Hence, in addition to separate probability distributions, the decision maker has to specify explicitly his/her utility function for each subpopulation separately.

In the Introduction, it was remarked that one of the main advantages of the simultaneous approach was that more realistic utility structures could be used. This is nicely demonstrated by defining the utility structure of the combined decision problem as an additive function of the following form:

$$u_{jhi}(t) = w_1 u_{jip}(t) + w_2 u_{him}(t), \qquad (2)$$

where $u_{jip}(t)$, $u_{him}(t)$ represent the utility functions for the separate placement and mastery decisions, and w_1 and w_2 represent nonnegative weights. The utility functions $u_{jip}(t)$ and $u_{him}(t)$ are assessed separately and then brought onto the same scale by use of the weights w_1 and w_2. A set of conditions sufficient for the existence of an additive value function may be found in Fishburn (1982), French (1986), Keeney and Raiffa (1976), and Krantz, Luce, Suppes, and Tversky (1971). Since utility must be measured at most on an interval scale, the utility function of (2) can always be rescaled (normalized) as follows:

$$u_{jhi}(t) = w u_{jip}(t) + (1 - w)u_{him}(t), \qquad (3)$$

where the weight w now should satisfy $0 \le w \le 1$. The utility function $u_{jhi}(t)$ now takes the following form:

$$u_{hji}(t) = \begin{cases} w u_{0ip}(t) + (1 - w)u_{0im}(t) & \text{for } j = 0, h = 0 \\ w u_{0ip}(t) + (1 - w)u_{1im}(t) & \text{for } j = 0, h = 1 \\ w u_{1ip}(t) + (1 - w)u_{0im}(t) & \text{for } j = 1, h = 0 \\ w u_{1ip}(t) + (1 - w)u_{1im}(t) & \text{for } j = 1, h = 1. \end{cases} \qquad (4)$$

In the following, we shall suppose that the treatments have been ordered in such a way that the treatments 0 and 1 can be considered as the "lower" and "higher" treatment, respectively. In general, students with high test scores on the placement test will be assigned to treatment 1, and vice versa. For instance, treatment 1 may contain less examples and exercises than treatment 0.

OPTIMIZING CUTTING SCORES FOR QUOTA-FREE PLACEMENT

As noted earlier, the optimal procedure from a Bayesian point of view is to look for a rule that maximizes the overall expected utility. Since we may confine ourselves to monotone rules, the expected utility of a random student from subpopulation i for the simultaneous approach is given by

$$E[u_{jhi}(T)|x_{ci},y_{ci}]$$

$$= \int_{-\infty}^{\infty} \int_{-\infty}^{x_{ci}} \int_{-\infty}^{y_{ci}} u_{00i}(t)\Omega_{0i}(x,y,t)dtdxdy +$$

$$\int_{-\infty}^{\infty} \int_{-\infty}^{x_{ci}} \int_{y_{ci}}^{\infty} u_{01i}(t)\Omega_{0i}(x,y,t)dtdxdy +$$

$$\int_{-\infty}^{\infty} \int_{x_{ci}}^{\infty} \int_{-\infty}^{y_{ci}} u_{10i}(t)\Omega_{1i}(x,y,t)dtdxdy +$$

$$\int_{-\infty}^{\infty} \int_{x_{ci}}^{\infty} \int_{y_{ci}}^{\infty} u_{11i}(t)\Omega_{1i}(x,y,t)dtdxdy. \tag{5}$$

Substituting the additive utility function of (4) into (5), and rearranging terms, yields

$$E[u_{jhi}(T)|x_{ci},y_{ci}] = w \int_{-\infty}^{\infty} E_0[u_{0p}(T)|x]q(x) +$$

$$(1 - w) \int_{-\infty}^{\infty} E_0[u_{0im}(T)|y]s_{0i}(y)\, dy +$$

$$\int_{x_{ci}}^{\infty} w\{E_1[u_{1ip}(T)|x] - E_0[u_{0ip}(T)|x]\}q_i(x)dx +$$

$$(1 - w) \left\{ \int_{y_{ci}}^{\infty} E_0[u_{1im}(t) - u_{0im}(t)|y]s_{0i}(y)dy + \right.$$

$$\int_{x_{ci}}^{\infty} \{E_1[u_{0im}(T)|x] - E_0[u_{0im}(T)|x]\}q(x)dx +$$

$$\int_{x_{ci}}^{\infty} \left\{ \int_{-y_{ci}}^{\infty} \{E_1[u_{1im}(t) - u_{0im}(t)|x,y]n_{1i}(y|x) - \right.$$

$$\left. E_0[u_{1im}(t) - u_{0im}(t)|x,y]n_{0i}(y|x)\}dy \right\} q_i(x)dx \bigg\}, \tag{6}$$

where $s_{ji}(y)$ and $n_{ji}(y|x)$ denote the probability function of Y and Y given $X = x$ in subpopulation i under treatment j, respectively, and where E_j indicates that the expectation has been taken over a distribution indexed by j ($j = 0,1$).

Before proceeding with the maximizatiion of (6), first some explanation will be given for the expression formulated in (6). First, in case of the expected utility of a random student from the ith subpopulation for the separate placement decision, $E_p[u_i(T)|x_{ci}]$, there are no utilities associated with the separate mastery decision implying that the second, fourth, fifth and sixth term of (6) disappear. It follows that (6) reduces to

$$E_p[u_{1i}(T)|x_{ci}] = w\left\{ \int_{-\infty}^{\infty} E_0[u_{0ip}(T)|x]q_i(x)dx + \right.$$

$$\left. \int_{x_{ci}}^{\infty} \{E_1[u_{1ip}(T)|x] - E_0[u_{0ip}(T)|x]\}q(x)dx \right\}. \qquad (7)$$

Furthermore, the expected utility of a random student from subpopulation i for the separate mastery decision, $E_m[u_i(T)|y_{ci}]$, follows immediately from (6) by realizing that both treatments coincide in this case implying that $n_{1i}(y|x) = n_{0i}(y|x)$ and $E_0[.] = E_1[.]$, in turn, implying that the fifth and sixth term in (6) vanish. Also, since there are no utilities associated with the separate placement decision in this case, the first and third term in (6) vanish. Taking into account the above-mentioned consequences imply that (6) reduces to

$$E_m[u_i(T)|y_{ci}] = (1 - w)\left\{ \int_{-\infty}^{\infty} E_0[u_{0im}(T)|y]s_{0i}(y)dy + \right.$$

$$\left. \int_{y_{ci}}^{\infty} E_0[u_{1im}(t) - u_{0im}(t)|y]s_{0i}(y)dy \right\}. \qquad (8)$$

From the expressions for the separate expected utilities stated above it can be concluded that the overall expected utility for the simultaneous approach actually equals the sum of the separate expected utilities in which the last two terms from (6) still have to be added. Henceforth, the last two terms are specific for the simultaneous overall expected utility.

Now, the decision procedure is viewed as a series of separate decisions, each of which involves one random student from the total population. Furthermore, it is assumed that the overall expected utility for the simultaneous approach, $E[u(T)|x_{c1},y_{c1}, \ldots, x_{cg},y_{cg}]$, is found by summing the expected utility for the simultaneous approach of a random student over all students. Under these assumptions, it follows that the overall expected utility for the simultaneous approach can be written as:

$$E[u(T)|x_{c1},y_{c1}, \ldots, x_{cg},y_{cg}] = \sum_{i=1}^{g} p_i E[u_{jhi}(T)|x_{ci},y_{ci}], \qquad (9)$$

where p_i is the proportion of students from subpopulation i in the total population, so $\Sigma_{i=1}^{g} p_i = 1$.

With quota-free placement, there is no constraint on the number of students that can be assigned to one of the treatments. Therefore, the values of the optimal cutting scores, say x'_{ci} and y'_{ci}, which maximize (9), can be obtained by maximizing (6) for each subpopulation i separately. The optimal decision rule can be derived by differentiating $E[u_{jhi}(T)|x_{ci},y_{ci}]$ with respect to x_{ci} and y_{ci}, setting the resulting expressions equal to zero, and solving for x_{ci} and y_{ci}.

However, before proceeding with this procedure, it is necessary to specify the probability, regression, and utility functions appearing in (6).

Bivariate Normal Model

In the following, we suppose that the variables X and Y have possibly different bivariate normal distributions under both treatments in each subpopulation i. Let ρ_{ji} denote the population correlation between X and Y under treatment j in subpopulation i, and let x_N and y_{Nj} denote the standardized scores of X and Y under treatment j ($j = 0,1$), respectively. Then it can be shown (see, e.g., Johnson & Kotz, 1970) that for the standardized bivariate normal distribution the conditional distribution of X_N given $Y_{Nj} = y_{Nj}$ is normal with expected value $\rho_{ji}y_{Nj}$ and variance $(1 - \rho_{ji}^2)$. Likewise, $n_{ji}(y_{Nj}|x_N)$ is normal with expected value $\rho_{ji}x_N$ and variance $(1 - \rho_{ji}^2)$.

The regression functions $E_{ji}(T|x)$ and $E_{ji}(T|x,y)$ of T on x and T on x and y under treatment j, are assumed to be linear in each subpopulation i; that is, they can be written as $\theta_{ji} + \Gamma_{ji}x$ and $\alpha_{ji} + \beta_{ji}x + \tau_{ji}y$, respectively. Using results from classical test theory, it follows that the regression coefficients can be written as:

$$\Gamma_{ji} = \rho_{ji}(\sigma_{Yji}/\sigma_{Xi})$$

$$\theta_{ji} = \mu_{Yji} - \Gamma_{ji}\mu_{Xi}$$

$$\beta_{ji} = (\sigma_{Yji}/\sigma_{Xi})\{(\rho_{ji} - \rho'_{ji}\rho_{ji})/(1 - \rho_{ji}^2)\} \qquad (10)$$

$$\tau_{ji} = (\rho'_{ji} - \rho_{ji}^2)/(1 - \rho_{ji}^2)$$

$$\alpha_{ji} = -\mu_{Xi}\beta_{ji} + \mu_{Yji}(1 - \tau_{ji}),$$

μ_{Yji}, μ_{Xi}, σ_{Yji}, σ_{Xi}, and ρ'_{ji} being the population means of Y and X, the population standard deviations of Y and X, and the reliability coefficient of Y under treatment j ($j = 0,1$) in subpopulation i, respectively. Assuming also linear regression for T on y under both treatments in each subpopulation i, and using Kelley's regression line (Lord & Novick, 1968, p.55), it follows

$$E_{ji}(T|y) = \rho'_{ji} y + (1 - \rho'_{ji})\mu_{Yji}. \qquad (11)$$

Linear Utility

Mellenbergh and van der Linden (1981) and van der Linden and Mellenbergh (1977) proposed a linear utility function for the separate decisions, which seems to be a realistic representation of the utilities actually incurred in many decision making situations. In a recent study, for instance, it was shown by van der Gaag (1989) that many empirical utility structures could be approximated by linear functions. They can in the case of multiple populations be defined in the following way:

$$u_{jip}(t) = \begin{cases} b_{0ip}(t_c - t) + d_{0ip} & \text{for } X < x_{ci} \\ b_{1ip}(t - t_c) + d_{1ip} & \text{for } X \geq x_{ci} \end{cases}$$

$$u_{him}(t) = \begin{cases} b_{0im}(t_c - t) + d_{0im} & \text{for } Y < y_{ci} \\ b_{1im}(t - t_c) + d_{1im} & \text{for } Y \geq y_{ci}, \end{cases}$$

where b_{0ip}, b_{1ip}, b_{0im}, and $b_{1im} > 0$.

For each action, this function consists of a constant term and a term proportional to the difference between the criterion performance t of a student and the minimum level of satisfactory criterion performance t_c. The parameters d_{jip} and d_{him} ($j,h = 0,1$) can, for example, represent the constant amount of costs of following treatment j and the costs of testing, respectively, and will in that case have a nonpositive value. The condition b_{0ip}, $b_{1ip} > 0$ is equivalent to the assumption that for assigning students to treatment 0 and 1, utility is a strictly decreasing and increasing function of t, respectively. Likewise, b_{0im}, $b_{1im} > 0$ expresses the assumption that the utility for failing and advancing the mastery test is a strictly decreasing and increasing function of t, respectively.

As Gross and Su (1975) and Petersen and Novick (1976) pointed out, the question whether decision rules are fair to the various subpopulations which can be distinguished depend within a decision-theoretic framework only on the chosen utilities. From this point of view, separate parameter values might be chosen in the linear utility model to allow for the fact that the students might belong to a disadvantaged or advantaged population (see also Mellenbergh & van der Linden, 1981). Suppose, for example, that population 2 is considered more advantaged than 1. Furthermore, it is assumed that incorrect decisions are considered worse for population 1 than for 2, while correct decisions are considered more valuable for population 1 than for 2. If so, b_{j1p} and b_{h1m} could be set higher than b_{j2p} and b_{h2m}, respectively, for every value of t ($j, h = 0,1$).

Now, substituting the assumed linear regression, bivariate normal probability, and linear utility functions in (6), differentiating with respect to x_{ci} and y_{ci}, setting the resulting expressions equal to zero, and solving for x_{ci} and y_{ci}, the optimal decision rule can be obtained. However, since the resulting system of equations cannot be solved analytically for x_{ci} and y_{ci}, the determination of the optimal cutting scores may be carried out via numerical approximation procedures such as the Newton iterative algorithm for solving nonlinear equations. For details of the derivations needed to apply Newton's iterative procedure, refer to Vos (1989).

Using the property that the standard normal distributions appearing in applying Newton's iterative algorithm can be approximated by logistic functions with a scale parameter equal to 1.7 (Lord & Novick, 1968, sect. 17.2), one obtains the optimal cutting scores x'_{ci} and y'_{ci}. The algorithm is implemented in a computer program called NEWTON available from the author.

DERIVATION OF OPTIMAL SEPARATE DECISIONS

The optimal separate mastery decision can be obtained by differentiating (8) with respect to y_{ci}, setting the resulting expression equal to zero, and solving for y_{ci}. Doing so, and using $s_0(y_{ci}) > 0$ and $w \neq 1$, it follows that

$$E_0[u_{1im}(t) - u_{0im}(t)|y_{ci}] = 0, \qquad (12)$$

which yields the same optimal cutting score y'_{ci} as the one given by van der Linden and Mellenbergh (1977). For the linear utility model, it follows from (12) that

$$y'_{ci} = \mu_{Y0i} + \{t_c - \mu_{Y0i} + (d_{0im} - d_{1im})/(b_{1im} + b_{0im})\}/\rho'_{0i}. \quad (13)$$

Similarly, the optimal separate placement decision, x'_{ci}, follows again by differentiating (7) with respect to x_{ci}, setting the resulting expression equal to zero, and solving for x_{ci}. Doing so, and using $q_i(x) > 0$ and $w \neq 0$, results in

$$E_1[u_{1ip}(T)|x_{ci}] - E_0[u_{0ip}(T)|x_{ci}] = 0. \quad (14)$$

Also, this optimal solution agrees with the one reached by van der Linden (1981). Adopting the linear utility model in (14), it follows that

$$x'_{ci} = \{d_{0ip} - d_{1ip} + t_c(b_{1ip} + b_{0ip}) - b_{1ip}\theta_{1i} - b_{0ip}\theta_{0i}\}/ (b_{1ip}\Gamma_{1i} + b_{0ip}\Gamma_{0i}). \quad (15)$$

As a final remark, it should be noted that the optimal separate cutting scores, unlike the expected utilities for the separate decisions, do not depend upon the value of w. On the other hand, the optimal cutting scores as well as the expected utilities for the simultaneous approach depend upon the value of w. To illustrate the models presented in this paper, a numerical example is given in the next section.

AN APPLICATION OF THE COMBINED DECISION PROBLEM

The procedure for computing the optimal cutting scores was applied to a sample of 59 freshmen in medicine. Both the placement and mastery test was composed of 21 free-response items on elementary medical knowledge with test scores ranging from 0–100. The treatments 0 and 1 consisted of an interactive video (IV) and a computer-aided instructional (CAI) program, respectively. Since the IV-program contained more examples and exercises, treatment 1 was considered as the "higher" treatment.

Due to previous schooling, the total sample of 59 students could be separated with respect to elementary medical knowledge into a disadvantaged and an advantaged population of 31 and 28 students referred to as populations 1 and 2, respectively. The normal models assumed for the distributions X_i and Y_{ji} ($j = 0,1; i = 1,2$) showed a satisfactory fit to the test data for a Kolmogorov-Smirnov goodness-of-fit test.

Table 19.1.   Statistics Placement and Mastery Tests (X and Y)

Statistic	Disadvantaged			Advantaged		
	X	Y		X	Y	
		Treatment			Treatment	
		0	1		0	1
Mean	55.965	63.266	62.148	59.832	66.125	67.233
Standard Deviation	10.821	10.144	11.245	11.674	10.517	12.523
Reliability		0.764	0.813		0.744	0.791
Correlation		$\rho_{01} = 0.786$	$\rho_{11} = 0.819$		$\rho_{02} = 0.725$	$\rho_{12} = 0.771$

The teachers of the course considered a student as having mastered the subject matter if he or she could answer correctly at least 55 percent of the total domain of items. Therefore, t_c was fixed at 0.55.

The means, standard deviations, and correlations between X and Y were computed for each subpopulation under both treatments using the unbiased maximum likelihood estimates of the sample means, sample standard deviations, and sample correlations, respectively. Furthermore, since the items were not scored as correct or false, the reliabilities of the test scores were estimated as coefficient α (Cronbach, 1951) for each subpopulation under both treatments. The results are reported in Table 19.1.

It is important to notice that the necessary statistics come from the correct experiment and not, for example, from ISSs in which students are already assigned to treatments on the basis of their scores on the placement test in question. In a proper experiment students from the same probability function of X are randomly drawn and assigned to treatments, after which their performances on the mastery test are measured.

Because the costs for testing are assumed to be equal for advanced and retained students, d_{h1m} is set equal to d_{h2m} ($h = 0,1$). Similarly, the costs of following the different treatments j ($j = 0,1$) are equal: $d_{j1p} = d_{j2p}$. Furthermore, it should hold that $b_{j1p} > b_{j2p}$ and $b_{h1m} > b_{h2m}$, taking into account the fact that population 2 was considered more advantaged than 1. Using the computer program NEWTON, the optimal cutting scores x'_{ci} and y'_{ci} were then computed iteratively with t_c as starting values. The criterion for convergence was that the absolute differences between two iteration steps for both x'_{ci} and y'_{ci} were smaller than 10^{-7}. The results are reported in Table 19.2 for 3 different values of the utility parameters as well as for $w = 0.5, 0.9,$ and 0.1 to illustrate the dependence of the results on the utility structure.

The table shows that the consequence of raising the value of w is

Table 19.2. Optimal Cutting Scores Quota-Free Placement with Linear Utility

No.	Utility Specifications Disadv.	Utility Specifications Adv.	w	Cutting Scores (x'_{ci}, y'_{ci}) Simultaneous Disadv.	Simultaneous Adv.	Separate Disadv.	Separate Adv.	Overall Expected Utility Simultaneous	Separate
(1)	$b_{01p} = 3.5$ $b_{11p} = 2$ $b_{01m} = 3$ $b_{11m} = 4$	$d_{01p} = -2$ $d_{11p} = -3$ $d_{01m} = -4$ $d_{11m} = -5$ $b_{02p} = 3$ $b_{12p} = 1$ $b_{02m} = 2$ $b_{12m} = 2.5$ $d_{02p} = -2$ $d_{12p} = -3$ $d_{02m} = -4$ $d_{12m} = -5$	0.5	$x'_{c1} = 46.38$ $y'_{c1} = 53.22$	$x'_{c2} = 43.81$ $y'_{c2} = 51.84$	$x'_{c1} = 46.10$ $y'_{c1} = 52.63$	$x'_{c2} = 43.82$ $y'_{c2} = 51.47$	21.09	20.87
(2)			0.9	$x'_{c1} = 46.12$ $y'_{c1} = 53.25$	$x'_{c2} = 43.82$ $y'_{c2} = 51.85$	$x'_{c1} = 46.10$ $y'_{c1} = 52.63$	$x'_{c2} = 43.82$ $y'_{c2} = 51.47$	14.92	14.87
(3)			0.1	$x'_{c1} = 55.19$ $y'_{c1} = 52.58$	$x'_{c2} = 45.30$ $y'_{c2} = 51.77$	$x'_{c1} = 46.10$ $y'_{c1} = 52.63$	$x'_{c2} = 43.82$ $y'_{c2} = 51.47$	27.43	26.87
(4)	$b_{01p} = 3.5$ $b_{11p} = 2$ $b_{01m} = 3$ $b_{11m} = 4$	$d_{01p} = 0$ $d_{11p} = 0$ $d_{01m} = 0$ $d_{11m} = 0$ $b_{02p} = 3$ $b_{12p} = 1$ $b_{02m} = 2$ $b_{12m} = 2.5$ $d_{02p} = 0$ $d_{12p} = 0$ $d_{02m} = 0$ $d_{12m} = 0$	0.5	$x'_{c1} = 46.14$ $y'_{c1} = 53.04$	$x'_{c2} = 43.46$ $y'_{c2} = 51.56$	$x'_{c1} = 45.87$ $y'_{c1} = 52.45$	$x'_{c2} = 43.46$ $y'_{c2} = 51.17$	24.94	24.72
(5)			0.9	$x'_{c1} = 45.89$ $y'_{c1} = 53.08$	$x'_{c2} = 43.46$ $y'_{c2} = 51.56$	$x'_{c1} = 45.87$ $y'_{c1} = 52.45$	$x'_{c2} = 43.46$ $y'_{c2} = 51.17$	17.96	17.92
(6)			0.1	$x'_{c1} = 55.09$ $y'_{c1} = 52.39$	$x'_{c2} = 45.54$ $y'_{c2} = 51.44$	$x'_{c2} = 45.87$ $y'_{c1} = 52.45$	$x'_{c2} = 43.46$ $y'_{c2} = 51.17$	32.06	31.53
(7)	$b_{01p} = 5$ $b_{11p} = 3$ $b_{01m} = 6$ $b_{11m} = 9$	$d_{01p} = -2$ $d_{11p} = -3$ $d_{01m} = -4$ $d_{11m} = -5$ $b_{02p} = 3.5$ $b_{12p} = 2$ $b_{02m} = 5$ $b_{12m} = 7$ $d_{02p} = -2$ $d_{12p} = -3$ $d_{02m} = -4$ $d_{12m} = -5$	0.5	$x'_{c1} = 46.87$ $y'_{c1} = 53.06$	$x'_{c2} = 43.30$ $y'_{c2} = 51.63$	$x'_{c1} = 46.06$ $y'_{c1} = 52.53$	$x'_{c2} = 43.99$ $y'_{c2} = 51.28$	51.59	50.72
(8)			0.9	$x'_{c1} = 46.12$ $y'_{c1} = 53.15$	$x'_{c2} = 44.02$ $y'_{c2} = 51.65$	$x'_{c1} = 46.06$ $y'_{c1} = 52.53$	$x'_{c2} = 43.99$ $y'_{c2} = 51.28$	29.78	29.60
(9)			0.1	$x'_{c1} = 57.69$ $y'_{c1} = 52.49$	$x'_{c2} = 49.04$ $y'_{c2} = 51.37$	$x'_{c1} = 46.06$ $y'_{c1} = 52.53$	$x'_{c2} = 43.99$ $y'_{c2} = 51.28$	74.05	71.84

generally a decrease of the optimal placement scores and a small increase of the optimal mastery scores. Thus, increasing influence of the utility associated with the mastery decision implies that students should be assigned sooner to the "lower" treatment. In particular, the optimal placement cutting scores should be raised considerably for $w = 0.1$. This can be argued by the fact that the increasing influence of the utility associated with the mastery decision implies that students should be assigned sooner to the "lower" treatment in order to prepare them better for the mastery test at the end of the treatment. Besides, this better preparation for the mastery test accounts for the fact that the optimal mastery scores can generally be set slightly lower with increasing w. Furthermore, inspection of Table 19.2 shows that both the optimal placement and mastery scores are lower for the advantaged than for the disadvantaged group. This is so because the disadvantaged students should be assigned sooner to the "lower" treatment. Also, they should stay longer in the instructional treatment to be sure that they have mastered the educational objectives.

In Table 19.2 the optimal cutting scores for the separate decisions are also displayed. The cutting scores optimizing the separate mastery and placement decisions were computed using (13) and (15), respectively. As can be seen from Table 19.2, the optimal cutting points for the separate model do generally not have large differences compared to those in the combined model for $w = 0.5$ and $w = 0.9$ for both subpopulations. However, for $w = 0.1$ the optimal cutting points for the placement decision of the combined model are substantially higher for both subpopulations. This can be explained by realizing that, as noted before, the psychometric portion of the separate model for optimizing the separate cutting scores does not depend upon the value of w. Furthermore, it has been argued before why the optimal cutting points for the placement decision of the combined model should be set rather high for $w = 0.1$.

In the Introduction, it was remarked that one of the main advantages of the simultaneous approach was the increase of the overall expected utility. This can be demonstrated by comparing the gain in overall expected utility of the simultaneous to the separate approach. In order to calculate the overall expected utility for the separate approach, first the expected utilities for the separate placement and mastery decisions were computed by substituting (15) and (13) into (17) and (18), respectively. Next, analogously to (9), the overall expected utility for the separate approach was calculated by summing the separate expected utilies for a random student over all students. It should be noted that the integrals appearing in computing the overall expected utility for the separate approach can be integrated analytically (see Vos, 1989).

Next, the overall expected utility for the simultaneous approach was calculated by substituting the optimal separate cutting scores from Table 19.2 into (9). The sixth term in the right-hand side of (9) has been computed using numerical integration methods, while the first five terms have been integrated analytically. A computer program called UTILITY available from the author has been written to calculate the overall expected utility both for the separate and simultaneous approach. Table 19.2 summarizes the results.

As can be seen from Table 19.2, the gain in overall expected utility for this specific example and chosen utility structures (1)–(9) is not very much. The gain is substantial only for utility structure (9) with $w = 0.1$. This can be explained by the fact that the utility associated with the mastery decision is dominating in this case. Now, due to the high optimal placement cutting scores for the combined model, most students will be assigned to the "lower" treatment implying that on the average they are better prepared for the end-of-treatment test. As a result, due to the high positive utility associated with the advance decision for this specific utility structure, the overall expected utility will be rather large.

Note that for both approaches the overall expected utility increases with decreasing w. This means that the utility associated with the separate mastery decision contributes the most to the overall expected utility.

DISCUSSION

In this chapter an approach to simultaneous decision making for combinations of elementary decisions was described. The approach was applied to the area of instructional decision making by combining two elementary decisions (viz., a placement and a mastery decision) into a simple ISS. It was indicated that the optimal placement cutting scores obtained by the simultaneous approach in some cases differed substantially from those obtained by the separate approach. In particular, if it was assumed that the influence of the utility function associated with the placement decision was small, it turned out that the cutting points for the placement decision yielded rather large differences.

The solutions given in this chapter only apply to treatment assignment problems followed by an end-of-treatment test. However, more complicated decision networks can be handled effectively within a decision-theoretic framework. Further examination of the "best" way to represent more complicated decision networks of combinations of elementary decisions seems a valuable line of research. By simultaneous optimization of such sequences of decisions, optimal decisions can be taken using the framework of Bayesian decision theory. Also, restrictions such as multivariate test data, quota restrictions, and multivariate criteria can be taken into account. Furthermore, the optimization methods can be readily generalized to more than two treatments by introducing a series of cutting scores on the placement test.

A final comment concerns the practicalities of assessing the weight w and utility functions in real-world situations. First, in Vos (1988) it is indicated how the parameters appearing in the separate linear utility functions can be assessed empirically. Basically, this methods boils down to first reducing the number of parameters in, for instance, $u_{him}(t)$ to two by making an admissable positive linear transformation (Luce & Raiffa, 1957). Next, in order to make the method work, the decision maker only has to specify two t-coordinates of the intersection of the utility lines associated with the advance and retain decision.

With respect to assessing the weight w ($0 \leq w \leq 1$), it should be noted that w represents the relative influence (in %) of the separate placement decision in the combined decision problem. For instance, if the decision maker perceives the separate decisions as equally important, then w should be set equal to 0.5. However, suppose he or she thinks the separate placement decision is three times as important as the separate mastery decision, then w should be given a value of 0.75.

REFERENCES

Cronbach, L.J. (1951). Coefficient alpha and the internal structure of tests. *Psychometrika, 16,* 297–334.

DeGroot, M.H. (1970). *Optimal statistical decisions.* New York: McGraw-Hill.

Ferguson, T.S. (1967). *Mathematical statistics: A decision theoretic approach.* New York: Academic Press.

Fishburn, P.C. (1982). *The foundations of expected utility.* Dordrecht: D. Reidel.

French, S. (1986). *Decision theory: An introduction to the mathematics of rationality.* Chichester: Ellis Horwood Limited.

Gross, A.L., & Su, W.H. (1975). Defining a "fair" or "unbiased" selection model: A question of utilities. *Journal of Applied Psychology, 60,* 345–351.

Hambleton, R.K., & Novick, M.R. (1973). Toward an integration of theory and method for criterion-referenced tests. *Journal of Educational Measurement, 10,* 159–170.

Huynh, H. (1976). Statistical considerations of mastery scores. *Psychometrika, 41,* 65–79.

Huynh, H. (1977). Two simple cases of mastery scores based on the beta-binomial model. *Psychometrika, 41,* 65–78.

Johnson, N.L., & Kotz, S. (1970). *Distributions in statistics: Continuous univariate distributions.* Boston: Houghton Mifflin.

Keeney, D., & Raiffa, H. (1976). *Decisions with multiple objectives: Preferences and value trade-offs.* New York: John Wiley & Sons.

Krantz, D.H., Luce, R.D., Suppes, P., & Tversky, A. (1971). *Foundations of measurement.* New York: Academic Press.

Lindgren, B.W. (1976). *Statistical theory* (3rd ed.). New York: Macmillan.

Lord, F.M., & Novick, M.R. (1968). *Statistical theories of mental test scores.* Reading, MA: Addison-Wesley.

Luce, R.D., & Raiffa, H. (1957). *Games and decisions.* New York: John Wiley & Sons.

Mellenbergh, G.J., & van der Linden, W.J. (1981). The linear utility model for optimal selection. *Psychometrika, 46,* 283–293.

Novick, M.R., & Petersen, N.S. (1976). Towards equalizing educational and employment opportunity. *Journal of Educational Measurement, 13,* 77–88.

Petersen, N.S. (1976). An expected utility model for 'optimal' selection. *Journal of Educational Statistics, 4,* 333–358.

Petersen, N.S., & Novick, M.R. (1976). An evaluation of some models for culture-fair selection. *Journal of Educational Measurement, 13,* 3–31.

van der Gaag, N.L. (1989, March). *Mastery decisions at the end of Dutch secondary education.* Paper presented at the Annual Meeting of the American Educational Research Association, San Francisco, CA.

van der Linden, W.J. (1980). Decision models for use with criterion-referenced tests. *Applied Psychological Measurement, 4,* 469–492.

van der Linden, W.J. (1981). Using aptitude measurements for the optimal assignment of subjects to treatments with and without mastery scores. *Psychometrika, 46,* 257–274.

van der Linden, W.J. (1985). Decision theory in educational research and testing. In T. Husen & T.N. Postlethwaite (Eds.), *International encyclopedia of education: Research and studies* (pp. 1328–1333). Oxford: Pergamon Press.

van der Linden, W.J. (1987). The use of test scores for classification decisions with threshold utility. *Journal of Educational Statistics, 12,* 62–75.

van der Linden, W.J. (1988). Applications of decision theory to test-based decision-making. In R.K. Hambleton & J.N. Zaal (Eds.), *New developments in testing: Theory and applications.* Amsterdam, The Netherlands: North-Holland.

van der Linden, W.J., & Mellenbergh, G.J. (1977). Optimal cutting scores using a linear loss function. *Applied Psychological Measurement, 1,* 593–599.

Vos, H.J. (1988). The use of decision theory in the Minnesota Adaptive Instructional System. *Journal of Computer-Based Instruction, 15,* 65–71.

Vos, H.J. (1989). *A simultaneous approach to optimizing treatment assignments with mastery scores.* Research Report 89–5 from the Division of Educational Measurement and Data Analysis, University of Twente, Enschede, The Netherlands.

Vos, H.J. (forthcoming). Simultaneous optimization of decisions using a linear utility function. *Journal of Educational Statistics.*

Vos, H.J., & van der Linden, W.J. (1987). Designing optimal rules for instructional decision making in CAI systems. In J. Moonen & T. Plomp (Eds.), *Developments in educational software and courseware* (pp. 291–298). Oxford: Pergamon Press.

appendix

Fifth International Objective Measurement Workshop University of California, Berkeley March 25–26, 1989

Session 1 Saturday March 25, 8:00–10:20

APPLICATIONS OF POLYTOMOUS RASCH MODELS

Chair: Geoff Masters, Australian Council for Educational Research

- *Calibrating for rehabilitation program evaluation and research*

  William P. Fisher, Marianjoy Rehabilitation Center, Wheaton, IL

- *Using partial information: The subset selection technique*

  Mark Frazier, University of California, Berkeley

- *Partial credit analysis of an employee benefits survey*

  Ellen Julian, National Board of Medical Examiners, Philadelphia, PA, and Ben Wright, University of Chicago

- *An application of the Rasch Rating Scale Model to adaptive attitude measurement*

  William R. Koch and Barbara G. Dodd, University of Texas at Austin

- *Methodological issues in the application of polytomous Rasch models to behavioral assessments*

Larry Ludlow, Boston College

- *Partial Credit modeling of biobehavioral data involving ordered stimuli*

David McArthur, VA Medical Center, Long Beach California, and Kenneth L. Casey, University of Michigan

Session 2   Saturday, March 25, 10:40–1:00

APPLICATIONS OF OBJECTIVE MEASUREMENT

Chair: Ellen Julian, National Board of Medical Examiners

- *A comparison of Item Characteristics Associated with Differential Item Functioning for Rasch and Mantel-Haenszel Detection Methodologies*

Nikolaus Bezruczko, University of Chicago

- *Loglinear Rasch analysis for detecting differential item performance*

Stephen Moore, University of California, Berkeley

- *Toward an understanding of psychometric structure in measures of personality*

Michael O'Brien, Fordham University, New York

- *Components of difficulty in spatial ability items*

Richard M. Smith and Gene A. Kramer, American Dental Association, and Anna T. Kubiak, ETS

- *Construct Generalization: A meta-analytic tool*

A. Jackson Stenner, MetaMetrics, Inc., Durham, NC

- *Application of a polytomous IRT model to attitude assessment in program evaluation.*

Mark Wilson, University of California, Berkeley

Session 3   Saturday, March 25, 2:00–2:30

COMPUTER PROGRAMS FOR TEST DEVELOPMENT AND ESTIMATION

Chair: Mark Wilson, University of California, Berkeley
(The demonstrations will be held concurrently.)

- *TESTCALC*

  Ivan Horabin

- *Loglinear item response theory modelling*

  Henk Kelderman, University of Twente, The Netherlands

- *Optimal item selection*

  T.J.J.M. Theunissen, CITO, The Netherlands

- *Logical constraints in test design*

  Huub Verstralen, CITO, The Netherlands

Session 4   Saturday, March 25, 2:30–5:00

MATHEMATICAL METHODS APPLIED TO PROBLEMS IN TEST DESIGN

Chair: Wim van der Linden, University of Twente, The Netherlands

- *Two-stage test construction by linear programming*

  Jos J. Adema, University of Twente, The Netherlands

- *Multi—objective test design with mathematical programming*

  Noud Gademann, University of Twente, The Netherlands

- *Optimizing item calibration designs*

  Wim J. van der Linden, University of Twente, The Netherlands

- *The Optimization of Decision Studies*

  Piet F. Sanders, Cito, The Netherlands

- *Golden section search strategies for computerized adaptive testing*

  Beiling Xiao, Iowa State University

Session 5   Sunday, March 26, 9:00–10:00

ITEM BANKING

Chair: George Ingebo, Portland Public Schools
Chad Karr, Portland State University

- **Rasch calibrated item banks**

  George Ingebo, Portland Public Schools, OR (Retired)

- **Automated test construction from a clustered item bank**

  Ellen Boekkooi-Timminga, University of Twente, The Netherlands

- **A one-step procedure for item banking with the Rasch Model**

  Matthew Schulz, Chicago Public Schools

Session 6   Sunday March 26, 10:30–12:00

MEASUREMENT MODELS FOR LEARNING AND INSTRUCTION

Chair: Geoff Masters, Australian Council for Educational Research

- **Test Anxiety and Item Order: New Parameters for Item Response Theory**

  Richard C. Gershon, Johnson O'Connor Research Foundation/ Northwestern University

- **Conjunctive Measurement Theory: Cognitive Research Prospects**

  Robert J. Jannarone, University of South Carolina

- **Loglinear Multidimensional IRT Models for Polytomously Scored Items**

  Henk Kelderman, University of Twente, The Netherlands

- **Using the Partial Credit Model to Define and Describe Achievement Grades: An Application**

  Geoff Masters, Australian Council for Educational Research

- **Simultaneous optimization of the Aptitude Treatment interaction Decision Problem with mastery scores**

  Hans J. Vos, University of Twente, The Netherlands

- **The Partial Order Model.**

  Mark Wilson, University of California, Berkeley

Session 7   Sunday, March 26, 1:30–3:30

ESTIMATING AND TESTING IRT MODELS

Chair: Henk Kelderman, University of Twente, The Netherlands

- **Comparison of efficiency of designs for IRT models**

  Martijn P. F. Berger, University of Twente, The Netherlands

- *Testing model fit in polytomous item response models*

  Cees A. W. Glas, CITO, The Netherlands

- *Conditional maximum likelihood estimation in conjunctive item response theory models*

  Henk Kelderman, University of Twente, The Netherlands
  Robert J. Jannerone, University of South Carolina

- *A Bayesian procedure for improving estimation of ability from inconsistent item responses*

  George Morgan, Australian Council for Educational Research

- *Constraint optimization: An alternative to Newton-Raphson in IRT estimation*

  Hoi K. Suen, Pennsylvania State University
  Patrick S. L. Lee, LaSalle University

Session 8   Sunday, March 26, 4:00–6:00

HISTORY AND PRINCIPLES OF MEASUREMENT

Chair: Ben Wright, University of Chicago

- *Historical views of the concept of invariance and measurement theory in the behavioral sciences*

  George Engelhard, Jr., Emory University, GA

- *The Historical roots of Rasch separability*

  William P. Fisher, Jr., Marianjoy Rehabilitation Center, Wheaton, IL

- *Representing the process of scale development: The structure of measurement*

  Arthur Ellen, University of Chicago

- *Rasch Models from objectivity: A Generalization*

  John M. Linacre, University of Chicago

- *Fundamental measurement of rank-ordered objects*

  John M. Linacre, University of Chicago

- *Deducing the Rasch model from concatenation*

  Ben Wright, University of Chicago

Author Index

Subject Index